The Essence of the
Christian Worldview

The Essence of the
Christian Worldview

MATT DeLOCKERY

WIPF & STOCK · Eugene, Oregon

THE ESSENCE OF THE CHRISTIAN WORLDVIEW

Wipf & Stock
An Imprint of Wipf and Stock Publishers
199 W. 8th Ave., Suite 3
Eugene, OR 97401

www.wipfandstock.com

PAPERBACK ISBN: 978-1-6667-0078-7
HARDCOVER ISBN: 978-1-6667-0079-4
EBOOK ISBN: 978-1-6667-0080-0

04/19/21

Contents

Acknowledgments

THERE ARE A NUMBER of people I want to thank, people who have made this project possible. To begin, I want to thank Mike Licona, who connected me with his former doctoral advisor, which enabled me to be accepted into Radboud University in Nijmegen to begin my studies. I want to thank Jan van der Watt for all his support, encouragement, and patience as he guided me through this process. I could not have asked for a better doctoral advisor.

I want to thank Blake Blount for reading parts of this book and offering suggestions. I especially want to thank Kevin Gibby, who read almost the entire book line-by-line, thought through every argument I made, and critiqued everything in-depth. It was not fun reading his critiques, but this book is much better (and much more readable) because of him.

Finally, I want to thank everyone who has financially supported my ministry, Why Should I Believe. If it were not for your generous contributions, I would not have been able to take the time to do this research.

Thank you all, very much!

1

Introduction

PROBLEM

If you were to ask someone who had been a Christian for a long time "Do you know what Christianity is?," the answer would probably be a resounding "Yes!" or "Of course!" You might even be given a look of indignation. After all, how could anyone not know what his or her own religion is?

But, suppose you were to ask that same person a slightly different question: "What is the essence of the Christian worldview?" or "If you were to boil Christianity down to its most basic level, what would it look like?" Here, the conversation might take a different turn. He or she might say something like "Christianity is the belief that Jesus Christ is the Son of God and has risen from the dead." You could ask, "So, is it a belief, then? I thought even the demons believe and shudder."[1] The person you're talking with might reply, "Yes, but they don't trust in Him." You could reply again, "So, all you have to do is believe in Jesus and trust him? Do you have to live in any certain way, or can you just do whatever you want?" They would certainly reply, "No, you have to follow his teachings." You might respond, "So, now Christianity is a belief, a trust, *and* a way of life?" This process could continue for some time, and the propositions about what is important to Christianity could

1. James 2:19.

keep piling up until it is described from every conceivable angle. But, with each new proposition, the conclusion becomes more and more ad hoc. Has this been thought out in advance, or are these propositions just being made up as the conversation rolls along? What is central to Christianity, really?

What if everything were turned around? Suppose a Christian wanted to learn about Islam and asked a Muslim, "What is the essence of Islam?" It is a non-trivial question to answer, because there are different sects, such as Sunni and Shia Muslims. How does one combine the beliefs of the different groups into one central statement (if such a thing is even possible)? The question that is really being asked is "What is so central to the faith that anyone in Islam must believe in, do, etc., in order to call himself or herself a Muslim?" This is the same question that was asked about Christianity. If a Muslim who did not know much about Christianity wanted to know what it is, how could a Christian explain it?

Laying aside the question of outsiders momentarily, even within Christianity, this is quite a problem. Large numbers of Christians have decided that they cannot work with one another because they have different theological beliefs. It is extremely common for churches and seminaries to allow people to teach only if they can sign the doctrinal statement of the particular group. This does not mean that churches, seminaries, and other ministries should not be selective in their teachers and leaders. They probably should. But, *on what basis* should they be selective? What is so central to Christianity that one should decide not to work with other people who call themselves Christians because they think or act differently? People are obviously using some sort of criteria to make their decisions, but what criteria are they using? Are they good criteria? Have they been well thought-out, or are they just made up along the way? When Christians make a decision[2] on whom they are willing to work with, they are making a decision about what is important to Christianity.[3] What actually is important to Christianity? What is its essence?

Paul said in 1 Cor 15:17, "If Christ is not raised, your faith is worthless, you are still in your sins." This is a nice and simple statement. If Christ is raised, then the Christian's faith is valuable; if Christ is not raised, then the Christian's faith is worthless. Ideally, in order to answer the questions

2. Refusing to decide whom to work with and thereby working with everyone is still making a decision. If a person driving a car approaches a stop sign and refuses to decide whether to stop or not, he still makes a decision. The car keeps moving forward, and he continues through the sign. So, a decision is still made.

3. Related to this is a second question, "Are there levels of importance within Christianity?" In other words, are some things very important and others less important, or is everything equal?

above, one would want something like Paul's statement in 1 Corinthians—a very simple and straightforward definition of the essence of the Christian worldview. This is what this study is trying to produce.

SOLUTION

"What is the essence of the Christian worldview?" is a very large question. As will be discussed in the next chapter, this book will focus on a smaller task: answering that question from the perspective of one of the most important figures in early Christianity, Paul. For those who think that the Bible is the word of God, that all the biblical authors are completely consistent with one another, and that these scriptures are the final authority on God's will for humanity, this will completely answer the question "What is the essence of the Christian worldview?" For those who think that church tradition plays a more important role, that the Holy Spirit has been guiding humanity into a more complete understanding of the Christian worldview, that Christianity is a matter of personal faith that varies from person to person, or any number of other views, this study will be a good start to understanding the question. But, it will not be the final word on the issue.

Ultimately, what will come out of this study will include Paul's answers to some of life's biggest questions: "Who are we?" "Where are we?" "What is wrong?" and "What is the solution?"[4] Paul will spend a lot of time talking about God, Christ, creation, and humanity. But, more importantly than just discussing these four (very large) topics, he will explain the relationships between them. "How are God and Christ related?" "What is God doing in creation (the world) today?" "What is humanity's role in creation?" and "What difference does this make in a person's day-to-day life?" He will talk about how theology and practice are connected and answer the question: "How does all this theology actually impact one's daily life?" And, he will answer something that is an even more fundamental question: "Why does it matter?"

4. N.T. Wright, *New Testament*, 123–24.

2

Approach

"What is the essence of the Christian worldview?" When one thinks about trying to answer this question, numerous problems present themselves. To begin with, is it even reasonable to think that there is such a thing as an essence of the Christian worldview? Christianity has been around for over two thousand years. Whose version of the Christian worldview should be accepted as canonical? Should anyone's? Perhaps faith is something personal, and each person's faith will be a little different. Perhaps the Holy Spirit will guide each person individually. Perhaps God is more concerned with people seeking Him than He is with there being a single "right" answer. Of course, all of that assumes that there actually is a God. Maybe there isn't. All of these questions and numerous others that one could ask means that answering the question "What is the essence of the Christian worldview?" is not a simple task.

Maybe the thing to do would be to try to narrow the task down and work towards a more modest goal. At least one way of addressing the question would be to look at the origin of Christianity and see what its founders thought. This would be something that people of most points of view would find useful. Some people think that Christianity was something started by God, so what one finds in the New Testament is the only thing that matters. These people would certainly find a study of what the founders of Christianity thought the Christian worldview was/is to be valuable. Some people think that everyone has an equal right to decide what Christianity is/should be. They might not value the founders' opinions more than anyone else's, but they are still opinions to be considered, so this task would be of some value. Others might be interested in this question for purely historical reasons, and this task would definitely address that.

There are many perspectives on this issue, and the three just listed don't cover them all. However, looking at the question "What is the essence of the Christian worldview?" from the perspective of the founders of Christianity seems to be valuable to a large number of people. Of course, there are still other important questions one could ask: "Is Christianity actually true?" "Does it matter?" "Does a concept like truth even apply to a worldview?" Looking at what those who founded Christianity thought the Christian worldview was does not address any of those questions. But, many people wonder about questions like those, and while this study will not answer them, it may help to clarify discussions about them.

In order to try to find the essence of the Christian worldview from the perspective of its founders, there are at least three possible investigations that could be conducted.[1] One could: 1) find the essence of the Christian worldview as described in a single letter or book,[2] 2) find the essence of the Christian worldview as conceived by a single New Testament author, or 3) find the essence of the Christian worldview in the early source documents.[3] The first task is primarily about looking behind the flow of thought of one letter or book to the underlying assumptions and theology. The second and third tasks become increasingly difficult. This is because one would have to do the same work of the first task for multiple works (second task) or for multiple works of multiple authors (third task) and then combine these, if possible, into a coherent whole.

In order to make as much progress as possible towards understanding the Christian worldview from the perspective(s) of its founders, it would

---

1. Others could be done, but these three keep one closest to the founding of Christianity. Looking at the Christian worldview from the perspective of the ecumenical creeds, for example, would be another task one could perform. This would be one way of looking at what the Christian worldview was like several centuries later on, as one moved further away from its original founding. This study will focus on a time closer to the founding of Christianity. However, it would be interesting to look at the Christian worldview from the perspective of the ecumenical creeds, compare it to those done on early Christianity, and contrast the results.

2. Not all letters or books would be good candidates for doing this study, because not all of them look at the Christian worldview from a high-level perspective.

3. Primarily, this would concern the works contained in the New Testament canon. However, many churches place a lot of weight on the church fathers from the late first to second centuries. In this case, these church fathers' views would need to be considered as well.

be wise to be strategic about what one investigates. Picking an unimportant writing from an author who was not influential would not be a good use of time. Rather, spending time investigating a key writing from someone who was quite influential in early Christianity would be much more productive. Choosing a key writing (Task 1) from an influential figure in early Christianity would move the whole project towards having a moderate to high level understanding of the thought of one author (Task 2) and shed a small to moderate amount of light on early Christianity (Task 3). Therefore, in this book, the focus will be on Paul. If he was not the most important theologian in the early church, he was certainly near the top of the list. Additionally, his church planting across the Roman world ensured that not only did Christianity spread quickly, it was was heavily influenced by his thought.

For this task, probably the best place one can look to find what Paul thought was essential to the Christian worldview is the letter to the Colossians. This letter is uniquely suited to that goal. Paul did not know the congregation at Colossae. He was confronted with problems and had to address them, but unlike a group with whom he was familiar, he could not assume they knew his general positions. Instead, he was forced to give a systematic overview and explain his views on Christianity before addressing their problems. If he had addressed only a single problem (as in the letter to the Galatians), then many aspects of Christianity would not be present, because the situation did not require it. Here, he had the opportunity to present the entirety of the Christian view.

Immediately, however, many would object to the choice of Colossians. One of the biggest problems is that many scholars today do not accept Paul as the author of Colossians.[4] The primary arguments are: 1) style—the style of Colossians does not fit with the style of the epistles generally accepted to have come from Paul;[5] 2) vocabulary—the vocabulary in Colossians, especially the many *hapax legomena* (words that only appear once in the New Testament but that appear in this letter), do not fit with accepted Pauline letters;[6] and 3) theology—certain theological aspects, such as the realized

---

4. Carson and Moo explain that there was no serious question about Pauline authorship before the twentieth century, but Bultmann and others began to speak of Colossians as deutero-Pauline. According to them, the evidence has not changed that much, rather the evidence is now seen as more weighty (*Introduction*, 331–32). For a history of the discussion on the authorship of Colossians, see Collins, *Letters*, 171ff.

5. Bujard, *Stilanalytische Untersuchunger*, 11. Sanders thinks "the stylistic and linguistic arguments against the authenticity of Colossians are limited to the first two chapters" ("Literary Dependence," 45).

6. Sanders suggests that "the extent of verbatim agreement with Paul's other letters is considerably more than double in Colossians what it is in Philippians. This probably indicates an amount that would not occur in a letter actually written by Paul"

eschatology of 3:1–4 and the lack of justification by faith, do not fit with accepted Pauline theology.[7]

Those in favor of authorship by Paul often counter these arguments as follows: 1) style—the objections assume first, that writers have to use the same language all the time to all people in all situations, and second, that Paul did not use a secretary (which he was known to do);[8] 2) vocabulary—the objections assume that Paul would not have used different terms if the situation required it;[9] and 3) theology—the objections assume that the letters to the Romans, Galatians, and Corinthians are the basis of all Paul's theology—which they may or may not be.[10] Supporters of Pauline authorship also cite specific evidence from other sections, such as the introduction and portions about Paul's life and ministry, as pointing towards genuine Pauline authorship.[11] What then does that mean for determining the author of Colossians?

("Literary Dependence," 31).

7. Horrell, "From ἀδελφοί to οἶκος θεοῦ," 305, and Vielhauer, *Geschichte der urchristlichen Literatur*, 197.

8. Hawthorne acknowledges the differences between Colossians and Paul's undisputed letters (especially in terms of style) but does not think the differences represent as large of a gap to overcome as is often thought (*Paul's Letter*, 34ff.). Stambaugh and Balch point out that use of a secretary was common (*New Testament*, 40).

9. DeSilva says that *hapax legomena* are "generally confessed to be insignificant even among advocates of pseudonymity. [Colossians] has no more *hapax legomena* than Philippians, and many of these unusual words occur either in the hymn of Colossians 1:15–20 (traditional material that would not be expected to reflect Paul's typical vocabulary) or in the treatment of the philosophy opposed (material that introduces the distinctive vocabulary of the rival teaching)" (*Introduction*, 696).

10. Bauckham points out something else interesting about the theology of Colossians. He says, "The large majority of NT letters, both those generally accepted as authentic and some that are often thought to be pseudepigraphal (Colossians, 1 Peter, Jude), take for granted the specific situations to which they are addressed, in the manner of authentic real letters. They do not, in the manner of pseudepigraphal letters . . . describe it for the benefit of readers who would otherwise not know it" ("Pseudo-Apostolic Letters," 490).

11. Consider the suffering of Paul described in 1.24. Dunn says, "One interesting corollary is that for such a theology [of Paul suffering for Christ] to be realistically put forward it was almost essential that Paul was still alive. If he was dead, then his sufferings were complete and so also were Christ's afflictions; and where was the end of all things? Here is a further slight indication that the letter was probably written while Paul was still alive, not by him, but with his approval" (*Epistles to the Colossians*, 117). Bruce thinks the use of the plural in 1.3 points towards Paul actually writing the letter. He says, "Even when someone else's name is conjoined with Paul's in the prescript of a letter, the thanksgiving which follows is normally expressed in the singular: 'I thank God.' This implies that the other person's name is conjoined with Paul's by way of courtesy; Paul is the real author of the letter. But in this letter, as in the two to the Thessalonians, the thanksgiving is expressed in the plural" (*Epistles to the Colossians*, 40).

For the purposes of this study, it doesn't matter whether Paul actually composed the letter. By ancient literary standards, a person could be the author of a letter without actually composing it.[12] As long as the letter came from the Pauline school of thought and is an expression of Pauline ideas, then it is still Pauline.[13] And, since this study is going to be focused on finding out what Paul thought was essential to the Christian worldview, it is only necessary to make sure that the work being investigated is truly Pauline.

Most of those who think someone other than Paul wrote the letter would still say that someone wrote the letter in general accordance with Pauline ideas.[14] Also, it must be remembered that this letter was part of the canon from early on, and therefore, it expresses the authentic teachings of early Christianity.[15] If this letter expressed a theology other than what was held by the early Christians (who were much closer to the founders of Christianity than modern scholars are), it is unlikely that they would have accepted Colossians. Therefore, while there are a lot of good points made by both sides in the debate over the authorship of the letter, it turns out that they really do not affect the outcome of this study. Because Colossians has both Pauline character and was part of the canon from early on, one can say that Colossians reflects Pauline thought. At worst, Colossians is Pauline

12. Brown says, "Although this issue is most often presented as one of Pauline authorship, as I have explained previously, the term 'author' offers difficulty. If the letter were written twenty years after Paul's death by a Pauline disciple seeking to present the thought of his master, in the ancient estimation Paul might very well be called the 'author,' i.e., the authority behind the work" (*Introduction*, 610, fn22). When one is asking "Who wrote Colossians?," one should take the time to also ask "Am I asking about the authorship according to modern literary standards or ancient ones?"

13. Even though he treats Colossians as deutero-Pauline, Brown says, "What is assured is that Col belongs in the Pauline heritage" (*Introduction*, 617). Carson and Moo say, "It is plain enough that there is a connection with Paul, but many recent scholars think that a follower of Paul rather than the apostle himself actually penned the book" (*Introduction*, 332). Strecker says that letters like Colossians "reflect the teacher-disciple relation, the 'Pauline school,' in which the apostle played the dominant role in relation to his coworkers" (*Theology*, 17). Sanders says of the author of Colossians, "His imitation of Paul is not that of a charlatan. He wished to say nothing other than what Paul himself would have said, and to that end he used Paul's own words" ("Literary Dependence," 44).

14. Dettwiler, for example, thinks that Colossians is a reformulation of Paul's ideas by one of his disciples shortly after his death. He acknowledges the deutero-Pauline nature of the letter but thinks that it is a positive and interesting fact, because it allows modern scholars to discover how a theological tradition was reworded to address a later situation ("L'Épître aux Colossiens," 27).

15. Kruger says, "We also have early evidence that Paul's letters were grouped together within a single manuscript. P46, dated c. 200, contains Romans, Hebrews, 1 Corinthians, 2 Corinthians, Ephesians, Galatians, Philippians, Colossians, and 1 Thessalonians" (*Canon Revisited*, 243). Additionally, it is worth noting that Colossians was included in Marcion's version of the Pauline corpus.

Christianity as Paul's followers saw it;[16] at best, Colossians is Pauline Christianity as Paul himself saw it. So, for the rest of this book, Paul will be described as the author. Whether it was actually Paul who wrote it, or whether it was one of his disciples who wrote it (either during his life or shortly thereafter), Paul was still the authority behind Colossians.

> Because it is so important that reliable information about Paul's views can be found in Colossians, it seems necessary that I share my own views. Personally, I think the best explanation of the data is that Timothy wrote the letter under the supervision of Paul. While the arguments against Pauline authorship are all based on assumptions, I do not think they should be so easily dismissed.
>
> It should be noted that the letter itself claims co-authorship. In v. 1, Timothy is named as a coauthor. However, the evidence for Timothy's inclusion goes beyond mere mention of him. In Colossians, when the body of the letter begins, its author uses the first person plural form of verbs. Verse 3 begins with εὐχαριστοῦμεν (we thank). By comparison, in 1 Cor 1:4, Sosthenes is named as a co-author. However, when Paul finishes the introduction and starts the letter itself (v. 4), he returns to the first person singular εὐχαριστῶ (I give thanks). Sosthenes is essentially an honorary co-author; Timothy is a legitimate co-author.[17]
>
> Additionally, at the end of the letter, in 4:18, Paul writes a greeting with his own hand. This would have either been written by someone trying to fake Pauline authorship, or it would have been actually penned by Paul himself. The latter option seems more likely, because if it were known that Paul didn't sign it himself, it would hurt the letter's credibility rather than help it. It seems more likely that someone other than Paul (like Timothy) actually wrote the letter, and Paul supervised it.
>
> If Timothy were Paul's disciple and wrote the letter under Paul's supervision, then the information in the letter would very closely represent Paul's thought. Paul's theology would form the basis of the letter's theology, because Paul taught Timothy. Paul put his signature at the end, which points towards Paul literally signing off on what the letter contained. Combined with the previous point, this means that Timothy probably actually wrote the letter, but Paul would have been ultimately responsible for its

---

16. Even if Colossians is an attempt by the disciples of Paul to accurately reflect his views, it is still a good source of his views.

17. For Timothy as a real contributor, see Bruce, *Epistles to the Colossians*, 40; Dunn, *Epistles to the Colossians*, 55; and Witherington, *Letters to Philemon*, 120. For Timothy mentioned as a courtesy, see Moo, *Letters to the Colossians*, 82.

contents. Therefore, it is accurate to say that the letter represents Paul's actual theology—even if it is expressed in different words.

Personally, I think this theory is the best explanation of all the data (including the general positions of scholars for or against Pauline authorship). Again, though, while this is my opinion of what probably happened, one does not need to agree with me for the argument in this book to be successful. All that must be true is that the letter represents Pauline theology—which it still would, even if Paul were already dead and his students were trying to accurately reflect his thoughts. So again, for the rest of this book, the name Paul will be used when referring to the author of the letter, because he is the ultimate authority behind it.

Now, even if the authorship of Colossians is not a problem, many would say that it would be better to look to Romans to find the essence of Paul's Christian worldview. After all, Paul had essentially the same opportunity when writing to the church in Rome as he did when writing to the church in Colossae. However, whether Romans is a better source than Colossians depends on what one is trying to find.

What this study is looking for is not a Christian theology but a Christian worldview. A Christian theology would explain both the major and minor points of Christianity and give details about each. It would also have sections on things that are relevant primarily (if not solely) to Christians. A worldview, on the other hand, would focus on the most essential elements of Christianity that would serve to compare it with other worldviews, as well as potentially be used to explain its essentials to new converts. An explanation of Christianity as a worldview is going to focus on the basics.

> A worldview is not an easy thing to define. Really, it is an ambiguous concept that basically covers everything in an individual's reality.[18] Sire lists eight questions that help one get an idea of what a worldview is. His basic questions are: "1. What is prime reality—the really real?, 2. What is the nature of external reality, that is, the world around us?, 3. What is a human being?, 4. What happens to a person at death?, 5. Why is it possible to know anything at all?, 6. How do we know what is right and wrong?, 7. What is the meaning of human history?, and 8. What personal, life-orienting core commitments are consistent with this worldview?"[19]

---

18. Vorgrimler, *Neues Theologisches Wörterbuch*, 681.

19. Sire, *The Universe Next Door*, 22-3. For another perspective, N.T. Wright, New Testament, 123-4 says that, "There are four things which worldviews characteristically do, in each of which the entire worldview can be glimpsed. First, . . . worldviews provide the *stories* through which human beings view reality . . . Second, from these stories one

A worldview is something that is very big; it encompasses everything in a person's reality. It is also something that gets at the very deepest questions that humans can ask—questions like "Who am I?" and "What is my purpose?" Now, it goes beyond the scope of this study to attempt a precise definition of "worldview." However, even without a precise definition, one can still say that worldviews are things that focus on the big questions of life and the big picture of reality. That is the purpose of this study—to look for that big picture view of Christianity (at least from Paul's perspective).

Related to the concept of worldview is that of narrative. Christopher Wright says, "Every human worldview is an outworking of *some* narrative."[20] Unfortunately, defining a narrative is just as difficult as defining a worldview. And, like worldview, a precise definition of narrative (or the related term, story)[21] goes beyond the scope of this study. However, unlike the term worldview, most people have an idea of what a narrative/story is.[22] It is this commonsense meaning of these words that will be used in this study. The reason that this matters is because "worldviews provide the *stories* through which human beings view reality . . . [and] from these stories one can in principle discover how to answer the basic *questions* that determine human existence: who are we, where are we, what is wrong, and what is the solution?"[23] For this study, narratives/stories will be important insofar as they help to explain the Christian worldview.

One of the reasons Colossians is an ideal place to look for the essence of the Christian worldview (according to Paul)[24] is that in the letter, Chris-

can in principle discover how to answer the basic *questions* that determine human existence: who are we, where are we, what is wrong, and what is the solution? . . . Third, the stories that express the worldview, and the answers which it provides to the questions of identity, environment, evil and eschatology, are expressed . . . in cultural *symbols*. These can be both artifacts and events - festivals, family gatherings, and the like . . . Fourth, worldviews include a praxis, a way-of-being-in-the-world. The implied eschatology of the fourth questions ('what is the solution?') necessarily entails *action*." Italics original.

20. Wright, *Mission of God*, 533. Italics original.

21. Ryan says that narrative and story are partial synonyms ("Toward a Definition," 22).

22. These two terms will be considered interchangeable for this study. They may not actually be interchangeable to those who study them, but the only purpose here is to help in the search for the essence of the Christian worldview. No precise definition should be inferred when either of these terms is used. For more information on narrative, see Toolan, *Narrative*, and Ryan, "Toward a Definition."

23. N.T. Wright, *New Testament*, 123; italics in original.

24. The ultimate goal is to find the essence of the Christian worldview. However, as discussed previously, this is such a big project, that it must be broken town into smaller projects and tasks. As described at the beginning of this chapter, in order to complete

tianity is being compared with another worldview.[25] As a result, one should expect that the emphasis in Paul's response is going to be on the most central aspects of Christianity and how they compare with an alternative.[26] In other words, Paul's response is going to focus on the Christian worldview rather than on a full Christian theology.

Beyond this, though, there is another important benefit in looking to Colossians for a Christian worldview rather than to Romans, and it has to do with filtering. Christian theology is an enormous topic. In order to find a Christian worldview—just the essential elements—one has to filter out what is more important from what is less important. How exactly should that filter be made? What criteria separate out what is more important from what is less important?

The benefit of using Colossians instead of Romans is that the filter has already been made and applied. With Colossians, Paul has already sorted out what he thinks is more important from what is less important. With Romans, the modern scholar would have to 1) get into the mind of Paul, 2) create a filter based on what Paul thinks is important, and 3) apply this filter to his letter to the Romans. None of those steps is easy. However, with Colossians, none of this is required, because Paul has already done it all. After all, if the goal is to understand what Paul thought, wouldn't it be best to let him filter out what is more important from what is less important?

There are a couple of downsides, however, to using Colossians. First, there is the obvious issue of authorship.[27] If one cannot be certain that Paul

---

the project of finding the essence of the Christian worldview according to the founders of Christianity or in early Christianity, one can subdivide this project into three tasks. Therefore, by studying Colossians, one is completing Task 1 (finding the essence of the Christian worldview in a single letter or book). If this is the best place to look for Paul's perspective, then one is also completing or almost completing Task 2 (finding the essence of the Christian worldview as conceived by a single author). Finally, since Paul was so important to early Christianity, great progress will also be made towards Task 3 (finding the essence of the Christian worldview in the early source documents).

25. Dibelius says that the Colossian church was confronted with the outside influence but was not yet overcome by it (*Paulus*, 127). If Dibelius is correct, and Paul argued in favor of Christianity, one can reasonably expect to find some arguments that favorably compare Christianity with another worldview. See also DeSilva, *Introduction*, 694.

26. The actual study will show that Paul does not spend much time on anything that isn't essential.

27. It may seem redundant to address the question of authorship again. This is such a big issue to many scholars that it does need to be addressed again. However, the current discussion is not about trying to determine who the author is. Rather, it is about trying to understand what effect the uncertainty in authorship has on the effectiveness of this study. In other words, if it is not certain that Paul is actually the author, how can one be sure that it is the essence of his worldview that one is finding by looking at Colossians?

was the author of Colossians, then it might not be Paul's actual thought that is being evaluated. Second, because Christianity is being compared with another worldview, one is going to get exactly that—Christianity compared with another worldview.[28] It is very possible that some important points of Christianity will be left out either because they do not compare well with the other worldview or because they are not critical in the explanation of Christianity to outsiders (even though they may be very important for believers).

Again, though, the concerns over authorship are probably not as problematic as they first appear. Most scholars believe that if Paul did not write Colossians, then it was probably written by one of his followers. So, since *someone* is going to have to filter Paul's theology from its long form to a more compact form, it seems better that the one to do it should be closer to Paul himself.[29] This favors the ancient author of Colossians, even if it were not Paul, over the modern scholar. Nor matter how good the modern scholar's exegetical skills may be, no one alive today knew Paul or knows anyone who knew Paul. This puts everyone in the modern world at a disadvantage.

As to the concern over leaving out some important points of theology, this is also not as big of a problem as it might appear at first. Some theological points might have been left out of Colossians because they did not compare well with other worldviews or because they had more relevance to believers rather than to outsiders. However, one should remember that the point is not to look at the whole of Paul's theology. The point is to look for the essence of the Christian worldview. Because of that, some parts of Paul's theology will be left out anyway.

However, because Paul will be comparing Christianity with another worldview, it is more likely that he will focus on the essentials of Christianity and therefore what constitutes the Christian worldview. Furthermore, because either Paul or one of his followers (rather than the modern scholar) is responsible for filtering Paul's theology, this brings the whole project one step closer to Paul's actual thought. So, when one considers all of the positives and negatives, even though there are some drawbacks, Colossians seems like the best place within the Pauline corpus to find the essence of his Christian worldview.

28. That means that the situation will determine Paul's response. Therefore, it is not a Christian worldview as such. Paul is not delivering a Christian worldview in a vacuum; rather, Paul is responding to certain challenges. However, by trying to understand *why* Paul responded the way he did, the hope is to be able to find what makes his message distinctively Christian and thereby find his Christian worldview through the way he argues.

29. As discussed previously, Colossians was thought to be canonical from early on. That means that early Christians who still had access to the apostolic tradition in oral form as well as contact with those who were not too many generations of disciples removed from the apostles (including Paul himself) considered it to be in line with Paul's thought.

So, how does one go about finding Paul's Christian worldview from Colossians? The first step is to do a detailed investigation of the letter. Essentially, this answers the question "What is Paul saying?" The second step is to look beneath *what* Paul is saying to ask the question "*Why* is Paul saying this?" This is about trying to understand the reasons for his positions. The third and final step is to separate what Paul thinks is essential to the Christian worldview from what he thinks isn't essential.

Steps 1 and 2 happen at the same time. Each section of the letter will be investigated one at a time in an effort to understand both *what* Paul was saying (Step 1) and *why* he was saying it (Step 2). There will be a significance section at the end of each chapter to summarize what can be learned about the "why?" part of Paul's thinking (Step 2).

This leads to the third step: taking everything the letter reveals about Paul's worldview and determining which elements are absolutely essential. There are two ways to do this. First, in Step 3a, all of the results from Step 2 will be gathered and combined. This will result in a picture of Paul's worldview based on the way he argued for Christianity over another philosophy.

Second, in Step 3b, Paul's thoughts will be evaluated according to standard theological categories. Everything that Paul thinks about God, Christ, humanity, etc,. will be gathered up and and evaluated one by one. The question here will be "If what Paul thinks about X were removed from his worldview, would his worldview then collapse?" So, for example, suppose Paul thinks that Christ is responsible for the creation of all things. The question would then be "What would happen if that were removed from Paul's worldview? If Christ were *not* responsible for the creation of all things, what would be the effect on Paul's Christian worldview? Would it collapse?"

This second method is like determining which supports are necessary to a building by (hypothetically) removing one of them at a time. If removing a support causes the building to collapse, then it was probably essential. The next step is to rebuild the building, add that support back in, and try another support. Once all Paul's thoughts from the letter have been evaluated, the ones that cannot be removed will be considered essential to his worldview. Finally, in Step 3c, the results from both these methods will be combined in order to produce a summary of Paul's Christian worldview.

The first two steps will take the majority of the book to complete. They will require detailed exegesis of the letter to the Colossians. The third step will be completed in the final chapter and hopefully result in the essence of the Christian worldview according to Paul. Now, it is time to begin Steps 1 and 2—working through the letter to understand what Paul was saying and why he was saying it.

3

Setting the Stage (1:3–8)

INTRODUCTION[1]

The city of Colossae was located in the Lycus River Valley in the south-west of what is modern-day Turkey. Colossae and the other cities in the valley, Laodicea and Hierapolis, were not evangelized by Paul, but by Epaphras (Col 4:12–13). It is possible that Paul visited the area on his way to Ephesus;[2] however, the letter itself says that he was largely unknown to the people in the church there (Col 2:1).[3] This will actually help in the search for what Paul considered to be the essence of the Christian worldview, because Paul cannot assume that the people there are already familiar with what he thinks on any given topic, since most of them don't know him. He will have to spell out everything completely, and that will make this investigation easier.

Looking for what Paul considered to be the essence of the Christian worldview will begin with the introduction to the letter to the Colossians.

1. If the reader is not familiar with Colossians, it would be a good idea to read it a few times first. This study assumes a general familiarity with the letter.

2. Bruce, "Colossian Problems: Part 1," 8.

3. For more background on the city of Colossae, see Bruce, "Colossian Problems: Part 1." For further information on introductory issues, see Brown, *Introduction*; Kümmel, *Einleitung*; and Michael Wolter, *Brief an die Kolosser*.

Paul addresses the Colossians in vv. 1–2, but vv. 3–8 will be the starting point for this search. Here, Paul does two things. First, he attempts to secure the good will of the audience and make them more receptive for the message that he is about to give them. Second, he gives a brief overview of the main points of his argument.[4] The latter will provide the first glimpse into Paul's thought.

A word of caution: one should not expect full clarity here. Paul will not be explaining any part of his worldview in detail at this point. He will be hinting at what is to come, but it will not be until the next section of the letter that he gets into anything in depth. Likewise, the search for the essence of the Christian worldview will not be completed here; it will merely begin here. However, Paul will give the readers some markers to look out for a little further down the road.

The main themes to keep an eye out for in this chapter are thankfulness, faith, love, and hope. Paul will also begin to get his readers thinking about God, Christ, and humanity, but he won't say much about those until vv. 9–14.

1:3[5]

εὐχαριστοῦμεν τῷ θεῷ πατρὶ τοῦ κυρίου ἡμῶν Ἰησοῦ Χριστοῦ πάντοτε περὶ ὑμῶν προσευχόμενοι

We thank God, the Father of our Lord Jesus Christ, always when we pray for you[6]

With his opening statement, Paul begins to soften the audience so that they will be more willing to listen to him. By telling the Colossians that he and Timothy thank God for them, he shows that he cares for them. However, while Paul's thanksgiving does attempt to win the audience, that is not all it does. Verse 3 begins a theme of thanksgiving that will continue throughout the letter.

There are seven places in Colossians where Paul speaks on thankfulness.

---

4. These two goals were typical for an exordium (introduction) to a speech, and while letters were not exactly like speeches, there were many similarities. See Cerutti, *Cicero's Accretive Style*, 151–52; Klauck, *Ancient Letters*, 209–10; and Stowers, *Letter Writing*, 34.

5. There is not much in vv. 1–2 that will be of use in this search. As such, those verses will not get their own section; rather, they will be discussed in looking at vv. 3–8.

6. Unless indicated otherwise, all translations are my own.

1. (1:3) Thankfulness towards God expresses Paul and Timothy's attitude when thinking about the Colossians. Paul wants the Colossians to do the same, and he is leading by example.

2. (1:12) The Colossians are told to thank the Father who qualified them to share in the inheritance.

3. (2:7) In the thematic statement, "abounding in thanksgiving" is one of the three descriptors of what it means to walk in Christ.

4-6.(3:15, 16, 17) Three times in the description of how the Colossians are to live their lives on a daily basis, Paul speaks to them of thankfulness.

7. (4:2) Immediately after the household code, Paul returns to thankfulness before closing the Christian living section, as well as the letter.

Paul's emphasis on thanksgiving, both in v. 3 and throughout the letter, was not merely reliance on the standard letter-writing style of the time.[7] If that is all it were, one might expect thanksgiving/thankfulness to make an appearance here in the introduction but then never appear again. Rather, the opposite is happening. Paul "is not telling his readers what a grateful man he is but is drawing their attention to the great thankworthy things God has bestowed on them."[8] There will be a consistent emphasis throughout the letter on what God has done for the Colossians, and Paul makes clear that thankfulness is the proper response.

However, the thankfulness that Paul will be encouraging throughout the letter is not merely something nice one says after receiving a gift. Rather, "acts of thanksgiving are acts of worship, and a life of worship is manifested in the way Christians are to live out their confession."[9] Notice in the verses above that all of them (except perhaps v. 3) are either about how one should live as a Christian or (in the case of 1:12) are about connecting Christian theology with Christian living. The connection between theology and lifestyle (or beliefs and actions) is first made here in the introduction, and because part of the point of the introduction is to bring up topics that will become important later, it would be good for the reader to remember this connection. One should expect Paul to go into more detail on all his introductory points later in the letter.

Something else important about 1:3 is the way it relates Jesus to God. Again, in the introduction, Paul gives very little detail about the points that

---

7. Arzt, "Epistolary Introductory Thanksgiving," 37, and O'Brien, *Introductory Thanksgivings*, 63.

8. Lenski, *Interpretation of St. Paul's Epistles*, 19.

9. Pao, "Gospel within the Constraints," 125.

he will cover (since it is only an introduction). However, one has only to read the letter at a surface level to know that Paul speaks of Christ in very exalted terms. In later chapters, there will be a lot of emphasis on who Christ is, what he has done, and how he is related to the Father. Paul is trying to get his readers to start thinking about Christ and his relationship to God. In 1:15–20, he will go into those topics in detail.

1:4

ἀκούσαντες τὴν πίστιν ὑμῶν ἐν Χριστῷ Ἰησοῦ καὶ τὴν ἀγάπην ἣν ἔχετε εἰς πάντας τοὺς ἁγίους

Since we heard of your faith in Christ Jesus and of the love you have for all the saints

Verse 4 is not a new thought; rather, it continues the thought of v. 3. Here, Paul explains *why* he is so thankful for the Colossians. Paul is thankful because of their *faith* and their *love*. His thought will continue into v. 5 with the third thing he is thankful for, their *hope*—the third cardinal virtue of early Christianity.[10]

Paul is also slowly introducing another theme that will become important later. He is not thankful that they have just some generic kind of faith, as if "sincere religious belief" is all that matters. No, the faith for which he is thankful is that their faith *in Christ Jesus*. This means that they are not just focusing on Christ as the object of their faith, but that they are also operating under his influence and control.[11] This places greater importance

10. Moo, *Letters to the Colossians*, 84, and Wilson, *Colossians and Philemon*, 86. O'Brien says these three virtues seem "to have been a sort of compendium of the Christian life current in the early apostolic church" (*Colossians-Philemon*, 11).

11. N.T. Wright says this phrase "could have the connotation of the sphere in which faith operates rather than, as an English reader tends to assume, the object of faith" (*Colossians and Philemon*, 51). O'Brien goes even further and completely rules out the possibility of ἐν Χριστῷ Ἰησοῦ (in Christ Jesus) as designating the object of the Colossians' faith (*Colossians-Philemon*, 11). Sumney, on the other hand, suggests that "it seems unwise to make a hard and fast division between these alternatives [object or sphere of faith]. Both belief in and dependence on Christ are important for the Colossians as it combats views the author thinks diminish the person and work of Christ" (*Colossians*, 34). Sumney's view makes sense, because while the Colossians' primary need is to live in the sphere of Christ, their belief in the centrality of Christ is being challenged, and so Christ as the object of faith may have special relevance here. However, some commentators, such as Witherington, see the ἐν (in) as a significant departure from Paul's typical phrase (faith in Jesus Christ, using the dative) (*Letters to Philemon*, 121). However, the only way one could make such a point would be if Paul were the sole author of Colossians. If someone else, like Timothy, were the author (with Paul as the supervisor), or if

on the forthcoming statements in the hymn about Christ's creation of the world. If Christ created all things and rules over all things, then his sphere of influence has no bounds.

However, even though Paul has given a direction for the faith that the Colossians have (Christ Jesus), he has not yet explained what that faith is. Is it a faith that Christ *has done* something? Is it a faith that Christ *will do* something? Is it a blind faith? Or, is it based on evidence? Again, Paul is just introducing the themes he wants to talk about here. He is putting the skeleton together, but so far, he hasn't put any meat on the bones.

In the second half of v. 4, Paul expresses his thankfulness for the love the Colossians have for all the saints (those who follow Christ). However, while ἀγάπη (agape/love) is a common word in Christian theological studies, it was not used much at the time of this letter.[12] Early Christians basically took this word and gave it their own meaning. Because of this, it will be better to wait until the Christian living section (3:1–4:6) to let Paul explain what he thinks it means. But, even though ἀγάπη (agape/love) is not being studied in detail here, it is worth noticing that Paul brought it up in the introduction to the letter. So, he must have thought it was important.

Now, the Colossians are not being praised for a generic love but for a love for all the saints. "Saints" is probably a reference to God's people rather than to any inherent moral qualities such people may possess.[13] The reference to the saints in v. 2, where Paul addresses the saints and faithful brothers in Christ at Colossae, suggests this. There, saints and faithful brothers are placed in parallel, which probably indicates that Paul thinks that they are the same group.[14] And, given that the letter is addressed to them and Paul

---

Paul had a coauthor, the point disappears, because style varies from author to author. Perhaps it is best to simply focus on the fact that the faith is in *Jesus Christ*.

12. Bauer et al say, "This term has left little trace in polytheistic Gk" (ἀγάπη, *Greek English Lexicon*, 6). Dunn says, "Of the different Greek words for 'love,' ἀγάπη was little used at the time: it appears only rarely in nonbiblical Greek before the second or third century AD and is relatively rare in the LXX, usually used there in reference to conjugal love" (*Epistles to the Colossians*, 57–58).

13. Moo, *Letters to the Colossians*, 84–85.

14. This is an example of Hebrew parallelism, which is a form of poetry that uses patterns in the words rather than meter or rhyme to make its point. Often there will be deliberate repetition between one line and another. This is something one regularly sees in the Old Testament and is probably best known from the book of Proverbs. For example, Prov 3:13 says, "Blessed is the man who finds wisdom and the one who gets understanding." Wisdom and understanding are being placed in parallel. This is not to say that they are different concepts; rather, by placing them in parallel like this, the author is emphasizing the point by saying the same thing in two different (though very similar) ways. If Paul is doing the same thing here in Colossians, then by placing "saints" and "faithful brothers" in parallel, he is showing that he thinks they mean the

is correcting their actions in the letter, he must not think of them as sin-
less. So, being called "saints" probably has nothing to do with people being
inherently moral. Rather, the emphasis on the word "saints" is on belonging
to a group of people: other followers of Christ. For the Colossians, this primarily meant other Christians with whom they would have interacted on a
regular basis, as well as members of other churches in the Lycus Valley and
throughout Asia Minor.[15]

Here, with his praise of the Colossians' ἀγάπη (agape/love) of all the
saints, Paul is beginning to introduce his idea of what interactions between
people should look like. He is introducing the idea of community. Again,
Paul has not defined ἀγάπη (agape/love). That comes later. For now, it is just
a placeholder—an empty shell that he will fill with content later. Right now,
he is simply introducing some of the main ideas.

1:5

> διὰ τὴν ἐλπίδα τὴν ἀποκειμένην ὑμῖν ἐν τοῖς οὐρανοῖς ἣν
> προηκούσατε ἐν τῷ λόγῳ τῆς ἀληθείας τοῦ εὐαγγελίου

> Through the hope that is laid up for you in the heavens, which
> you heard before in the word of truth, the gospel

The third member of the triad, hope, stands apart from the other two. Look
at how Paul connects the three parts, and focus on the words that connect
the three parts: ἀκούσαντες τὴν πίστιν ὑμῶν . . . καὶ τὴν ἀγάπην . . . διὰ
τὴν ἐλπίδα (because we heard of your faith . . . *and* love . . . *through* hope).
It is significant that the first two terms are connected with a καὶ (and), but
hope stands in relation to the other two by means of a διὰ (through). Some
want to say that hope is linked to faith and love in a causative way; the
Colossians' faith and love is *because* of the hope laid up for them in heav-
en.[16] Other commentators think it is better to say that faith and love "spring
from" hope.[17] However, the way to get at the relation between these three
virtues is not by an analysis of the prepositions but by looking at the meaning of the term that stands apart from the other two, hope.

---

same thing. The repetition is being used for emphasis, much like wisdom and understanding in Prov 3:13.

15. Dunn, *Epistles to the Colossians*, 58, and Moo, *Letters to the Colossians*, 85.

16. Bing, "Warning in Colossians 1:21–23," 80, and Moo, *Letters to the Colossians*,
85.

17. Dunn, *Epistles to the Colossians*, 58; and N.T. Wright, *Colossians and Philemon*,
52.

Hope, here, is τὴν ἐλπίδα τὴν ἀποκειμένην ὑμῖν ἐν τοῖς οὐρανοῖς (the hope that is laid up for you in the heavens). ἀποκειμένην (laid up) is very important to understanding hope, because the fact that it is "laid up/stored" for the Colossians means that this hope is objective rather than subjective.[18] What Paul has in mind is not a *feeling* of hopefulness but rather some true statement about external reality that will impact the Colossians' future. This hope exists, in some way, ἐν τοῖς οὐρανοῖς (in the heavens).[19]

Now, this objective hope, this true statement about external reality that will impact the Colossians' future, is not the same kind of hope held by the Greeks. Schnelle says that "in Greek thought the future and thus hope were perceived as both attractive and threatening."[20] In other words, the version of hope that they had was more like possibility. Things in the future could go very well, or they could go very badly. Because there was possibility, there was hope, but there was also fear and danger. For the Christian, on the other hand, because hope is a concrete thing and not a subjective *feeling* of hope, there would not be danger or need for fear.

There is a profound theology in this word, hope, that sets Christianity apart from the alternative philosophy at Colossae and from many other religions as well. "From the very beginning, Paul reminds his readers that their hope lies in what God has done for them in Christ and not in their own capacities or abilities . . . . Their lives have now become part of the story of the gospel, God's gracious deliverance in Christ."[21] If Christianity is actually based on what God has done for humanity rather than on what humans can do for themselves, then this is a big difference between the Christian worldview and any other alternative. Now, Paul has not said anything definitive on this subject yet, but he does hint at this possibility by referring

18. Thompson, *Colossians and Philemon*, 20; Witherington, *Letters to Philemon*, 121; Wolter, *Brief an die Kolosser*, 52; and N.T. Wright, *Colossians and Philemon*, 51.

19. On the basis of the plural form "heavens," Dunn thinks that the Jewish belief in the multiple regions of heaven is in view. He says, "If the usual topography is in mind here, the implication would be that the lower reaches of heaven were populated by (normally hostile) 'principalities and powers,' with God and his angels in the upper regions or beyond all the heavens. The hope, then, would be for a destiny that outmaneuvers and defeats these powers and reaches right into the presence of God" (*Epistles to the Colossians*, 59–60). Ultimately, Dunn's view on ἐν τοῖς οὐρανοῖς (in the heavens) makes the Colossians' hope sure, because it is founded on the sovereignty of God. This certainly fits with the theology one finds in Colossians, especially the verses about the powers and authorities in ch. 1–2. However, unless there is additional confirmation elsewhere in the letter that this view of heaven is actually what is meant by the plural "heavens," it might be best not to make that assumption. The point is that the hope Paul is talking about is based on the sovereignty of God.

20. Schnelle, *Theology*, 581, and Dunn, *Epistles to the Colossians*, 58.

21. Thompson, *Colossians and Philemon*, 19.

to the concrete hope that is laid up for the Colossians in the heavens. This reference to something firm and sure that believers can put their trust in but that Paul does not explain creates suspense. It makes the reader want to find out more about what Paul might mean and whether such hope could be real.

It is time now to return to faith and love and to determine their relationship to hope. If Christian hope is laid up for the Colossians in the heavens and is an objective or concrete kind of hope, how does that lead to faith and love?

Unfortunately, at this point, Paul has not given the readers any more details. He has only said that hope is laid up for them in the heavens (and thus is probably a concrete sort of thing). And, he says that faith is in Christ Jesus, and the Colossians' love is directed towards all the other saints/faithful brethren. However, while Paul has not given his readers many details, he is telling his audience where he will go. One should, therefore, expect to find more on 1) what this hope really is, 2) who Christ is and what he has done, and 3) what it means to have ἀγάπη (agape/love) for others. All that is certain so far is that faith and love are somehow "caused by" or "spring from" hope, hope seems to be a concrete or objective thing rather than mere wishful thinking, and hope makes Christianity different from other worldviews.[22]

In the last half of v. 5, Paul grounds the hope the Colossians have in "the word of truth, the gospel." Each of these three words is linked to the others with the genitive case, which makes it more difficult to pinpoint their exact relationship to one another.[23] However, even if it is not possible to determine *how* they are to be linked grammatically, one should note that "word," "truth," and "gospel" *are* being linked. What Paul is doing here is grounding the Christian message in its truth. It is not mere wishful thinking or a "technique for changing people's lives."[24] Rather, Paul's claim is that the Christian message is actually true, and because of that, people should pay attention.

Finally, Paul says that the Colossians have heard of this ἦν (before), but it is not clear to what "before" refers. It is possible that the reference is to when the Colossians first heard the gospel from Epaphras, but the Greek simply refers to an earlier, unspecified date, i.e. "recently."[25] It might be best

---

22. Paul may have said in 1 Cor 13 that love is the greatest of the three virtues, but here he says that hope is the most foundational. Without hope, there would be no reason to have faith and no example of what it means to love. Hope appears to be what makes faith and love possible.

23. Moo, *Letters to the Colossians*, 86.

24. N.T. Wright, *Colossians and Philemon*, 52.

25. Dunn, *Epistles to the Colossians*, 60, and Wilson, *Colossians and Philemon*, 89.

to not try to make anything more of this than to simply say that the Colossians already were familiar with the gospel that Paul was giving them.

1:6–8

τοῦ παρόντος εἰς ὑμᾶς καθὼς καὶ ἐν παντὶ τῷ κόσμῳ ἐστὶν
καρποφορούμενον καὶ αὐξανόμενον καθὼς καὶ ἐν ὑμῖν ἀφ' ἧς
ἡμέρας ἠκούσατε καὶ ἐπέγνωτε τὴν χάριν τοῦ θεοῦ ἐν ἀληθείᾳ
καθὼς ἐμάθετε ἀπὸ Ἐπαφρᾶ τοῦ ἀγαπητοῦ συνδούλου ἡμῶν ὅς
ἐστιν πιστὸς ὑπὲρ ὑμῶν διάκονος τοῦ Χριστοῦ ὁ καὶ δηλώσας
ἡμῖν τὴν ὑμῶν ἀγάπην ἐν πνεύματι

which has come to you just as indeed in the whole world it is bearing fruit and increasing—just as it also does among you, from the day you heard and understood the grace of God in truth, just as you learned it from Epaphras our beloved fellow slave, who is a faithful servant of Christ on your behalf and has made known to us your love in the Spirit.

τοῦ παρόντος εἰς ὑμᾶς (which has come to you) at the beginning of v. 6 points back to τῷ λόγῳ τῆς ἀληθείας τοῦ εὐαγγελίου (the word of truth, the gospel, at the end of v. 5). Verse 5 connected the gospel with hope, and v. 6 says that the gospel (the word of truth and the source of hope) has come to the Colossians.

Now, according to Paul, this gospel has been proclaimed in the whole world. This does not mean, however, that everyone in the entire world has heard the message. This phrase probably has an eschatological meaning. Wright says, "From his perspective as a converted Pharisee the important point was that the salvation promised in the Old Testament had now been unleashed upon the world irrespective of geographical or racial barriers."[26] This seems reasonable, given that Paul is going to speak about the breaking down of barriers in 3:11. Additionally, this is probably meant to point towards the truth of the Christian message, since it is spreading worldwide and is not merely a local belief.[27] If the creator of the cosmos is really behind this message, then one would think that it should be for everyone and not just a local group.

Paul also points out that the Colossians have another witness to the truth of the gospel—their own experience. The gospel has been bearing fruit

---

26. N.T. Wright, *Colossians and Philemon*, 53.

27. Moo, *Letters to the Colossians*, 89; O'Brien, *Colossians-Philemon*, 13; and Sumney, *Colossians*, 37.

and increasing among them. Therefore, of all people, Paul says, you Colossians should know that this gospel is real, because you have experienced the results firsthand.

However, καρποφορούμενον καὶ αὐξανόμενον (bearing fruit and increasing)[28] is something that *happens* among the Colossians. It is not something they actually *cause*. It is the gospel, not the Colossians, that is bearing fruit and increasing. "This keeps the emphasis on what God is doing."[29] This would imply to the Colossians that if they leave the gospel for any alternative, the bearing fruit and increasing that has been occurring will stop, because these things come from God.

Lest there be any confusion about to which message Paul is referring, back in v. 5, Paul reminded the Colossians that the message he is preaching is the one that they "heard before." This is the one that they heard from Epaphras, who will be described as τοῦ ἀγαπητοῦ συνδούλου ἡμῶν (our beloved fellow slave)[30] and πιστὸς ὑπὲρ ὑμῶν διάκονος τοῦ Χριστοῦ (a faithful servant of Christ on your behalf) in v. 7. Paul is describing Epaphras like this to set him up as an example worth following.

Here in v. 6, one finds a second reference to the Colossians' hearing of the message, "since the day you heard and understood the grace of God in truth." There are two things to notice here. First, there is the repetition of "truth." It is debated whether the phrase ἐν ἀληθείᾳ (in truth) modifies ἠκούσατε καὶ ἐπέγνωτε (you heard and understood) or τὴν χάριν τοῦ θεοῦ (the grace of God),[31] but the fact that one sees ἀληθείᾳ (truth) in both vv. 5 and 6 is probably not an accident. Paul is emphasizing that the *true* path is the one through the gospel and not any other.

The second thing one should notice is the way Paul describes the message the Colossians have heard. In v. 5, Paul refers to the message they heard before as the εὐαγγέλιον (good news). Here, it is described as τὴν χάριν τοῦ θεοῦ (the grace of God). The word χάριν (grace) is not the focus here; rather, it is θεοῦ (God).[32] By describing the message as τὴν χάριν τοῦ θεοῦ (the

28. This is a phrase which many commentators consider to be reminiscent of Genesis 1, for example, Moo, *Letters to the Colossians*, 88; O'Brien, *Colossians-Philemon*, 13; and N.T. Wright, *Colossians and Philemon*, 53. Moo says, "To be sure, the verb 'bear fruit' does not occur in the Old Testament formula, but Paul may have substituted this verb (and placed it first) because it conveys better than 'multiply' the results of the gospel in the lives of believers" (*Letters to the Colossians*, 88).

29. Sumney, *Colossians*, 38.

30. There will be a lot more on slavery in the chapter on 3:18–4:1. There is a reason for this language, and it will be discussed in detail.

31. Wilson, *Colossians and Philemon*, 94.

32. Schweizer says this is much like the single occurrence of "Spirit" in v. 8 ("Christus und Geist," 308).

grace of God), Paul is making it clear that what the Colossians have heard has *God* as its source.

Now, beyond reminding the Colossians that the message they heard before is the one which comes from *God* and is the *true* message, Paul goes to extra lengths to make sure the Colossians cannot possibly misunderstand which message he is talking about and why it is better. Paul creates structure in these verses in order to emphasize these points. Between these two verses, there are three instances of καθὼς (just as). They are as follows:

1. καθὼς καὶ ἐν παντὶ τῷ κόσμῳ ἐστὶν καρποφορούμενον καὶ αὐξανόμενον

2. καθὼς καὶ ἐν ὑμῖν ἀφ' ἧς ἡμέρας ἠκούσατε καὶ ἐπέγνωτε τὴν χάριν τοῦ θεοῦ ἐν ἀληθείᾳ

3. καθὼς ἐμάθετε ἀπὸ Ἐπαφρᾶ τοῦ ἀγαπητοῦ συνδούλου ἡμῶν

1. Just as indeed in the whole world it is bearing fruit and increasing

2. Just as also it does among you, from the day you heard and understood the grace of God in truth

3. Just as you learned from Epaphras our beloved fellow slave[33]

Paul is telling the Colossians that bearing fruit and increasing cannot be separated from the gospel. He essentially says, "This gospel *works*! Who would know this better than you? This gospel has worked *for you*! So, if you Colossians want to continue bearing fruit and increasing, you need to stick to what you were taught—*without any changes!*"

The structure here serves to link the three statements so that they cannot be separated from each other. Now, this gospel is further defined as the one they learned from Epaphras. "The term 'learned' (ἐμάθετε) probably indicates that Epaphras had given them systematic instruction in the gospel rather than some flimsy outline and that these Colossians had committed themselves as disciples to that teaching."[34] So, it's not like the Colossians didn't understand the message. They had been well taught. What they needed, then, was not more instruction. They needed commitment.

Even though he has not made his arguments yet, here in the introduction, Paul is setting the stage for what is to come: comparing Christianity with another worldview. The message the Colossians heard from Epaphras

---

33. While this is often translated as "fellow servant," the word here actually means "fellow slave." Again, there will be a long discussion on slavery in the chapter on household code in 3:18–4:1. Following that discussion, it will make more sense why Paul refers to people as fellow slaves.

34. O'Brien, *Colossians-Philemon*, 15.

is the gospel, it is the word of truth, it comes from God, and it bears fruit and increases in the whole world, as well as among them. Anything else would be less than the gospel, less than the word of truth, not from God, not bearing fruit and increasing, not spreading through the whole world, and not having born fruit among them.

Before concluding, it is necessary to say something about the Holy Sprit, or rather lack thereof, in this letter. The brief reference to the "spirit" in v. 8 is the only reference to the Holy Spirit in the entire letter, and it is only a probable reference at that. One cannot be *completely* certain that it is, in fact, a reference to the Holy Spirit, even though it *probably* is. While there is not much to say about this here (since no information is given), this absence will become important when it comes time to break down the essentials of the Christian worldview. One will need to ask why Paul left the Holy Spirit out of his explanation.[35]

SIGNIFICANCE

Paul's introduction to this letter begins his comparison of the Christian worldview with the alternative one on offer in Colossae. Even though that other worldview will not be discussed until ch. 2 of the letter, he is nevertheless preparing his argument here by outlining what is special about Christianity.

Paul begins with the topic of thankfulness, and even though this topic is not discussed much in vv. 3–8, there is more emphasis on thankfulness in this letter than in any other of his letters.[36] But, thankfulness implies a wider narrative. In order for one to be genuinely thankful, something must have happened which leads to thankfulness. This wider narrative has not yet been discussed, but it will be in the next section of the letter.

Paul also talks about Christianity as if it is based on truth. He does not speak as if Christianity is merely a nice set of things to believe or actions to perform in order to make one happy. It is not merely "useful," nor is it a means to an end. If Paul thinks Christianity is based on truth, then he is saying that it is based on the way the world actually is. Whether he is saying the alternate worldview at Colossae is false or mere preference has yet to be determined. But, he says, Christianity is true.

35. There will be a whole section addressing this question in the last chapter.

36. O'Brien says, "Thanksgiving appears in Colossians twice as often as in 2 Corinthians and three times more frequently than in the other letters of the Pauline corpus" (*Introductory Thanksgivings*, 63).

As a result of Paul's claim to truth, any of the specific claims that he makes (such as that God exists, that Jesus rose from the dead, or that Christianity actually works in the life of the Christian) are now open to question. If they were merely things to believe that ultimately carry no meaning, then it would not matter if they are true. But, now that he has claimed that Christianity is true, they matter a great deal. Paul has opened up Christianity to being proven false.

That means if someone is thinking about becoming a Christian, he or she would do well to look around at the world and ask the question "Does Christianity look like it's true?" If Christianity is true, then it is of supreme importance, and one should commit his or her entire life to it. If Christianity is not true, then there is no reason to pay attention to it, and it can be safely ignored—or perhaps fought against, if one thinks it is a danger to others.

If one decides that Christianity is likely to be true and then follows its teachings, that person's life will be centered around responding to whatever it is that Christianity is about, which remains to be seen. So far, all that is certain is that faith, love, and hope are important, and thankfulness ties in with them somehow.

In addition to faith, love, hope, and thankfulness, Paul leaves his readers with the topics of God, Christ, and humanity. He has mentioned these briefly, but he has said very little about them. The reader is left wondering about four questions: 1) Who is Christ? 2) How does Christ relate to God? 3) What has Christ done? 4) How should humanity respond? In 1:9–14, Paul is going to start talking about some of these big questions as he shows the Colossians what it looks like to walk in a manner worthy of the Lord.

4

Walking in a Manner Worthy
of the Lord (1:9–14)

INTRODUCTION

In vv. 3–8, Paul introduced some of the main themes of the letter. In vv. 9–14 he begins to address specific topics. However, these verses start with διὰ τοῦτο (for this reason), meaning they build on the previous section of the letter.[1] Like every section of the letter, this section builds on what has come before and prepares the reader for what comes after.

The themes in vv. 9–14 are even more densely packed together than they were in vv. 3–8. About every one and a half verses, Paul shifts from one theme to another. However, these themes are not separate from one another, and this adds a level of complexity. It is almost necessary to hold all of them in one's head at the same time in order to understand any of them. Fortunately, though, they can be broken down and simplified. If the reader knows what is coming before diving into the verses themselves, it should not be difficult to follow Paul's train of thought.

There are three main divisions of vv. 9–14. The first division is vv. 9–10a. Here, Paul talks about the interaction of beliefs (theory) and actions

---

1. Donelson, *Colossians*, 17; Lightfoot, *St. Paul's Epistles*, 203; MacDonald, *Colossians and Ephesians*, 47; Moo, *Letters to the Colossians*, 92; and Sumney, *Colossians*, 44.

(practice) and how to know God himself. The two things he says that are relevant to pleasing God are the knowledge of God's will (theory) and walking in a manner worthy of the Lord (practice). Paul explains how *knowing* what God wants a person to do (theory) and then actually *living it out* (practice) lead to a person improving morally and knowing God himself better.

The second division of vv. 9–14 is vv. 10b–12a. This section builds on vv. 9–10a. It answers the question "If a Christian is supposed to 'walk in a manner worthy of the Lord' (practice), what does that actually look like? How can a person walk/live in a worthy manner?" Paul will give four actions that describe what walking in a manner worthy of the Lord looks like. They are: 1. bearing fruit, 2. increasing (in the knowledge of God), 3. being strengthened, 4. giving thanks. In ch. 3 of the letter, Paul will break down the Christian life into specific actions one should take, but here he gives the general categories.

The third and final division of vv. 9–14 is vv. 12b–14. In these verses, Paul talks about what God has done for the Colossians and explains why they should be thankful. Furthermore, because of what God has done for them, they should *want* to walk in a manner worthy of the Lord.

All these divisions are closely connected, and these verses get fairly detailed. However, knowing what is ahead will make everything much more clear. These divisions and how they connect to one another will be discussed in part or in whole several times over the course of the chapter. For now, just remember that there are three main divisions: 1) beliefs and actions, 2) worthy living, 3) God and humanity.

1:9

> διὰ τοῦτο καὶ ἡμεῖς ἀφ' ἧς ἡμέρας ἠκούσαμεν οὐ παυόμεθα ὑπὲρ ὑμῶν προσευχόμενοι καὶ αἰτούμενοι ἵνα πληρωθῆτε τὴν ἐπίγνωσιν τοῦ θελήματος αὐτοῦ ἐν πάσῃ σοφίᾳ καὶ συνέσει πνευματικῇ
>
> and for this reason, from the day we heard, we have not ceased to pray for you, asking that you may be filled with the knowledge of his will in all spiritual wisdom and understanding

In v. 9, Paul tells the Colossians that he and Timothy have been praying for them. They have been doing this since they heard of the Colossians' *faith* in Christ Jesus and the *love* they have for all the saints because of the *hope* laid up for them in the heavens (vv. 4–5). However, their prayers have not been for action on the Colossians' part (something they should do) but rather for action on God's part (something Paul prays God will do). The use of the passive πληρωθῆτε (be filled) indicates that God is the actor. This means that the Colossians do not attain this knowledge for themselves; rather, God grants it to them.[2] But, what is this knowledge?

The word ἐπίγνωσιν (knowledge) itself actually gives a clue as to its meaning, because this is not the normal word for knowledge but a compound noun that probably serves to point back to God.[3] In other words, this knowledge is not a generic knowledge about the world. Rather, this is knowledge about or directed towards God. Now, this conclusion cannot be reached on the basis of ἐπίγνωσιν (knowledge) alone, although this word does point in that direction. However, the qualifying phrases that follow, "of his will" and "in all spiritual wisdom and understanding," do bring one to the conclusion that knowledge about or directed towards God is what is meant here.

The first phrase, "of his will," helps to describe what this knowledge is. Very simply, it is knowledge of God's will. But, that fact carries with it two significant theological implications. First, knowing the will of God is important for the very fact that it is *God's* will. "For a theist who believes that God's active purpose determines the ordering of the world, lies behind events on earth, and shapes their consequences, one of the most desirable objectives must be to know God's will."[4] This would be enough all by itself to make the knowledge Paul is talking about important. However, something else about this phrase is just as significant.

"Knowledge of God's will" points towards the revelation of God to man. There do not seem to be many ways one can gain knowledge about a transcendent being. Looking at the actions of such a being and trying to infer something about him/her/it might be one of the best ways, but this is very limited. Knowing something about that being would be greatly aided if he/she/it simply revealed things to humanity. Knowledge of God's will points towards exactly that. It points towards God revealing something about his desires that humanity would have little or no access to otherwise. This is what Paul is praying for when he prays for the Colossians to be filled (πληρωθῆτε) with the knowledge of God's will. He is praying that God *give* the Colossians knowledge about his will. Of course, that says something

---

2. Sumney, *Colossians*, 45.

3. MacDonald says, "The compound noun translated as knowledge here, ἐπίγνωσις, can mean full or complete knowledge or insight. But it seems more likely that the addition of ἐπί to the general term γνωσις in this case serves the grammatical purpose of expressing knowledge directed toward a particular object, i.e., God's will" (*Colossians and Ephesians*, 47).

4. Dunn, *Epistles to the Colossians*, 69.

important about Christianity. If the Christian God is the kind of God that gives knowledge about himself, then Christianity is a religion of revelation.

The other phrase that describes how Paul wants the Colossians to be filled (πληρωθῆτε) is "in all spiritual wisdom and understanding." Like "of his will," this phrase explains more about Paul's prayers for the Colossians to be filled (πληρωθῆτε) with God's knowledge. These two phrases are parallel to one another and describe what Paul wants for the Colossians. He wants them to be filled with the knowledge 1) of God's will and 2) in all spiritual wisdom and understanding. But what does that second phrase mean?

Wisdom and understanding are essentially two ways of saying the same thing.[5] The important part of this phrase is actually the word πνευματικῇ (spiritual). There may be a connection here with the phrase "your love in the spirit" in the previous verse (v. 8). If the reference to spirit in v. 8 is a reference to the Holy Spirit, then "the writer's interest will not simply be in a wisdom that is an innate capacity of the human spirit but in a wisdom that is provided by a relationship to God in Christ."[6]

However, even if these two uses of spirit/spiritual are not meant to be connected, Paul is still setting up a contrast that he will explore later. When he compares Christianity with the "philosophy" in ch. 2 of the letter, he will talk about Christianity as the path laid out by God, and therefore it is heavenly and spiritual. By contrast, the philosophy is a path created by men, and therefore it is earthly and has no more than a "shadow of the things to come" (2:17).

Here, though, Paul is not making that argument—at least not yet. He is merely hinting to his readers about some of the topics he will address in an effort to better prepare them for the argument to come. For now, one can simply think of the word πνευματικῇ (spiritual) as a reemphasis of what the passive πληρωθῆτε (be filled) means: it means that the knowledge comes *from God.*

The phrase "in all spiritual wisdom and understanding," therefore, is meant to describe what knowledge the Colossians are to be filled with. They are to be filled "in all *spiritual* wisdom and understanding" rather than "in all *earthly* wisdom and understanding." And, with the combination of the phrases "of His will" and "in all spiritual wisdom and understanding," Paul is emphasizing the revelation of God to man. But, once God gives revelation, what should man do?

5. This is just like "saints" and "faithful brothers" in the last chapter. This is another example of Hebrew parallelism. It is Paul saying the same thing in two slightly different ways in order to emphasize that thing's importance.

6. Lincoln, "Spiritual Wisdom of Colossians," 213, and Bruce, "Colossian Problems: Part 4," 46.

1:10

περιπατῆσαι ἀξίως τοῦ κυρίου εἰς πᾶσαν ἀρεσκείαν ἐν παντὶ
ἔργῳ ἀγαθῷ καρποφοροῦντες αὐξανόμενοι τῇ ἐπιγνώσει τοῦ
θεοῦ

So as to walk in a manner worthy of the Lord, fully pleasing
to him: bearing fruit in every good work and increasing in the
knowledge of God

περιπατῆσαι ἀξίως τοῦ κυρίου (so as to walk in a manner worthy of the
Lord) is the reason Paul is praying for the Colossians.[7] He wants them to
walk in a manner worthy of the Lord. This is part of a larger theme that
spans several verses. Paul wants them to be filled with the knowledge of
God's will (v. 9) so as to walk in a manner worthy of the Lord (v. 10a). Then,
vv. 10b-12 describe what walking in a manner worthy of the Lord looks like.
But, what is a "walk"?

At its essence, a "walk" is "a metaphorical expression for moral and
ethical behavior."[8] It describes how a person lives life. In this verse, "walk"
is modified with two additional phrases: ἀξίως τοῦ κυρίου (in a manner
worthy of the Lord) and εἰς πᾶσαν ἀρεσκείαν (fully pleasing to him). ἀξίως
τοῦ κυρίου (in a manner worthy of the Lord) indicates that the way one
lives life should be aimed at being worthy of the Lord. It is not OK to just
do whatever one wants. One's moral and ethical behavior need to be worthy
of the Lord.

εἰς πᾶσαν ἀρεσκείαν (fully pleasing to him) explains the goal of one's
efforts. ἀρεσκεία essentially means "desire to please."[9] Though this word was
often employed in a negative sense in secular Greek, "it could also be used
in a positive sense, and frequently in Hellenistic Judaism referred to what
was 'well-pleasing to God.'"[10] The person who is following God should be
trying to please God or live a life that is well-pleasing to God.

Very simply, the first half of this verse is saying that a person should
live his or her life in a manner that would please God. However, things are
not as simple as just "trying to do one's best to make God happy." The previous verse (v. 9) said the Colossians have to be filled with the knowledge of

7. O'Brien says, "The infinitive construction indicates the purpose for which the
readers are to be filled with a knowledge of God's will, namely 'to walk worthily of the
Lord'" (*Colossians-Philemon*, 19).

8. Gurtner, "Colossians," 593. Dunn points out that describing one's conduct as a walk
is atypical of Greek thought but is characteristically Jewish (*Epistles to the Colossians*, 71).

9. Bauer et al., ἀρεσκεία, *Greek English Lexicon*, 129.

10. O'Brien, *Colossians-Philemon*, 22.

God's will in order to be able to walk in a manner pleasing to the Lord. That means that the Colossians need God's help to live in a manner pleasing to God.

So, Paul wants his readers to be able to live a worthy life—one that is pleasing to the Lord. How should they go about doing that? In the second half of v. 10, Paul begins his explanation of what it actually looks like to walk in a manner worthy of the Lord. This explanation will consist of four participles[11] stretching through v. 12. They are: 1) καρποφοροῦντες (bearing fruit), 2) αὐξανόμενοι (increasing), 3) δυναμούμενοι (being strengthened), 4) εὐχαριστοῦντες (giving thanks). Each of these describes *how* the Colossians are to walk in a manner worthy of the Lord. Paul will describe each of these in turn, although he treats the first two as a pair.

Alhough the first two participles, καρποφοροῦντες and αὐξανόμενοι (bearing fruit and increasing), appear here in v. 10, it is not the first time they have made an appearance in the letter. In v. 6, Paul said the word of truth, the gospel, was bearing fruit and increasing in the whole world. Here in v. 10, he is saying the Colossians are (or should be) bearing fruit and increasing. What Paul is doing is connecting the "word of truth, the gospel" to the Colossian Christians. The Colossians should be doing at least some of the same things that the gospel is doing: they are both to be bearing fruit and increasing.

Turning to the meaning of the participles themselves, Paul further explains the first one, καρποφοροῦντες (bearing fruit), as occurring ἐν παντὶ ἔργῳ ἀγαθῷ (in every good work). Because it is about "works" that humans do, καρποφοροῦντες (bearing fruit) is about human actions. Furthermore, because the works the Colossians are supposed to do are "good" works, that means the Colossians must improve the way they act; they must become morally mature.[12] They cannot simply learn about God's will and think that they are done. They must *live out* God's will.

What Paul is telling the Colossians is that if they are filled with the knowledge of God's will, this should manifest itself in the way they live their daily lives.[13] Knowledge of God's will combined with an appropriate

---

11. A participle is a word formed from a verb that is often (but not always) used to describe another word, for example; the "running" man. Running is a participle that is based on the verb "to run." Here, it is being used to describe what type of man this is. It is the "running" man. It could also be the "laughing" man, the "crying" man, or the "hungry" man. All of the words in parentheses are participles.

12. If Paul thought they were already morally mature, the letter would look much different.

13. Sumney says, "Perhaps this indicates that the gospel finds its real fulfillment in the way it works in people, leading them to live worthy lives" (*Colossians*, 48).

response on the part of the believer should lead to moral maturity. And, moral maturity reveals God to those who see the Colossians' actions. Since the way the Colossians are to live is based on God's will, living the lives God wants them to will directly reveal him to the people around them. Then, they will bear fruit—just like the gospel has done (v. 6).

Connected with bearing fruit is the second participle, αὐξανόμενοι (increasing). Like bearing fruit, it is not merely that the Colossians are to increase in some abstract manner; rather, they are to increase τῇ ἐπιγνώσει τοῦ θεοῦ (in the knowledge of God). But what does that actually mean? Moo provides two options. He says, "The relationship could be one of sphere, paraphrased nicely in the NLT: 'you will learn to know God better and better.' Or the *in* could have instrumental force: growing takes place by means of our knowledge of God."[14] So, which is it? In order to answer this question, one must first answer another question: "What is the relationship between knowledge in v. 9 and knowledge in v. 10?"

It may seem a little confusing for Paul to say knowledge is one of the elements of a Christian's walk, because one's walk is a consequence of one's knowledge (v. 9). It seems circular, or at least it does at first. Upon closer inspection, one sees that the two instances of "knowledge" are actually different. In v. 9 it is "knowledge of his will," and in v. 10 it is "knowledge of God." If one were to focus on just the main ideas of vv. 9–10, something like this would result: "asking that you may be filled with the knowledge of His will . . . so as to walk in a manner worthy of the Lord . . . increasing in the knowledge of God." When looking at it this way, it appears that the knowledge in v. 9 is what begins everything, walking worthily in v. 10 is what humans should do after receiving that knowledge, and the knowledge in v. 10 results from walking worthily. That means that the first knowledge (knowledge of his will) enables one to have the second knowledge (knowledge of God).

Returning to Moo's options, the first option, using the instrumental force of "in," would mean that the phrase "in the knowledge of God" provides the means by which one does something. Therefore, growing would take place *by means of* the knowledge of God. The problem with this is that the context implies that one is attempting to grow in the knowledge of God. So, using the instrumental force of "in" would result in one reasoning in a circle: increasing in one's knowledge of God will increase one's knowledge of God. While that may be true, it's not very helpful. Perhaps, Paul meant something else.

On the other hand, if one uses the relationship of sphere, then the phrase "in the knowledge of God" means that growth takes place in the

---

14. Moo, *Letters to the Colossians*, 97.

sphere/realm/category of the knowledge of God. Moo said above that this would result in something that meant "you will learn to know God better and better."[15] When this is combined with v. 9, it would mean something more like "knowledge of God's will helps one to know God himself better." This makes much more sense.

Now, suppose one were to take this a step further and integrate this meaning into the meaning of the first participle (bearing fruit). What would happen? The result of this would be a statement that means something like: "the knowledge of God's will helps one to live a life worthy of the Lord—a life that is pleasing to him. And, living this life, in turn, helps one know God better." This seems to be what Paul is getting at in vv. 9–10.

What one sees in vv. 9–10 is a good example of the interaction of beliefs and actions that will feature throughout the letter. Each of the two elements Paul has presented impacts the other. 1) Knowledge of God's will enables the Christian to know how to 2) live a life that is worthy of the Lord and pleasing to him. And, 2) living a life that is worthy of the Lord helps a person to 1) know God's will better. Additionally, when both of these parts are put together, a person comes to know God himself better. But, how does that actually work? How does living a life worthy of the Lord help one to know God better?

Perhaps the way to look at this is to look at the interrelationship between theory and practice. Not only does understanding theory improve one's ability to perform more effectively, one's attempts at performing improve one's understanding of theory. Imagine a gymnast attempting to learn a complicated motion. Understanding how the motion is supposed to work (theory) will enable him or her to attempt the motion in the best way possible. However, practice also helps to understand how the motion is supposed to work (theory). It is not that practice changes physics or the way the motion is supposed to be performed. The physics remain constant. But, practice helps the gymnast to *understand* the physics better. In the same way, God's will is like theory and the Colossians' efforts are like practice. God's will does not change, but the Colossians' understanding of it does. Their knowledge of theory (God's will) helps them to be able to practice (walk in a manner worthy of the Lord) more effectively. And, as they practice, they understand the theory (God's will) at a deeper level.

On the surface, this process sounds something like this:[16]

---

15. Moo, *Letters to the Colossians*, 97.

16. Graphics created by Melissa Tertichny.

UNDERSTANDING GOD'S WILL

WALKING IN A MANNER WORTHY OF THE LORD

However, cycling back and forth between understanding God's will (theory) and walking in a manner worthy of the Lord (practice) is not a circle that goes around and around. Instead, the imagery is more like a spiral.[17] That means that if the Colossians are doing what Paul is suggesting, they should actually be improving and not just coming back to the same place they were before. What happens is that each trip around the spiral moves the Colossians upwards in their knowledge of God's will and their ability to live it out.[18] And the upward direction is the knowledge of God himself.

17. There are many similarities between the imagery of a spiral and Aristotle's virtue ethics. It would be interesting to investigate the similarities and differences between the two. Unfortunately, though, that goes beyond the scope of this study.

18. O'Brien says, "Since the participles which define the walking worthily are all in the present tense and stress the notion of progress, it is probably right to conclude that the Colossian Christians would receive further knowledge as they were obedient to the knowledge of God they had already received" (*Colossians-Philemon*, 23). Whether additional knowledge is received or the received knowledge is better understood (or both), the idea here is that of progress.

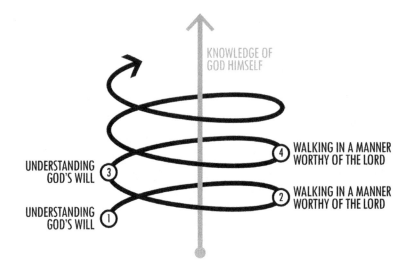

Later in the letter, Paul will explain in detail what it means to live as a Christian. But, given the upward spiral he is describing here, it is clear that Paul did not think of the Christian life as merely following a set of rules or getting one's ticket to heaven or any number of other things that people often think about Christianity today. Paul's view of Christianity was not a static life but rather a dynamic interaction with God that involves both seeking to understand his will, his mind, and what he wants for humanity and then trying to live that out.

1:11

ἐν πάσῃ δυνάμει δυναμούμενοι κατὰ τὸ κράτος τῆς δόξης αὐτοῦ εἰς πᾶσαν ὑπομονὴν καὶ μακροθυμίαν μετὰ χαρᾶς

Being strengthened with all power, according to his glorious might, for all endurance and patience with joy

The third element of a walk that is pleasing to the Lord highlights the manner in which one is to complete this walk. It is to be done in the power that comes from God rather than in one's own strength. The participle δυναμούμενοι (being strengthened) is in the passive voice, which points toward God as the one who is providing the strength. With this phrase, though, there are two modifiers that explain it further: κατὰ τὸ κράτος τῆς δόξης αὐτοῦ (according to his glorious might) and εἰς πᾶσαν ὑπομονὴν καὶ μακροθυμίαν μετὰ χαρᾶς (for all endurance and patience with joy).

The first of these, κατὰ τὸ κράτος τῆς δόξης αὐτοῦ (according to his glorious might), serves to reemphasize the fact that God is the one who is providing strength to the Colossians. The passive voice of the participle δυναμούμενοι (being strengthened) and the fact that this strengthening occurs according to his glorious might points again to God as the source of strength. After all, if the Colossians are to be strengthened, that strength has to come from somewhere. Are they supposed to strengthen themselves with "all power"? No. Just as they were to increase in the knowledge of *God's* will, so they are to be strengthened with *God's* strength. Once again, Paul reminds the Colossians of the importance of their relationship with God.

The second modifier, "for all endurance and patience with joy," is a little more difficult. Working backwards, one must ask the question, does "with joy" modify ὑπομονὴν καὶ μακροθυμίαν (endurance and patience) in v. 11 or εὐχαριστοῦντες (giving thanks) in v. 12? The answer to this question will help determine the emphasis of these last two participles.

There are reasons why one might connect "with joy" in either direction,[19] and if one were to look at these two verses in a vacuum, "with joy" would make more sense attached to v. 11. After all, "patient endurance was a stoic virtue, but joy in the midst of suffering (Acts 16:25) was unique to Christianity."[20] However, considering the context of Colossians and the themes throughout the letter, that may not be the best option. "With joy" basically serves the function of emphasizing whichever of the two phrases to which it is attached. Either it emphasizes the need for joy in the midst of patient endurance (probably as one undergoes persecution), or it emphasizes the need for joy as one thanks God.

The problem with the former is that the need for patient endurance in the face of persecution is not really a theme in this letter.[21] Even if Paul thought it was important, it is not in view here. However, the need for thankfulness is in view. In the sections to follow, Paul goes on to describe

19. Lightfoot argues that "with joy" must be connected with v. 11, because when it is connected with v. 12, "the emphatic position of μετὰ χαρᾶς [with joy] cannot be explained; nor indeed would these words be needed at all, for εὐχαριστοῦντες [giving thanks] is itself an act of rejoicing" (*St. Paul's Epistles*, 206). On the other hand, Sumney says, "A good case can be made for either option . . . . Though social and economic persecution was a daily reality for many in the early church, interpreting that experience is not a focus at this point in Colossians. Thus, the writer probably does not highlight the need for joy in the face of persecution" (*Colossians*, 51).

20. Bruce, *Epistles to the Colossians*, 48.

21. Paul does talk about filling up what is lacking in Christ's afflictions in 1:24 and asks the Colossians to remember his chains in 4:18. However, these instances of suffering are not major themes but make smaller points in service of the major themes. Furthermore, these are about Paul's suffering, not the Colossians' suffering.

what God has done for the Colossians. He describes the redemption and forgiveness that come from God through Christ, shows how everything the Colossians have comes through their relationship with the creator and renewer of the cosmos, and then emphasizes that those who were hostile to God now have been reconciled to Him. The entire letter drives home just how much has been done for the Colossians that they could not have done themselves. This lends itself more towards thanksgiving than it does to patient endurance.

However, while the phrase "with joy" does serve to emphasize "giving thanks," that does not mean that "endurance and patience" is meaningless. In reality, it is quite important. The primary point Paul is making to the Colossians is to "be strengthened with power" which comes from God *for* endurance and patience. Endurance and patience is the reason *why* God strengthens the Colossians. The point of the four participles is to explain how one can walk in a manner worthy of the Lord. Therefore, since "endurance and patience" are the reason the Colossians are strengthened, they indirectly explain how to walk in a manner worthy of the Lord. Paul is telling them that this walk is something that will take time and will not be easy. It is something to which they will have to continually apply themselves and for which they will need God's help. God is strengthening the Colossians, because the road ahead will be difficult.

1:12

> [μετὰ χαρᾶς] εὐχαριστοῦντες τῷ πατρὶ τῷ ἱκανώσαντι ὑμᾶς εἰς τὴν μερίδα τοῦ κλήρου τῶν ἁγίων ἐν τῷ φωτί
>
> [with joy] giving thanks to the Father who has qualified you to share in the inheritance of the saints in light.

The last of the four participles that describes what it means to walk in a manner worthy of the Lord is εὐχαριστοῦντες (giving thanks). This participle actually bridges two of the main thoughts Paul is explaining in vv. 9–14. In order to understand how everything is connected, it would be helpful to step back for a minute and look at what is going on.

Verses 9–10a were about the upward spiral (see diagram on p. 34).[22] Paul was describing the interaction between beliefs and actions (or theory and practice) that helps a person know God better. God gives a person

---

22. One might also ask whether there is a downward spiral to correspond to the upward one. This is an interesting question, and it will be addressed later in the letter when Paul discusses the actions that displease God.

some amount of knowledge about his will (theory). Hopefully, the person then tries to live according to God's will (practice). By living out God's will (practice), the person will understand God's will better than the first time (theory), and this will enable him or her to live it out (practice) even better than the first time. This results in a spiral that moves in an upward direction, in which a person continually learns more and more about God's will and becomes better and better at putting it into practice. The ultimate result of this upward spiral is knowing God himself better.

Verses 10b–12a are about how to actually make this upward spiral happen. Paul uses four participles to explain what things a person should actually be doing to make his or her walk (the way one lives) better, i.e., how to make it a walk that is worthy of the Lord and pleasing to him. At this point, though, Paul is really only explaining how beliefs and actions interact. He is not getting into specific actions one should or should not do in one's daily life. That will happen in ch. 3 of the letter.

The Christian life, in Paul's view, is not merely a static existence in which one simply obeys a list of rules. Rather, the Christian life is a dynamic walk whereby each day, month, and year present different challenges and opportunities, because as the Christian matures, he or she will be in a different relation to both the world around and to God above. It is not that God is changing or that the world is (necessarily) changing. The Christian, however, is changing. The four participles that describe the Christian life point to it being a process, and those who follow it will need to be strengthened by God to complete it.

However, as Christians continue on their walk, they should be εὐχαριστοῦντες (giving thanks) for everything that has been done on their behalf. The fourth and final participle describes what gives Christians the motivation to keep moving forward. Thankfulness answers the question "Why?—Why would anyone want to walk the path that God has put in front of him or her?" Paul's answer is "because of what God has done for you."

Appropriately, vv. 12b–14 are about what God has done for the Colossians (and all Christians). Verses 10b–12a and 12b–14 are bridged by εὐχαριστοῦντες (giving thanks). Giving thanks is one of the four participles—one of the things that the Colossians should be doing in order to walk in a manner worthy of the Lord. However, it also introduces what the Father has done on their behalf. Really, it belongs with both the material that comes before it *and* the material that comes after it. This seems to be Paul's design. The question still remains, though, "Why should the Colossians be thankful?"

Verse 12 says, εὐχαριστοῦντες τῷ πατρὶ τῷ ἱκανώσαντι ὑμᾶς εἰς τὴν μερίδα τοῦ κλήρου τῶν ἁγίων ἐν τῷ φωτί (giving thanks to the Father who has qualified you to share in the inheritance of the saints in light). Something has been done for the Colossians: the Father has "qualified" them. Specifically, the Father has qualified them to share in the inheritance with the saints in light. This represents "an act of divine grace whereby they were 'qualified or made fit' (ἱκανώσαντι) to share in an inheritance for which they had previously been unqualified."[23] Paul is also setting up a contrast to be made later in the letter between the God who qualifies (1:12) and the men who disqualify (2:18). The main point, though, is that God has qualified the Colossians.

What is interesting about the tense of the verb "qualify" is that it speaks to something that has already taken place. God has *already* qualified them.[24] This is something that will continue into v. 13. Everything that has been done on the Colossians' behalf has already taken place. This is not something they have to wait for the next life to receive, nor is it something they can only obtain if they do certain things that please God. God has already given them this qualification.

While what it means to be qualified is not described here, the *object* of the qualification is. Understanding what the Colossians are qualified *into* will help to explain what it means to be qualified. Now, in contrast to a description of what it might mean to be qualified by a modern Westerner who thinks in individualistic terms, one finds something here that is decidedly Eastern and group-oriented. The Colossians are not qualified to be fit for a status, position, or rank that only people who have done a certain thing or who have reached a certain level of achievement can get into. Rather, they have become part of a people. They have been made part of a group.

The phrase εἰς τὴν μερίδα τοῦ κλήρου means "'to have a share in the κλῆρος,' i.e. the inheritance of God's people."[25] Sumney says, "This language transports us to the exodus and the land of Israel as an inheritance for Israel from God. The land is often called the inheritance of Israel (e.g., Deut 3:18; 19:14; Josh 13:7). So this is a known way to speak of receiving the blessings that God has reserved for God's people."[26]

Something very important is happening here. Paul is starting to talk about the Colossians in very Jewish terms. Commentators often note the

---

23. Dunn, *Epistles to the Colossians*, 75.

24. O'Brien says, "The aorist tenses point to an eschatology that is truly realized (i.e. God had *already* qualified [ἱκανώσαντι] the Colossians to share in the inheritance, he had *already* delivered [ἐρρύσατο] them from this alien power and had *already* transferred [μετέστησεν] them to his Son's kingdom), while by contrast, the present tense of verse 14, 'we have' [ἔχομεν], stresses the continued results of the redemption wrought in the past" (*Colossians-Philemon*, 26).

25. O'Brien, *Colossians-Philemon*, 26.

26. Sumney, *Colossians*, 53.

Jewishness of the word ἱκανώσαντι (qualification).[27] Additionally, what the Colossians are qualified into is a group, specifically, those who receive an inheritance from God. As Sumney said above, this was commonly understood by Jews to refer to the promised land. Now, because of the context in which the inheritance is described as the land (the books of Deuteronomy and Joshua), the exodus and entrance into the promised land are part of the picture that is being painted. And, this is not simply a random reference to the exodus that shows up out of nowhere. The exodus is about to feature in the next two verses.

What is happening is that Paul is taking very important Jewish ideas and applying them to the Colossians. Paul is saying that the Colossians are part of a special people who have received something special from God. The difference is, "[t]he inheritance to which Paul refers belongs to a higher plane and a more lasting order than any earthly Canaan."[28] The inheritance the Colossians have received is not land but something much greater (to be described in vv. 13–14). God has qualified them to belong to his people. He has qualified them, brought them into his family, and given them a share of the inheritance. For this, the Colossians should give thanks.

One final question about this verse still remains: "Who are the holy ones in light?" There have been two major views on this.[29] The older view was that the holy ones/saints are humans—people of God in the Old Testament or the first Jewish Christians the Gentiles are now joining. The newer view is that the holy ones/saints are angels—God's holy ones in the realm of light. Although there are good reasons to prefer the older view that the saints are humans,[30] neither one makes much difference for understanding

27. For example, Bruce, *Epistles to the Colossians,* 50; Dunn, *Epistles to the Colossians,* 75–76; O'Brien, *Colossians-Philemon,* 26; and N.T. Wright, *Colossians and Philemon,* 61.

28. O'Brien, *Colossians-Philemon,* 26.

29. Bruce, *Epistles to the Colossians,* 49.

30. When one combines Paul's reference to the Colossians as saints in 1:2 with the pronoun usage in 1:12–14, it looks like the Colossians have been made saints, whereas previously they were outside the people of God as a result of being Gentiles. Notice in 1:12 how Paul says that the Father has qualified "you," and in v. 13–14, he switches to the first person plural "we" and "us" when describing what God has done. Keener says, "In the Old Testament, the 'saints' or 'holy' or 'set apart ones' were Israel. Israel's 'inheritance' was first of all the Promised Land but in Jewish tradition pointed toward the ultimate possession of the world to come" (*IVP Bible Background,* 570). Considering first that the audience was primarily Gentiles, second, that Paul will speak of the mystery among the Gentiles in 1:27, and third, that here he makes it clear that the Gentile Colossians were being incorporated into a people of whom they were never a part before (God's people), it seems better to think of the people in view as the human family of God rather than the company of angels.

what Paul thought was essential to the Christian worldview. The main point is that the Colossians are given an inheritance with those who are called "saints" and thereby share with them "in light." This is likely meant to contrast with the forthcoming references to the "domain of darkness" in v. 13, as well as the description of the Colossians' former life as "alienated and hostile in mind in the doing of evil deeds" in v. 21.

1:13

ὃς ἐρρύσατο ἡμᾶς ἐκ τῆς ἐξουσίας τοῦ σκότους καὶ μετέστησεν εἰς τὴν βασιλείαν τοῦ υἱοῦ τῆς ἀγάπης αὐτοῦ

who has delivered us from the domain of darkness and has transferred us into the kingdom of his beloved Son

In v. 13, Paul continues to explain to the Colossians *why* they should give thanks to God. Many commentators have noted the similarity between the statement about deliverance and language about the exodus.[31] However, beyond the mere fact that the language of the exodus is used, the more interesting point is *why* it is used. Bruce says, "If deliverance were necessary, their former existence was one of bondage."[32] Sumney elaborates on this and says, "This statement envisions people imprisoned by these powers in a realm dominated by evil. Those who have been captured by evil—and this included all people—are incapable of freeing themselves because these powers possess such strength."[33]

The imagery of deliverance from evil is also evident in the phrase ἐξουσίας τοῦ σκότους (domain of darkness). This is actually the same phrase used in Luke 22:53 for the sinister forces that oppose Christ.[34] Probably even more interesting is that the word used here for the powers of evil, ἐξουσίας (domain),[35] is also used in the hymn (v. 16) as part of what Christ created.[36] The Colossians have been transferred out of the domain of darkness and into the kingdom of light, the kingdom of God's beloved Son.

---

31. For example, Dunn, *Christology in the Making*, 77; Gurter, "Colossians," 593; Keener, *IVP Bible Background*, 570; Moo, *Letters to the Colossians*, 103; and N.T. Wright, *Colossians and Philemon*, 62.

32. Bruce, "Colossian Problems: Part 4," 53.

33. Sumney, *Colossians*, 56.

34. Bruce, "Colossian Problems: Part 4," 51.

35. It is translated here as "domain," though it can also mean "authority" as it is translated in the hymn.

36. The importance of this will be investigated when looking at the hymn.

The imagery of both the exodus (deliverance) and the domain of darkness communicates that the Colossians were prisoners of one side but were rescued by God and transferred to his side.

However, it does not appear that all problems have been solved. As far as this verse says, the domain of darkness still exists, and it is still a reality in the Colossians' lives.[37] All that has been said in this verse is that the Colossians have been transferred out of the domain of darkness. Paul does not say that the domain itself has been destroyed or its rulers judged, nor does he say that the domain of darkness has been emptied of its other occupants. Furthermore, there is nothing in the surrounding verses that suggests everyone has been transferred out of the domain of darkness. This probably means that Paul thinks there are people still living in the domain of darkness.

What Paul is doing here is dividing the world into two camps, kingdoms, or domains. Those in the domain of darkness live under its rulers and follow its code of conduct. The other camp, by contrast, is characterized by light, is ruled by God's beloved Son, and has its own way of life. This sort of contrast was not uncommon. Malherbe says that moralists around this time and before made heavy use of certain rhetorical conventions, including the image of the two ways. That was "the image of a man at a crossroads, challenged to choose between a life of virtue and one of vice."[38] Paul is not yet challenging them to choose one way over the other, but he is describing what the two ways look like and showing them that one of them is clearly the better choice.

Paul is beginning to set up the contrast of being "in Christ" with the obvious contrary position of not being "in Christ." Here, he is describing Christianity as a completely different path from others that are on offer. By contrasting the kingdom of God's beloved Son with the domain of darkness, Paul is not merely setting up Christianity as a nice set of things to believe or a slight modification of the way one lives or thinks. Rather, Paul sees it as an entirely new existence and an entirely new way of life. By speaking of Christianity and its alternative at the kingdom level and telling the Colossians that they have been delivered from their previous darkness, he does not leave the possibility open to the Colossians to believe just the theological and ignore the practical. He also does not leave it open to live the Christian life on any basis other than on Christian theology. The entire way for which

37. Dunn says, "The darkness has not been stripped of its authority and banished; rather, it can now be legitimately and authoritatively resisted" (*Epistles to the Colossians*, 78).

38. Malherbe, *Moral Exhortation*, 135.

he is arguing is one unit, and he will soon make the case that that is the superior of the two ways.[39]

1:14

ἐν ᾧ ἔχομεν τὴν ἀπολύτρωσιν τὴν ἄφεσιν τῶν ἁμαρτιῶν

in whom we have redemption, the forgiveness of sins

In v. 14, Paul continues the exodus theme with his use of τὴν ἀπολύτρωσιν (redemption)—a word which has a long history in the story of Israel. Keener says, "'Redemption' meant freeing a slave by paying a price for that slave; in the Old Testament, God redeemed Israel from their slavery in Egypt by the blood of the firstborn and the lamb."[40] Witherington says that the verbal cognate for redemption occurs frequently in Deuteronomy and "denotes the ransom or release or deliverance of a captive from either war or some sort of slavery, like the release of the Israelites from bondage. The believer before conversion is therefore in a form of bondage, enslaved by and in darkness."[41]

Paul is continuing to draw on exodus language (as he did with deliverance from the domain of darkness) to make a point about the Colossians, their situation, and Christ. "Their situation before Christ is compared to one of captivity, and the one after Christ is characterized by deliverance and redemption. The imagery here is that of rescue and the purchasing of freedom—the believers have been emancipated."[42] Given the echoes of the promised land in 1:12 and the redemption of Israel here, it may be that the kingdom of God's beloved Son is being thought of as the *new* promised land.[43]

At the most basic level, what is happening is that Paul is borrowing language from the most dramatic event in Israel's history and using it to show that something of at least that level of significance is happening here.[44]

---

39. Sumney says, "The language of v. 13 has a distinctly political ring with its talk of rescue from one ruler and transfer into the dominion of a different king . . . . One's allegiance must shift to the king of a new realm. This requires the believer to relativize all other allegiances and commitments" (*Colossians*, 58).

40. Keener, *IVP Bible Background*, 571.

41. Witherington, *Letters to Philemon*, 126.

42. Sumney, *Colossians*, 59.

43. Dunn, *Epistles to the Colossians*, 81.

44. Of course, Paul has already used language reminiscent of the beginning of Genesis ("bearing fruit and increasing") and will shortly use a lot of cosmic language in the hymn. Putting these together with the exodus language of 1:12–14, it looks like Paul is saying that something has happened that is unparalleled in significance.

He makes it clear what that thing is by defining the redemption further, not as some new promised land, but as the forgiveness of sins. The Colossians have indeed been redeemed, but it is from a different type of slavery. Instead of being slaves to other humans, the Colossians have been slaves to sin.

There are two more things that can be gleaned from this verse. First, forgiveness occurs only in Christ. Verse 14 starts with ἐν ᾧ (in whom), signifying that redemption is to be found in Christ. Second, the redemption is not something the Colossians have to wait for; it is something they already have. The use of the word ἔχομεν (we have) indicates that the Colossians already possess this redemption.[45]

Paul ends (or rather pauses) his train of thought rather abruptly here. There are still questions that he has not answered. For example, *why* is redemption found in Christ and not somewhere else? If the Colossians are already experiencing the redemption now, why do they still experience trouble in their lives? Presumably they still do, otherwise either the rest of the letter would look very different, or they might not even need a letter at all. However, Paul does not answer these or any other questions—at least not yet. Up to this point, he has been constructing an outline to be filled with content as the letter progresses. With these verses, Paul is basically saying, "This is what the situation is. This is what God has done for you. And, all of it happens in and only in Christ." The next section of the letter will explain why Paul thinks this is the case.

SIGNIFICANCE

As Paul moves from the introduction to the body of the letter, he begins to explain in detail some of the themes he merely hinted at previously. There are four main points of significance in this section of the letter.

First, Christianity is a religion of revelation. God is a transcendent being that man could not access or interact with if God did not allow it. However, what Paul says is that God gives knowledge of his will to humanity. God *wants* humans to know about himself, and through the process of living according to his will, they come to actually know him.

Second, it appears that humans have to be reshaped or fixed. If humans are supposed to learn to walk in a manner worthy of the Lord and become fully pleasing to him, they must not have reached those goals yet. However, while what this walk looks like has not yet been described, the broad outline has been. Christians are to bear fruit, increase in the

---

45. O'Brien, *Colossians-Philemon*, 82.

knowledge of God, be strengthened with the strength that comes from God, and give thanks to God.

Third, there is a strong connection between beliefs and actions. There are several ways in which they are connected, the simplest of which is living out one's beliefs. Christianity makes statements about the way the world actually is, which implies that the follower of Christianity should live in a manner consistent with the true nature of reality. Beliefs and actions are also connected in the upward spiral that describes how one moves towards walking in a manner worthy of the Lord. Knowing God's will leads to walking better, and walking better leads to knowing God's will better (now that one has practiced living it out). The person who is following God will be constantly moving upwards on the spiral.

Finally, everything that happens with the Christian is part of a bigger picture. Paul explained that there are two camps, the domain of darkness and the kingdom of God's beloved Son (Christ's kingdom). Christians were prisoners of the former but have been delivered by God through Christ into the latter. Importantly, the reason they were prisoners in the first place is because of sin (redemption is described as the forgiveness of sins). There is something larger going on here, and this is an important piece, but it looks like there is still more to come.

5

The Hymn: Introduction

INTRODUCTION

The observant reader will notice that beginning with v. 15, the letter starts to sound a little different. Many scholars think that there is something here known as a hymn and that this represents the foundation on which the theology for the rest of the letter is built. If this is true, then the hymn will be absolutely essential for understanding Paul's thoughts on the Christian worldview. Therefore, before it will possible to proceed investigating this section of the letter verse by verse, it is necessary to pause for a minute and first look at two questions: 1) What is a hymn? and 2) Is the material in Col 1 a hymn?

WHAT IS A HYMN?

In the ancient world, a hymn was a speech or piece of writing that praised a god and was often directed to that god.[1] While both the Christian and Greco-Roman versions of hymns stress divine actions and/or power/deeds, Christian hymns were most often an act of thanksgiving.[2] It sounds strange

1. Pernot, "Rhetoric of Religion," 242.
2. Pernot, "Rhetoric of Religion," 244.

to modern ears to think of hymns as addressing God. In the modern world (at least in the West), hymns are still about God and what he has done for believers, but frequently, people think of them in terms of poetry set to music.

However, hymns in the ancient world were not necessarily poetry set to music, and they may or may not have been sung by a congregation. What counted as a hymn was a fairly broad category,[3] but the question of whether they were sung or not is actually irrelevant to our purposes. Most important to what makes a hymn here is its purpose. *Why* was it written?

Primarily, hymns were meant to instruct one another in the faith.[4] Colossians 3:16 says that hymns (along with psalms and spiritual songs)[5] should be used for teaching and admonishing one another. In other words, they should be used for helping one another to become better people. This means that a hymn would likely contain wisdom/doctrine that could/should be used as the foundation for Christians helping one another. A hymn, then, is less like a song and more like a theological piece of material that was used for teaching and instruction. Perhaps, although the technical word is hymn, it would be easier for modern readers to think of the word creed. A creed (like the Apostles' Creed) is a theologically dense and highly formulated piece of material used for teaching and instruction.[6] And, while it is possible to set a creed to music, the point is primarily to communicate information.

Later in the letter, Paul will say that hymns are to be used for teaching and helping one another to be better people (Col 3:16). In his mind, then, hymns form a rule, standard, or foundation on which people should base their lives. Therefore, if there is a hymn in the letter, it would be very important. It would provide a foundation for the theology of the entire letter.[7] It

3. Collins says hymns encompass "a variety of materials which are essentially separable from the literary contexts in which they are found and which are characterized by their distinctive vocabulary and rhythmical cadence" (*Letters That Paul Did Not Write*, 190).

4. Malan, "Church Singing," 517.

5. There have been attempts to divide such poetical compositions into ψαλμοῖς, ὕμνοις, and ᾠδαῖς πνευματικαῖς (psalms, hymns, and spiritual songs) as described in Colossians 3:16, but the distinction is not technical, and cannot be pressed rigidly. See Buttrick, *Interpreter's Dictionary*, 2:668, and Hastings, ed., *Dictionary of the Bible*, 2: 441.

6. Briggs says, "Creedal forms in the New Testament are indications of likely self-involvement" (*Words in Action*, 215). What is important about this is that by reciting a hymn/creed, believers were not merely repeating a series of theological statements but actually involving themselves in and committing themselves to its meaning.

7. One brief example of how Paul will refer back to the content of 1:15–20 throughout the letter can be seen in his argumentation against the philosophy in ch. 2. 1:19 says, "Because in him all the fullness was pleased to dwell"; 2.9–10 says, "Because in him all the fullness of deity dwells bodily, and you have been filled in him who is the head of

is, therefore, essential to understand whether there is a hymn in Colossians, and if so, what it says.

IS THE MATERIAL IN COLOSSIANS 1 A HYMN?

The idea in the modern era that these verses represent a hymn started with Eduard Norden in 1923,[8] and since that time, "scholars have widely agreed that this passage quotes (perhaps with modifications) a self-contained christological statement that probably arose as part of an early church liturgy."[9] Traditionally, determination of the presence of a hymn as well as its boundaries has centered on questions of pronoun use; vocabulary, content, and style; and structure. Each of these will be considered in turn.

Pronoun Use

Here is an outline of pronoun use in the supposed hymn and surrounding verses:

Verses	Pronoun Use
vv. 11–12	second and third person
vv. 13–14	first and third person
vv. 15–20	third person only
vv. 21–23	second and third person (with one first person)

There is something different about vv. 15–20: they use only the third person. Consider for a moment what each of these pronouns is and when they are used. First person pronouns are "I" and "we;" second person pronouns are "you" (both singular and plural); and third person pronouns are "he," "she," "it," and "they." First and second person pronouns are used primarily in conversation. Third person pronouns are used when referencing external material or talking about things/ideas that don't directly relate to one of the people in the conversation.

---

all rule and authority." Paul almost directly quotes from 1:15–20, modifies it slightly to further explain what he thinks in means, and then uses it to make an argument about why the way of Christ is better than the way offered by the philosophers. This will be discussed in detail later, but this is only one of many examples of how Paul refers back to these verses throughout the rest of the letter.

8. Ralph Martin, "Reconciliation and Forgiveness," 61. For the original statement, see Norden, *Agnostos Theos*, 253.

9. Hay, *Colossians*, 50.

The way these pronouns are being used suggests a conversation is taking place. In vv. 11–14, Paul is talking to the Colossians (using first and second person pronouns), and he is referencing external material (third person pronouns). Then, in vv. 15–20, he drops all of the first and second person and uses only third person. He is referencing external material *only*. Finally, in vv. 21–23, he switches back to using second person (with one first person) in addition to the third person. It's like he's talking to them, then wants to reference something, then comes back to the conversation. This strongly indicates that Paul is referencing external material. But, it goes further than that.

Verse 21 starts with the words καὶ ὑμᾶς (and you). These words are emphatic and serve to apply what has just been said to the Colossians.[10] This makes it even more clear that Paul is referencing external material, because now he is bringing the conversation back around to the Colossian community. Unlike vv. 13–14 and 21–23, there is no reference to the Colossian community in vv. 15–20.[11] In these verses, Paul shifts to something completely external.

If a hymn has been inserted into the text, this is the sort of thing that one would expect. The information in vv. 15–20 might be related in some way to either the author or the audience, but it is not *about* them.[12] Given that vv. 15–20 are the only verses in this section that use the third person *exclusively*, it seems very possible that these verses consist of information that Paul is using to make a point in his letter to the Colossians, rather than information that forms part of his dialogue with them.

Vocabulary, Content, and Style

The next thing to consider in determining whether there is or is not a hymn in these verses is the actual material in the verses. To begin with, there are a large number of terms here which are uncharacteristic of the Pauline

---

10. O'Brien, *Colossians-Philemon*, 64. Moo says that with this reference to the Colossians, Paul is highlighting the "transition from the theological assertions of the 'hymn' to its application" (*Letters to the Colossians*, 139).

11. Leppä, *Making of Colossians*, 84. To be clear, there is a reference to the church in v. 18. However, this is a reference to the church in a general way rather than the specific church at Colossae. So, Leppä's point is still valid.

12. This may seem like a small point to make, but in reality, it is not. If the author uses the third person for a section of his letter to the Colossians, then it does not mean the conversation has totally stopped; he may just be referring to something else that he wants to talk to them about.

letters.[13] Lohse highlights many of the terms in the hymn, including εἰκὼν τοῦ θεοῦ (image of God), ἀοράτου (invisible), θρόνοι (thrones), κυριότητες (dominions), ἀρχή (beginning), πρωτεύων (preeminent), κατοικῆσαι (to dwell), ἀποκαταλλάξαι (to reconcile), εἰρηνοποιήσας (making peace), and αἵματος τοῦ σταυροῦ αὐτοῦ (blood of his cross), and he points towards their unusual nature.[14] Some of these terms occur only once in the New Testament, while others appear only a few times and/or carry a different meaning here than they normally do. An usually high concentration of terms not found in other Pauline writings suggests the use of outside material.

Related to the use of uncommon vocabulary is the presence of a higher density of theological concepts than the immediate context.[15] It is difficult to quantify exactly how much more tightly theological concepts are packed into vv. 15–20, but one does get a sense that these verses are much more theologically developed that those surrounding vv. 15–20. For example, it was possible to discuss the five verses of vv. 9–14 in a single chapter. It will take three chapters (in addition to this introductory chapter) to discuss the six verses of vv. 15–20. Once the discussion of vv. 15–20 begins, it will not be difficult to see why so much space is needed. Those verses are *much* more theologically dense than anything else seen so far (or to be seen in the rest of the letter).

Besides the vocabulary, there are stylistic indicators that these verses stand out from the surrounding context and might represent a hymn or other material inserted into the letter. For example, Leppä says, "Verse 1:15 begins with a relative pronoun 'who' (ὅς) which is typical of hymns (cf. Rom 4:25, Phil 2:6, 1 Tim 3:16, and Heb 1:3)."[16] This and other stylistic indicators point to a structure that exists in the hymn, although, because these indicators are primarily structural in nature, they will be discussed in the next section.

---

13. Leppä, *Making of Colossians*, 84.

14. Lohse, *"Briefe an die Kolosser,"* 78–79.

15. Christian Stettler points towards concepts such as salvation, reconciliation, and the future hopes of Christians (*Kolosserhymnus*, 77).

16. Leppä, *Making of Colossians*, 84. Leppä's point that certain indicators like the relative pronoun ὅς (who) are typically used in other hymns is also supported by Neufeld, though Neufeld focuses on other elements. Neufeld says that while relative clauses may be used to introduce credal material, one might also recognize formulary material by "the use of ὅτι [because], the double accusative, and the infinitive to express a statement which is quoted directly or indirectly" (*Earliest Christian Confessions*, 42).

Structure

In order to be able to ask "Is there structure in these verses?," it would be helpful to know precisely what is meant by structure. The easiest way to think about structure is to think about modern music. The popular songs one hears on the radio are almost almost always divided into verses. Each of these verses usually has a clear theme that separates it from the other verses, and those verses also have their own theme. One often finds other elements of structure in pop songs, such as a word that occurs at the end of one line will rhyme with a word that occurs at the end of another line. People do not usually speak in verses with rhyming words, so the listener can tell that the words have been structured in order to form a song.

Similarly, in order to answer the question "Is there structure in these verses?," one will be looking for the same sorts of things. Does it look like Paul has just continued his writing as if nothing has changed, or has he added elements that make it different from normal speech (like a songwriter does)?

There are a number of different elements in these verses that suggest they contain structure one would not find in normal spoken or written words. The most important elements in vv. 15–20 are the two "strophes" introduced by the relative ὅς ἐστιν (who is) clause in vv. 15a and 18b. That statement needs some explanation. First, a "strophe" is basically the same thing as a "verse" in a pop song. However, since this is a biblical text, and it is already divided into verses, it would be confusing to refer to a verse that contains multiple verses. Therefore, going forward, "verse" will continue to refer to the numbered verses with which people are familiar in the Bible, and "strophe" will refer to sections of text—like the "verses" in pop songs.

Second, a relative clause is a part of a sentence (but not a full thought) that refers back to something else. Relative clauses usually start with who, whose, that, which, where, or when, and they define or identify the noun that precedes them. They are used to explain something else that isn't in that sentence. Now, both vv. 15a and 18b start with relative clauses. What makes this interesting is that both of these relative clauses start new thoughts, and yet they refer back to something else that isn't even part of these verses (vv. 15–20)—verses that are very different from the material around them.

Additionally, Leppä says, "Both strophes include a causal clause beginning with ὅτι (1:16, 19)."[17] In other words, there is more structure here than simply the way these two supposed strophes start. Besides, simply being able to divide a series of verses into two sections does not make them into

---

17. Leppä, *Making of Colossians*, 84.

strophes, i.e., it does not necessarily mean that there is a hymn here. However, the more the two parts are structured similarly, the more one starts to think that they were composed this way intentionally.

It would take a long time to list out all of the structural elements of these verses. Perhaps the simplest way to point out the many similar elements of structure would be to look at it visually. Below is a rough outline of vv. 15–20 that shows many of the structural elements. This does not consider parallel themes or more detailed structural similarities. Those will be considered as these verses are investigated in detail. These are just the main elements.

Greek Text

15   *ὅς ἐστιν
        1) εἰκὼν τοῦ θεοῦ τοῦ ἀοράτου
        2) *πρωτότοκος πάσης κτίσεως
16   *ὅτι ἐν αὐτῷ ἐκτίσθη τὰ πάντα ἐν τοῖς οὐρανοῖς καὶ ἐπὶ τῆς γῆς τὰ
              ὁρατὰ καὶ τὰ ἀόρατα εἴτε θρόνοι εἴτε κυριότητες εἴτε ἀρχαὶ εἴτε
              ἐξουσίαι· τὰ πάντα δι' αὐτοῦ καὶ εἰς αὐτὸν ἔκτισται

17   - καὶ αὐτός ἐστιν πρὸ πάντων
        - καὶ τὰ πάντα ἐν αὐτῷ συνέστηκεν
18a   - καὶ αὐτός ἐστιν ἡ κεφαλὴ τοῦ σώματος τῆς ἐκκλησίας

18b   *ὅς ἐστιν
        1) ἀρχή
        2) *πρωτότοκος ἐκ τῶν νεκρῶν
19   ἵνα γένηται ἐν πᾶσιν αὐτὸς πρωτεύων
20   *ὅτι ἐν αὐτῷ εὐδόκησεν πᾶν τὸ πλήρωμα κατοικῆσαι καὶ δι' αὐτοῦ
              ἀποκαταλλάξαι τὰ πάντα εἰς αὐτόν εἰρηνοποιήσας διὰ τοῦ αἵματος
              τοῦ σταυροῦ αὐτοῦ [δι' αὐτοῦ] εἴτε τὰ ἐπὶ τῆς γῆς εἴτε τὰ ἐν τοῖς
              οὐρανοῖς

English Translation

15   *Who is
           1) the image of the invisible God,
           2) the *firstborn of all creation
16   *because in him were created all things in the heavens and on the earth,
                      visible and invisible, whether thrones or dominions or rulers or
                      authorities, all things through him and for him were created.

17a   - and he is before all things,
              - and in him all things hold together,
18a   - and he is the head of the body, the Church.

18b   *Who is
           1) the beginning,
           2) the *firstborn from the dead,
19   in order that he might in all things be preeminent.
20   *because in him all the fullness was pleased to dwell and to
                      reconcile [through him] all things to him, whether things on the earth or
                      things in the heavens, making peace by the blood of his cross.

Look at the layout of these verses, and compare the parts that have a * or a number. It is hard to look at something like this and say that there is not a definite structure to these verses. This sort of structure does not exist in the verses surrounding vv. 15–20. Even if other parts of the letter have structure, the only thing that matters for determining whether these verses are a hymn is the immediate context. The point is to try to determine if the same verses that have unusual vocabulary and a shift in the use of pronouns also have definite structure. After looking at them, it would appear that they do.

Finally, what might be the purpose for the structure of these verses? Bailey says that the "parallelism found in many creeds invites the interpreter to compare or think about the relationship between the parallel parts."[18] He cites Rom 10.9[19] as an example and says, "one is compelled to think about the use of the parallel verbs 'confess' and 'believe.' Why does a person *confess* that Jesus is Lord and *believe* that God raised him? Are these verbs interchangeable? Why are they given in the order that they are, considering that a person usually believes before she or he confesses?"[20] Bailey's observation about structure in Romans has direct application here. In what way does Christ being the image of God correspond to his being the

18. Bailey and Vander Broek, *Literary Forms*, 85.

19. "Because if you confess with your mouth that Jesus is Lord, and believe in your heart that God raised him from the dead, you will be saved" (Rom 10:9).

20. Bailey and Vander Broek, *Literary Forms*, 85.

beginning/source? How do the two uses of πρωτότοκος (firstborn) relate to one another? And, how do other parts of the two main strophes compare? The audience was likely meant to ask questions like these.

SIGNIFICANCE

In looking at the pronoun use; the vocabulary, content, and style; as well as the structure of Colossians 1:15–20, it turns out that all these elements point in the same direction. Verses 15–20 were an early Christian hymn that was inserted into the context. There would be more room to debate this if only some of the indicators surveyed pointed toward this conclusion, but in this case, all of them do. For this reason, there is almost no debate among scholars today that there is a hymn in these verses.[21] Martin says that since Norden originally suggested that these verses represent a hymn, "scholars have widely agreed that this passage quotes (perhaps with modifications) a self-contained christological statement that probably arose as part of an early church liturgy."[22]

Considering that ancient hymns were meant to instruct persons in their faith and deliver theological teaching, it is very likely that this hymn forms the basis of much of the theology in the letter. As such, it would be a good idea to investigate the hymn's theology in detail. That investigation will be the focus of the next three chapters.

---

21. Scholars who think that 1:15–20 are a hymn inserted into the letter include (but are not limited to): Alkier, *Die Realität der Auferweckung,* 64; Bruce, *Epistles to the Colossians,* 54; Collins, *Letters That Paul Did Not Write,* 190; Dettwiler, "Verständnis des Kreuzes Jesu," 85; Harris, *Colossians and Philemon,* 37; Koester, *Introduction,* 269; Leppä, *Making of Colossians,* 84; Neufeld, *Earliest Christian Confessions,* 42; Norden, *Agnostos Theos,* 253; Robinson, "Formal Analysis," 275; Hanna Stettler, *Heiligung bei Paulus,* 549; O'Brien, *Colossians-Philemon,* 64; Thompson, *Colossians and Philemon,* 27–28; and Witherington, *Jesus the Sage,* 269. More could be added easily.

22. Ralph Martin, "Reconciliation and Forgiveness," 61. Evaluating whether something is or is not a hymn is a difficult process. This chapter has briefly worked through the main methods used by scholars to ask whether something is a hymn in order to show the reader that *all* of them point towards the existence of a hymn in 1:15–20. Had there been conflicting results between the different indicators (pronoun use, vocabulary, content, style, and structure), this chapter would have needed to be much longer. The reason this chapter is as short as it is, is because all of the indicators point in the same direction. As a result, there is very little disagreement among scholars that there is a hymn in 1:15–20.

6

The Hymn: Christ and Original Creation (1:15–16)

INTRODUCTION

The christological hymn begins with vv. 15–16. Verse 15 will make two statements about Christ: 1) he is the image of the invisible God, and 2) he is the firstborn of all creation. The first statement describes how Christ relates to God, and the second statement describes how Christ relates to creation. The second statement will be further explained by v. 16.

The last chapter showed that ancient hymns were highly dense theological statements; every word and phrase carried a lot of meaning. In this chapter (as well as the other chapters on the hymn), there will be extra focus on the details so that the hymn's theology will be clear. These details will be important, because as the last chapter also explained, hymns were used for instruction and theological education. Paul will be using this hymn precisely for that in the rest of the letter. With this hymn, he is laying the foundation for the arguments he will be making later.

In addition to the detailed focus on the content of the hymn, there will also be an emphasis on structure. Part of this is because hymns are generally highly structured pieces of material (and this one is no exception). As will become clear in the coming chapters (especially the next two), this structure was not accidental or developed just for style. The structure of this hymn was developed with purpose, and it carries meaning. Therefore, the hymn's structure will be discussed in the process of looking at its content and then summarized at the end of each chapter with a diagram.

The key to getting the most out of this chapter (as well as the rest of the hymn) is patience. The arguments are going to get very detailed, and those details might become overwhelming. However, while it certainly would be easier to move through this part of the investigation more quickly, it would not be wise to do so. Because Paul will base so many of his later arguments on the statements made in the hymn, every little detail here matters.

Paul is essentially laying the foundation for a house, and like the foundation of a house, it is critical that it be accurate. Suppose a builder makes the foundation for a house just an inch or two higher on one side than the other. It may not seem like a big deal at the time, and someone walking by may not even notice. However, when the framing for the house is added, everything will be an inch or two off. Then, the floors will be an inch or two off. Then, the walls will be an inch or two off. Nothing in the house will line up correctly, because the foundation was not laid accurately. Like the foundation of a house, it is critical to get the foundation of theology correct, because everything built on it later will depend on the accuracy of that foundation.

1:15A

> ὅς ἐστιν εἰκὼν τοῦ θεοῦ τοῦ ἀοράτου
>
> who is the image of the invisible God

The first question to answer is "To what does ὅς ἐστιν (who is) refer?" There are only four personal subjects in the preceding verses which could grammatically be the referent of a relative clause: the Father, the Son, Paul, and the Colossians. To begin with, Paul is not referring to himself or the Colossians as the image of the invisible God. If he were, the rest of the letter would look very different. That leaves only two choices: the Father and the Son. For ὅς ἐστιν (who is) to refer to the Father, one of two things would have to happen. The first option is God would have to be referred to as the image of his invisible self, which makes no logical sense. This would mean that God is the visible version of his invisible self—so God would have to be both visible and invisible at the same time. The other option is that God and the Father are different. If this were the case, then the letter has stepped into either polytheism or gnosticism.[1] However, if Paul were suggesting that either of these two were true, then the rest of the letter would look very different.

The only remaining option is the Son. There are two strong reasons to think that this is the correct option. First, the two strophes[2] that begin with ὅς ἐστιν (who is) are parallel to one another, which implies that they both refer to the same person. The second strophe speaks of this person as the πρωτότοκος ἐκ τῶν νεκρῶν (firstborn from the dead). This is not Paul or the Colossians, and unless Paul is suggesting a wildly different theology than either Judaism or early Christianity would recognize, this does not refer to the Father. It can refer only to Christ.

Second, the entire letter is focused on the person and work of Christ. At this point, there have been only hints of the importance of Christ. However, as one moves through the rest of the letter, this will become more clear. In 1:22, Paul says Christ has died in order to reconcile people to God and make them holy, blameless, and above reproach before him. In 2:8, Paul will argue against the philosophy because it is "according to the traditions of men and according to the elemental forces of the world and not according to Christ." He will then spend the rest of the chapter explaining to the Colossians how much Christ has done for them and why the philosophy doesn't measure up.

From the beginning of ch. 3 to the end of the letter, Paul will describe how Christians should live: they should focus on the things above, where Christ is seated at the right hand of God (3:1–4). In Christ, all the traditional divisions between groups (Greek, Jew, circumcised, uncircumcised, barbarian, Scythian, slave, and free) have been broken down (3:11). Christ brings peace (3:15), and he should be the reason for everything that one does (3:17)—which includes the way one treats others in the household (3:18–4:1). Everything in the whole letter is focused on who Christ is, what he has done, and why both of those things make a difference. God is behind it all, but the focus is on Christ and his actions. Christ and his actions are described in the hymn, and then Paul uses the rest of the letter to explain the implications of who Christ is and what he has done.

So, because it makes no sense to think that the hymn could refer to Paul, the Colossians, or God the Father, as well as the fact that there are two strong reasons to think that it does refer to Christ, it makes the best sense to think Christ is the focus of the hymn. He is the one to whom ὅς ἐστιν (who is) refers. Because there is such strong evidence that Christ is the focus of

---

1. Gnosticism will be discussed in more detail later.

2. Remember, a strophe is like a verse in a pop song. It has multiple lines and (usually) a single subject. In this case, a strophe will contain one or more biblical verses.

the hymn, there is next to no argument about this point among commentators. The focus for this hymn is on God's beloved Son (v. 13).

The second question is "What does it mean to be the image of the invisible God?" To answer that, it will be necessary to understand what the word "image" meant.

Representations of people and gods were common in the ancient world and were regularly painted, sculpted, and placed on coins. Strictly speaking, though, it was not the individuals themselves who were represented. The role of an object (like a statue) was to display the value, status, and social connections surrounding the individual for whom it stood.[3] Macdonald says that "there were practically only two anthropomorphic types available for the primitive Greek artist—the nude male and the draped female. The artist was therefore compelled to resort to symbolism in order to differentiate his divine figures."[4] The artist, it seems, was not so much trying to represent the actual likeness of a person or god but rather to communicate something about his or her attributes. An image was more about a person's internal identity than what the person (or god) actually looked like.

This same pattern held true with the use of images on coins. In other words, it was not just divinities that were placed on (Greek) coins but their attributes as well.[5] This idea was not unique to the Greeks but continued through Roman times. Coin imagery was chosen to be a credit to the emperor and his reign, and coins reflected the general values, assumptions, and goals of the regime.[6] That means that the imagery placed on coins during the Roman period was meant more as a means of communication of ideas rather than actual reality. In other words, an image was not meant to be a photograph that shows exactly the way one would see a person (or god) if one were to see him face to face. It was meant to be more like a portrait filled with symbolism and meaning.

The emphasis on communicating meaning through symbols in imagery was not even something unique to Greco-Roman culture. Walton says that in the ancient Near East, "The representations of the king were not intended to capture his physical features. In an image it was not physical likeness that was important, but a more abstract, idealized representation of identity relating to the office/role and the value connected to the image."[7] He says further that, "In both Egypt and Mesopotamia an idol contained

3. Steiner, *Images in Mind*, 11.

4. Macdonald, *Uses of Symbolism*, 16.

5. Rüpke, ed., *Blackwell Companion*, 143.

6. Longfellow, *Roman Imperialism*, 40.

7. Walton, *Ancient Near Eastern Thought*, 212.

the image of the deity. This allowed the image to possess the attributes of the deity, function as mediator of worship to the deity, and serve as indicator of the presence of the deity."[8]

The points that Walton makes about the Ancient Near East are very similar to the ones the other authors make about the Greco-Roman view of images. Images were meant as a way to symbolize something about the people or gods they were trying to represent. However, Walton does go a step further and say that because of this representation, the image was able to serve as "a mediator of worship to the deity." Not only was the image a symbol of who the god actually was, but it was a symbol of the god's presence and could be viewed as a mediator. In the ancient world, then, the image of a god was a representation (or perhaps a mediator) of a particular god.

Jewish thought fits right in with both Ancient Near Eastern and Greco-Roman thought.[9] However, it is difficult to say precisely what it meant to Jews for *man* to be in image of God, because ten of the seventeen occurrences of "image" in the Hebrew Bible refer to various types of physical images, two occurrences refer to man as an image or "shadow," and the last five occur in Genesis 1–9.[10] In other words, all of the references that could shed light on what it means for *man* to be made in the image of God occur in early Genesis. So, there are really no uses of the word in another context that can help scholars better understand what it means.

Wenham says, "The strongest case has been made for the view that the divine image makes man God's vice-regent on earth. Because man is God's representative, his life is sacred: every assault on man is an affront to the creator and merits the ultimate penalty (Gen 9:5–6). But this merely describes the function or the consequences of the divine image; it does not pinpoint what the image is in itself."[11] Because it is not possible to give a clear meaning to the word "image" from the Hebrew scriptures, it would probably be best to start with the general meaning of the word that was held across the ancient world and see if the context changes the meaning. In the ancient world, an image of a god was a representation or mediator of that god.

In Colossians, the hymn opens with the statement that Christ himself is the image of the invisible God.[12] If Christ as the image of the invisible

8. Walton, *Ancient Near Eastern Thought*, 212.

9. Walton, *Ancient Near Eastern Thought*, 212.

10. Wenham, *Genesis 1–15*, 29.

11. Wenham, *Genesis 1–15*, 31–32.

12. Technically, v. 13 is referring to God's beloved Son, but there are no scholars who attempt to say that this is someone other than the Christ of the opening of the letter.

God means that he is the representation or mediator of God, then there is a point being made here about the relationship between Christ and God. Bruce says, "To call Christ the image of God is to say that in Him the being and nature of God have been perfectly manifested—that in Him the invisible has become visible."[13] Bruce makes two interesting points that should be considered.

First, he says that Christ as the image of God implies that God has been perfectly manifested in Christ. This sounds reasonable, because if the image were only a partial manifestation, then the text should say something like "who is the *reflection* of the invisible God" or "who is *like* the invisible God." It would probably be too much to say that Christ is not merely a partial representation of God on the basis of this phrase alone. However, there will be other places in the letter, especially the language about "fullness," that will support this point. For now, the idea that Christ "fully" or "perfectly" represents God will be held tentatively.

The second point Bruce makes is that in Christ, the invisible has become visible. This passage, however, is not making a statement about God as invisible; it is making a statement about Christ as the representation of God. "The phrase 'the invisible God' indicates divine transcendence, even remoteness, in some contrast to earlier phrases about God as Father."[14] Claiming that Christ reveals God probably does indicate that God is somehow *above* humanity and needs to be revealed—or that Christ somehow reveals him better or in a more special way. However, if the inability of man to see God were the point in contention, there would be more in the hymn and/or the letter about the invisibility/transcendence of God. It is more likely that the point Paul is making is about Christ revealing God. "To say that Christ is the *image* of God means that, in some way, the unseen or invisible God becomes visible, moves into our sphere of sense perception, in the life of this human being."[15] This is the point the hymn (and, by extension, Paul) is making. Christ is how one "sees" God.

1:15B

πρωτότοκος πάσης κτίσεως

the firstborn of all creation

---

13. Bruce, "Colossian Problems: Part 2," 101.

14. Hay, *Colossians*, 55.

15. Thompson, *Colossians and Philemon*, 28. Italics in original.

The phrase "firstborn of all creation" has been no stranger to controversy and interpretative difficulties. Col 1:15 was one of the most prominent texts in the Arian controversy over the deity of Christ, and the same question they wrestled with back then is the same one anyone hoping to understand this verse must wrestle with today: "Is Christ part of creation or not?" The meaning of the phrase πρωτότοκος πάσης κτίσεως (the firstborn of all creation) is based on three things: 1) the meaning of the word πρωτότοκος (firstborn), 2) the genitive construction of πάσης κτίσεως (of all creation), and 3) the relationship of v. 16 to v. 15.

The first question to ask is "What does the word πρωτότοκος (firstborn) mean?" When discussing this question, many commentators refer to Ps 89:27: "And I will make him the firstborn [πρωτότοκος in LXX], the highest of the kings of the earth."[16] It is easy to understand why this is so, because the passage clearly uses πρωτότοκος (firstborn) in a non-biological way that is similar to the passage in Colossians. The reason this is non-biological is that Ps 89:27 places "firstborn" in parallel with "the highest of the kings of the earth," which means that "firstborn" is explaining David's position. For "firstborn" to be referring to biological birth, David would have had to have been the biological offspring of God, which is not what this psalm is saying. That means that the question of whether Christ is a part of creation or not, cannot be decided by simply saying, "The passage says he is the firstborn; firstborn means birth; therefore, Christ is part of creation." πρωτότοκος (firstborn) can refer to literal birth, but it does not have to. It can also refer to one's position, i.e., one's first-ness.

In the New Testament, πρωτότοκος (firstborn) generally does not refer to literal birth. In fact, the only passage in the New Testament in which it unequivocally refers to literal birth is Luke 2:7,[17] where Mary is described as giving birth to Jesus and laying him in a manger. Primarily, the word firstborn emphasizes the first part of the word; it is about being *first* rather than being *born*.[18] To view firstborn as primarily referring to literal birth (thereby implying that Christ is part of creation) would demand emphasis on the latter half of the word, -τοκος (born).[19] This would go against the general use

---

16. For example, Bruce, "Colossian Problems: Part 4," 59; Harris, *Colossians and Philemon*, 39; MacDonald, *Colossians and Ephesians*, 58; Moo, *Letters to the Colossians*, 119; Sumney, *Colossians*, 65; Lukyn Williams, *Epistles of Paul*, 41; and Witherington, *Letters to Philemon*, 134.

17. Kittel and Friedrich, eds., *Theological Dictionary*, 6:876.

18. Kittel and Friedrich, eds., *Theological Dictionary*, 6:878–9.

19. O'Brien suggests that Rom 8:29 might be an exception to the observation that πρωτότοκος (firstborn) does not refer to literal birth, because this indicates that Christ is the eldest of the family. He says that if πρωτότοκος (firstborn) were stripped away

of the word.[20] Had the author of the hymn wanted to say that Christ was the first created being, there was another option for that. He could have simply used the word πρωτοκτίστος (first-created). However, he did not.

Significantly, there is another instance of πρωτότοκος (firstborn) in the hymn, which will help explain this one. In v. 18, Christ is described as πρωτότοκος ἐκ τῶν νεκρῶν (firstborn from the dead). This almost certainly has a metaphorical meaning, for what could it mean to literally come out of a woman's womb after one has become a grown man? And would the phrase ἐκ τῶν νεκρῶν (from the dead) imply that this grown man literally coming out of a woman's womb occurred when she was dead? This is probably not what was meant. Later elaboration on the phrase in the second strophe makes it clear that "firstborn from the dead" refers to Christ's resurrection. His death and resurrection occurred after he was already a grown man, so biological birth is not in view. Furthermore, this is essentially the same question Nicodemus asks in John 3, and Jesus' answer points towards a metaphorical birth rather than a biological one. There is nothing that would suggest that biological birth is in view here.

Everything about the word πρωτότοκος (firstborn) itself suggests that the metaphorical meaning is more likely in view than the biological meaning. First, πρωτότοκος (firstborn) never had to mean literal birth in the Old Testament. Second, there is only one time in the New Testament when it

---

from the context and used only by itself, then Christ could be seen as part of the creation (*Colossians-Philemon*, 44). However, O'Brien's potential objection does not stand up well under scrutiny. Even if Christ is being described as the head of the family, this is not a family that has been physically born. This family is one that has been raised from the dead and has experienced new birth. Being the firstborn in a family that is unified by having been raised from the dead would not show that Christ was a created being—human, yes; created, no. Even on the view of Christ which holds that he existed without creation, he still became human. O'Brien himself recognizes that while this objection could work in theory, it is not very strong. He continues on to say that the option he suggests does not seem possible because of the ὅτι (because) and the commentary (v. 16) on the title that follows. Both of these things make it difficult to separate the two verses thematically. In the end, it seems that this difficulty with the phrase πρωτότοκος πάσης κτίσεως (firstborn of all creation) might have been expected by the hymn's author(s), and so the commentary which follows it (v. 16) was likely meant to address the problems he/they anticipated.

20. Kittel and Friedrich, eds., *Theological Dictionary*, 6:878–9. That is not to say that in this passage πρωτότοκος (firstborn) could not mean something other than what it usually means. After all, in the introduction to this study, it was made clear that immediate context would take precedence over general usage. This point is merely saying that emphasizing the latter half of the word, -τοκος (born), would be to go against the grain. If there is reason in the context to think that that is what the author of the hymn meant, then that is what he meant. The question is, then, "Is there a reason to think that the hymn's author was using πρωτότοκος (firstborn) in a non-standard way?"

certainly refers to literal birth (Luke 2:7).[21] Third, its general usage in the New Testament emphasizes the first part of the word (πρωτό-, first) rather than the last part (-τοκος, born). Fourth, and most importantly, the parallel usage in the hymn points to a metaphorical meaning rather than a literal one. Therefore, for all these reasons, πρωτότοκος (firstborn) probably refers to Christ's "first-ness" rather than to a literal birth.

Now that the meaning of the word πρωτότοκος (firstborn) has been investigated, it is time to move on to the next part of determining what it means for Christ to be πρωτότοκος πάσης κτίσεως (the firstborn of all creation). Is he part of creation or not?

The second question to ask is: "What does the genitive construction of πάσης κτίσεως (of all creation) mean?" Helyer says:

> Several possibilities present themselves: 1) It could be a partitive genitive, so that *prototokos* [firstborn] would be included in some way in the class of creatures; 2) It could be a genitive of comparison, which would exclude the *prototokos* [firstborn] from the same; 3) It could be a genitive of place, defining the sphere of the firstborn's authority; 4) it could be an objective genitive, in which case the action implied in *prototokos* [firstborn] terminates on all creation.[22]

These will be investigated one at a time, starting with the least likely.

Wallace defines the genitive of place as "the genitive substantive [which] indicates the place *within which* the *verb* to which it is related occurs."[23] As an example he gives Luke 16:24, "Send Lazarus in order that he might dip the tip of his finger *in water* . . . ."[24] The genitive of place means that the action of the verb is *located* in a certain place. In Colossians, this would mean that as the "firstborn" of all creation, Christ would have been the "first one *born in*" creation. This essentially says the same thing as the partitive genitive, i.e., Christ is a *part* of creation. Between the two options for the genitive (partitive and place), saying that Christ is part of creation makes better sense than to say that the location in which he was born was creation. Furthermore, Wallace says of the genitive of place, "This usage is rather rare in the NT and ought to be suggested only if no other category fits."[25] Because of this, if Christ is part of creation, the partitive genitive should be preferred over the genitive of place.

21. There, the context made it clear that literal birth was in view.

22. Helyer, "Arius Revisited," 63.

23. Wallace, *Greek Grammar*, 124. Italics in original.

24. Wallace, *Greek Grammar*, 124. Bolding changed to italics.

25. Wallace, *Greek Grammar*, 124.

The next option to consider is the genitive of comparison. This means exactly what it sounds like it means. It is making a simple comparison between two things. This view "does not distinguish Christ from various individual created things but compares him to all created things as a group. . . . It seeks to set Christ in the highest rank in relation to all created beings— which includes all beings except God."[26] However, this does not say whether Christ is *part* of the group "all created beings." It merely says that he is in the highest rank. He could either be *part* of that group (a created being), or he could be *outside* that group (an uncreated being).

Now, to say that a simple comparison is being made without going any further might be fine for many passages, but it seems unlikely here. This section of the hymn intends to explore and explain Christ's relationship to creation, and the whole hymn itself explains who Christ is and what he has done. To leave unanswered what is perhaps the biggest question one could ask—"Is Christ part of creation or not?"—in a passage that raises that very question *and* tries to settle such issues is hard to believe. It is much more likely that the hymn's author had an opinion about that question, and an answer can be found in this passage, rather than that he simply ignored the question.

Furthermore, it might be fine to stop with a genitive of comparison if the context did not have more information that could help to further define Christ's relationship to creation. But, there is more information. So, why stop looking for an answer until all of the possibilities have been exhausted? It is probably worth investigating whether the hymn says he is higher than creation as a *part* of creation or higher than creation while existing *outside* of creation. So, the genitive of comparison could work, but it should not be chosen unless it is not possible to decide between the partitive and objective genitives.

So, what about the final two options: the partitive genitive (Christ is part of creation) and objective genitive (Christ is outside creation)? In order to decide between them, there are two questions that need to be answered. First, does the word πρωτότοκος (firstborn) itself imply a partitive or objective genitive? And second, what impact does v. 16 have on the meaning of πρωτότοκος (firstborn)?

Really, the first question has already been answered in the discussion on the meaning of the word πρωτότοκος (firstborn). Everything that could impact the meaning of the word itself pointed away from a literal birth and towards a metaphorical meaning. That means that in this passage, the meaning of the word πρωτότοκος (firstborn) points away from the partitive genitive and towards the objective genitive.

26. Sumney, *Colossians*, 65.

To answer the second question, "What impact does v. 16 have on the meaning of πρωτότοκος (firstborn)?," it is necessary to first ask "What is the relationship of v. 16 to v. 15?"

It might be a little confusing where the investigation is right now. So, before moving forward, here is a reminder. The original question was, "Is Christ part of creation or not?" The meaning of the phrase πρωτότοκος πάσης κτίσεως (the firstborn of all creation) is based on three things: 1) the meaning of the word πρωτότοκος (firstborn), 2) the genitive construction of πάσης κτίσεως (of all creation), and 3) the relationship of v. 16 to v. 15. Number 1 has already been answered, and Number 2 is currently being discussed. However, the relationship of v. 16 to v. 15 is actually part of both Numbers 2 and 3. Understanding how v. 16 is related to v. 15 will help determine whether the genitive construction of πάσης κτίσεως (of all creation) is a partitive genitive or objective genitive (Number 2), and it will also answer Number 3. So, this is the final piece of the puzzle, and it will count towards both Numbers 2 and 3. Now, back to the investigation.

The fact that there is a causal ὅτι (because) and an entire verse elaborating on what was said in v. 15 indicates that something needs more explanation. The questions are "What needs more explanation?" and "What does v. 16 modify?" There are three options: v. 16 can modify just εἰκὼν (image), just πρωτότοκος (firstborn), or both εἰκὼν (image) and πρωτότοκος (firstborn). The content of v. 15 and v. 16 will determine which is best.

Verse 16 starts by linking Christ to creation (in him all things were created), then lists the things in creation which he is responsible for creating (all things in heaven and on earth, visible and invisible, etc.), then links him to creation again (all things were created through him and for him). Verse 16 emphasizes that nothing in all of creation is excluded from the things that were created "in him." It makes no difference whether the created things themselves are heavenly or earthly, seen or unseen. Everything, even the rulers and authorities, were created in him.

So, how does this modify v. 15? Does it modify both the statements about Christ or just one of them? Well, it definitely refers to Christ as the firstborn of all creation. Whatever one thinks is the precise meaning of v. 16, it would be hard not to connect the emphasis on creation in v. 16 with Christ's relationship to creation in v. 15. So, if v. 16 modifies Christ as the firstborn over all creation, the only question left is, does v. 16 *also* modify Christ as the image of the invisible God?

The simple answer to this question is no. Describing Christ as *being* the visible manifestation of an invisible God has nothing to do with his *act* of creating everything. One is a description of his relationship to the invisible God, and the other is a description of something he has done. Now, perhaps the invisible God is responsible for creating as well. But, even if that were the case, that is not the description being given here. Christ as the image of the invisible God merely says that he is the visible representation of the invisible God.

Furthermore, the focus in v. 16 is on making sure the reader knows that Christ is responsible for everything in creation. It details the contents of creation and then names Christ as the agent who is responsible for their creation. The content of v. 16 does not have anything to do with the content of the statement that Christ is related in a particular way to God. It focuses entirely on his relationship to creation. The first statement about Christ (image of the invisible God) shows how he is related to God. The second statement about Christ (firstborn of all creation) shows how he is related to creation.

That means that v.16 modifies only the phrase πρωτότοκος πάσης κτίσεως (firstborn of all creation). So, then, does it point towards Christ as a part of creation (partitive genitive) or as outside it (objective genitive)? Verse 16 explains *why* Christ is described as the firstborn of all creation: because he created *all things that have been created*. That means that the content of v. 16 points toward Christ as outside creation (objective genitive) rather than Christ as a part of creation (partitive genitive). He could not have been part of creation if he created all things that were created. However, some might want to ask one final question: "Could Christ have been created by God first, and then he created everything else afterwards?"

Due to the content of v. 16, this is not a real option. Here's why. Verse 16 describes how Christ is responsible for the creation of *all things*. For him to have been first created by God and then create all things, Christ would have had to create himself; he would have had to bootstrap himself into existence. That simply breaks logic. To create oneself, Christ would have had to already exist. But, then, he would have already existed and would not need to be created. So, the options are either: 1) Christ was uncreated, or 2) Christ was part of creation (whether directly created by God or not). And, since v. 16 says that he was responsible for the creation of all things, then he was not part of creation. That leaves only oe option: Christ was uncreated.

This can be confusing, so going through it briefly one more time might be helpful. According to v. 16, Christ could not have been created—even by God. If God had created Christ, and then Christ created everything else after that, then Christ would still be a part of creation. Maybe Christ would not be a part of *his own* creation, but he would still be a part of creation, because he would have been a part of *God's* creation. However, since v. 16 goes to great lengths to make clear that Christ was responsible for the creation of *all* things—whether visible/invisible, earthly/heavenly, etc.—that means that Christ was not part of *anyone's* creation. Christ is, therefore, an uncreated being. Because of this, it would be better to translate πρωτότοκος πάσης κτίσεως as "firstborn *over* all creation" rather than "firstborn *of* all creation" to emphasize his supremacy and make clear that Christ is not a created being.

Now, maybe Christ actually is a created being and isn't creator at all. Maybe none of this is true, and Paul and the hymn's author were simply wrong. However, the point here is to investigate the letter as it stands in order to understand Paul's thoughts. And, the hymn's thoughts all point in a single direction; Paul is quoting that hymn as support for his views. Therefore, in Paul's view, Christ is not created. Christ is uncreated, and he created all things that have been created.

In looking at Christ's relationship to creation, there have been three points of focus: 1) the meaning of the word πρωτότοκος (firstborn), 2) the genitive construction of πάσης κτίσεως (of all creation), and 3) the relationship of v. 16 to v. 15. All three have pointed to Christ *not* being a part of creation. In Paul's view, then, Christ was uncreated and stands on the creator side of the creator/creation divide. Christ is the creator of all things, while he himself is uncreated. Paul believes Christ is the uncreated creator.

1:16

> ὅτι ἐν αὐτῷ ἐκτίσθη τὰ πάντα ἐν τοῖς οὐρανοῖς καὶ ἐπὶ τῆς γῆς τὰ ὁρατὰ καὶ τὰ ἀόρατα εἴτε θρόνοι εἴτε κυριότητες εἴτε ἀρχαὶ εἴτε ἐξουσίαι τὰ πάντα δι' αὐτοῦ καὶ εἰς αὐτὸν ἔκτισται

> because in him all things were created in the heavens and on the earth, visible and invisible, whether thrones, whether dominions, whether rulers, whether authorities, all things were created through him and for him

Before looking into the meaning of any of the words or phrases in v. 16, there are two structural elements that need to be pointed out. First, there is parallel content between the first and last lines of the verse:[27]

> ὅτι ἐν αὐτῷ ἐκτίσθη τὰ πάντα
> τὰ πάντα δι' αὐτοῦ καὶ εἰς αὐτὸν ἔκτισται

---

27. O'Brien calls this a chiasmus (*Colossians-Philemon*, 36–37). Sumney, however, calls this an inclusio, because "the material that lies between these parallel statements does not manifest the consistent parallels needed for a chiasm" (*Colossians*, 65). Whichever is the correct term, it is clear that the content of v. 16 is bounded by statements that locate creation "in Christ."

> because in him all things were created
> all things were created through him and for him

The second structural element is the chiasm in the expansion of τὰ πάντα (all things).[28] Notice how "heavens" pairs with "invisible," and "earth" pairs with "visible."

A ἐν τοῖς οὐρανοῖς
    B καὶ ἐπὶ τῆς γῆς
    B' τὰ ὁρατὰ
A' καὶ τὰ ἀόρατα

A in the heavens
    B and on the earth
    B' visible
A' and invisible

These structural elements are meant to make particular points in the explanation of Christ's relation to creation. Both of these will feature in the discussion of v. 16.

There are three main things to notice about v. 16. First, v. 16 describes original creation. The second main strophe of the hymn (vv. 18b–20) will talk about how Christ has acted to put everything back as it should be. However, this strophe is talking about the creation of things *in the beginning*.[29] Second, Christ is responsible for creation. In the first and last lines of v. 16, the author says this three times in order to make the point clear. *Christ* is the one responsible for creation. Third, "all things" were created by Christ; nothing was left out. Now, why think these things are the points v. 16 is making?

The first point is that v. 16 is describing original creation. There are two instances of the verb "to create": ἐκτίσθη and ἔκτισται. However, the difference in verb tense between these two instances of "create" makes two different points. The aorist tense in the first instance points towards the historical act of creation, but the perfect tense of the second points towards creation's ongoing existence.[30] ἐκτίσθη (aorist tense) says that all things were created in

---

28. O'Brien says there have been attempts to find a chiasm in the second set of terms (thrones, dominions, etc.), but there is too little agreement on what they mean to be able to do anything more than speculate (*Colossians-Philemon*, 37).

29. Dunn says, "Even as christianized, the two strophes seem to be structured on a protology/eschatology, old cosmos/new cosmos distinction, with the future eschatological emphasis limited to the second" (*Epistles to the Colossians*, 92).

30. Sumney says, "Perhaps the use of the perfect tense shows the author thinking that Christ continues to work as creator not just of the things that already exist, but

the past at some point, but it does not give any further information. ἔκτισται (perfect tense) says that all things were created and completed in the past, and the effects of that creation are felt in the present. With the second verb, the hymn's author is saying to his audience: "If you look around you at everything in creation, this was all created by Christ. He created it, and it is the world you are living in now. Christ both ἐκτίσθη (created, aorist tense) this world, and because he ἔκτισται (created, perfect tense) it, you are now able to live in it. Of course, he didn't just create this world. He created all things."

What is also significant about these verbs is that both of them occur in the passive voice. This shows that it is God who is creator.[31] However, as the rest of the verse will emphasize, this was not a solo act.[32] "God creates, but Christ is the agent of creation."[33]

The second thing to notice about v. 16 is that Christ was responsible for creation. To emphasize his point, the author of the hymn makes three statements describing *how* Christ is related to creation. All things were created ἐν αὐτῷ (in him), δι᾽ αὐτοῦ (through him), and εἰς αὐτὸν (to/for him). The author is being redundant in order to emphasize the point that the one responsible for creation is Christ.

Now, it would be nice to try to break down exactly what each of these three prepositions (in, through, and to/for) means. However, the author may not have intended for that to be done. The three prepositions used in v. 16—ἐν, δι᾽, and εἰς (in, through, and to/for)—will be repeated in the exact same order in vv. 19–20. There, they will be used to explain that the fullness of God was pleased to dwell *in* him, and to reconcile all things *through* him and *to* him.

The parallel structure between these two strophes makes it unlikely that the prepositions were being used in highly specific ways. What is more likely is that, by reusing the same prepositions, the author of the hymn was creating a parallel structure that was meant to communicate an important theological point, namely, that Christ is related in the same way to the original creation as he is to the reconciliation of creation.

If that is the case, then these three prepositions are used to do two things. First, they are used to create parallel structure to show that in the same way that Christ was supreme over original creation, he is also supreme over the reconciliation of creation. This is a point that will return in v. 18d,

---

also of the things God intends to bring about through Christ" (*Colossians*, 69). This is a theme that will return in v. 17.

31. MacDonald, *Colossians and Ephesians*, 60, and O'Brien, *Colossians-Philemon*, 45.

32. The prepositions especially work to emphasize this point. They will be discussed in the next paragraph.

33. MacDonald, *Colossians and Ephesians*, 60.

which says, "that in all things he might be preeminent." Second, these three prepositions are being used to make redundantly clear that all things were created *in relation to* Christ. Redundancy is a big part of v. 16 (as the third point the author is making with this verse will show). The author does not want to take any chances at being misunderstood. He wants his point to be crystal clear. Christ is responsible for creation—*all* of it.

Therefore, the best way to understand these prepositions—ἐν, δι', and εἰς (in, through, and to/for)—is that the hymn's author was trying to come at the issue of Christ's relationship to creation from every angle. And, from every angle, the picture looks the same: Christ is responsible for creation.

The third thing to notice about v. 16 is "all things" were created by Christ; nothing was left out. τὰ πάντα (all things) is used in both the first and last lines of this verse.[34] However, beyond the simple repetition of τὰ πάντα (all things), it is the material in the middle that is meant to emphasize Christ's responsibility for *all* creation. This is done first by means of the chiasm discussed above:

A ἐν τοῖς οὐρανοῖς
   B καὶ ἐπὶ τῆς γῆς
   B' τὰ ὁρατὰ
A' καὶ τὰ ἀόρατα

A in the heavens
   B and on the earth
   B' visible
A' and invisible

"Heavens" and "invisible" are meant to correspond in the same ways as "earth" and "visible." This results in a double statement about what Christ created. Since heavens and invisible refer to the same part of creation, this is a redundancy that the author is using for emphasis. And since earth and visible both refer to the same part of creation, this is also a redundancy that the author is using for emphasis. However, there is still more here.

"Heavens and the earth" was a common Jewish way of referring to all of creation. Think back to Genesis 1: "In the beginning, God created the heavens and the earth." Just as Genesis 1 is giving credit to God for all of creation, so Christ is being given credit here for all of creation. Of course, that also means that Christ is being given credit for something that is usually attributed only to God: the creation of the heavens and the earth.

34. N.T. Wright thinks that the inclusion of the article in τὰ πάντα (all things) indicates "that Paul sees this created world as a single whole (i.e. 'the totality')" (*Colossians and Philemon*, 71).

In tandem with "heavens and the earth," Christ is said to have created all things "visible or invisible." What is significant about this is that, like "heavens and the earth," there is nothing that would fall outside of one of the categories of either "visible" or "invisible." In case one didn't get the Jewish reference to all of creation with "heavens and the earth," one finds a more Greek description of "all things" with "visible and invisible." Furthermore, "visible/invisible" are an "A/~A" statement.[35] Since the set is something paired with its negation, it would be logically impossible for anything to exist outside of one of the two parts. Here, the hymn's author is using a more Greek way to make the point that Christ created "all things."

Following the heavens/earth, visible/invisible chiasm, v. 16 continues to list the things that Christ created. However, instead of using more language to describe "all" things, the author focuses on a specific category of things. He says Christ created all things, εἴτε θρόνοι εἴτε κυριότητες εἴτε ἀρχαὶ εἴτε ἐξουσίαι (whether thrones, whether dominions, whether rulers, whether authorities).

Much time has been spent in an attempt to identify these four terms: θρόνοι (thrones), κυριότητες (dominions), ἀρχαὶ (rulers), and ἐξουσίαι (authorities). Many commentators think these powers refer to angelic beings. Dunn thinks these four terms represent a hierarchy of heavenly powers in which "thrones" is superior to "dominions," and so on. He thinks that all four terms refer only to the invisible, heavenly realm, which means that he sees this as an emphasis on the unseen side of creation (perhaps in response to the Colossians' situation).[36] Similarly, O'Brien thinks that "four classes of angelic powers are listed . . . . They probably represent the highest orders of the angelic realm."[37]

Because some scholars think that these terms refer to angelic beings only, their resulting discussions are centered around the nature of these beings, i.e., whether they are good or bad.[38] Other scholars think that these

---

35. "A/~A" means "A and not A." It is a philosophical way of saying "everything." One might say "all colors that are red or not red." All colors would be covered by that statement. Every color falls into one of those categories. Either it is red, or it is not red. The same thing holds true here. Either something is visible, or it is invisible. Everything falls into one of those two categories. So, this is a Greek way of saying Christ created "all things," because nothing could be left out of an A/~A statement.

36. Dunn, *Epistles to the Colossians*, 92.

37. O'Brien, *Colossians-Philemon*, 46–47.

38. Witherington thinks they they must have originally been good, since the Son created them, and they fell after their original creation (otherwise they would not need reconciling to God) (*Letters to Philemon*, 134). On the other hand, in surveying the uses outside of Colossians, Carr says, "We may conclude that the terms θρόνοι, κυριότητες, ἀρχαὶ, and ἐξουσίαι [thrones, dominions, rulers, and authorities], far from conveying to

words represent spiritual powers, but that these spiritual powers are connected with earthly powers.[39] The exact identity of these powers is highly
debated, because "some of the terms Paul uses belonged to complex meta-
physical systems in contemporary non-Christian thought. As a result, it is
not easy to separate the different terms clearly."[40] Unfortunately, that means
that an exact identification of these terms may not be possible at present.
However, it is not necessary to understand their exact identity in order to
understand how they relate to Paul's Christian worldview. For that, one only
needs to understand what they stood for.

The powers discussed here—θρόνοι (thrones), κυριότητες (dominions), ἀρχαὶ (rulers), and ἐξουσίαι (authorities)—are important because
they are powers that are *above* the Colossians but *under* Christ. Because
Christ is responsible for their creation, he is over them.[41]

Both ἐν τοῖς οὐρανοῖς καὶ ἐπὶ τῆς γῆς τὰ ὁρατὰ καὶ τὰ ἀόρατα (in
the heavens and on the earth, visible and invisible) and εἴτε θρόνοι εἴτε
κυριότητες εἴτε ἀρχαὶ εἴτε ἐξουσίαι (whether thrones, whether dominions,
whether rulers, whether authorities) are meant to do similar things. The former is meant to refer to all creation and thereby emphasize the point already
made: Christ is responsible for *all things* in creation; nothing is excepted.
The latter points specifically at the power structures in creation, whether

---

the Colossians the idea of hostile forces of the universe or of malevolent spirits, would
have at most described beings whose status was neutral, requiring definite signs from the
context to be interpreted in an evil sense" (*Angels and Principalities*, 52). Even if evil powers
are in view and in need of reconciliation (as Witherington says), very probably, these terms
refer to all powers, whether good or evil. The point being made is that Christ created all
things, and since original creation would have been prior to any fall (at which point, some
would say that certain of the powers *became* evil), this would have included *all* powers.

39. Sumney says, "While these titles clearly designate heavenly beings, they probably have an additional point of reference. These names also designate visible social and
political offices, structures, and realities . . . . Other Christians, notably the author of Revelation, see direct connections between the supernatural powers that oppose Christians
and the powers that literally rule the earth" (*Colossians*, 67). Similarly, N.T. Wright says,
"For Paul spiritual and earthly rulers were not sharply distinguished. In his view, earthly
rulers held authority only as a trust from the creator" (*Colossians and Philemon*, 72).

40. N.T. Wright, *Colossians and Philemon*, 72.

41. Now, it is theoretically possible that the Colossians could actually have been
some of these powers. If these words refer to earthly powers (or both heavenly powers
and earthly powers combined), then there would be at least some people on earth that
would fall into one of these categories. However, it is unlikely that any/many of the Colossians were in this category for two reasons. First, Christians in the first century rarely
had any political or earthly power. Second, and more importantly, in ch. 2, Paul will talk
about how Christ disarmed the rulers and authorities and triumphed over them. It also
looks like these same powers were working against the Colossians. As such, it seems
unlikely that they would have been in one of these four categories themselves.

spiritual, earthly, or the combination of the two. Christ is responsible for the creation of all things—including all of the powerful beings/people in creation. This will become an important point in ch. 2

Finally, at the end of v. 16, there are two more statements about Christ's relationship to creation.[42] The second of the three statements, that all things were created δι᾽ αὐτοῦ (through him), primarily echoes the first statement. It is the third statement that is different: τὰ πάντα . . . εἰς αὐτὸν ἔκτισται (all things were created to/for him). Up to this point, much of what has been said of Christ could have been said of Wisdom in Jewish thought. However, this third statement, that everything that was made in creation was made *for* him, goes beyond anything found in such literature.[43]

> The LORD possessed me [wisdom] at the beginning of his work, the first of his acts of old . . . then I was beside him, like a master workman, and I was daily his delight, rejoicing before him always.[44]

> For she [wisdom] is a breath of the power of God, and a pure emanation of the glory of the Almighty; therefore nothing defiled gains entrance into her . . .[45]

Many commentators think that statements like these lie behind some of the concepts in the hymn. For example, Witherington says that "the parallels between this hymn and the Wisdom of Solomon are so numerous that they must be listed at the outset of the discussion."[46] He then goes on to list the parallels in chart form. He is far from alone, however. Most (if not all) scholarly treatments of this hymn mention the Jewish concept of the Wisdom of God as a conceptual background to the material in the hymn.

A full investigation into the nature of Wisdom goes beyond the scope of this study, but that level of detail is not needed. It is enough to say that there was a common Jewish belief at the time of this letter that Wisdom came from God, was responsible (at some level) for creation, and is connected with the concept of the εἰκὼν (image). It is not necessary to go further, because the idea of Wisdom has not been lifted straight out of Jewish thought. Here, Wisdom is a springboard from which the author of the hymn leaps in order to make his point. Moo (with O'Brien) says that "the

---

42. The first of the three statements was at the beginning of the verse.

43. Moo, *Letters to the Colossians*, 124, and O'Brien, *Colossians-Philemon*, 47.

44. Prov 8:22, 30, ESV.

45. Wis 7:25, RSV.

46. Witherington, *Jesus the Sage*, 266–67.

statement that all things were made *to* him or *for* him (τὰ πάντα δι' αὐτοῦ καὶ εἰς αὐτὸν ἔκτισται), goes far beyond anything ever said of Wisdom."[47]

Rather than strictly identifying Christ as Wisdom, what the author of the hymn does is to draw on some of the Wisdom concepts and to combine them with other concepts, such as those of εἰκών (image) and λόγος (word/reason), in order to make his point. Loader says, "Wisdom brings two important emphases to Christology. 1) It allowed early Christians to express the relationship of the Son to the Father in ways which went beyond an obedient chosen man and exalted one with the authority of the Son of Man. 2) A synthesis of wisdom and eschatological sonship christology might be expected to result in the view that the Son is sent by the Father, to perform the deeds and functions of the Son of Man, only developed more fully."[48]

Wisdom thought was appropriated by the author of the hymn (and, by extension, Paul) as a way of making certain points. The desire appeared to be to portray Christ as something more than simply an obedient human, and existing categories (like Wisdom) were used to aid in this task. In some places, the author simply followed Wisdom thought (e.g., Christ was in the beginning with God); in others, he surpassed Wisdom thought (e.g., the goal of creation was *for* Christ, because nothing like this was ever said of Wisdom). O'Boyle summarizes this by saying: "It seems that, while there is an element of uniqueness involved in talking about the pre-existence and incarnation of a personal being who took on flesh and became Jesus the Messiah, the sapiential material with its exalted praise of Wisdom helped prepare the way for such an idea."[49]

This final statement, that creation was made *for* Christ, portrays Christ as the *goal* of creation. He is the end for which it was made. Certainly, it is odd for a person to be the goal or purpose of creation. However, Christ is no ordinary person. So far, Christ has been described as the image of the invisible God—the way one sees God. And, he has been described as the firstborn over all creation—the uncreated creator. So, while it does sound a little odd, perhaps there is a reason for it. But, what does it actually mean to say that Christ is the goal or purpose of creation?

Wright says, "Verse 16 thus moves the thought of the poem from the past (Christ as agent of creation) to the present (Christ as the one to whom the world owes allegiance) and to the future (Christ whose sovereignty will

47. Moo makes this point and references O'Brien (*Letters to the Colossians*, 125). O'Brien says, "Paul's teaching about Christ as the goal of all creation . . . finds no parallel in the Jewish Wisdom literature or in the rest of the extant Jewish materials for that matter " (*Colossians-Philemon*, 47).

48. Loader, "Apocalyptic Model," 542–43.

49. O'Boyle, *Towards a Contemporary Wisdom Christology*, 73.

become universal)."[50] O'Brien says, "It needs to be remembered that the One of whom Paul speaks in this vein had recently been crucified as a common criminal in Jerusalem. However, he had risen victoriously from the dead and revealed himself to Paul as Son of God. To him as the goal, the whole of creation, and therefore history as well, moved. It was the Father's intention that all things should be summed up in Christ."[51] Finally, Sumney says that "Christ is the intended goal of creation. Perhaps this indicates that the cosmos should conform to his character."[52]

Each of the three views above looks at v. 16 in general and the final statement in particular a bit differently, but taken together, they present a multi-faceted view of what the hymn is saying. Wright emphasizes that the position of Christ as supreme is consistent through time—through past, present, and future. O'Brien reminds the reader that though the hymn is talking about a transcendent being, this same being also lived, died, and was resurrected as Jesus of Nazareth. Sumney looks ahead to both the present and future implications for Christians. If Christ is the intended goal of creation and the one to whom the cosmos should conform, most of all that means that those who follow him should and will conform to his character.

50. N.T. Wright, *Colossians and Philemon*, 73.

51. O'Brien, *Colossians-Philemon*, 47. On a somewhat unrelated note, it is possible that this provides a bit of insight into the resurrection of Jesus. If Christ is responsible for all things in creation, that would include the earth and all matter. The termination of biological functions for Jesus of Nazareth would not have been a huge problem to overcome for the one responsible for all creation. The creator of all things would have had no problem reanimating a body that he created. It is not as if the entirety of God's wisdom and power existed in the physical location occupied by Jesus of Nazareth. God was still active elsewhere (such as when the centurion's servant was healed without Jesus being present). The death of Jesus did not mean that God's Wisdom somehow died, too. One might say that Wisdom lived on, resurrected the body of Jesus, and continued to indwell it in its new, glorified state.

52. Sumney, *Colossians*, 69.

DIAGRAM[53]

An important part of understanding the hymn is understanding its under-lying structure, because structure carries meaning. With each successive chapter on the hymn, more will be added to the diagram. Here is what has been discovered so far:

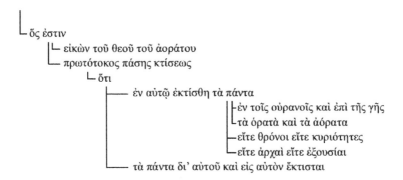

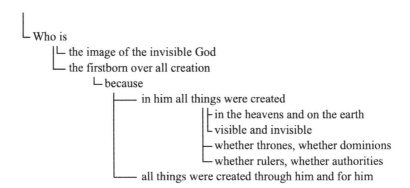

---

53. A diagram like this one shows how all the individual units of these verses are related to one another. The word order has been (and will be) kept as close as possible to the original. The lines indicate what modifies what. The ὅς ἐστιν (who is) refers back to God's beloved son in v. 13, so it points upwards and off the diagram. In turn, ὅς ἐστιν (who is) is modified by two statements about Christ, but both statements are independent of one another, so they point back to ὅς ἐστιν (who is) with separate lines. Verse 16 starts with a ὅτι (because), but it only modifies πρωτότοκος (firstborn) and not εἰκὼν (image). Therefore, it does not have a line pointing back to εἰκὼν (image). ἐν τοῖς οὐρανοῖς καὶ ἐπὶ τῆς γῆς τὰ ὁρατὰ καὶ τὰ ἀόρατα (in the heavens and on the earth, visible and invisible) share a line modifying τὰ πάντα (all things), because they are one unit.

SIGNIFICANCE

The focal point of this section of the hymn is the two statements made about Christ in v. 15: 1) he is the image of the invisible God, and 2) he is the first-born over all creation. The first statement about Christ explains that he is the visible representation of the invisible God. In other words, if one wants to "see" God, he needs to look at Christ. Christ reveals God. This also means that if one attempts to see God by some other means than Christ, then one loses his best chance of seeing the invisible God.

The second statement about Christ says that he is responsible for the creation of *all things*. However, Christ himself was not created. That means that Christ is the uncreated creator. He has existed from eternity past; created everything in existence; and is the reason, purpose, and goal for which everything was created.

Things get really interesting, though, when these two statements are considered together. The first statement shows how Christ is related to God, and the second shows how he is related to creation. By describing Christ as *related* to the invisible God, the hymn sounds like it is describing him as a distinct person. If that is true, then he cannot actually *be* the invisible God. However, the phrase "firstborn over all creation" and its explanation show Christ is uncreated and place him on the creator side of the creator/creation divide. So, one statement is saying that he is God,[54] and the other statement is saying that he is distinct from God. With these two statements, it sounds like the hymn is expressing early binitarian/trinitarian thought.[55]

Now, just because this thought is not expressed in the same manner as it would be in later centuries (using the language of "persons" and "natures"), that does not mean that it is only partially complete. These are some of the earliest statements that explain who Christ is, and they reflect a thought that is based on pictures. An "image" is literally the ancient version of a picture. Before cameras existed, a representation of something or someone had to be painted, carved, or otherwise represented. Similarly, describing someone as the "firstborn" carried with it the idea of a firstborn son who was the beginning of the offspring and was superior to all those who would follow (because it was first).[56]

---

54. It is hard to see how uncreated creator could mean anything else.

55. There is no discussion of the Holy Spirit in Colossians (outside the brief, though probable, reference in v. 8), so this would only be binitarian thought. However, it is expressing what would later be trinitarian thought and is consistent with it, even if the focus is only on God and Christ. The Holy Spirit is not ruled out; he is just not in focus.

56. Even though Christ is described as the firstborn in a metaphorical (rather than biological) way, the imagery behind the firstborn is still that of literal birth. The

Later language on this subject was more propositional, such as describing God as three persons in one nature. Both "person" and "nature" have very technical definitions, and the description of the trinitarian God based on those definitions is not immediately clear to the average person. This can be seen in many Christians today who claim orthodoxy, but in an effort to explain the Trinity, they rely on metaphors whose meanings were denounced as heresy by early church councils.[57] An explanation of the Trinity with propositional language is not simple to understand.

This was an early explanation of the nature of Christ that was given in more pictorial language. It did not require technical language the average person wouldn't know immediately,[58] and so communication of the basic idea was fairly straightforward. Not surprisingly, questions arose, like "Is Christ a *second* God?" Later trinitarian (and incarnational) language was created in an attempt to answer questions like these. Whether the original authors had answers to these questions or not is something that is probably impossible to know. However, just because the early Christians (like the author of the hymn) did not formulate their thoughts in the same manner as later Christians would (using propositional language rather than pictorial language), that doesn't mean that they didn't hold binitarian/trinitarian views. From the two propositions in v. 15, it would appear that at least the author of the hymn and Paul did.

The hymn also describes Christ as supreme over all creation, and as such, there will be at least one immediate effect on all Christians. As implied in v. 16, if Christ was responsible for the creation of all other rulers and authorities in the cosmos, then that means that those other rulers and authorities are really all sub-rulers and sub-authorities. The ultimate authority is Christ, which means that if one follows Christ, one can follow sub-rulers and sub-authorities only as long as they do not come into conflict with Christ. However, if they do conflict, and the Colossians are truly following Christianity, they will obey Christ. This will become important later in the letter.

Christ's supremacy, however, is not something specific only to the time of the letter. If Christ really is the creator of the cosmos, then his supremacy is for all time and all people in all places. The supremacy of an earthly (and

---

metaphorical meaning of supremacy comes from the idea of "first-ness."

57. For example, one will commonly hear Christians say that God is like water which can exist as ice, water, or water vapor. Or, they will say that one man can simultaneously be a father, a husband, and a son. Unfortunately, both of these analogies actually represent modalism rather than the Trinity. Less commonly, one might hear that God is like a three-leaf clover which has three leaves but is still one clover. This is also not the Trinity; it is partialism.

58. Not to mention the fact that it hadn't been developed yet.

mortal) ruler might be based on winning a war or being born into the ruling family. However, if Christ's supremacy is based on his creation of the cosmos, he could not lose that supremacy unless there were another being capable of overthrowing him. Given that he created all other beings in existence (that are not part of the Binity/Trinity, even though they are not separate beings), that seems unlikely. That means, then, that Christ's supremacy is universal in both time and scope; it is not culture- or time-specific.

Finally, if actions are based on beliefs (as discussed in vv. 9–10), then Christ's supremacy is going to have an impact on how Christians are to live their lives. Whatever Christ commands and however he directs Christians to live will necessarily be their highest calling, since there is no one greater. What this looks like has not yet been discussed, but since actions (practice) are based on beliefs (theology), who Christ is will impact how one should live.

7

The Hymn: Christ's Current Activities (1:17–18a)

INTRODUCTION

Verses 17–18a is a highly debated section structurally. Part of this has to do with the fact that there are themes in this section that resonate with material in both vv. 15–16 and 18b-20. This has led some to call this section a second strophe in a three-strophe hymn and others to call it a transitional strophe in a two-strophe hymn. Before looking at the content of these verses, though, some basic structural considerations need to be made.

In addition to structural considerations, how these verses fit into the overall structure will be very important theologically. The first strophe of the hymn focused on original creation—what Christ did *in the beginning*. The last strophe of the hymn will focus on the other main phase of Christ's actions in the world. Between the two main phases of Christ's actions in the world, there is a reference to the church. What could that mean?

STRUCTURE

- 17a   καὶ αὐτός ἐστιν πρὸ πάντων
- 17b   καὶ τὰ πάντα ἐν αὐτῷ συνέστηκεν
- 18a   καὶ αὐτός ἐστιν ἡ κεφαλὴ τοῦ σώματος τῆς ἐκκλησίας

- 17a   and *he is* before all things
- 17b   and in him all things hold together
- 18a   and *he is* the head of the body, the Church

The first thing to notice is the appearance of καὶ (and) at the beginning of each of the three statements. This places all three in parallel and suggests that they should be treated as a single unit. Second, the first and third statements resemble each other in that they make statements about Christ in the form of καὶ αὐτός ἐστιν . . . (and he is . . .). Third, the very next thing in the hymn is ὅς ἐστιν ἀρχή πρωτότοκος ἐκ τῶν νεκρῶν (who is the beginning, the first-born from the dead), the phrase which so closely parallels the opening of the hymn in v. 15. Because v. 18b begins the last strophe, it is unlikely that this section continues beyond v. 18a. When all these points are taken together, it makes the best sense if these three statements are taken together and treated as a unit. The question is "How do they fit in with the rest of the hymn?"

The problem with trying to attach these three statements solely to either the first or last strophe is that the themes are different. While the content of the first statement is fairly similar to that of the first strophe, the content of the second and third is not. Similarly, when one looks at the last strophe, the first statement does not fit well, even if the second and third might. It seems more likely that the three statements of vv. 17–18a were meant to stand between the first and last strophes and to connect them, as well as to make their own point. So, do these statements represent a full, middle strophe, or are they more of a transitional strophe (only semi-independent)?

The first and last main strophes have certain structural elements in common. Each of them has these five elements: 1) ὅς ἐστιν (who is), 2) first statement about Christ, 3) second statement about Christ—including the use of the word πρωτότοκος (firstborn), 4) causal ὅτι (because), and 5) description of how Christ fulfills the role of πρωτότοκος (firstborn), using the prepositions ἐν, δι', and εἰς (in, through, and to/for). Verses 17–18a have none of these elements used to distinguish the other two strophes as such.

While these verses share elements from each of the two main strophes, they do not share the features that so decidedly define the first and last strophes. One cannot, therefore, consider these verses to be a third main strophe. Instead, it is better to think of them as a transitional strophe between the two main strophes.

1:17

καὶ αὐτός ἐστιν πρὸ πάντων καὶ τὰ πάντα ἐν αὐτῷ συνέστηκεν

and he is before all things, and in him all things hold together

Verse 17a is frontloaded with a reference to Christ,[1] and one finds another reference to Christ, ἐν αὐτῷ (in him), in v. 17b. Additionally, there is continued emphasis on τὰ πάντα (all things) and on Christ's ultimacy in relation to τὰ πάντα (all things). However, at first glance, there does not seem to be much new theology in either of the first two statements. There is the continued emphasis on Christ's relationship to creation, although most of what is said in these two statements seems to reflect back on the previous two verses. But, is that true? Is that all there is to v. 17?

The first statement, καὶ αὐτός ἐστιν πρὸ πάντων (and he is before all things), is meant to refer back to the first strophe of the hymn. So, there is really nothing new in that statement, although it plays an important role in connecting the theology of the first strophe with what is to come. However, the second statement, καὶ τὰ πάντα ἐν αὐτῷ συνέστηκεν (and in him all things hold together), begins to take the reader into new areas.

The real key to the significance of the second statement is in the time element of συνέστηκεν (cohere/hold together). This word speaks to Christ's involvement in creation in an ongoing sense. It literally says that creation could not hold together without his involvement. Now, this word συνέστηκεν (cohere/hold together) is found in Platonic and Stoic thought on creation, and many commentators think that this hymn might relate to or modify that thought.[2] Because of that, the first two statements are often seen as focusing on Christ's relationship to creation and are therefore closely connected, while the third one is viewed as different.

---

1. MacDonald says, "The 'he' in this case is most likely emphatic. It means he himself—he and no other" (*Colossians and Ephesians*, 60). The same point will also apply to the αὐτός (he) at the beginning of v. 18.

2. For example, Bruce, "Colossian Problems: Part 2," 104; Donelson, *Colossians*, 26–27; MacDonald, *Colossians and Ephesians*, 61; and Sumney, *Colossians*, 70.

If the first two phrases are taken together, then the second phrase probably "is yet another way that Christ's almost immeasurable superiority to all other powers is evident; they could not even continue their existence without the cohesion and stability with which Christ undergirds the whole cosmos."[3] This would certainly fit with the theology of the hymn—especially with the purposefully redundant emphasis in the first strophe that Christ is responsible for all things in creation (including all other powers). The fact that he is responsible for their continued existence is not so much a new point to make but more of an add-on that continues a theme already discussed. Considering how densely packed the theology of the hymn is, one wonders if this is all the transitional strophe was meant to communicate.

On the other hand, what if the second phrase were considered to be more closely linked to the third phrase rather than the first? If this were the case, then συνέστηκεν (cohere/hold together) would not be a reference to Christ actively holding the world together in the sense that it would cease to exist if he did not keep it in existence.[4] Rather, "in him all things hold together" would be a statement saying that Christ is actively involved in the world and is responsible for holding all things together in the sense of shaping history.[5] In other words, he would not be a sort of deistic creator that made the cosmos and then left it to run on its own. This statement would mean that the creator is *currently* involved in his creation. How interesting is it that the next (and final) statement in the transitional strophe makes reference to the church? So, what does the third phrase mean, and how exactly does it connect with the one that comes before it?

1:18A

κεφαλὴ αὐτός ἐστιν ἡ κεφαλὴ τοῦ σώματος τῆς ἐκκλησίας

and he is the head of the body, the church

---

3. Sumney, *Colossians*, 70.

4. Although, the author of the hymn would probably think this is true as well.

5. Even though συνέστηκεν (cohere/hold together) was used in Platonic and Stoic thought, that does not mean that the word is being used the same way here. The immediate context of the letter in general and the hymn in particular is more important for determining the meaning of the word as it is used here. Given the points that are about to be made about Christ and the Church as well as this transitional stophe's purpose in the hymn, it makes much better sense to think of συνέστηκεν (cohere/hold together) as referring to the way the creator is currently acting in the world.

The third statement says that Christ is the head of the body, the church. To begin with, the head-body metaphor does not mean the same thing here as it does elsewhere in the New Testament. Here, it does not refer to who has what role in the church (with each person being a different part of the body). Instead, it is about how the church relates to Christ.[6] In other words, instead of making the point that everyone in the church is part of a whole and that everyone needs to work with one another, the use of the head-body metaphor here is describing how the church as a whole relates to Christ. Christ is the head, and the church is the body.

With the head-body metaphor, the hymn ascribes a level of importance to the church that is not found in the rest of creation. In the first strophe, it is made clear that Christ created everything in the cosmos, including all other powers and authorities. He is their creator. However, while Christ is still the creator of those who are a part of the church, he is also their head. Christ is the head, and the church is the body. This places the church in a special role that is unique when compared with the rest of creation. No one else can claim to be Christ's body, besides the church.

There is something else interesting here. In vv. 13–14, the Colossians were told that they had been rescued from the domain of darkness and transferred into the kingdom of God's beloved Son, and it is in his Son that they have redemption, the forgiveness of sins. It is significant that not only does this letter emphasize that the Colossians are part of the church, it also emphasizes that there is hostility between the world and God.[7] However, as members of the church, the Colossians have been removed from the domain of darkness.[8] They are now part of the kingdom of Christ.

So, what does it mean for the Colossians to be transferred from one kingdom to another while they are still living their same lives in their same communities? What has really changed since they were transferred into the kingdom of Christ? Obviously, they have not been physically taken out of the world—otherwise, how could they receive a letter? Instead, the transfer of kingdoms is at least partially related to whom a person follows.[9] Christ is now their head, and they are his body. They have a new leader. Additionally, this means that if they have been transferred from one kingdom to the other, it is very likely that other people are still a part of this domain of darkness while on earth. In the picture of the world that the hymn and

---

6. Roose, "Hierarchisierung der Leib-Metapher," 118.

7. 1:13–14 and 1:21–23 especially highlight this.

8. More will be said on this in 1:21–23.

9. It is more than just this, though. What has changed as result of being transferred into the kingdom of Christ will be discussed numerous times throughout the letter.

the surrounding verses are painting, there are people living side by side in the same communities who are a part of different kingdoms. They have allegiance to different leaders, and they play for different teams.

To continue with this line of thinking, consider that the Colossians were transferred into the kingdom of God's beloved Son, and it is they who have "redemption, the forgiveness of sins" (vv. 13–14). As a result of this transfer, they are now part of his body, the church. That means that the body of people that have "redemption, the forgiveness of sins" is the church. This should make a strong point to the Colossians about their connection with Christ. If they have an intimate connection with the creator of the universe who is responsible for their redemption (as part of the church), what more could anyone else offer? The most important thing they have (redemption) comes from Christ.

The church, therefore, is the body of people that has been transferred from the domain of darkness into Christ's kingdom, and Christ is the head of this body of people. But, how does this connect with the phrase that comes before it? In what way is the church connected with Christ's continued actions in the world?

To ask those questions is to be halfway to an answer. Verse 17b says that Christ is continually involved in his creation. The very next phrase says that he is the head of the body, the church. The juxtaposition of these two concepts seems to indicate that the way that Christ is working in the world now is through the church. Christ is the head and is therefore responsible for leadership and guidance. What is significant is that the church is the body, which means that its members are to follow his guidance and carry out his wishes. If Christ is still working in creation, and those who are a part of the church are taking his orders, the most likely conclusion is that Christ is working in the world through the church.

It will not be until the final strophe of the hymn that Christ's current actions in the world are described. For now, all that can be said is that Christ is working in the world through the church. What Christ is doing and how the church participates in that will be discussed in the next chapter.

DIAGRAM[10]

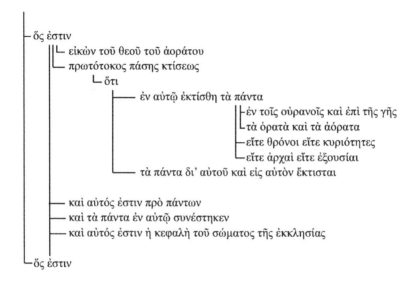

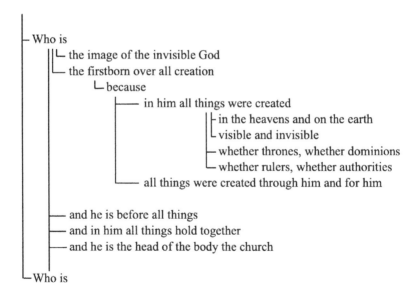

10. The reason vv. 17–18a are connected to both of the ὅς ἐστιν (who is) clauses is because they connect the two main strophes. They do not refer directly back up to v. 13 and are not a main strophe. They are a transitional strophe.

SIGNIFICANCE

The discussion of Christ as the creator of all things centers on what he did a long time ago. That is why his act of creation is described in the past tense; it is finished. However, in v. 17b, the hymn says καὶ τὰ πάντα ἐν αὐτῷ συνέστηκεν (and in him all things hold together). With συνέστηκεν (hold together), the focus moves into the present tense. Christ is said to be responsible for the *ongoing* activities in the cosmos, and then immediately after that, he is described as the head of the church—which is his body. Christ ruling over the church puts the focus not on a timeless statement of his position in relation to creation. Rather, it places Christ into history and into this world.[11] If Christ is continuing to act in creation, then the church must be a part of that. After all, does not the body do what the head directs it to do?

These verses do not represent merely a way to get from the first main strophe to the second, i.e., they are not verses that serve a grammatical purpose but have very little to add theologically. Rather, these verses serve to tie together two very important phases in the history of God's actions in the world and explain what God is doing *now*. The first strophe speaks to the original creation of the cosmos in, through, and for Christ. This transitional strophe explains that Christ is working in the world through the church. The last strophe will focus on the other main phase in Christ's actions in the world. Given the structure of the hymn, that means that the last strophe must balance the first strophe. Whatever it is, therefore, is something of equal importance to original creation. What one finds in this transitional strophe, then, is that the church is the way Christ is working to move from what happened in the first strophe to what happens in the last strophe.

The church is made up of those people who have been rescued from the domain of darkness and transferred into Christ's kingdom. The church is the place where redemption and forgiveness happen, and the members of the church are the ones who experience it. They are also the ones responsible for acting in the world on behalf of Christ.

---

11. Gabathuler, *Jesus Christus*, 176.

8

The Hymn: Christ and the Reconciliation of Creation (1:18b-20)

INTRODUCTION

Verse 18b starts with the second ὅς ἐστιν (who is) that begins the second main strophe of the hymn. Like the first strophe, this one has two primary parts: 1) the ὅς ἐστιν (who is) combined with two statements about Christ and 2) the ὅτι (because) with the reasoning that follows explaining *why* the two statements about Christ are true/possible. There are more features than this, and they will be discussed when looking at the verses in detail. However, these two primary parts explain how this strophe is shaped and show where the investigation will be headed.

As discussed previously, the relative clause ὅς ἐστιν (who is), with its two statements about Christ, represents a main structural element of the hymn.[1] Furthermore, the two main strophes have parallel structure, which means that the themes of this strophe should be expected to balance the themes of the first one. The first main strophe was about Christ's relationship to God and Christ's original creation of all things. This strophe will reveal more about who Christ is, as well as show what he has done to repair creation.

1. For more information, look at the chapter on the introduction to the hymn, in the section on structure.

In vv. 13–14, Paul said that the Colossians have been transferred from the domain of darkness into the kingdom of God's beloved Son. And, it is there that they have redemption, the forgiveness of sins. Verse 18a further defined the kingdom of God's beloved Son as the church, which is Christ's body. This final strophe of the hymn will finish answering the question all of Paul's readers must have had: "How is all of this possible?"

1:18B-D

> ὅς ἐστιν ἀρχὴ πρωτότοκος ἐκ τῶν νεκρῶν ἵνα γένηται ἐν πᾶσιν αὐτὸς πρωτεύων
>
> who is the beginning, the firstborn from the dead, that in everything he might be preeminent

ἀρχή usually means "beginning" or "ruler."[2] These are accurate translations; however, simply calling Christ the "beginning" is fairly nebulous. What exactly does that mean? Looking at the immediate context, there is actually another use of the word in the hymn itself that might help explain ἀρχή (beginning) further. In v. 16, the plural form ἀρχαὶ (rulers) is used to refer to the rulers over whom Christ is supreme. Very likely, the hymn author intends "to set Christ above all the beings in v. 16 by assigning to him this same designation and giving it in the singular. That is, rather than a plurality of beings in this classification, as there is for all those in v. 16, Christ is uniquely the Ruler and thus the one to whom all the others are subordinate."[3] It is unlikely that this use is accidental, especially given the theme of the superiority of Christ that runs throughout the hymn. As a result, ἀρχή (beginning/ruler) carries at least the overtones of Christ's role as *the* ruler and *the* authority in contrast to the other (lesser) rulers and authorities.

However, there is a further question to ask. Even if one could say that ἀρχή means beginning or ruler, one must still ask "Beginning of what?" or "Ruler of what?" After all, if Christ is the beginning or ruler, he has to be the beginning or ruler of something or someone. Dunn connects ἀρχή

---

2. Bauer et al., ἀρχή, *Greek English Lexicon*, 137–38. O'Brien says that ἀρχή (beginning/ruler) has basically to do with "primacy, whether in a temporal sense or with reference to authority and sovereignty" (*Colossians-Philemon*, 50).

3. Sumney, *Colossians*, 72. He goes on to say that this is "a minor point in comparison with the emphasis on Christ as the creator of the new life through the resurrection." Even so, noticing this helps one to understand some of the nuance for the meaning of this word, as well as why the author of the hymn chose it.

(beginning/ruler) with the statement that follows and says that it refers to Christ as "the new beginning of resurrection."[4] A number of scholars, however, have turned to Genesis, because there is a verse there that uses both ἀρχή (beginning) and πρωτότοκος (firstborn) together in a way similar to how they are used in the hymn. Gen 49:3 in the LXX says,[5] "Reuben, you are my firstborn [πρωτότοκος]; my might and the beginning [ἀρχή] of my strength, preeminent in dignity and preeminent in power." Because of the way ἀρχή (beginning) is being used here, it carries with it the connotation not just of "beginning" but of "founder."[6] Since Reuben is the first of Jacob's children, that means that he began or "founded" a new group of people— even though he was not actively involved in the process. If this is the meaning behind ἀρχή (beginning), then instead of calling Christ the *beginning*, it might be better to call him the *beginner*—of a new people.

If ἀρχή (beginner/founder) carries the same meaning for Christ as it did for Reuben, then that would mean that Christ began a new group of people. One must then ask "Which group did he found?" In the hymn, there are only two "groups" mentioned: the rulers and authorities in v. 16 and the church in v. 18. Now, because Christ is the creator of all things, he is the creator of both groups. However, the church has been further described as the body of which Christ is the head. The church is much more personally related to Christ, so much so that it is described as being his body. It seems better, then, to say that while Christ is the *creator* of the rulers and authorities, he is the *founder* of the Church.

Calling Christ the founder of the church explains one of the statements about Christ, but what about the other statement? What does it mean to call Christ the πρωτότοκος ἐκ τῶν νεκρῶν (firstborn from the dead)? It is universally agreed among commentators that this phrase refers to the resurrection of Jesus. Really, it is hard to see how this phrase could refer to anything else, especially considering that v. 20 talks about the blood of Christ's cross. However, even if this definitely refers to Christ's resurrection, that still does not explain how it is being applied here.

> By looking at the word "resurrection," one is entering into the discussion of the afterlife that had been going on for quite some time (and continues still). Importantly, there is debate over whether the background for the usage of "resurrection"

4. Dunn, *Epistles to the Colossians*, 97.

5. The LXX is the earliest translation of the Old Testament (and some other books) into Greek that has survived today. It is helpful to scholarship in many ways, including comparing Old Testament and New Testament terminology (since the New Testament is written in Greek).

6. Moo, *Letters to the Colossians*, 129, and Sumney, *Colossians*, 73.

in Colossians is more appropriately Jewish or Greek in origin. This needs to be discussed briefly in order to understand what is meant when the hymn says πρωτότοκος ἐκ τῶν νεκρῶν (first-born from the dead). Whether or not Christ actually did rise from the dead is another topic entirely.[7]

The Jewish concept of resurrection is often thought to have begun during the Babylonian exile with Ezekiel's vision of the valley of dry bones. This outlook, Vermes says, "developed along two separate paths in the post-exilic period (after 539 BC)"[8]—the first path through Isaiah and Daniel, the second path through the Wisdom of Solomon and the Greek Apocrypha in the Septuagint.[9] Lapide agrees with Vermes when he says that it is a historical fact that the resurrection of the dead was not solidified into a doctrine of Judaism until a relatively late time.[10] However, Lapide also says that most rabbis claim "that the faith in the resurrection of the dead is much earlier than the Maccabees, that it is as old as Judaism itself. In this respect, one midrash asserts that Abraham, when he was about to sacrifice his son Isaac at the command of God, did it because 'He considered that God was able to raise men even from the dead' (Heb. 11:19)."[11]

The reason why there is disagreement among those who investigate the belief in the resurrection within Judaism is partly due to the fact that the ideas of the afterlife developed over time. Raphael says that in a period of three centuries (following the Babylonian exile), three important developments took place in Jewish afterlife eschatology. "First, resurrection transformed the understanding of Sheol into an intermediate realm where the righteous await divine redemption at the end-of-days. Second, the doctrine of resurrection envisioned that the result of God's divine judgement would occur within a postmortem realm. And finally, with the Book of Daniel, divine retribution developed a dualistic aspect to it, teaching that eventually there would be a postmortem judgment for both the righteous and the wicked.[12]

---

7. If one wishes to look into the historical question of whether Jesus of Nazareth rose from the dead or not, the most comprehensive study is Licona, *Resurrection of Jesus*.

8. Vermes, *Resurrection*, 10.

9. The more traditional Jewish path envisaged a bodily resurrection, while the Hellenistic one thought of the soul being liberated from the body.

10. Lapide, *Resurrection of Jesus*, 54.

11. Lapide, *Resurrection of Jesus*, 55.

12. Raphael, *Jewish Views*, 73.

The Greek view of the afterlife is quite different. Cullmann says of the idea of the afterlife found in Plato's *Phaedo*, "Our body is only an outer garment which, as long as we live, prevents our soul from moving freely and from living in conformity to its proper eternal essence. It imposes upon the soul a law which is not appropriate to it. The soul, confined within the body, belongs to the eternal world. As long as we live, our soul finds itself in a prison, that is, in a body essentially alien to it. Death, in fact, is the great liberator."[13]

Cullmann says further that "the contrast between the Greek idea of the immortality of the soul and the Christian belief in the resurrection is still deeper. The belief in the resurrection presupposes the Jewish connection between death and sin. Death is not something natural, willed by God, as in the thought of the Greek philosophers; it is rather something unnatural, abnormal, opposed to God. The Genesis narrative teaches us that it came into the world only by the sin of man. Death is a curse, and the whole creation has become involved in the curse. The sin of man has necessitated the whole series of events which the Bible records and which we call the story of redemption. Death can be conquered only to the extent that sin is removed."[14]

Given the conceptual difference between the Greek and the Jewish view,[15] it makes better sense to think that in Colossians, it is the Jewish version that is in view. Some, like Bedard, try to make a case that the Greek version makes a better background for early Christian belief in the resurrection, but their arguments are not convincing.[16]

---

13. Cullmann, *Immortality of the Soul*, 19–20. There is more to the concept of the afterlife in *Phaedo* than this, but this is enough for a brief comparison of a few ideas between Greek and Jewish thought.

14. Cullmann, *Immortality of the Soul*, 28.

15. One should note that not all Jews in the first century believed in the resurrection. Vermes confirms what one finds in the New Testament when he says that the Pharisees believed in the resurrection, while the Sadducees did not (*Resurrection*, 11). Lapide adds that both the chief Pharisaic schools (those of Hillel and Shammai) believed in the bodily resurrection (*Resurrection of Jesus*, 57).

16. Bedard says, "What is amazing about this story [Er from Plato's *Republic*] is that, with a few modifications, this could be a Jewish apocalyptic revelation worthy of Enoch. Many of the common themes in Jewish apocalyptic are found in this story, including a cosmological survey, development of belief in life after death and the increasing significance of the individual in resurrection, judgment and eternal bliss. Particularly significant is the belief that existence as a disembodied soul is only temporary and that the soul must return to some sort of bodily form" ("Hellenistic Influence," 178). While Bedard thinks that this story could form the background to Christian thought, there are problems with this. In his supposed parallel, even though one returns to a bodily form,

Beyond all this, however, Greek ideas of the afterlife make no sense when applied to Colossians—especially the hymn. In looking at the hymn, Jewish resurrection explains πρωτότοκος ἐκ τῶν νεκρῶν (firstborn from the dead) better and answers the question "Why did Christ have to die?" However, it would not make sense to call the Greek version of the afterlife a resurrection from the dead and try to fit it into the hymn. If "Greek resurrection" were in view in Col 1:18 and the shedding of the body were already inevitable (since everyone dies), there would have been no need for Christ to die, because everyone would eventually die and shed their bodies anyway. They then would be "resurrected" upon death as people always had been, without Christ having had to do anything. Furthermore, it makes no sense to call Christ the πρωτότοκος ἐκ τῶν νεκρῶν (*firstborn* from the dead) unless he were the *first* to die and be reborn (which he would not be in the Greek view, but would be in the Jewish view). He could only be called the firstborn if he were doing something unique when compared to all those who had died before him. It makes better sense, then, to think one is looking at the Christian version of Jewish resurrection.

In the first strophe, Christ is called the πρωτότοκος πάσης κτίσεως (firstborn over all creation); here, he is the πρωτότοκος ἐκ τῶν νεκρῶν (firstborn from the dead). Given the parallel structure of the hymn, that means πρωτότοκος ἐκ τῶν νεκρῶν (firstborn from the dead) is just as important as πρωτότοκος πάσης κτίσεως (firstborn over all creation). So, what makes Christ's resurrection from the dead as significant as his creation of all things?

If the resurrection being discussed here is mostly in line with the Jewish concept of resurrection, then, it would not have been something expected to happen to a single individual.[17] Imagery used as the foundation of resurrection theology, like Ezekiel's valley of dry bones, suggested a multitude of people. Given that Jewish thinking on the resurrection viewed

---

that form is not progression on to a glorified state but *reincarnation* to live this life again. Additionally, while this might occur in a human form, it might also occur in an *animal* form. Furthermore, one might note the judgment here is based on simple works rather than on being part of the people of God or connection with any Christ-like figure. Even if it were technically possible for Christian belief in the resurrection to have come out of the Greek view, the Jewish view is much closer to the Christian view. For that and other reasons, it seems better to assume a Jewish background to Christian resurrection thought.

17. For more information on this, see the excursus above.

it as an eschatological event in which many (if not all) participated,[18] and that Christ is described here as a founder of a group over whom he is said to be the "firstborn," then it looks like the imagery behind Christ's resurrection points towards those who are a part of Christ's group, the church, as being resurrected with him.[19]

When one combines ἀρχή (beginner/founder) with πρωτότοκος ἐκ τῶν νεκρῶν (firstborn from the dead), the picture that results is that through his death and resurrection, Christ began a new group, the church. At this point in the hymn (and at this point in the letter), nothing more is said than that Christ's resurrection has happened. Basically, what the hymn does is explain what this particular piece of the puzzle is and how it fits in with everything around it. The significance of this puzzle piece has not yet been discussed; however, the rest of both the hymn and the letter will explore what Christ's resurrection means to individuals and creation.

At the end of v. 18, one finds the phrase ἵνα γένηται ἐν πᾶσιν αὐτὸς πρωτεύων (that in everything he might be preeminent). Up to this point, the second main strophe has been parallel with the first. However, this structure is broken with the introduction of a ἵνα (that/in order that) clause for which there is no parallel in the first strophe.

In the passage, this phrase is being used as a purpose clause. It declares that Christ can now be said to be first ἐν πᾶσιν (in everything), which probably means more than just the immediate context of the second strophe is in view. Considering that the two πρωτότοκος (firstborn) statements feature so prominently in the hymn, it is likely that these statements (and, by extension, the entire hymn) explain Christ's primacy, his first-ness.

18. Donelson, *Colossians*, 27; Dunn, *Epistles to the Colossians*, 98; Moo, *Letters to the Colossians*, 129; O'Brien, *Colossians-Philemon*, 51; and N.T. Wright, *Resurrection*, 726–27. Wright says, "'Resurrection' was a key part of the 'eschaton'; if it had happened to one man whom many had regarded as Israel's Messiah, that meant that it had happened, in principle, to Israel as a whole. The Messiah represented Israel, just as David had represented Israel when he faced Goliath. Jesus had been executed as a messianic pretender, as 'king of the Jews,' and Israel's god had vindicated him. This, apparently, was how Israel's god was fulfilling his promises to Israel. Again and again the early Christians emphasized that Jesus was raised from the dead *by god*, and by 'god' they meant Israel's god, YHWH. They saw the resurrection as a life-giving act of the covenant god, the creator who had always had the power to kill and make alive, who indeed was different from the other gods precisely in this respect. The resurrection was the sign to the early Christians that this living god had acted at last in accordance with his ancient promise, and had thereby shown himself to be God, the unique creator and sovereign of the world" (*Resurrection*, 726).

19. Paul will speak directly to those who are part of the church dying and rising with Christ later.

The phrase ἵνα γένηται ἐν πᾶσιν αὐτὸς πρωτεύων (that in everything he might be preeminent) is most probably meant as a summary statement: "Christ is first in both original creation and in the reconciliation of creation."[20] The hymn is not finished, and there are still many important topics to cover, but the second πρωτότοκος (firstborn) statement has just been made, so now it is possible to state that Christ is first in everything. This statement, the repeated use of τὰ πάντα (all things), and all-encompassing language like ἐν τοῖς οὐρανοῖς καὶ ἐπὶ τῆς γῆς (in the heavens and on the earth) are meant to make clear what this statement summarizes: in all things, Christ is first. The importance of Christ's "first-ness" will feature both in Paul's comparison with the philosophy in ch. 2 and with his explanation of the Christian life in ch. 3.

1:19

ὅτι ἐν αὐτῷ εὐδόκησεν πᾶν τὸ πλήρωμα κατοικῆσαι

because in him all the fullness was pleased to dwell

It is important to notice that this verse starts with a ὅτι (because). The same thing was true of v. 16 in the first strophe, and just like in the first strophe, this ὅτι (because) is meant to show that what follows will give the reasoning behind what has just been said about Christ. That means that vv. 19–20 explain how v. 18 is possible.

However, unlike with the first strophe, it will not be necessary to determine whether the material that follows relates to only one of the statements or to both of them. The two statements are being considered as a unit, because while they do have somewhat separate meanings ("beginner/founder [of a people]" and "firstborn [of many] from the dead"), they make more sense together. By rising from the dead and bringing others with him, Christ

---

20. There is some tension between: 1) the fact that this phrase is a purpose clause, 2) that this phrase is used as a summary statement, and 3) that Christ is already the ἀρχή (beginning), so why would he need to *become* preeminent? The resolution to this tension will be found in v. 19. There, the hymn will say that God was pleased to dwell in Christ and reconcile all things through him. God made Christ the ἀρχή (beginning) and πρωτότοκος ἐκ τῶν νεκρῶν (firstborn from the dead) *so that* (purpose clause), in combination with his original creation of all things, *in everything he might be preeminent* (summary statement). That reconciles nos. 1 and 2. As far as no. 3, if one thinks of ἀρχή not as "beginning" but as "founder" (as discussed above), then it makes perfect sense to say, "God made Christ the founder of a new people." Therefore, the tension between these three points will be removed by v. 19, which says that God was pleased to do these things through Christ.

began a new group of people, the church.[21] These two statements are not separable in the way that "image of the invisible God" and "firstborn over all creation" are. Therefore, since these two statements function as a single unit, everything that follows will be considered to modify them together.

The first thing that needs to be investigated is the word πλήρωμα (fullness). Now, the concept of fullness was one that was well understood in Greco-Roman times, albeit in a different context. Küchler says that the image of fullness has been found on coins that come from Jewish areas, and, given that coins were used to circulate messages widely, it is very likely that "fullness" was a common idea/image. One of the ways this message was transmitted was through the use of the cornucopia, which communicated fertility, abundance of blessings, and prosperity/wealth—all of which come from the divine world.[22] If, therefore, the linguistic metaphor of fullness was already understood, the receptive ground was already prepared. It would have been relatively easy for Christians to take the idea of fullness as overflowing abundance and use it in a different context. So, what does πλήρωμα (fullness) mean in this context?

The πλήρωμα (fullness) is said to dwell in Christ, and because this phrase starts with a ὅτι (because), whatever this fullness is, it contributes to the reason that Christ can be said to be the beginning and the firstborn from the dead. In this context, there are two primary options for translating the phrase εὐδόκησεν πᾶν τὸ πλήρωμα κατοικῆσαι: 1) "all the fullness was pleased to dwell . . . ," or 2) "God was pleased that all his fullness should dwell . . . ."[23] As should be immediately clear, the issue surrounding the translation of this phrase is whether the fullness is God's fullness or not.

Moo explains the support for both options: "In favor of the former rendering [all the fullness was pleased to dwell] is: (1) the fact that we do not need to supply a subject (the alleged subject, 'God,' last occurs in v. 15 and then not as a subject); and (2) 'fullness' is clearly the subject of the verb 'dwell' in the parallel passage in 2:9. In favor of the latter rendering [God was pleased that all His fullness should dwell] is: (1) the masculine form of the participle 'making peace,' which would normally echo the form of the subject of the main verb ('God' being masculine); (2) the awkwardness of the combination of 'all the fullness was pleased . . . to reconcile.' However,

---

21. There are other things that his resurrection accomplished, but the point is that the beginning of the Church is inseparable from Christ's resurrection.

22. Küchler, "Aus seiner Fülle," 138–39.

23. Moo, Letters to the Colossians, 131.

both these latter problems are considerably alleviated if we take 'all the fullness' to mean, as we probably should, 'God in all his fullness.'"[24]

There are, however, two additional reasons to think that it is God's own fullness that was pleased to dwell in Christ. First, if fullness is a separate entity, then it would probably be a personal one, because, according to the passage, the fullness was "pleased." It seems unlikely that the fullness could be some kind of impersonal force, because impersonal forces are not usually thought to experience pleasure.

On the other hand, if πλήρωμα (fullness) refers to "God in all His fullness," then there is no problem, because God is a personal being and capable of being pleased. Rather than implying a new personal entity called "fullness" (which would be a serious move away from the theology of the hymn as well as the rest of the letter), or an impersonal force that has the ability to experience pleasure, it seems simpler to understand πλήρωμα (fullness) as referring to God in His fullness.

Second, if the Jewish background that has been present up to this point is still present in this verse (i.e., if there has not been a radical shift at the beginning of v. 19), then it makes better sense for God to be the subject of εὐδόκησεν (was pleased) than it would for an impersonal "fullness" to be the subject. In support of the Jewish background continuing here, one could point out that "the verb 'pleased' is regularly used in the LXX with God as the subject to describe his good pleasure."[25] Fullness in the Old Testament was thought of as God's fullness rather than as an impersonal force.

So, to suggest that God is the subject of εὐδόκησεν (was pleased) and that πλήρωμα (fullness) refers to God in His fullness, is really to continue the same theological thoughts one sees in the Old Testament—the same thoughts that form the background of the hymn. This points toward God as the subject of εὐδόκησεν (was pleased), because it does not require a radical shift in thought. Therefore, for all the reasons given above, the best way to translate this verse is probably, as Moo said, "God was pleased that all his fullness should dwell."[26]

> There has been a lot of speculation about whether the use of the word πλήρωμα (fullness) means that there was an early form of Gnosticism at Colossae that Paul was countering. This is

24. Moo, *Letters to the Colossians*, 131.

25. Dunn, *Theology of Paul*, 204.

26. Moo, *Letters to the Colossians*, 131. Of course, this still leaves questions like: "If God was *pleased* to dwell in Christ and to reconcile all things through him, could it have been done differently? Could God have created all things without Christ? Could God have reconciled all things without Christ?" Questions like these will be addressed in the conclusion of this book, after the whole letter has been investigated.

because, as Wilson says, "The word πλήρωμα [fullness] is a technical term, particularly in Valentinianism, for the totality of the intermediary powers or emanations produced by the supreme transcendent being, or for the region which they inhabit."[27] However, he is quick to add, " . . . but that does not mean that it has to be understood in a Gnostic sense here."[28] Bruce agrees with Wilson and says, "No doubt the word πλήρωμα [fullness] had a special sense (or senses) in Gnostic terminology, but it does not follow that the present occurrence originally bore that special sense (or senses)."[29]

Besides the lack of requirement that πλήρωμα (fullness) must refer to gnostic thought, there are good reasons to think that it does not imply Gnosticism here. Hay says that, "Unlike later Gnosticism, the hymn makes no distinction between God and the 'fullness,' nor does it suggest that in his life on earth Jesus departed from the divine 'fullness' or 'emptied' himself of it. Christ is distinguished from God as 'image,' but he is not represented as an inferior; on the contrary, all the plenitude of divine being dwells in him."[30] If the later gnostics thought of the fullness as separate from God (as Hay says), then this cannot be the same fullness that is being used here. Furthermore, in 2:9, Paul speaks again of this πλήρωμα (fullness), and says that it is τῆς θεότητος (of deity), which rules out that this was a separate fullness and not God's fullness. In the hymn (as well as in the rest of the letter), there is no indication that the fullness is separate from God. Rather, it is most likely that the fullness that is described here is God's fullness, which would point away from Gnosticism.

27. Wilson, *Colossians and Philemon*, 152.

28. Wilson, *Colossians and Philemon*, 152.

29 Bruce, "Colossian Problems: Part 2," 108. He continues, "The word is used by Paul and other New Testament writers in a variety of senses. Conceivably it may have been used in a technical sense by the false teachers at Colossae, and there may be some allusion to that technical sense here, but nothing can be established as a matter of fact on the bare ground of its being conceivable." To that point, there are other uses for the word πλήρωμα (fullness). For example, in classical Greek, Wilson says it "can be used of the complement of a ship, its crew or its cargo" (*Colossians and Philemon*, 152). Given that there are other options for what the word might mean (including the normal sense of the word *fullness*), it seems premature to jump to the conclusion that it must have a gnostic origin without additional data.

30 Hay, *Colossians*, 62. Melick says that, "In Gnostic schemes, in general, the term 'fullness' (πλήρωμα) referred to the totality of the emanations from God. The emanations, or 'aeons,' were spiritual and separate from the material world. Although these emanations came from God, they were not considered part of God" (*Philippians*, 223).

Finally, if Colossians is (as many scholars consider it to be) either one of the last of Paul's letters or one of the first of the non-Pauline letters, then the date at which this letter would have been written is likely too early to have been addressing the problem of Gnosticism. Donelson says, "The notion of God's fullness will become famous in Christian Gnostic circles. But the peculiar problems involved in Gnostic speculations probably have not yet emerged. Instead, the author is addressing again the whole question of the sufficiency of Jesus. Does Christ possess in himself adequate power against all the forces in the world? Should we add other allegiances to our allegiance to Christ?"[31]

If one looks at the hymn and its context, Donelson's point makes sense. The hymn does not address questions of a fullness that is separate from God or other gnostic issues. Rather, the focus is, as Donelson says, on the supremacy and sufficiency of Christ. He is shown to be preeminent in all things (v. 18) and the hymn is directed at making this point. It is possible that πλήρωμα (fullness) has a polemical thrust,[32] but if it does, it is only incidental. The focus is on who Christ is and what he has done. For all of these reasons, it seems highly unlikely that the gnostic ideas of πλήρωμα (fullness) are present in Colossians. The point is that *God* dwells in Christ. The language about the "fullness" is meant to explain that everything is to be found in Christ, and nothing is lacking. In other words, there is nothing of God that a person can find elsewhere that cannot be found in Christ.

Now, God was not merely "pleased"; He was pleased *to dwell*. Because of the wording of 1:19 (God's fullness "was pleased to dwell"), many see a parallel with Ps 68:16 (LXX 67:17).[33] It says, "Why do you look with hatred, O many-peaked mountain, at the mount that God *desired* for his abode, yes, where the Lord will *dwell* forever?" Verses like Jer 23:24 point to God filling the whole earth;[34] however, Ps 68:16 suggests that he was present in the temple in a special way.

In Judaism, while the temple was functioning, it was the primary place where one met God. However, this was something that would begin to change with time, especially after the temple was destroyed. Coloe says:

---

31. Donelson, *Colossians*, 28.

32. Moo, *Letters to the Colossians*, 132.

33. Hay, *Colossians*, 62; Heil, *Colossians*, 72; MacDonald, *Colossians*, 63; and Moo, *Letters to the Colossians*, 133, for example.

34. "'Can a man hide himself in secret places so that I cannot see him?' declares the Lord. 'Do I not fill the heavens and the earth?' declares the Lord" (Jer 23:24).

Judaism had once looked to the Ark, the Tabernacle, and especially the Temple as the visible point of contact between God
and humanity. Through the processes of their history, especially
with the loss of the Solomonic Temple, Israel moved away from
emphasizing the cultic presence of God, towards a more personal and covenant-based presence of God's Spirit placed within
(Ezek 36:26; 37:12). In the later Wisdom tradition, God's presence in Israel was personified in Lady Wisdom and embodied
in the Torah. Sinai and Wisdom traditions came together in a
reformulation of Israel's claim to possess divine revelation.[35]

Coloe speaks of a continuing belief in Judaism of the presence of
God in some way. The primary thought seems to have been of God dwelling in the temple, although after its destruction, Jewish thinkers proposed
other modes of God's presence, such as the presence of his Wisdom. Given
that Wisdom thought forms an important part of the background for this
hymn,[36] it should not be surprising that one finds God's presence featuring
prominently. What is surprising, and what goes beyond anything seen so far
about Wisdom, is that God's presence is being described here as dwelling
not in a place but in a person. The implication of this is that God's fullness
dwelling in Christ means that Christ is fulfilling the role of the temple.

One of the most important things about the temple is that it was where
God's presence dwelled in a special way. That means that if one wanted to
"meet" God, the temple was the place to do it. Verse 19 says that, like Solomon's temple, God's special presence was in Christ. If that is true, then it

---

35. Coloe, *God Dwells with Us*, 214.

36. For more on Wisdom, see the excursus at the end of the discussion on v. 16.

looks like the same can now be said of Christ: he is where one meets God.[37] The hymn is describing Christ as the new temple.[38]

However, even beyond saying that Christ is where one *does* meet God (because God's fullness dwells in him), it is also possible to say that Christ is where one *needs* to meet God. After all, if God has chosen to specially dwell in a given place (in this case, a person), it is only logical to think that this is where God wants humans to meet him. That would logically imply that humans *should* meet him there. The only reason to think that humans should meet God elsewhere is if their chosen meeting place is more important than God's. It seems unlikely that either the hymn's author or Paul would think this. They would almost certainly say that if God has chosen a place to meet, then that is where the meeting should take place.

Before going any further, it is important to understand whether looking at the parallel passage in 2:9 will be of any use in explaining the meaning of 1:19. Here are the two verses side by side:

1:19—ὅτι ἐν αὐτῷ εὐδόκησεν πᾶν τὸ πλήρωμα κατοικῆσαι
because in him all the fullness was pleased to dwell[39]

37. One of the main centers of such discussion is the fourth gospel. Coloe (*God Dwells with Us*, 214) and Kerr (*Temple of Jesus' Body*, 82), for example, argue that the fourth gospel presents Jesus as the replacement for the temple. However, not all discussion on this topic is centered there. Beale says, "Colossians 1:19 refers to Christ as the end-time temple. Paul applies the psalmist's reference to God dwelling in Israel's temple [Ps 67(58):16–17) (LXX)] to God now dwelling in his son, apparently as the expression of the latter-day temple in which God's presence fully resides" (*Temple*, 267). Sanders believes that "Jesus' demonstrative action in the temple and his saying against the temple (whether a prediction or a threat)" is representative of his eschatological expectation that the kingdom was at hand and the old temple was to be replaced by a new one (*Jesus and Judaism*, 77). If Sanders is right and a new temple was part of an eschatological expectation (see also Beale, *Temple*, 226), then one is not limited to either the fourth gospel or even statements like Col 1:19, and many eschatological texts become relevant. Simply by the fact that the temple is where one encounters God in a special way, the Colossian hymn is presenting Christ as the temple. If someone wishes to suggest that this is not the case, there is no need to argue the point, because temple language is not featured in Colossians. However, given Judaism's long history of viewing God as dwelling in the temple and the statement here that God's fullness was pleased to dwell in Christ, it does seem appropriate to describe Christ as the temple.

38. Beyond saying that Christ is being *described* as the temple because God's fullness dwells in him, one could also say that Christ *functions* as the Temple. To do this would require a comparison of what Christ does to what the temple did. This goes beyond the scope of this study. However, if one wanted to do this, one might start by looking into the things that Christ accomplished, such as reconciliation between God and humanity (1:20, 21–23), and then comparing them to what the temple accomplished.

39. As discussed previously, the best translation of this verse is: "Because God was pleased for all his fullness to dwell in him." However, in order to make a better comparison between 1:19 and 2:9 for those who do not read Greek, the translation has been

2:9—ὅτι ἐν αὐτῷ κατοικεῖ πᾶν τὸ πλήρωμα τῆς θεότητος
σωματικῶς
because in him all the fullness of deity dwells bodily

So, 2:9 is very closely related to 1:19. The question is, is it of any use in explaining 1:19?

Most commentators think that the hymn was written by someone other than Paul.[40] That would mean that 2:9 would be Paul's interpretation of 1:19. However, since understanding things from Paul's point of view is the goal of this study (rather than simply looking for the theology of the hymn without any purported Pauline additions), 2:9 is useful. The question is, does 2:9 change the meaning of 1:19 (from Paul's point of view) at all?

Really, if 2:9 does anything, it only strengthens the above interpretation of 1:19—that it was God's fullness dwelling in Christ. Essentially, 2:9 is 1:19, with two parts added to explain what might have been questionable about 1:19. τῆς θεότητος (of deity) makes it clear that it really was God's fullness that was indwelling Christ. σωματικῶς (bodily) takes things a little further than 1:19 and says that this indwelling was in bodily form. What these additions actually mean will be discussed when looking at 2:9. The only important thing now is that 2:9 does nothing to change the above interpretation of 1:19 to something different. So, what does 1:19 mean?

Verse 19 says that God in all his fullness was pleased to dwell in him (Christ). This statement is situated between a reference to Christ's

temporarily changed to something that shows how similar the two verses are. Even without being able to read Greek, the reader can still compare the Greek verses to see how similar they are. The first three words are identical. Then, 1:19 has εὐδόκησεν (was pleased), while 2:9 does not. Next, both verses have πᾶν τὸ πλήρωμα (all the fullness). Finally, 1:19 has κατοικῆσαι (to dwell) while 2:9 has κατοικεῖ (dwells) a little earlier in the sentence. These are the same word; they are just in different tenses. The real differences between these verses are τῆς θεότητος (of deity) and σωματικῶς (bodily). These will be discussed in detail when looking at 2:9.

40. The reasons for this are part of the reasons they think it is a hymn in the first place. The vocabulary, style, and content are different from what is generally considered Pauline. On a related note, there is better reason to think the hymn was something given to the Colossians by Epaphras when he first evangelized them, than that it was something composed by Paul or Timothy for the purpose of this letter. If Paul was trying to keep the Colossians from leaving Christianity, he would have more success by reminding them of what they already believed and emphasizing that position's truth/value than he would by giving them a new argument. In 2:6–7, Paul will encourage the Colossians to remain in the faith *just as they were taught*. His argument would be stronger if the hymn were something given to them on a prior occasion. This is not definitive, but it makes better sense than the view that Paul (or Timothy) wrote this hymn for this occasion.

resurrection in v. 18 and the reference to his death on a cross in v. 20. What is interesting is that Christ is not only being described as a first-century Jew who walked in Palestine and died on a cross, but he is also described as the uncreated creator in the first strophe. It is clear that the author of this hymn has stepped into incarnational theology of some sort. Christ is placed beyond the realm of humans or angels and into the realm of God; yet, he still lived and died as a human. What should one make of this?

Certainly, there is incarnational thought here. However, much like the binitarian/trinitarian[41] thought of the first strophe, the incarnational thought in this strophe is given in pictorial terms. It is like the Old Testament describing God as a rock. Obviously, God is not literally a rock, and everyone who heard or hears a statement like this knows that. However, the word "rock" is metaphorical language that is meant to communicate important things *about* God—namely, He is strong, He is powerful, He can be relied upon, etc. If one were to attempt to describe these same characteristics about God in propositional terms, he or she would have to make statements like "God has the ability to be causally active in time and space in such a way that no other force, personal or impersonal, has the ability to overpower His causal actions."

Saying "God is a rock" is communicating something about God in pictorial terms. Explaining these same concepts in propositional language also communicates something about God; it just does it differently. So, when someone looks at the hymn and says that there is not genuine binitarian/trinitarian or incarnational thought here, he or she might not have taken into account the method of communication. The two statements made about Christ in the first strophe make very clear that Christ is both God *and* distinct from God (firstborn over all creation/uncreated creator *and* image of the invisible God). However, this figure who was both God and yet distinct from God also died on the cross and rose from the dead. There is, therefore, genuine binitarian/trinitarian thought in the first strophe and genuine incarnational thought in the last strophe.

41. Some Christians might object to the idea of binitarian thought (two persons in the Godhead instead of three). However, outside the single (and only probable) reference to the Holy Spirit in 1:8, the only two divine characters in this letter are God and Christ. The Holy Spirit is not present here; so, one cannot speak of a Trinity. Nevertheless, binitarian thought is how the church moved towards trinitarian thought in the centuries after Christ. Once the deity of Christ was established, the Holy Spirit was brought in afterwards. The thought here is binitarian, although it is consistent with trinitarian thought. The only question is whether Paul or the author of the hymn would have continued on to trinitarian thought like later Christians did. Unfortunately, that is not something that can be gleaned from this letter.

Again, whether the author of the hymn or Paul understood these concepts in the same way as later theologians in church history, one can only speculate. However, just because one does not see binitarian/trinitarian and incarnational thought communicated with propositional language, one should not assume that the author of the hymn and/or Paul did not have a full understanding of those concepts. Perhaps, even if the more complicated thought were known, the author of the hymn and Paul might simply have chosen to put the explanations in a form that would be more easily communicated. Again, one can only speculate. But, either way, both binitarian/trinitarian and incarnational thought are definitely communicated in this hymn.

As pointed out previously, v. 19 explains v. 18. It is connected to v. 18 with a ὅτι (because), which means that the material that follows v. 18 explains why Christ was the beginning and the firstborn from the dead. Verses 19–20 explain why Christ was able to be the founder of a new people, the church.

So far, v. 19 has said that God in all his fullness was pleased to dwell in Christ. However, this is about to be expanded. God was pleased to dwell in Christ, but he was also pleased to do something else.

1:20

> καὶ δι' αὐτοῦ ἀποκαταλλάξαι τὰ πάντα εἰς αὐτόν εἰρηνοποιήσας
> διὰ τοῦ αἵματος τοῦ σταυροῦ αὐτοῦ [δι' αὐτοῦ] εἴτε τὰ ἐπὶ τῆς
> γῆς εἴτε τὰ ἐν τοῖς οὐρανοῖς
>
> and through him to reconcile all things to him, whether things
> on the earth or whether things in the heavens, making peace by
> the blood of his cross

Verse 20 cannot be investigated on its own, because it is neither a complete thought nor a complete sentence. The only verb in the verse is ἀποκαταλλάξαι (to reconcile), but it is an infinitive and cannot stand on its own. The last verb that could stand on its own was εὐδόκησεν (was pleased) in v. 19. However, εὐδόκησεν (was pleased) is followed by two infinitives: κατοικῆσαι (to dwell) and ἀποκαταλλάξαι (to reconcile). These infinitives are parallel to one another and are both governed by εὐδόκησεν (was pleased).[42] That means, then, that the basic structure of vv. 19–20 looks like this:

---

42. Bruce, "Colossian Problems: Part 4," 74; Dettwiler, "Verständnis des Kreuzes Jesu," 88; Hay, *Colossians*, 62; and Moo, *Letters to the Colossians*, 133.

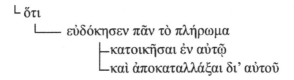

∟ ὅτι
    ∟── εὐδόκησεν πᾶν τὸ πλήρωμα
        ⊢κατοικῆσαι ἐν αὐτῷ
        ∟καὶ ἀποκαταλλάξαι δι' αὐτοῦ

∟ because
    ∟── God was pleased for all His fullness
        ⊢ to dwell in him
        ∟ and to reconcile through him

God was pleased for all his fullness to do two things: to dwell and to reconcile. Verse 19 described the first action God was pleased to carry out in Christ, and v. 20 describes the second action God was pleased to carry out in Christ.

However, there is one more structural element to keep in mind. Everything in vv. 19–20 is still governed by the ὅτι (because) at the beginning of 1:19, which means that these verses explain v. 18. They explain why Christ can be the firstborn from the dead and the founder of a new group, the church. He could do these things because God's fullness was pleased to dwell in him *and* to reconcile all things through him.

Before it is possible to understand reconciliation, it is important to notice that something seems to be missing. How is it that in the first strophe Christ created all things (presumably in harmony), and in the second main strophe, they are now in need of reconciliation? What happened in the intervening time? Most likely, between these two times there occurred a state of estrangement or disharmony (often referred to as the "fall") that necessitated reconciliation. It is not possible to go into much detail about this, because no details are given. However, it is possible to say that at some point, all things went from existing in a single kingdom,[43] Christ's kingdom, to two kingdoms: the domain of darkness and Christ's kingdom (1:13). "Reconciliation" is the divine response to this separation.

As to the question of a "fall," many commentators think that such a state of estrangement occurred.[44] It is important to point

43. Or, camp, team, side, etc.

44. Dunn, *Epistles to the Colossians*, 102; Hay, *Colossians*, 63; House, "Doctrine of Salvation," 326; Moo, *Letters to the Colossians*, 133; O'Brien, *Colossians-Philemon*, 53; and N.T. Wright, *Colossians and Philemon*, 76, for example.

out that everything about a "fall" in Colossians is *implied*. There is no explanation of such a theological concept in the letter. Such a concept does, however, seem to be necessary for both the hymn and the letter to be logically coherent. After all, if Christ is responsible for creating everything and then later on it needs to be reconciled, then there really are only two options. Option 1: Christ created the cosmos in a state of disharmony from which it needed to be reconciled. Or, Option 2: Christ created the cosmos in a state of harmony; at some point disharmony entered the cosmos, and then reconciliation was needed in order to restore the original harmony.

While Option 1 is possible, it does seem to go against the spirit of the letter. The way Christ is spoken of in the letter does not make him out to be the sort of creator who would create disharmony. Obviously, whether Christ actually is the sort of creator who would create disharmony or not is another question, but it does not appear that the letter points in that direction. Because of this, Option 2 seems to be the better choice. That means that at some point after original creation, all or part of creation took a step down—from perfection to non-perfection (assuming, among other things, that harmony is better than disharmony).

Historically, this change in the state of the cosmos has been referred to as the "fall." How much thoughts on the fall that became more widespread later were present in the minds of the author of the hymn or Paul at the writing of Colossians is not something the text will answer. However, there does not seem to be a better term to use for this intermediate change in the cosmos's state of affairs between a perfect and complete creation (which the text seems to imply) and one which is somehow less than perfect and complete. If one state of affairs has dropped down a level from the state previous to it, "fall" seems like at least a decent way of describing it. So, the word "fall" will continue to be used for this change in the cosmos's state of affairs, but the reader should know that this in no way is intended to assume any later theological ideas.

The word ἀποκαταλλάξαι (to reconcile) is further explained by the words εἰρηνοποιήσας διὰ τοῦ αἵματος τοῦ σταυροῦ αὐτοῦ (making peace by the blood of his cross).[45] This accomplishes two things. First, it explains that "making peace" is what was needed. There were parties which were

---

45. O'Brien, *Colossians-Philemon*, 56; Sumney, *Colossians*, 76–77; and Wall, *Colossians and Philemon*, 77.

hostile to one another, and making peace/ending hostilities is what happened so that reconciliation could occur. Second, it shows that the means by which the peace was achieved was by the blood of Christ's cross. Christ's death on the cross was what was required to make this peace possible—even though nothing more is said about exactly how his death accomplished that.

So, what is reconciliation, then? The word itself "comes not from the sacrificial cult but from the discourse of political negotiation. Parties engaged in hostile conflict have been reconciled to each other."[46] It is possible that two hostile parties might become reconciled to each other willingly, but it did not necessarily have to be that way. In the political world of the first century, "having made peace" might more readily be understood as the "cessation of war."[47] For example, Rome claimed to bring peace to the whole world, yet it did so through the defeat of others.[48] In other words, Rome defeated all its enemies, and when the war was over and Rome was victorious, it declared peace.

However, just because people in the first century would be familiar with the Roman idea of making peace, it does not follow that Christ would bring peace in the same way. After all, Tacitus quotes the Caledonian chieftain Calgacus as saying that the Romans make a desert and call it peace.[49] There is no indication in the letter that Christ is making a desert. So, if reconciliation and making peace happen via the defeat of the opposing parties, the letter will have to explain what that means.

There are, then, two different options for reconciliation and peacemaking. Peace can occur when both parties are willing, or it can occur when the stronger party decides to make peace (i.e., cessation of war) and the weaker party has no choice but to accept the "peace" imposed on it. The questions for this passage are, who are the parties involved, and what sort of peace is made?

There are two places in the immediate context outside the hymn that point towards parties that need reconciliation. In vv. 21–22, the Colossians will be said to have been "alienated and hostile in mind in the doing of evil deeds" but now are "reconciled." The two parties here are God and the Colossians, and the Colossians function as a specific instance of a reconciled party. However, the Colossians (and even all humanity) do not qualify as "all things," which is what Christ is said to have reconciled.[50]

46. Thompson, *Colossians and Philemon*, 33.

47. Dunn, *Epistles to the Colossians*, 103.

48. Sumney, *Colossians*, 77.

49. Tacitus, *Agricola* 30.

50. The verse says that τὰ πάντα (all things) have been reconciled to him, and then

The material before the hymn, in vv. 13–14, probably holds the answer. The language about the domain of darkness and the kingdom of God's beloved Son divides everything in the cosmos into two camps—those with Christ and those not with Christ. This is the most likely referent for what has been reconciled. As discussed above, with the fall, everything in creation split into two camps. With the blood of Christ's cross, everything has been/ will be reconciled back into one camp.

The reconciliation of all things does not, however, imply a universal salvation. To say that universal salvation is meant here would be to render other parts of the letter unintelligible. What, for example, could it mean for Paul to continually tell the Colossians to remain "in Christ"? If everyone will be saved anyway, why would they need to do that? What would be the purpose in telling the Colossians to seek the things above (3:1–4) if they will share in those things whether they follow Christ or not? Why would Paul bother with polemic against the alternate philosophy, if all roads lead to God? Reconciliation of all things must mean something other than a universal salvation.

Given the context of the hymn, it seems most likely to think that reconciliation is about restoring the harmony of original creation. In the beginning, all things were created in, through, and for Christ, and all things were in harmony and existed in Christ's kingdom. At some point, the cosmos was thrown into disharmony, and a second sphere/kingdom/camp came into existence: the domain of darkness. Through his death on the cross, God acted decisively through Christ to bring all things back into their original creational order.

Reconciliation, then, is the return of the entire cosmos to the sphere/ kingdom/camp of Christ[51]—to its original creational order. There appears

---

it elaborates further εἴτε τὰ ἐπὶ τῆς γῆς εἴτε τὰ ἐν τοῖς οὐρανοῖς (whether things on the earth or whether things in the heavens). So, more than just humanity is in view here. τὰ πάντα (all things), with its further description, must include everything. Presumably, that would mean not just humans but also the rulers and authorities from v. 16 (which may not be human), as well as any other parties that are not mentioned.

51. There is debate on whether the reconciliation is to God or to Christ. In favor of "to God," Moo cites unusual language and the focus of the hymn itself (*Letters to the Colossians*, 132). In favor of "to Christ," Sumney suggests that because the prepositional phrase "through him" comes before the infinitive "to reconcile," it is emphatic, and the emphasis therefore remains on Christ as the agent (*Colossians*, 133–34). However, it might be good to ask the question, "Is this a distinction without a difference?" If Christ is God's agent for both the creation and reconciliation of all things, would not everything then be reconciled (at least indirectly) εἰς (to) God just as it was created (at least indirectly) εἰς (to/by) God? Either everything is reconciled to God through Christ (as His agent), or everything is reconciled to Christ (who is the agent of God). Both of these say essentially the same thing. If, however, one thinks of reconciliation

to be something that happens to those in the church that is above and beyond reconciliation. It has not yet been defined, but it involves walking in a manner worthy of the Lord and knowing God himself. This was described in the upward spiraling process in 1:9–12, and it will be explained more fully later (especially in 3:1–4:6).

Now, since the kingdom that needs to be reconciled is the domain of darkness, and one does not see universal salvation in Colossians, it is not possible to arrive at the conclusion that all things will participate in this "something special" that happens to those who are part of the church. All things will be reconciled but, as was pointed out earlier, reconciliation and making peace can happen even if the other party does not want peace. This "something special" that involves walking in a manner worthy of the Lord and knowing God himself is something that happens only to those who are a part of the church. Those who are not part of the church will be reconciled, but they will not experience this other thing (which will be defined later in the letter).

So, what determines whether an individual human participates in this other thing, in addition to reconciliation? If the two options for reconciliation are not merely part of the background imagery, then there are two different ways for individuals to be reconciled: willingly and unwillingly. If these are the options, then humans can either participate willingly as part of the church, or they can choose the unwilling submission of a defeated foe.[52] From the exhortations later in the letter, it would appear that humans do have the ability to choose between the two options. Otherwise, why would Paul tell them that they *should* follow the way of Christ rather than the

---

as the return of all things to their original intended order, the question of whether all things are reconciled to God or to Christ changes. All things will return to the kingdom of Christ, and there will no longer be a domain of darkness whose members are hostile to God and Christ. So, instead of asking, "Are all things reconciled to God or to Christ?" one might ask, "In the beginning, were all things created in relation to God or to Christ?" This question does not entirely make sense, because all things were created in relation to both (although in different ways, because of Christ's relationship to God). What is probably more useful to say (as well as what the text is intending) is that the reconciliation of all things means the return of the cosmos and everything in it to its intended creational order (although, because some choose not to be reconciled willingly, this reconciled order might look a little different than the original order). This will be made a little more clear when exactly what went wrong is investigated.

52. There is no mention of whether any other part of "all things" has such a choice. For example, one is not told whether angelic creatures would have the same options (if such a thing is necessary or even possible). The only thing that is clear about "all things" is that "all things" will be reconciled.

alternative philosophy? Or, why would he tell them they *should* do or not do certain actions?[53]

Before concluding the investigation of the second strophe and moving on to the big picture ideas, there are two final structural features one should notice. The first is the parallel use of prepositional phrases in the first and second strophes. In the first strophe, all things were created ἐν αὐτῷ, δι' αὐτοῦ, καὶ εἰς αὐτὸν (in him, through him, and to/for him). Here in the second strophe, God's fullness was pleased to dwell ἐν αὐτῷ (in him) and all things were reconciled δι' αὐτοῦ (through him) and εἰς αὐτόν (to him). In both strophes, these prepositional phrases are meant to emphasize that, in all ways, all things exist in relation to Christ—both in original and reconciled creation. Through the continued use of τὰ πάντα (all things), as well as εἴτε τὰ ἐπὶ τῆς γῆς εἴτε τὰ ἐν τοῖς οὐρανοῖς (whether on the earth or whether in the heavens), the hymn is making redundantly clear that all things exist in relation to Christ.

Really, the hymn could have been shorter if its author simply wanted to communicate content. However, with the addition of the heaven and earth language, the extra prepositional phrases, and the ἵνα (in order that) clause, the hymn grows longer. But, all of that additional material exists to add emphasis and make the unmistakeable (and quite forceful) point that Christ really is supreme and nothing and no one (other than the invisible God) stands above or beside him. Since the author of the hymn and, by extension, Paul did not want the reader to miss that point, one should make sure not to miss it.

The last thing to cover before looking at the full diagram of the hymn and the significance of this chapter are some big picture ideas. Now, it was said previously that vv. 19–20 both explain v. 18. The fact that God in all his fullness was pleased to dwell in Christ and reconcile all things through and to him explains how Christ could be the founder of a new group.

At first glance, though, this doesn't seem to make a lot of sense. After all, forming a new group is easy, right? And, if one were an authority figure like Christ obviously is (first strophe), couldn't he just get a group of people together and declare them to be a new group? In many senses, that seems possible. However, there is a little more to this group than that.

Verses 13–14 explain that those who are a part of Christ's kingdom have been delivered from the domain of darkness and transferred into Christ's kingdom, the church.[54] Along with this transfer, they have also been

53. Free will, however, is not a topic of discussion in this letter. The only things that are definitive are that all things will be reconciled by Christ and that something special happens to those who are a part of the church.

54. For an explanation on why Christ's kingdom is the church, see discussion of v. 18a.

redeemed, which is further described as the forgiveness of sins. So, bringing someone into the church is not as simple as just saying: "You're a part of the church now." Christ has to redeem them (which includes forgiving their sins) and transfer them between domains/kingdoms.

So, how is Christ able to accomplish all of this? This question gets at the logic behind the hymn itself as well as how the hymn is being used in the letter. Ultimately, what happens is that Paul makes a statement in vv. 13–14 about what God has done through Christ. Then, the hymn explains how and why Christ was able to accomplish this.

Here are the two points made in vv. 13–14:

Verses 13–14	
1) God transferred some people from the domain of darkness into Christ's kingdom.	v. 13
2) Christ redeemed the people entering his kingdom and provided forgiveness for their sins.	v. 14

Everything starts with Number 1: God transferred some people from the domain of darkness into Christ's kingdom. Now, this transfer involved Number 2: Christ redeemed the people entering his kingdom and provided forgiveness for their sins. These are the two overarching points. The hymn explains how these things are possible, and each of the two main strophes does it in a different way.

Here is how the logic of the letter works, using the content from the first strophe:

Verses 13–14 and Verses 15–16	
1) God transferred some people from the domain of darkness into Christ's kingdom.	v. 13
2) Christ redeemed the people entering his kingdom and provided forgiveness for their sins.	v. 14
3) Christ is the image of the invisible God and firstborn over all creation	v. 15
4) Christ created everything that has been created.	v. 16

The first two points are exactly the same as they were in vv. 13–14. But now, one can see that vv. 15–16 explain how vv. 13–14 are possible. 1) God transferred some people from the domain of darkness into Christ's kingdom. This transfer involved 2) Christ redeeming the people entering his kingdom and providing forgiveness for their sins. Christ was able to do this because 3) he is the image of the invisible God (and, therefore,

God's representative), and he is the firstborn over all creation. Christ is the firstborn over all creation because 4) he created everything that has been created.

The flow of logic in the second main strophe is very similar. It starts with the same two points from vv. 13–14, because they are what the hymn is helping to explain. However, instead of points 3 and 4, it uses two new points to explain how Christ can accomplish Numbers 1 and 2. Here is how the logic of the letter works with the second main strophe:

Verses 13–14 and Verses 18b–20	
1) God transferred some people from the domain of darkness into Christ's kingdom.	v. 13
2) Christ redeemed the people entering his kingdom and provided forgiveness for their sins.	v. 14
5) Christ rose from the dead and founded a new group of people, the church.	vv. 18b-d
6) God's fullness was pleased to dwell in Christ and to reconcile all things through him.	vv. 19–20

Again, just like with the first strophe, the two points that start everything off are from vv. 13–14. Then, the hymn explains how vv. 13–14 are possible. The flow of logic goes like this: 1) God transferred some people from the domain of darkness into Christ's kingdom. This transfer involved 2) Christ redeeming people entering his kingdom and providing forgiveness for their sins. Christ was able to do this because 5) he rose from the dead and founded a new group of people, the church. Christ was able to do these things because 6) God's fullness was pleased to dwell in him and to reconcile all things through him.

The reader should notice that in all the tables, the first two points are identical. Again, this is because they come from vv. 13–14, and both main strophes of the hymn explain how Christ was able to accomplish these things. Therefore, it is the latter two points in the two logical progressions that really explain how and why Christ was able to accomplish Numbers 1 and 2. Numbers 3 and 4 were explained in vv. 15–16, and Numbers 5 and 6 were explained in vv. 18b-20.

Seeing how the hymn logically explains vv. 13–14 should help the reader understand how some of the big theological pieces of Paul's Christian worldview fit together. This is not all of his worldview (or even all of his theology), but it should help connect some of the dots. It is now time to look at the full diagram of the hymn and see how all the pieces of the hymn fit together.

DIAGRAM[55]

Here is the full diagram of the hymn:

```
┌─ ὅς ἐστιν
│    │└─ εἰκὼν τοῦ θεοῦ τοῦ ἀοράτου
│    └─ πρωτότοκος πάσης κτίσεως
│         └─ ὅτι
│              ├──── ἐν αὐτῷ ἐκτίσθη τὰ πάντα
│              │      ├─ἐν τοῖς οὐρανοῖς καὶ ἐπὶ τῆς γῆς
│              │      └─τὰ ὁρατὰ καὶ τὰ ἀόρατα
│              │      ├─εἴτε θρόνοι εἴτε κυριότητες
│              │      └─εἴτε ἀρχαὶ εἴτε ἐξουσίαι
│              └──── τὰ πάντα δι' αὐτοῦ καὶ εἰς αὐτὸν ἔκτισται
│
│    ├──── καὶ αὐτός ἐστιν πρὸ πάντων
│    ├──── καὶ τὰ πάντα ἐν αὐτῷ συνέστηκεν
│    ├──── καὶ αὐτός ἐστιν ἡ κεφαλὴ τοῦ σώματος τῆς ἐκκλησίας
│
└─ ὅς ἐστιν
     │└─ ἀρχή
     └─ πρωτότοκος ἐκ τῶν νεκρῶν
          │└─ ἵνα γένηται ἐν πᾶσιν αὐτὸς πρωτεύων
          └─ ὅτι
               └──── εὐδόκησεν πᾶν τὸ πλήρωμα
                      ├─κατοικῆσαι ἐν αὐτῷ
                      └─καὶ ἀποκαταλλάξαι δι' αὐτοῦ τὰ πάντα
                         │└─ εἰς αὐτόν
                         └─ εἰρηνοποιήσας διὰ τοῦ αἵματος τοῦ σταυροῦ αὐτοῦ
                              ├─ εἴτε τὰ ἐπὶ τῆς γῆς
                              └─ εἴτε τὰ ἐν τοῖς οὐρανοῖς
```

55. The word order in vv. 19–20 has been changed somewhat in order to highlight the structure of the verses.

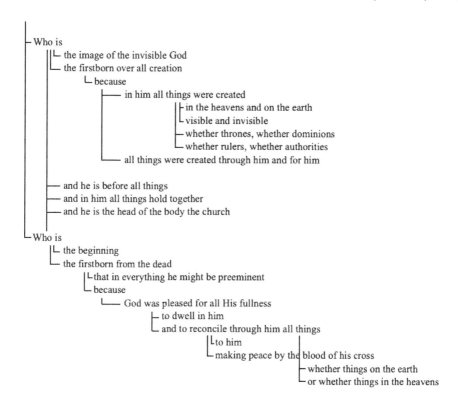

SIGNIFICANCE

The final strophe of the hymn shows what Christ has done to repair what went wrong with original creation. In the beginning, all things were created by, through, and for Christ. Everything existed in harmony and in proper relation to its creator. However, with the fall, all of that changed. A second kingdom came into existence, the domain of darkness, and disharmony entered creation. Christ's death on the cross and subsequent resurrection made it possible for him to end the disharmony in creation and return everything to its proper creational order.

The reason Christ could do all this is because God's fullness was pleased to dwell in him and to reconcile all things through him. God's fullness dwelling in Christ describes him as the new temple—the place where God has chosen to meet man. This represents genuine incarnational thought: God was actually *in* Jesus of Nazareth.[56] Because of this, if one wishes to meet God, he needs to meet him in Jesus rather than anywhere else.

It is both who Christ is and his work on the cross that allow him to return everything to its original creational order (reconciliation). Everyone and everything will be returned; however, something special happens to those who are a part of the church. This includes reconciliation, but it goes beyond merely returning to one's place in the cosmic order. This has not been described yet, except to say that those people who follow Christ and are a part of the church will walk in a manner worthy of the Lord and come to know God himself (1:9–10). Paul will progressively add to this description in the next sections of the letter (1:21–2:5 and 2:6–2:23). However, not until ch. 3 will Paul finish his explanation of what this something special is that happens to those who are a part of the church.

Now, the importance of the Church was already discussed in looking at 1:17–18a, but that importance could not be fully explained until the final strophe. A big part of what makes the church so special is the role it plays in creation. Verses 17–18a said that the church is responsible for helping Christ with his continuing work in creation. However, not much more could be said at the time, since there had not yet been any mention of what Christ is doing in creation. So, what is Christ doing in creation?

In the first strophe, two statements were made about Christ. First, he was said to reveal God (image of the invisible God). By looking at Christ, one can know what the invisible God is like. Second, he was said to be responsible for the creation of the entire cosmos (firstborn over all creation,

---

56. Some will wonder whether God *still* dwells in Jesus. Did the indwelling continue beyond the grave? That is not discussed in the hymn, but it will be discussed later in the letter.

or, alternatively, the uncreated creator). Everything was made by, through, and for him. The first strophe, then, gives two things that Christ is responsible for: 1) revealing God and 2) creating all things in the beginning.

Those who are a part of the church are only capable of participating in one of these two things. Creating all things in the beginning has already been completed; it is not possible to go back and be a part of it. Revealing God, on the other hand, is something that those in the church *can* do. Granted, it will be on a limited basis, since those in the church are not the image of the invisible God. However, showing who God is and what he is like by the way they live *is* something the church can do. This will be an important topic of discussion in ch. 3 and 4, but for now, it is enough to say that the church can share with Christ in revealing God. If Christ continues to reveal God, and the church is to share in Christ's current activities in the world, then this is probably part of the church's job, too.

In the second main strophe, there are two more statements made about Christ. He is said to be 3) the founder of a new group (the church) and 4) the firstborn from the dead. Again, these are not things that humans can simply mimic. Christ has already risen from the dead, and this new group has already been started. So, like creating all things in the beginning, these are past events that cannot be copied. However, if one looks at what Christ is actually accomplishing by his resurrection from the dead and founding of the church, one finds something in which Christians can participate.

What Christ is doing through his resurrection from the dead and founding of the church is working to fix what is wrong with creation. Verses 13–14 said that all humans were born into the domain of darkness; they have to be *transferred* into the kingdom of God's beloved Son. By rising from the dead and founding the church, Christ is working to free humans from darkness and death. Specifically, in vv. 13–14, one sees humans taken from captivity and condemnation to redemption and forgiveness. This is something that Christ does, but humans can participate in it.

Those who are a part of the church participate in Christ's work because they are part of those people who are transferred from the domain of darkness into Christ's kingdom and redeemed and forgiven for their sins (vv. 13–14). They also participate in the spiraling upward process that leads to them knowing God more fully, as well as walking in a manner worthy of the Lord (vv. 9–12). Christ is working to fix what is wrong with creation, and by having what is wrong with them fixed, Christians are participating in Christ's work. It is possible that Christians might also help with these same things in the lives of others, but that is not something that has been discussed up to this point.

Finally, even though it is not one of the four statements about Christ, it needs to be asked whether the church can participate in reconciliation. Reconciliation was described as the returning of all things to their original creational order. The next section of the letter will explain that reconciliation has already happened for those who are a part of the church. However, the facts that moral exhortation is needed and the domain of darkness still exists point toward the fact that reconciliation has not been completed for everyone. Christ's death and resurrection, therefore, are an announcement that reconciliation of *all* things will take place in the future. Some people have already been reconciled, but the reconciliation of all things is yet to come.

The final reconciliation of all things does not appear to be something with which the church can help. It seems like something for which Christ has already accomplished all the necessary prerequisites; he is just waiting to fully implement it. However, it may be possible for people to be used in a limited capacity to help others towards reconciliation in this life (as well as that "something special" that happens as a part of the church).[57] This will take the church beyond merely *participating* in Christ's work into actually *helping* Christ with his work. Again, this will be discussed later in the letter. Paul is just laying the theological foundation now. He will discuss how to live it out later.

Some of the things one sees in the hymn are unique to Christ. Only Christ created all things in the beginning, and only Christ can accomplish the final reconciliation of all things. However, the church can participate in some of Christ's work on a limited basis. Those in the church are resurrected by Christ and participate in what Christ is doing in the here and now through the spiraling upward process (1:9–12). This points towards the importance of how Christians should live. While no specific actions have been discussed yet, if Christians' lives are supposed to change as a result of following Christ, then there is some sort of connection between participating in what Christ is doing and how Christians live their daily lives.

This final strophe of the hymn shows how Christ is working to fix what is wrong with creation. The end of the domain of darkness has already been announced, because all things will be finally reconciled (returned to their original creational order). Christ is also fixing what is wrong with humans by resurrecting them from the dead so they can be brought into his kingdom, the church, where they will be redeemed and forgiven for their sins.

---

57. To whatever extent creation is reconciled, the church might be able to help with that (although this is not a topic in the letter).

The hymn in 1:15–20 shows the reader two things: 1) who Christ is and 2) what he has done. These two things explain why Paul thinks Christ is so important, and it will be the foundation for his arguments in favor of Christianity throughout the rest of the letter.

9

Reconciliation through Christ (1:21–2:5)

INTRODUCTION

In this section, Paul will conclude his argument in favor of Christianity. In 1:3–8, he introduced some of his general thoughts to the Colossians. In 1:9–14, he explained how the Colossians can walk in a manner worthy of the Lord, and he told them how God has transferred them, through Christ, from the domain of darkness into the kingdom of His beloved Son. The hymn in 1:15–20 showed how all of that was possible by explaining who Christ is and what he has done. Here, in 1:21–2:5, Paul will explain to the Colossians how what Christ has done applies to their own lives, as well as where following Christ will take them. This will conclude Paul's argument in favor of Christianity. In the next section, 2:6–23, he will compare the Christian worldview with the alternative philosophy and show why he believes Christianity is superior.

Verses 21–22 pick up the flow of thought before the hymn, from vv. 13–14. In vv. 13–14, the Colossians were said to have been delivered from the domain of darkness and transferred into the kingdom of God's beloved Son. There, they find redemption, the forgiveness of sins. In vv. 21–22, one finds a very similar message: the Colossians were enemies of God, but through Christ, they have now been reconciled and made holy. The intervening hymn explains who Christ is and why he has the ability to do this, and with v. 21, one sees how that applies to the Colossians and to all Christians. Because Christ is the creator of all things as well as the reconciler of all of creation, his work is not for a limited group of people or for a limited time in history. Christ's work is for all people, at all times, in all places.

1:21–22

καὶ ὑμᾶς ποτε ὄντας ἀπηλλοτριωμένους καὶ ἐχθροὺς τῇ διανοίᾳ ἐν τοῖς ἔργοις τοῖς πονηροῖς νυνὶ δὲ ἀποκατήλλαξεν ἐν τῷ σώματι τῆς σαρκὸς αὐτοῦ διὰ τοῦ θανάτου παραστῆσαι ὑμᾶς ἁγίους καὶ ἀμώμους καὶ ἀνεγκλήτους κατενώπιον αὐτοῦ

and you were once alienated and hostile in mind in the doing of evil deeds, but now he has reconciled you in the body of his flesh through death in order to present you holy and blameless and above reproach before him.

The use of the third person in the hymn is immediately changed with the opening words of v. 21, καὶ ὑμᾶς (and you). This returns the focus to the Colossians. Additionally, these verses take the form of a "once, but now" (ποτε . . . νυνὶ δὲ) contrast "between the readers' pre-Christian and pagan past on the one hand, and their present standing in Christ on the other."[1] This highlights the change that Christianity has made in the Colossians. The previous and current states of the Colossians are described in vv. 21–22 and represent parallel descriptions of their standing before God pre- and post-conversion.[2]

1:21   καὶ ὑμᾶς ποτε ὄντας
ἀπηλλοτριωμένους
καὶ ἐχθροὺς τῇ διανοίᾳ ἐν τοῖς ἔργοις τοῖς πονηροῖς
1:22   νυνὶ δὲ
ἀποκατήλλαξεν . . .
ἁγίους καὶ ἀμώμους καὶ ἀνεγκλήτους

1. O'Brien, *Colossians-Philemon*, 64. Dunn says, "'But now' (νυνὶ δὲ) is a genuine Paulinism to express this moment of divine reversal" (*Epistles to the Colossians*, 107).

2. These verses have been modified in order to highlight the parallels between them. ἐν τῷ σώματι τῆς σαρκὸς αὐτοῦ διὰ τοῦ θανάτου παραστῆσαι ὑμᾶς (in the body of his flesh through death in order to present you) was removed from the middle of v. 22, and κατενώπιον αὐτοῦ (before him) was removed from the end of v. 22 to focus on the nature of the Colossians before and after the work of Christ. The removed words explain how this transformation took place, as well as indicate its goal. Their significance will be discussed later.

1:21   and you were once
        alienated
        and hostile in mind in the doing of evil deeds
1:22   but now
        he has reconciled you . . .
        holy and blameless and above reproach

The status of the Colossians' relationship to God is described by ἀπηλλοτριωμένους (alienated) and ἀποκατήλλαξεν (reconciled). They were once alienated, but now they are reconciled. All of the terms that follow these two describe the Colossians themselves, but ἀπηλλοτριωμένους (alienated) and ἀποκατήλλαξεν (reconciled) describe the Colossians' relationship to God.

	Before Christ	After Christ
Relationship to God	alienated	reconciled
Description of the Colossians	hostile in mind in the doing of evil deeds	holy and blameless and above reproach

Additionally, the way the secondary terms in each description are connected is important. In 1:22, each of the terms is separated by a καὶ (and), so one finds three distinct (though related) terms in a list format. However, the terms in 1:21 only *look* like a list in many English translations (the translation above corrects this). In reality, the terms in 1:21 are not a list at all. Unlike the description of the Colossians post-conversion, the two terms which describe their former life are separated by ἐν (in). They were hostile in mind ἐν (in) the doing of evil deeds. In other words, ἐν τοῖς ἔργοις τοῖς πονηροῖς (in the doing of evil deeds) describes *how* the Colossians were hostile in mind.

Prior to their reconciliation through Christ, the Colossians were enemies of God.[3] "The word ἐχθροὺς [hostile] is best understood in an active sense because of the following τῇ διανοίᾳ [in mind], to denote a conscious antagonism to the only true God, i.e. 'hostile in mind.'"[4] Paul is not describing the Colossians as well-meaning people who have simply wandered off the path by accident and made a few mistakes. Rather, they were actively

3. Dettwiler points out that unlike the hymn, Col 1:21–23 makes explicit reference to the state of adversity prior to reconciliation ("Lettre aux Colossiens," 117–18).

4. O'Brien, *Colossians-Philemon*, 66. Sumney says, "This alienation and hostility are 'with respect to your inner being.' διανοίᾳ, often translated 'mind,' refers to the whole of one's being" (*Colossians*, 82).

hostile to God. Additionally, the combination of the perfect passive participle ἀπηλλοτριωμένους (were alienated) with the present participle of the verb ὄντας (to be) shows that this was the continuous state of the Colossians prior to their conversion.[5]

Something to notice in the description of ἐχθροὺς (hostile) with τῇ διανοίᾳ (in mind) is the connection of beliefs and actions. The Colossians were actively hostile to God in their minds, and this showed itself through their doing of evil deeds. In other words, their internal attitude toward God manifested itself in their external actions. This connection between the internal and the external was already featured in 1:9–12 as the Colossians were filled with the knowledge of God's will (internal), then practiced living out God's will (external), which led to them understanding God's will (internal) better than they did originally. However, 1:9–12 and 1:21–23 are not the only places where the connection of beliefs and actions will appear. This connection will return again many times throughout the rest of the letter.[6]

The second part of the ποτε . . . νυνὶ δὲ (once . . . but now) construction shows the state of the Colossians *after* encountering Christ. There are three terms used to describe the Colossians, ἁγίους καὶ ἀμώμους καὶ ἀνεγκλήτους (holy and blameless and above reproach). The first two, ἁγίους καὶ ἀμώμους (holy and blameless) are often thought to be hinting at a sacrificial metaphor, while ἀνεγκλήτους (above reproach) and the verb παραστῆσαι (to present) are thought to point towards a judicial metaphor. While there is some disagreement about which metaphor goes with which word, the point is still clear: Paul wants to present the Colossians as faultless, i.e., with nothing bad in them.[7]

---

5. MacDonald, *Colossians and Ephesians*, 71; Dunn, *Epistles to the Colossians*, 105; and O'Brien, *Colossians-Philemon*, 66.

6. It is worth noting that, while this is an important theme in Colossians, it is not unique to this letter. For example, in the gospels, one finds the connection of a person's identity with his works. The metaphor of a good tree bearing good fruit and a bad tree bearing bad fruit is a recurring theme that illustrates that a person's actions are not disconnected from the person but rather are a reflection of who he or she really is (Matt 7:15–20, 12:33–37; Luke 6:43–45). Furthermore, not only was this theme not unique to this letter, it was not even unique to Christianity. Malherbe says the idea that "one's speech should agree with one's deeds" was "common wisdom" and not limited to the NT authors (*Moral Exhortation*, 38ff.).

7. N.T. Wright thinks "the words translated 'present,' 'in his sight,' and 'without blemish' all evoke the language of Jewish sacrificial ritual" (*Colossians and Philemon*, 82). O'Brien thinks that ἀνεγκλήτους (above reproach) and παραστῆσαι (to present) point toward the judicial metaphor but they control the meaning of the other two words, so "it is doubtful, however, whether thoughts of sacrifice are really present in this clause at all" (*Colossians-Philemon*, 68–69). Dunn thinks "there is an implicit . . . interplay between the idea of Christ's death as sacrifice (1:20) and the presentation of

However, the verb παραστῆσαι (to present) points towards the Colossians' faultless state as a future goal rather than a present reality. They are not yet holy, blameless, and above reproach; rather, Christ has reconciled them in order to παραστῆσαι (present) them as holy, blameless, and above reproach. The same verb will also be used in a very similar way in v. 28, which helps to clarify this verse. In v. 28, Paul says that he warns and teaches everyone so that "we may present" (παραστήσωμεν) everyone perfect in Christ. In v. 28, Paul's goal is to present the Colossians before God in a worthy manner. Both verses describe this faultless state as a future towards which the Colossians are headed.[8] That means they are not faultless yet.

At this point, the past, present, and future states of the Colossians have been described. In the distant past, the Colossians were alienated and hostile to God (1:21). In the more recent past, they were reconciled to God (1:22). In the present, they are walking a path that leads to moral improvement (1:9–12). Finally, in the future, they will be presented to God as holy and blameless and above reproach (1:22).[9] The question to ask is "How can the Colossians be presented as faultless/perfect? The letter itself says that their past was filled with hostility to God and evil deeds." The simple answer is, through Christ's reconciliation.[10] However, actually reconciling God and man is no simple task.

The Colossians had a relationship with God that was characterized by hostility, and they needed peace with him. This was accomplished by God redeeming them and providing forgiveness through Christ (v. 14). However,

---

those who are unblemished as a sacrifice to God. In other words, there is an echo of the Pauline idea of sacrificial interchange, where the spotless sacrifice by dying as a sin offering is somehow interchanged with the blameworthy sinner and its spotlessness transferred to the sinner" (*Epistles to the Colossians*, 109–10).

8. Verses 22 and 28 will be compared in more detail after looking at v. 28.

9. There has been and will be a lot of discussion about Colossians representing a partially-realized eschatology. It should not come as a surprise that at some point, that eschatology will be fully-realized. What has been declared in advance, will be obtained in reality. What the Colossians are currently becoming, they one day will be. The language of standing before the judge/king is not emphasizing judgment but the realization of the hope they have and the promises that have been made to them.

10. There are some textual issues with this word. Metzger says, "The conflicting textual phenomena of this verse are difficult to resolve. On the one hand, the reading ἀποκατήλλαξεν [a different form of "to reconcile"] is well supported and provides acceptable sense. On the other hand, however, if this were the original reading, it is exceedingly difficult to explain why the other readings should have arisen" (*Textual Commentary*, 554–55). Because of the uncertainty regarding the original form of the verb καταλλάσσω (to reconcile), it is probably best to say that the Colossians were reconciled through Christ's "body of flesh by his death" and attempt to draw no further inferences from the word itself. The context will need to provide the meaning that the word cannot.

what happened to the Colossians was not as simple as God saying, "You are forgiven." What God did for them through Christ was to fix what was wrong with them. They were resurrected from the dead with Christ and thereby became part of a new group of people, the church (1:18). This put them on an upwards path on which they continually know God better and better (1:9–12). Finally, in the future, they will be presented holy, blameless, and above reproach before God (1:22).

Christ is therefore critical to the peace process. This was not merely the end of a war in which everyone goes home still mad at the other side. Christ actually ended the hostility—and that meant fixing what was wrong with the Colossians.

It makes more sense now why Paul would insert the hymn where he did. He placed it right between a high-level explanation of what God has done for humanity through Christ (vv. 13–14) and how what Christ has done works out in the lives of individual believers (vv. 21–23). The point is, if Christ is not who the hymn says he is, then he could not have made peace between God and man. But, if he is who the hymn says he is, and if the Colossians are looking for a true relationship with God, Paul is making it clear that they should look to Christ—the one who made peace between them and God. The follow-up question then is "*How* did Christ actually make the reconciliation happen?"

There is a phrase in v. 22 that gives further information that helps answer that question. The reconciliation happened ἐν τῷ σώματι τῆς σαρκὸς αὐτοῦ διὰ τοῦ θανάτου (in the body of his flesh through death). διὰ τοῦ θανάτου (through death) points to Christ's death on the cross. In v. 20, the hymn said Christ's death on the cross is the means by which all things, whether on the earth or in the heavens, were reconciled. Paul is reminding the Colossians that the reconciliation they have received came through the death of Christ.

The phrase τῆς σαρκὸς αὐτοῦ (of his flesh) was added to avoid a potential ambiguity with ἐν τῷ σώματι (in the body). There is another "body" in v. 18—Christ's body, the church. Paul wants to make it clear that it was Christ's *physical* body that accomplished the reconciliation and not Christ's *spiritual* body, the church.[11] The church has in no way accomplished reconciliation for itself. Christ provided the reconciliation, and the church received it.

---

11. Witherington, *Letters to Philemon*, 139; also Dunn, "'Body' in Colossians," 169. Witherington thinks there is also the possibility that the emphasis on the word "body" here refers to the philosophy and its "denigration of the physical body" (*Letters to Philemon*, 139). If this was in the back of Paul's mind, it wouldn't change the meaning of this verse, but it would give it a secondary application.

Verses 21–22 give further clarification of the reconciliation described in v. 20. According to v. 20 (in combination with vv. 13–14), not all beings currently exist in the kingdom of Christ. Everything was created in the kingdom of Christ, but as a result of the fall, a second kingdom, the domain of darkness, came into existence. Furthermore, it is implied that humans exist in the domain of darkness by default;[12] they have to be *transferred* into the kingdom of Christ. Reconciliation is the return of all things into their creational order (under Christ), whether they want to return or not.

There is something, though, that sounds a little odd about these two uses of the word "reconciliation." In 1:22, Paul speaks of reconciliation as positive; yet in 1:20, it does not carry that connotation. In 1:20, reconciliation can be either positive or negative (for the individual). Reconciliation has been announced by the death of Christ (1:20), but it has not yet been applied to everyone. If it had, there would not still be a domain of darkness (1:13), nor would people live in hostility to God and do evil deeds (1:21). In contrast, reconciliation for the Colossians (1:22) is decidedly positive. They are on good terms with God, are part of the church, and can expect to be presented before him holy, blameless, and above reproach. This is not the picture of reconciliation given in v. 20 (which can be either positive or negative).

The difference between these two views on reconciliation definitely seems to be whether one is part of the church or not. If one is part of the church (like the Colossians), the good kind of reconciliation can be expected. However, if one does not become part of the church and remains in the domain of darkness, the bad kind of reconciliation is probably to be expected. But, it seems like there is still maybe a little more to the different types of reconciliation than just whether one is a part of the church or not.

It seems like there may be a time element to reconciliation. In other words, "*When* is a person reconciled?" Verse 22 speaks of the Colossians' reconciliation in the past tense; it has already happened for them. However, reconciliation must not be something that happens in this life to those who are in the domain of darkness. Otherwise, why are they still able to be hostile to God and do evil deeds? They must not have been brought back into their original creational order (reconciled), not yet.

Because of this, it looks like there is indeed a time element to reconciliation. Those who are reconciled during this life become part of the church, have a good relationship with God, spiral up (1:9–12), and are one day presented to God as holy, blameless, and above reproach. Those who are not reconciled during this life remain in the domain of darkness and experience a different future. This has not been described, but even if they

---

12. For more details, see the excursus on the fall in the discussion of 1:20.

simply miss out on all the things that happen to those who are part of the church, it seems like a pretty negative future.

At the most basic level, in vv. 21–22, one can see that the Colossians were previously hostile toward God, but now have been reconciled and brought into the body of Christ. Their actions were evil, but now they are on the path toward good. All of this comes about through the work of Christ, which he accomplished in the body of his flesh through death. Christ is the sole point on which the Colossians' lives have turned. Both their relationship to God and their moral lives have changed as a result of their connection with Christ.

1:23

> εἴ γε ἐπιμένετε τῇ πίστει τεθεμελιωμένοι καὶ ἑδραῖοι καὶ μὴ μετακινούμενοι ἀπὸ τῆς ἐλπίδος τοῦ εὐαγγελίου οὗ ἠκούσατε τοῦ κηρυχθέντος ἐν πάσῃ κτίσει τῇ ὑπὸ τὸν οὐρανόν οὗ ἐγενόμην ἐγὼ Παῦλος διάκονος

> if you continue in the faith, stable and steadfast, not shifting from the hope of the gospel that you heard, which has been proclaimed in all creation under heaven, and of which I, Paul, became a minister

The conditional statement in v. 23, εἴ γε ἐπιμένετε τῇ πίστει . . . (if you continue in the faith . . .) raises questions about the nature of the Colossians' standing before God. Paul says that if the Colossians do not remain in the faith, then they will lose something. Specifically, the text is pointing to the Colossians' presentation before God as holy, blameless, and above reproach (v. 22). Does that mean: 1) Christ will not *present* them before God or 2) Christ will not present them *holy, blameless, and above reproach*? In other words, if the Colossians fail to remain in the faith, does it mean that they will lose their current relationship to God (Number 1) or does it mean that they will not become as good of people as they could have been (Number 2)?

This issue is further complicated by the fact that vv. 21–22 said the Colossians were already reconciled to Christ at the time of the writing of this letter. The ποτε . . . νυνὶ δὲ (once . . . but now) construction in vv. 21–22 makes it clear that their current state is that of reconciled people. They ποτε (once) were alienated, νυνὶ δὲ (but now) they are reconciled. However, v. 23 says they will only be presented as holy, blameless, and above reproach, *if* they continue in the faith. So, the two options above are tied in with the fact that the Colossians are already reconciled to God. But how?

Commentators frequently mention that the statement that begins with εἴ γε (if) expresses more confidence than doubt.[13] However, even with Paul's confidence, interpreting it is not straightforward. Melick says:

> There are three possible interpretations about why Paul used the first-class condition. The options are: that Paul actually placed a condition on the believers so that they might lose their salvation if they did not continue in the faith; that the clause refers to the "blameless" presentation of the believers at the day of the Lord; or that Paul assumed all believers would continue in the faith and that was an evidence that they were, in fact, genuine in their commitment.[14]

Commentators spend a lot of time arguing over these three options. However, the attempts to distinguish between them miss Paul's point (or at least his emphasis). These attempts really seem to be addressing the underlying question "What is the minimum one must do to be saved?" Perhaps another way to put it would be "How far could one stray from Christ, and/or how little commitment is required to be saved?" There is nothing in this letter indicating that Paul is interested in answering this question. He is instead answering the questions "What is the right path?" and "What does that path look like?"

Another way to illustrate this would be to imagine two camps, one for those who follow Christ and one for those who do not (the kingdom of Christ and the domain of darkness). In this letter, Paul is attempting to describe what each camp looks like and explain why the Christ camp is better. He is not, however, trying to inform the Colossians what will happen to those who travel back and forth between the two camps (never really choosing a side) or to those who insist on sitting in the middle between the two. He is saying that all good things (such as holiness) exist in the Christ camp only. Whatever Paul might think about the indecisive people who never really choose a camp, it seems unlikely that he would have good things to say about them, considering how firm he is on his position that one only finds relationship with God through Christ. Whichever side they ended up on, it

13. For example, Dunn, *Epistles to the Colossians*, 110; Melick, *Philippians*, 233; O'Brien, *Colossians-Philemon*, 69; and Witherington, *Letters to Philemon*, 140. Melick explains, "His words, 'if you continue,' are significant. They are part of a first-class conditional sentence in Greek. Some have suggested that the construction implies an element of doubt. However, there is no doubt about the outcome of the condition. Paul fully expected them to continue in the faith" (*Philippians*, 233).

14. Melick, *Philippians*, 234.

is hard to image that Paul thinks God would be pleased with those who refuse to choose a side. The Colossians have heard arguments from Epaphras,
the philosophers, and now Paul. They have the ability to make an informed
decision.

Paul inserted the christological hymn into the letter to make it clear
that following Christ is the only way forward. In ch. 2, he will begin to
compare Christianity with the alternative philosophy. Here, he is starting to
introduce the Colossians to the idea that they will have to choose one way or
the other, and (Paul argues) the way of Christ is how they will be presented
holy, blameless, and above reproach. Because of this, it seems at least likely
that Paul is not answering the question commentators are asking, "Can one
lose one's salvation?" If this is true, then this verse represents a simple statement that even though another group is claiming to be able to provide what
one needs (access to God, salvation, etc.), the only path forward is in Christ.

There are two other things to think about that might help in determining what this verse means. First, what is the "goal?" What is it that the Colossians specifically, and Christians in general, should be moving towards?
In 1:9–10, Paul described the Colossians' relationship with God as a "walk."
This is contrary to many modern Christians who act as if their relationship
with God is more of a means to an end—the end being a blissful existence
in heaven when they die. The difference between the two thoughts is that for
one, the goal is a place; for the other, the goal is a person. Continuing this
thought, if the Colossians' relationship with God is more like a walk with
a person, a continual interaction that has the potential to grow over time,[15]
why should this end (or begin) at death?

If one thinks of the Colossians' relationship with God as a walk that
begins in this life and continues into the next, that changes how one thinks
about this passage in two ways. First, to turn away from Christ is to turn
away from one's only chance of a positive relationship with God. The question most people are asking is "Can people lose their salvation if they leave
Christ for another worldview?" The only way this question makes sense is
if one considers salvation to be more about a place than a person. To reflect
the personal nature of salvation, one should rephrase the question to ask, "If
people leave Christ for another worldview, will they still have a relationship
with God through Christ?" This makes the question more accurate relative
to the content of Colossians, but the question itself becomes a bit nonsensi-
cal. If one *leaves* Christ, in what way could he or she still have a relationship
with God *through* Christ?[16]

15. Think of all the passages where one is told to grow, increase, be filled, etc.

16. The gospel of Matthew has Jesus saying: "But whoever denies me before men, I

This means that one cannot simply "lose" his or her salvation like one can lose his or her car keys. Nor is one's salvation something that could be taken away by someone else. After all, the hymn made it clear that Christ is supreme over all creation and even created all the other powers and authorities. No one has the power to take the believer's salvation away. This relationship with Christ is one in which the believer has been resurrected with Christ.[17]

If it is possible to end one's relationship with Christ, one does not "lose" it; one would have to throw it away. One would have to abandon his or her relationship with Christ and walk away from him, because there is no indication in the letter that Christ is going to end it, and no other beings have the power to end it. So, *if* it can be ended, it would have to be as a result of the Christian actively throwing it away. But again, Paul does not seem interested in addressing whether that is possible (at least not in this passage). Here, he is simply making the point that all good things are to be found in Christ, so if you want them, you need to look to Christ.

There is a second thing to think about in order to understand Paul's conditional statement (if you remain . . .). Some of the thought on how to interpret this statement attempts to separate the beliefs of individuals from their actions. It suggests that some people might believe in Christ but turn away from him and therefore not become perfected. They would still be reconciled, but they would not become holy, blameless, and above reproach.

However, 1:9–12, as well as 1:21–22, have already shown that beliefs are connected to actions. This is a theme which will show up again and again throughout the letter: actions are connected to beliefs and are inseparable from them. If one stays attached to Christ, good actions will follow; if one departs from Christ or never becomes joined to Christ, then bad actions will follow. This means that the only way for one to become holy is to have right beliefs, which center around the person and work of Christ and the relationship to him. If one is willingly reconciled to Christ and remains in him, the holiness and blamelessness is certain (although part of it remains in the future).[18]

Paul also tells the Colossians not to shift from the hope of the gospel (ἀπὸ τῆς ἐλπίδος τοῦ εὐαγγελίου). This reminds them of the "hope" that

---

also will deny before my Father who is in heaven" (Matt 10.33). While this comes from outside Colossians, it is consistent with the idea of Christ presenting before the Father those who are in him and continue in the faith. It also suggests what appears to be the content of the conditional statement: if one does not remain in Christ, Christ will not present him before the Father.

17. This was discussed in 1:18, but it will feature in both ch. 2 and 3.

18. The already/but not yet theme common in Pauline thought is present in Colossians. It will return again, especially in ch. 3.

they have in Christ—the hope that is a concrete future reality, rather than wishful thinking about the future.[19] Then, he reiterates that this hope is found in the gospel they already received.[20] In other words, they should not turn to something new.

Following this, Paul takes a brief shot at the philosophy by saying that the gospel they have already received has been proclaimed in all creation under heaven (κηρυχθέντος ἐν πάσῃ κτίσει τῇ ὑπὸ τὸν οὐρανόν). In other words, the Christian gospel is something that is a worldwide gospel and not merely some local thing. The "real" gospel, he implies, is one that would apply to all people, at all times, and in all places—like one would expect, if Christ really did create all things and reconcile all things.[21] It is not merely some local novelty. Finally, Paul says that he is a minister of this gospel, but that will not be discussed right now. Paul's role in the spreading of the gospel will be a subject throughout the rest of ch. 1 and the beginning of ch. 2.

The primary message of v. 23 is that the only way to have a relationship with God is through Christ, and the only way to become holy is through Christ. This theological point foreshadows the critiques of the philosophy that will begin in ch. 2. The Colossians were in danger of potentially being led astray, and Paul wishes to explain why they should remain in Christ. In Paul's view of Christianity, everything one needs is found in Christ and nowhere else, and one should follow Christ both fully and exclusively. Paul is not addressing the question of people who follow Christ halfway or for only a limited time.

1:24–25

νῦν χαίρω ἐν τοῖς παθήμασιν ὑπὲρ ὑμῶν καὶ ἀνταναπληρῶ τὰ ὑστερήματα τῶν θλίψεων τοῦ Χριστοῦ ἐν τῇ σαρκί μου ὑπὲρ τοῦ σώματος αὐτοῦ ὅ ἐστιν ἡ ἐκκλησία ἧς ἐγενόμην ἐγὼ διάκονος κατὰ τὴν οἰκονομίαν τοῦ θεοῦ τὴν δοθεῖσάν μοι εἰς ὑμᾶς πληρῶσαι τὸν λόγον τοῦ θεοῦ

Now I rejoice in my sufferings for your sake, and in my flesh I am filling up what is lacking in Christ's afflictions for the sake of his body, that is, the church, of which I became a minister

19. Also, 1:5.

20. Also, 1:6.

21. The gospel had not *actually* been preached to the whole world by this point. However, it was a gospel without boundaries. Paul will say in 3:11 that it was for all peoples, whether Greek or Jew, circumcised or uncircumcised, barbarian, Scythian, slave, or free.

according to the stewardship of God, which was given to me for
you to make the word of God fully known

In these verses, there is a phrase that is difficult to understand. Paul says he
is ἀναταναπληρῶ τὰ ὑστερήματα τῶν θλίψεων τοῦ Χριστοῦ (filling up what
is lacking in Christ's afflictions). Furthermore, it seems he rejoices in his
own sufferings because of this. One unlikely interpretation of this is that
there was something lacking in the effectiveness of Christ's death on the
cross that required Paul to fill in the gaps. Were this the case, Paul's emphasis in the letter on the sufficiency of Christ would make no sense.

The most common way of understanding τὰ ὑστερήματα τῶν θλίψεων
τοῦ Χριστοῦ (what is lacking in Christ's afflictions) is the paradigm of the
messianic woes.[22] The messianic woes essentially are "the apocalyptic
thought that there is an appointed sum of suffering that must be endured
in order to trigger the final events of history; the thought then is that the
death of Christ has activated the first trigger, but those sufferings are not yet
complete, otherwise the second and final trigger would have been activated
too."[23] In this view, then, "Jesus, the Messiah, had suffered on the cross; now
his people, the members of his body, had their quota of afflictions to bear,
and Paul was eager to absorb as much as possible of this in his own 'flesh.'"[24]
Paul therefore would be suffering so that the Colossians and others did not
have to suffer. Since there was a specific amount of suffering that had to
occur, if Paul received it, then they wouldn't have to.[25]

There is another possibility, though. It could be that the filling up
what is lacking in Christ's afflictions refers "to the completing of the *effect*
of Christ's sufferings, in the sense that the suffering of Christians in His

22. Commentators who suggest the way to interpret this phrase as either the mes-
sianic woes or a predetermined amount of suffering the church must go through in-
clude Bruce, *Epistles to the Colossians*, 83; Dunn, *Epistles to the Colossians*, 115; O'Brien,
Colossians-Philemon, 78; Sappington, *Revelation and Redemption*, 189; Witherington,
Letters to Philemon, 144; N.T. Wright, *Colossians and Philemon*, 92; and Yates, "Note on
Colossians 1:24," 88.

23. Dunn, *Epistles to the Colossians*, 116.

24. Bruce, *Epistles to the Colossians*, 83.

25. Behind this view could be the idea of limited goods. Malina says the people
in Paul's world (the ancient Mediterranean) believed there was a limited amount of
everything in the world (contrary to the view after the Industrial Revolution that there
can always be more of something). On this view, if one person became rich, someone
else would become poor. So, others would suspect the newly rich person of taking for
himself what belonged to others (*New Testament World*, 89–90). Potentially, that idea
could lie behind this view. There was a limited amount of suffering that had to be filled
up. Christ suffered a lot, and Paul was glad to suffer as much as possible to reduce the
amount the Colossians had to suffer.

name contributes to the effectiveness—the availability, as it were—of His constructive sufferings."[26] In other words, the sufferings could be a means of expanding the gospel to new places. In support of this view, the book of Acts explains that suffering would be involved in Paul's calling to take the gospel to the Gentiles.[27]

Unfortunately, Paul does not go into detail about what his current sufferings actually involved. In 4:18, he asks the Colossians to remember his chains, indicating that he was in prison. This was done in the process of living out his calling as a minister of the gospel (1:25), but not much more can be learned from the letter.

What is important to understand is that Paul said he was suffering *on the Colossians' behalf.* This does three things. First, it connects Paul and his ministry with the Colossians. Paul just got done telling them in v. 23 that they will be presented holy, blameless, and above reproach to God *if* they continue in the faith. Paul is letting the Colossians know that even though the path they are walking is difficult, they are not alone in it. Paul is walking with them and even suffering on their behalf. Now, he may or may not have been suffering for the Colossians specifically. It could be Paul was suffering as a part of his calling to reach the Gentile world, and because the Colossians were part of that world, his suffering was for them (at least in part). But, even in this case, the Colossians would be part of the group for which he was suffering, so it would correct to say that he was suffering for them.

The second thing Paul's suffering does builds on the first point. Not only does Paul's suffering connect Paul and his ministry with the Colossians, it reminds the Colossians that they are a part of something bigger than just what they experience in their daily lives. By willingly and joyfully suffering for something greater, Paul personally demonstrates the heavenly focus that he wants the Colossians to have.

Finally, it is very possible that Paul would have needed to give the Colossians a reason to listen to him. The Colossians had never actually met Paul, and even though he was an apostle, Paul's relationship with the Corinthians shows that that wasn't always enough. Besides, giving his audience

---

26. C.F.D. Moule, "'Fulness' and 'Fill,'" 85, and Schreiner, *Paul,* 102.

27. In Acts 9, when Saul is blinded and the Lord appears to Ananias in a vision to lay hands on him to receive his sight, Ananias objects. However, the Lord responds, "Go, for he is a chosen instrument of mine to carry my name before the Gentiles and kings and the children of Israel. For I will show him how much he must suffer for the sake of my name" (9:15). The point is not that Saul/Paul is called to suffer off by himself somewhere and occasionally preach the gospel. Rather, Paul is to preach the gospel, and suffering will be involved in the process. Additionally, Paul's own statement in Col 1:28–29 says that the purpose of his suffering is to aid the preaching of the gospel. Preaching Christ to present everyone mature in Christ is the reason he labors.

a reason to trust him would not have been unexpected for someone like Paul.[28] For all three of these reasons, then, if Paul were able to connect with his audience through his sufferings, he would have been able to tackle the problems in Colossae and put the Colossians' focus back onto the true gospel.

Something important for both ancient and modern audiences is that one finds evidence here that Paul really believed what he said. People don't usually suffer for something they don't believe. A person could be mistaken about his beliefs (and whether Paul was mistaken is a different question), but the fact that Paul was willing to suffer for Christianity increases the likelihood that he actually believed what he was saying.

Now, the purpose of all this suffering is πληρῶσαι τὸν λόγον τοῦ θεοῦ (to make the word of God fully known). However, when Paul says he is suffering to make sure the word of God is fully known, he has something specific in mind. He will explain what this is in the next two verses.

1:26–27

τὸ μυστήριον τὸ ἀποκεκρυμμένον ἀπὸ τῶν αἰώνων καὶ ἀπὸ τῶν γενεῶν νῦν δὲ ἐφανερώθη τοῖς ἁγίοις αὐτοῦ οἷς ἠθέλησεν ὁ θεὸς γνωρίσαι τί τὸ πλοῦτος τῆς δόξης τοῦ μυστηρίου τούτου ἐν τοῖς ἔθνεσιν ὅ ἐστιν Χριστὸς ἐν ὑμῖν ἡ ἐλπὶς τῆς δόξης

the mystery which has been hidden for ages and generations but has now been revealed to his saints, to whom God willed to make known how great are the riches of the glory of this mystery among the Gentiles, which is Christ in you, the hope of glory

In v. 25, Paul said the purpose of his suffering was to make the word of God fully known. In v. 26, Paul further describes the word of God as τὸ μυστήριον (the mystery).[29] Now, this word μυστήριον (mystery) could refer

---

28. Malherbe says, "Philosophers frequently found it necessary to justify their activity as moral reformers. Given the practical and nontechnical nature of much of philosophy, during the first and second centuries A.D. large numbers of charlatans for their own profit invaded the cities . . . . Genuine philosophers developed a manner of self-description that contrasted themselves to their competitors, clarified their motivations, and asserted their superiority over the majority of people" (*Moral Exhortation*, 34).

29. Dunn says about the prominence of revelation/knowledge language, "This need not imply a strong 'Gnostic' or hidden knowledge content in the teaching and praxis being confronted at Colossae; of the words [used,] only σοφία [wisdom] (2:23) appears within the explicitly polemical section (2:8–23), and somewhat surprisingly, ἀποκαλύπτω/ἀποκάλυψις [to reveal/revelation] not at all" (*Epistles to the Colossians*, 113).

to two different things. It could be "an eschatological mystery, a concealed intimation of divinely ordained future events whose disclosure and interpretation belong to God alone."[30] Alternatively, τὸ μυστήριον (mystery) could mean "some sort of heavenly journey, revelation, or esoteric knowledge," and this may be what the philosophers at Colossae believed.[31] The former idea of μυστήριον (mystery) was about God revealing some part of His plan to humanity. The latter idea of μυστήριον (mystery) was about humans getting to take a spiritual journey or learn secret knowledge as the key to something greater.

In these verses, Paul is claiming that Christianity had a mystery. This would not have been uncommon in the ancient world. There was a whole class of religions at the time called the "mystery" religions (which, not surprisingly, had mysteries they would reveal only to members). However, in these verses, Paul does not describe τὸ μυστήριον (the mystery) as a spiritual journey or secret knowledge that would lead the Colossians up to a higher spiritual plane. Rather, he speaks of τὸ μυστήριον (the mystery) in a way more similar to the first category, God revealing something about his plan for humanity. But, Paul goes beyond this.

This μυστήριον (mystery) is not about something in the future for which the Colossians are to wait. Rather, this μυστήριον (mystery) is about something that was previously in the future but now has entered the world. It is the realization of what once was a future μυστήριον (mystery). And, this mystery is not a set of facts or the key to something greater. It is the something greater. It is Χριστὸς ἐν ὑμῖν ἡ ἐλπὶς τῆς δόξης (Christ in you, the hope of glory).

The revelation of this mystery carries with it an extra level of significance for the Colossians because they were Gentiles. After all, Paul says in v. 27 that "Christ in you, the hope of glory" was a mystery ἐν τοῖς ἔθνεσιν (among the Gentiles). But now, he is telling the Colossians that they get to share in this mystery.

Part of what God is doing through Christ is including persons previously thought to be outside God's promises, i.e., the Gentiles. "Had this grace

30. O'Brien, *Colossians-Philemon*, 84. It is commonly noted that μυστήριον (mystery) corresponds to the Aramaic word translated "secret," frequently found in the book of Daniel. See Bruce, *Epistles to the Colossians*, 84–85; Moo, *Letters to the Colossians*, 155; O'Brien, *Colossians-Philemon*, 84; Wiley, "Study of 'Mystery,'" 351, and others. However, Israel and her neighbors' uses of this word were not exactly the same. Gladd says, "The content of the term in Daniel, differing greatly from the ANE [Ancient Near East—meaning neighboring peoples to ancient Israel], is God's eschatological kingdom and related events" (*Revealing the Mysterion*, 50).

31. Roberts, "Jewish Mystical Experience," 179; Dunn, *Epistles to the Colossians*, 120; and Sappington, *Revelation and Redemption*, 186.

[incorporation into the body of Christ] been shown to believing Jews alone, it might not have excited such wonder; they, after all, were the messianic people. But non-Jews are included as well, and included on an equal footing with Jews."[32] The inclusion of the Gentiles in the body of Christ prepares the way for the statement in 3:11 that there is no distinction between peoples, no matter their background, in the body of Christ. "The true people of God consist of those who put their faith in Christ. This fact the author stresses by calling Christ the Gentiles' hope of glory, that is, their participation in the future glory of the end-time is not bound up with their inclusion in the Jewish nation."[33]

Christ and his relationship to the believer is the essence of the mystery. The mystery is Χριστὸς ἐν ὑμῖν (Christ in you).[34] "The phrase 'in you' assigns the letter's readers a position of astonishingly high status. Not only are they recipients of God's revelation; they are also a significant part of the mystery itself, part of God's plan for the whole world."[35] God reveals himself to the believer, but he also works in the believer through Christ. This is the same point as the one made in 1:18 when Christ is described as the head of the body, the church. Both explain that Christ is working in the world through the church. The "mystery" of "Christ in you" is that the creator of the universe is working in and through the Christian believer.

Before continuing, it is important to clarify one point. The idea of "Christ in you" does not refer to the creation of a physical place inside the body of the believer where a little Jesus lives.[36] Rather, what is meant by this phrase is that Christ now operates in the *sphere* of the Christian believer. Instead of the Jewish God working primarily in and through the nation of Israel, Paul is saying that he now works in and through Christians—like the Colossians. The church as the body of Christ is now how the creator is operating in the world. "Christ in you" means that Christ is working in and

---

32. Bruce, *Epistles to the Colossians*, 85.

33. Roberts, "Jewish Mystical Experience," 179.

34. There is debate over whether "you" here is a reference to the Gentiles (which would mean that the mystery is about the Gentiles becoming part of the body) or whether "you" means Christ in the believer (implying that the mystery is about receiving the Holy Spirit). Sumney says, "Verse 28's reference to the judgment confirms that this expression looks to the Parousia. Since 'hope of glory' points to the Parousia, it casts an eschatological hue on the context, increasing the likelihood that 'Christ in you' refers to possession of the Spirit, because the coming of the Spirit is an eschatological phenomenon. Yet so is the entrance of Gentiles into the people of God. Perhaps it is best, therefore, to allow some multivalence to the expression 'Christ in you'" (*Colossians*, 106).

35. Sumney, *Colossians*, 107.

36. The letter would look a little cartoonish if it did.

through the church. To the Colossians, "Christ in you" meant that God was "affecting change" and "making things happen" through them.[37]

1:28–29

ὃν ἡμεῖς καταγγέλλομεν νουθετοῦντες πάντα ἄνθρωπον καὶ διδάσκοντες πάντα ἄνθρωπον ἐν πάσῃ σοφίᾳ ἵνα παραστήσωμεν πάντα ἄνθρωπον τέλειον ἐν Χριστῷ εἰς ὃ καὶ κοπιῶ ἀγωνιζόμενος κατὰ τὴν ἐνέργειαν αὐτοῦ τὴν ἐνεργουμένην ἐν ἐμοὶ ἐν δυνάμει

whom we proclaim, warning every man and teaching every man in all wisdom in order that we may present every man perfect in Christ. For this purpose I also toil, striving with all his energy that he powerfully works within me.

The main point of these two verses is Paul's explanation of the purpose of his ministry. This is summed up in the words ἵνα παραστήσωμεν πάντα ἄνθρωπον τέλειον ἐν Χριστῷ (in order that we may present every man perfect in Christ). Paul's goal was to present the believer τέλειος (perfect) in Christ. Bauer et al. have four definitions for τέλειος. "1) pert. to meeting the highest standard, *perfect,* 2) pert. to being mature, *full-grown, mature, adult,* 3) pert. to being a cult initiate, *initiated,* 4) pert. to being fully developed in a moral sense, *perfect, fully developed.*"[38] All four of these say basically the same thing, although the initiation into a cult sounds a bit different. However, it can fit with the other three if one thinks of it as passing all the necessary requirements in order to join a cult/religious group

---

37. This raises the questions, "*How* does Christ work in the believer? How does he actually *help* an individual? What does that look like?" Col 1:9 says that the believer will be "filled with the knowledge of his will in all spiritual wisdom and understanding." So, part of it must be that believers are given more knowledge about which direction to go/ what the right way looks like. Col 1:11 says that believers will be "strengthened with all power, according to his glorious might, for all endurance with joy." So, in some way, then, Christ gives strength to the believers to continue down the right path. Col 2:19 speaks of growing "with a growth that is from God." So probably, God is responsible for growth somehow, and the important thing to do would be to stay close to Christ. But how does all of this help? The letter to the Colossians gives an overview of the Christian worldview according to Paul, but it is too short to do anything but paint with broad strokes. Very probably, there would be more on how Christ works in the believer in a discussion of the Holy Spirit; however, there is only one direct reference to the Spirit in Colossians (1:8, and it is only a probable reference at that). This is both an interesting and important question, but it extends beyond what can be gained from the letter to the Colossians alone.

38. Bauer et al., τέλειος, *Greek English Lexicon,* 995–6.

as a full member. The believer who is τέλειος is complete, fully mature, perfect—not lacking anything.

There is a strong connection here with v. 22, although there is one important difference: there are two different parties trying to present the Colossians as faultless/perfect.[39] In v. 22, Christ reconciled the Colossians to present them holy, blameless, and above reproach. In v. 28, Paul warns and teaches everyone so that "we" (Paul and Timothy) may present them perfect in Christ. Immediately, it sounds a little odd to have two different parties seemingly doing the same thing. However, looking at the actions of the two parties will clarify what is going on.

In v. 22, Christ *reconciled* the Colossians so that their future state would be faultless/perfect. In v. 28, Paul and Timothy are *warning and teaching everyone* so that their future state will be faultless/perfect. The Colossians were previously alienated and hostile in mind in the doing of evil deeds (v. 21), and they will one day be faultless/perfect (v. 22, 28). Getting from their prior state to their future state involves two things: 1) reconciliation (accomplished by Christ) and 2) moral improvement during this life (contributed to by Paul and Timothy).[40] Both Christ and Paul/Timothy are involved in helping the Colossians on to their final state; they just have different roles.

The point of vv. 28–29 is to show that Paul's goal is to present everyone perfect in Christ. Everything else revolves around this. ὃν ἡμεῖς καταγγέλλομεν (whom we proclaim), refers to Christ and reiterates that Christ is the one Paul (and Timothy) are telling everyone about, because it is only in Christ that everything in ch. 1 is possible. νουθετοῦντες πάντα ἄνθρωπον καὶ διδάσκοντες πάντα ἄνθρωπον ἐν πάσῃ σοφίᾳ (warning every man and teaching every man in all wisdom) shows that Paul thinks there are serious consequences to rejecting Christ. This will become a topic of discussion in 3:5–8 when Paul speaks of the coming wrath of God.

εἰς ὃ καὶ κοπιῶ ἀγωνιζόμενος κατὰ τὴν ἐνέργειαν αὐτοῦ τὴν ἐνεργουμένην ἐν ἐμοὶ ἐν δυνάμει (For this purpose I also toil, striving with all his energy that he powerfully works in me) says that proclaiming Christ is the reason Paul is doing everything that he is doing. There is also

39. "Holy, blameless, and above reproach" are probably saying the same thing as "perfect," and the differences between them are likely differences of nuance rather than substance. This would be like the descriptions of "all things" in v. 16: "in the heavens and on the earth" and "visible and invisible." It is two different ways of saying the same thing. "Perfect" and "holy, blameless, and above reproach" are two different ways of saying the Colossians will be presented as "fully-formed, complete, and lacking nothing."

40. Whether moral improvement in this life is necessary for Christians to reach this final "perfected" state is a topic that will be addressed later. All that is being said here is that moral improvement is what happens, and Paul and Timothy are helping the Colossians with it. It is not being described as necessary.

a reference back to v. 11, in which Paul said that one of the characteristics of walking in a manner worthy of the Lord is to be strengthened by God for the journey. Here, Paul is saying that God is strengthening him in the same manner that he told the Colossians should happen with them.

What one sees in vv. 28–29 is the continuation of a logical sequence of thought. Paul begins in 1:9–14 with the interrelationship of beliefs and actions (the upward spiral). He also explains that the good position the Colossians are in right now is a result of what God has done for them through Christ. They have been transferred from the domain of darkness into the kingdom of God's beloved Son. Then, in the hymn, Paul shows how all of this is possible by explaining who Christ is and what he has done, including both the creation and reconciliation of the cosmos and mankind. And, in 1:21–23, Paul reminds the Colossians that it was through Christ that they were reconciled to God.

Pulling all of this together in 1:24–29, Paul tells the Colossians of a mystery that has been hidden for ages and generations. Christ, who has God's fullness dwelling in him, dwells in the believer. It should be remembered that Christ is *the* way the Colossians can know God most fully (image of the invisible God), and knowledge of God and actions are interconnected (1:9–12). Therefore, it is only through "Christ in you" that the Colossians are able to become τέλειος (perfect). Paul here is completing his explanation of why Christianity is *the* way to become reconciled to a good relationship and walk with God. This is possible because the creator and reconciler of humanity has made it possible.

2:1–5

θέλω γὰρ ὑμᾶς εἰδέναι ἡλίκον ἀγῶνα ἔχω ὑπὲρ ὑμῶν καὶ τῶν ἐν Λαοδικείᾳ καὶ ὅσοι οὐχ ἑόρακαν τὸ πρόσωπόν μου ἐν σαρκί ἵνα παρακληθῶσιν αἱ καρδίαι αὐτῶν συμβιβασθέντες ἐν ἀγάπῃ καὶ εἰς πᾶν πλοῦτος τῆς πληροφορίας τῆς συνέσεως εἰς ἐπίγνωσιν τοῦ μυστηρίου τοῦ θεοῦ Χριστοῦ ἐν ᾧ εἰσιν πάντες οἱ θησαυροὶ τῆς σοφίας καὶ γνώσεως ἀπόκρυφοι τοῦτο λέγω ἵνα μηδεὶς ὑμᾶς παραλογίζηται ἐν πιθανολογίᾳ εἰ γὰρ καὶ τῇ σαρκὶ ἄπειμι ἀλλὰ τῷ πνεύματι σὺν ὑμῖν εἰμι χαίρων καὶ βλέπων ὑμῶν τὴν τάξιν καὶ τὸ στερέωμα τῆς εἰς Χριστὸν πίστεως ὑμῶν

For I want you to know how great a struggle I have for you and for those at Laodicea and for all those who have not seen me face to face that their hearts may be encouraged, being knit together in love, to reach all the riches of full assurance of understanding

> and the knowledge of God's mystery, which is Christ, in whom
> are hidden all the treasures of wisdom and knowledge. I say this
> to you in order that no one may delude you with plausible argu-
> ments. For even though I am absent in body, yet I am with you
> in spirit, rejoicing to see your good order and the firmness of
> your faith in Christ.

Paul begins these verses by explaining how much he cares for the Colossians
and for those at Laodicea. He already told the Colossians this in v. 24 when
he said he was suffering for their sakes. However, he is telling them this
again as a way of reemphasizing that he has their best interests at heart in
preparation for what is coming in ch. 2. He will be telling them some things
that will not be easy to hear.

Paul is in the middle of a struggle for the Colossians (v. 1) in which
he is trying to help them move in the right direction. This is complicated
by the fact that he has not met many of the people to whom he is writing.[41]
Paul's struggle (v. 1) has three parts, which he describes in vv. 2–3. These are:
1) "that their hearts may be encouraged, being knit together in love," 2) "to
reach all the riches of full assurance of understanding and the knowledge
of God's mystery, which is Christ," and 3) "in whom are hidden all the treasures of wisdom and knowledge."

The first part speaks to the interactions within the community. Christianity is not an individual pursuit; it is something one does with others.
That is why Paul hopes their hearts will be knit together in love. The Christians at Colossae should be part of a community.

Additionally, when Paul speaks of the "heart," he is not referring to
warm, fuzzy feelings. "To speak of the heart in the ancient Mediterranean
world is to refer to the whole of the human capacity for thought, judgment,
and emotion."[42] Paul repeatedly refers to Christ as the solution to what's
wrong with humanity. Here, he is saying that the whole of the person is
where that solution will be applied. Christianity, therefore, is not simply
a weekly meeting to attend, a set of prayers to say, or a series of beliefs to
accept. Christianity is something that affects the entire life of the believer;

---

41. However, Paul is not alone in this struggle. In 4:12–13, Paul will tell the Colossians that Epaphras (who probably founded this church) sends his greetings and is just
as concerned for them as Paul is. These greetings are to those at Colossae, Laodicea, and
Hieropolis. These are the three cities of the Lycus River Valley and were all located close
to one another. Besides the fact that they were probably founded around the same time
by Epaphras, it would not be surprising if they all were familiar with the philosophy
Paul describes in this letter. So, while this letter is specifically addressed to the Colossians, it would probably be of value to the Christians in all three cities.

42. MacDonald, *Colossians and Ephesians*, 85.

there is no part of the believer's life that is left out. And, believers' whole lives are to be encouraged and knit together in love within the community.

In the second part of this summary statement, Paul says he hopes for the Colossians "to reach all of the riches of of full assurance of understanding and the knowledge of God's mystery, which is Christ."[43] The fact that these things are described as riches simply points to them having worth.[44] What is significant is that when Paul tells the Colossians that "full" assurance is to be found in Christ, one finds a return of the πλήρωμα (fullness) theme. This is something that started in 1:9 and has been continuing regularly ever since. The Colossians are to be "filled" with the knowledge of his will (1:9), the "fullness" of God dwells in Christ (1:19), Paul is "filling up" what is lacking in Christ's afflictions (1:24), Paul is working to make the word of God "fully" known (1:25), and finally here, Paul hopes for "full" understanding by the people who have accepted the message (2:2). Running parallel to this are the continued statements involving πάντα (all), the most recent of which is found here in 2:2 and another which will show up in 2:3. The Colossians are being told repeatedly and in various ways that the *full* version of what they seek and *all* things they need are to be found in Christ.

In the third and final part of this statement, Paul says that in Christ "are hidden all the treasures of wisdom and knowledge." This is interesting, because in the second part of this statement, Paul hoped for the Colossians "to reach all of the riches of full assurance of understanding and the knowledge of God's mystery, which is Christ."

This insistence on all knowledge and wisdom being found in Christ is preparing the reader for what is to come in just a few verses, because it speaks against the philosophy at Colossae. In Paul's view, there is no other path to God than through Christ, and there cannot be more than one path, because there is only one Christ. There is only one image of the invisible God, there is only one creator of all things, there is only one head of the church, there is only one in whom God's fullness dwells, and there is only one through whom heaven and earth are reconciled by death on a cross. As a result of this, all wisdom, knowledge, salvation, and perfection are to be found in Christ and in Christ alone. That is why Paul says in 2:3 that in Christ "are hidden all the treasures of wisdom and knowledge," and then

---

43. Dunn says, "The awkward insertion of 'Christ' at the end of 2:2 has the effect (no doubt deliberate) of focusing attention back onto Christ, thus introducing what is a very tight and effective summary of the main emphases of the distinctive christology so far put forward in the letter" (*Epistles to the Colossians*, 131).

44. MacDonald, *Colossians and Ephesians*, 86.

he goes on in 2:4 to warn the Colossians about those who would attempt to delude them with plausible-sounding arguments.[45]

> It is interesting that Paul says that both wisdom and knowledge are to be found in Christ, because while these are similar terms, they are not exactly the same. Definitions for wisdom include "the ability to make sound judgments on what we know, especially as it relates to life and conduct"[46] and "the ability to direct one's mind toward a full understanding of human life and toward moral fulfillment."[47] In the Judeo-Christian tradition, wisdom was often described as a practical knowledge or skill (as of a tradesman or of a godly person in making moral choices).[48] The common theme is that wisdom is practical. The one who is wise is more able to complete tasks well and/or make good moral choices.
>
> Knowledge, in the Old Testament, is often grounded in experience and is intensely relational. "Knowledge can be passed on to another, but the knowledge is still passed on as an experience rather than an argument."[49] In the New Testament, knowledge is often experiential and relational, however, often "the NT uses knowledge in a more theoretical sense, consistent with its range of meaning in Greek. For instance, knowledge of Jesus is insight into a revealed truth, namely, that Jesus, against appearances, is actually the eternal Word of God."[50]
>
> While these definitions are not limited to Colossians, the use of these words in Colossians is consistent with these definitions. Probably, the purpose behind using both of these words which have such close meanings is to say that everything that one can know about the divine and how to live as a result of that knowledge is to be found in Christ.

This is why Paul has such a struggle for the Colossians (v. 1). Those who follow the alternate philosophy are attempting to lead the Colossians away from Christ.[51] And because Paul thinks the only path to God is through Christ, he is greatly concerned for the Colossians.

---

45. Beasley-Murray says, "Paul's immediate declaration that in Christ 'all the treasures of wisdom and knowledge' are hidden (verse 3) is intended to counter the idea that more is available than that which has been made known to the Church" (*Baptism*, 470).

46. Freedman, ed., *Anchor Bible Dictionary*, 1380.

47. Elwell and Comfort, eds., *Tyndale Bible Dictionary*, 1304.

48. Hahn, ed., *Catholic Bible Dictionary*, 954.

49. Hahn, ed., *Catholic Bible Dictionary*, 519.

50. Freedman, ed., *Anchor Bible Dictionary*, 777.

51. Paul will compare the alternate philosophy directly with Christianity in 2:6–23.

This brings back a recurring theme in the letter: the connection of beliefs and actions. Paul is concerned about what the Colossians believe, because what they believe will affect what they do. And, it is only possible for them to become holy, blameless, and above reproach (v. 22) as well as perfect (v. 28) *if* they remain in Christ (v. 23). All the good things Paul wants for the Colossians are only to be found in Christ, and if they are led astray with wrong beliefs, then their actions will be led astray as well. If that happens, then there will be no more upward spiraling (vv. 9–12), because that can happen only when a person acts on the knowledge that is given by God. Walking in a manner that is pleasing to God happens when a person follows the path that God sets in front of them.

Paul has taken the entire first chapter to clearly lay out who Christ is and why he is so important. And he is struggling for them, because they are in danger of being led astray with plausible arguments.

Verse 4 is essentially an introduction to the comparison Paul is about to make between Christianity and the alternate philosophy. "*Pithanologia*, 'plausible arguments,' is the antithesis of the rhetorical term *apodexis*. The latter refers to 'demonstration,' that is, a convincing conclusion drawn from accepted and logical premises. The opposite is a plausible sounding but ill-founded conclusion."[52] This portrayal of the alternate philosophy's position gives an indication of where Paul's argument is headed. He has spent the entire first chapter explaining the foundations of his own position; in ch. 2, he will compare Christianity with the other philosophy.

Finally, in v. 5, Paul reminds the Colossians again that he cares for them. By telling them that he rejoices over their good order and firmness of faith, he is also reminding them that they should stand strong in what they know to be true and encouraging them to do so. This ends the section in which Paul lays out his views on Christianity. Now, he will move into the section in which he compares Christianity with the alternative on offer in Colossae.

SIGNIFICANCE

In 1:21–2:5, Paul continues the thought from 1:13–14. There he said the Colossians had been transferred from the domain of darkness into the kingdom of God's beloved Son. The hymn (1:15–20) showed how this transfer was possible. It explained who Christ is and what he did that enabled the reconciliation of all things to God through Christ.

---

52. Witherington, *Letters to Philemon*, 149; Dunn, *Epistles to the Colossians*, 133; and Keener, *IVP Bible Background*, 573.

With v. 21, Paul begins to explain how everything that Christ has done applies to the Colossians. They have been reconciled to God through Christ, and it is through Christ that they are becoming perfect and complete, lacking nothing. For humans to be able to be presented before God in this manner, their hostility toward God, as well as the separation that exists between them and God, must end. Paul says that this reconciliation between God and humanity can happen through Christ and only through Christ. Because of this, Christianity is not something that is merely a list of beliefs to accept or actions to perform. Christianity affects the entire life of the person. It is about who a person is and how that person relates to God.

This section also returns to a theme that will be prevalent through the rest of the letter, which is "Christ in you" (the believer). This does not refer to Christ physically living inside a person, nor does it refer to some sort of super-spiritual thing that is entirely beyond comprehension (although it is a spiritual thing). Rather, it means that the creator and reconciler of the heavens and the earth is acting in the world through those who follow him (the church, vv. 17–18a). Christ works *in* and *through* Christians. It is hard to imagine a greater statement of importance for those who follow Christ than this. This is something that makes both Christianity and the Christian special and unique.

Because there is only one Christ, and only one way for all of this to be possible, Paul is insistent that Christianity is the only true way to God. Here, he concludes his explanation of the Christian position and will soon show why he thinks the alternative at Colossae (and indeed, any alternative) cannot match up.

10

Christianity vs. the Philosophy (2:6–23)

INTRODUCTION

In the first chapter of the letter, Paul explains why he thinks the Colossians should continue to follow Christianity. In ch. 2, he compares Christianity and the philosophy, the alternate worldview on offer in Colossae.

Paul lays out the main themes he wants to cover in the rest of the letter in the thematic statement (2:6–7). The thematic statement has two main parts: 1) receiving Christ—"Therefore, as you have received Christ"—and 2) living a Christ-like life—"so walk in him." These two parts of the thematic statement correspond to the subjects Paul will cover in the rest of the letter. 2:8–23 relates primarily to the first statement and explains what it means to have received Christ, and 3:1–4:6 relates primarily to the second statement and tells the Colossians how they should live.

However, 2:8–23 is not solely about the Christian worldview. It is about the Christian worldview in comparison with the alternate philosophy. Paul laid out a theological foundation in the previous part of the letter, so there is no need for him to repeat himself. However, what he does need to do is show the Colossians why Christianity is superior to the alternate philosophy.[1] That is his focus in this chapter.

1. The general nature of his arguments means that they would apply to every other

2:6–7

ὡς οὖν παρελάβετε τὸν Χριστὸν Ἰησοῦν τὸν κύριον ἐν αὐτῷ
περιπατεῖτε ἐρριζωμένοι καὶ ἐποικοδομούμενοι ἐν αὐτῷ καὶ
βεβαιούμενοι τῇ πίστει καθὼς ἐδιδάχθητε περισσεύοντες ἐν
εὐχαριστίᾳ

Therefore, as you received Christ Jesus the Lord, so walk in him,
rooted and built up in him and established in the faith, just as
you were taught, abounding in thanksgiving.

These two verses begin with something that many gloss over upon first
reading them. At the beginning of 2:6, Paul uses the word παρελάβετε (received). παρελάβετε (received) is commonly understood to be a technical
or semi-technical term used to refer to content that has been delivered as
part of tradition.[2] There is actually a double reference to the tradition that
has been delivered to the Colossians. Verse 7 also refers to this tradition
by saying: καθὼς ἐδιδάχθητε (just as you were taught). The two of these
point to the apostolic tradition concerning Christ Jesus the Lord that was
originally delivered by Epaphras.[3]

The double reference in these verses to the receiving of tradition
("received" in 2:6 and "just as you were taught" in 2:7) shows that Paul is
strenuously emphasizing that the correct views are those the Colossians had
previously received. Given the emphasis on traditions about Christ, it would
not be surprising if the christological hymn in 1:15–20 were part of the traditions about Christ that the Colossians had received from Epaphras. If so,
then Paul's inclusion of it is an attempt to return them to the foundations
of their faith.

The core content of the traditions communicated to the Colossians
is described in 2:6. The Colossians received "Christ Jesus the Lord." There
are two points made about Jesus in this statement: 1) he is Lord, and 2) he
is Christ. While it would take a lot to explain the meaning behind both of
those terms, it really isn't necessary. This short formulation is like a summary statement that probably "gathers up all that Paul has previously said
about Christ in Colossians"[4] and represents the theology that the Colossians
were in danger of rejecting.[5]

worldview as well.

2. Beasley-Murray, *Baptism*, 470; Dunn, *Epistles to the Colossians*, 138; MacDonald,
Colossians and Ephesians, 88; and O'Brien, *Colossians-Philemon*, 105.

3. Lane, "Creed and Theology," 218.

4. O'Brien, *Colossians-Philemon*, 106.

5. Wolter, *Brief an die Kolosser*, 117.

However, this is not only a statement abut theology. It is a statement about the connection of beliefs and actions (or, theology and praxis). Paul uses this statement about Jesus as both Lord and Christ as his basis for telling the Colossians to "walk in him." Once again, Paul connects beliefs and actions.

Before discussing how life in Christ is described in the thematic statement, it is important to point out that this life happens ἐν αὐτῷ (in him). Paul is emphasizing the importance of Christ for Christianity and for the Colossians. Everything that happens to them or for them happens ἐν αὐτῷ (in him). If there were no Christ, there would be no Christianity, and none of the things that Paul lists in 2:7 would apply to them.

In 2:7, Paul gives a series of four participles that further explains what it means to "walk in him." This is actually the second time he gives such a list in the letter. In 1:10, Paul explains how Christians are to walk in a manner worthy of the Lord and does so using a series of four participles. Significantly, in both cases, the series of participles ends with the theme of thanksgiving.

These two lists are not exactly parallel, however. The four participles in ch. 1 describe what a life that is pleasing to the Lord should look like. Here, all four participles are centered on holding firmly to the foundation that the believer has in Christ. Even the command to be thankful focuses on helping to solidify the foundation, because it reminds the Colossians what has been done on their behalf. In ch. 3, Paul will go into more detail about what it means to walk in a Christian manner, but in ch. 2, the focus will be on comparison of Christianity with the alternate philosophy. Essentially, ch. 1 focuses on theology, ch. 2 applies that theology to the believer, and ch. 3 explains how the believer should live as a result.

With a closer look at the participles, one notices something about their tenses and voices. Consider the following:

Tenses and Voices of the Four Participles	
1. ἐρριζωμένοι (rooted)	The Colossians were rooted (perfect tense) by God (passive voice) in Christ (implied by connection with ἐποικοδομούμενοι/built up).
2. ἐποικοδομούμενοι (built up)	The Colossians are currently being built up (present tense) by God (passive voice) in Christ.
3. βεβαιούμενοι (established)	The Colossians are currently being established in the faith (present tense) by God (passive voice).
4. περισσεύοντες (abounding)	The Colossians should currently (present tense) be abounding in thanksgiving to God. However, this is something that should come from them (active voice).

The tenses and voices of these four participles give a brief account of the relationship between God and the Colossians as a result of the actions of Christ. God has done everything the Colossians need. He *has* rooted them (in Christ), he *is* building them up, and he *is* establishing them in the faith. The proper response of the recipients of this divine action is to abound in thanksgiving (in the present). In other words, Paul is saying, because of everything God has done and is doing for you Colossians, you should be thankful. The Colossians should recognize the source of everything they have received. Because Jesus really is supreme and the Colossians really have and do receive everything they need from him, it is imperative that they recognize this.

Beyond simple analysis of the verbs, one can better understand the images presented here by looking at how metaphors are used to communicate ideas. Lackhoff and Johnson say, "*Nonmetaphorical* concepts are those that emerge directly from our experience and are defined in their own terms. . . . *Metaphorical* concepts are those which are understood and structured not merely on their own terms, but rather in terms of other concepts. This involves conceptualizing one *kind* of object or experience in terms of a *different* kind of object or experience."[6] This means that the metaphors in Colossians 2 are not describing what Christ has *actually* done for the believer. Christ does not literally attach plant roots to the Colossians. Rather, Paul is conceptualizing one kind of object (what Christ has done) in terms of a different kind of object (ideas the Colossians are familiar with). Christ is responsible for the growth of the Colossians, and, as such, they need to stay attached to him if they wish to continue to grow.

Lackhoff and Johnson say further that, "Abstract concepts are not defined by necessary and sufficient conditions. Instead they are defined by clusters of metaphors. Each metaphor gives a partial definition. These partial definitions overlap in certain ways, but in general they are inconsistent, and typically have inconsistent ontologies."[7] This makes sense when one thinks about the three metaphors that describe what Christ has done for the believer (the first three). "Being rooted" and "being built up" are contrary metaphors. The former produces an image of roots going down and the

---

6. Lackhoff and Johnson, "Metaphorical Structure," 195. Italics in original.

7. Lackhoff and Johnson, "Metaphorical Structure," 200. Dunn says of the metaphors in ch. 2, "With the kaleidoscope of metaphors which Paul used to express these fundamental transformations (of cosmos and history as well as of individuals) some overlap and inconsistency was inevitable. Confusion only arises if the metaphors are treated as literal statements" (*Epistles to the Colossians*, 162).

latter of a building or structure going up. How can the believer be expected to go both up and down at the same time?[8]

The answer is that these metaphors are each meant to give a partial definition/explanation of what happens to believers in Christ.

What Happens to Believers in Christ	
1. ἐρριζωμένοι (rooted)	As a plant draws its strength from the soil, so the believer should be connected *into Christ* and draw his strength *from Christ*. This means trusting Christ and relying on him for all the believer's spiritual needs.
2. ἐποικοδομούμενοι (built up)	The Colossians will be built up through Christ. If they remain *in him*, they will experience the growth that they desire. They need look nowhere else.
3. βεβαιούμενοι (established)	Remaining *in Christ* will produce the security the Colossians seek. There is no need to look to the στοιχεῖα (elemental forces of the world, v. 8) or anywhere else for confirmation of faith. The Colossians are established *in Christ*.

The simple explanation of these metaphors is that *everything* the Colossians seek (strength, growth, and security) is to be found in Christ.[9] And, if everything is to be found *in him*, there is no need to seek it elsewhere. All the Colossians need to do is remain firm in their faith in him (first three participles), as well as thank him for what he has done (fourth participle).

What the thematic statement teaches is that, in Paul's view, the Christian worldview rests on the sufficiency of Christ. While this seems like an obvious point to make, if it truly were that obvious, the letter to the Colossians would not have been needed. There is a difference between Christ being important (perhaps simply as the founder of Christianity) and Christ being *everything* one needs spiritually.

The coming sections will show that the philosophy promised things that the Colossians thought they needed. Paul strongly objected. All the Colossians' spiritual needs are to be found in Christ. As they have received Christ, they need to continue to walk in him. The life of the believer,

---

8. O'Brien says, "Repeatedly in ancient literature the images of being rooted and built up are linked with reference to buildings . . . . The metaphors are joined so as to describe the solid foundation upon which believers' lives are to be based" (*Colossians-Philemon*, 107).

9. This is reflective of what the Colossians seek. The four participles in ch. 1 explain what a life pleasing to the Lord looks like. What one seeks and how one should live are not the same thing.

therefore, involves trusting Christ, staying connected to him, and thanking him for what he has done.[10]

2:8

βλέπετε μή τις ὑμᾶς ἔσται ὁ συλαγωγῶν διὰ τῆς φιλοσοφίας καὶ κενῆς ἀπάτης κατὰ τὴν παράδοσιν τῶν ἀνθρώπων κατὰ τὰ στοιχεῖα τοῦ κόσμου καὶ οὐ κατὰ Χριστόν

See to it that no one takes you captive through philosophy and empty deceit, according to human tradition, according to the elemental forces of the world, and not according to Christ

Everything from here to the end of ch. 2 is centered around this philosophy and why Paul thinks the Colossians should reject it. The place to start the investigation into why Paul thought they should reject the philosophy is with the word "philosophy" itself.

Moreland and Craig say, "The word [philosophy] comes from two Greek words *philein*, 'to love,' and *sophia*, 'wisdom.' Thus a philosopher is a lover of wisdom. Socrates held that the unexamined life is not worth living, and the ancient Greek philosophers sought wisdom regarding truth, knowledge, beauty and goodness. In this sense, then, philosophy is the attempt to think hard about life, the world as a whole and the things that matter most in order to secure knowledge and wisdom about these matters." In modern times, they say, "Philosophy often functions as a second-order discipline. For example, biology is a first-order discipline that studies living organisms, but philosophy is a second-order discipline that studies biology."[11] When one reads about the philosophy that Paul was opposing, it should be kept in mind that he was talking about the first-order discipline that thought about life, the world, and things that matter most, rather than the second-order discipline that served to study the meaning and impact of other subjects.

In ancient times, there was a great deal of overlap between philosophy and religion. Part of the reason for this was because religion was understood differently than it is now. Hadot says, "The philosophical way of life never entered into competition with religion in antiquity, because at the time religion was not a way of life which included all of existence and all of inner

---

10. περισσεύοντες ἐν εὐχαριστίᾳ (abounding in thanksgiving) is the only one of the four participles that has an active voice. Therefore, this is the only thing the Colossians are required to do: be thankful. This implies, however, that they do not seek fulfillment elsewhere. Seeking elsewhere what Christ has already provided is not being thankful.

11. Moreland and Craig, *Philosophical Foundations*, 13.

life, as it was in Christianity. It was, rather, philosophical discourse which could collide with the received ideas on the gods within the city, as it did in the case of Anaxagoras and of Socrates."[12] Armstrong says that philosophy was an attempt to arrive at an account of reality by the use of human reason, with no assistance from anything other than human sources.[13] On this definition, one could say that religion had a similar task, only it primarily accepted information from non-human sources.

It might be best, therefore, not to try to differentiate too much between religion and philosophy in the ancient world. The word φιλοσοφία (philosophy) "carried a wide range of meanings describing all sorts of groups, tendencies and viewpoints within the Greek and Jewish worlds."[14] Josephus apparently thought that the term philosophy was flexible enough to be used to describe the Pharisees, Sadducees, and the Essenes.[15] Lohse says, "Hellenistic Judaism and also the mystery religions liked to call themselves 'philosophy,' and with this self-designation they obviously sought to woo and attract the world surrounding them—whoever opens himself up to such a philosophy will receive—through religious experience and cultic act—supernatural knowledge by virtue of which he will be in a position to comprehend the meaning of his life as well as of all life."[16] Philosophy, then, was a much broader term in ancient times than it is now, and it referred to something closer to what is often thought of today as a "worldview."

Given the broader definition of philosophy used in ancient times, it would probably be best not to read too much into the term "philosophy" used in 2:8 and instead simply regard it as Paul's way of referring to the other viewpoint/worldview in Colossae. Even without focusing on the term, though, it is still possible to understand something important about Paul's thoughts on this alternate view simply by the way he refers to it. Notice, the threefold use of κατά (according to) in v. 8:

> βλέπετε μή τις ὑμᾶς ἔσται ὁ συλαγωγῶν διὰ τῆς φιλοσοφίας καὶ κενῆς ἀπάτης
>> κατὰ τὴν παράδοσιν τῶν ἀνθρώπων
>> κατὰ τὰ στοιχεῖα τοῦ κόσμου
>> καὶ οὐ κατὰ Χριστόν

---

12. Hadot, *What Is Ancient Philosophy?*, 272.

13. Armstrong, *Introduction to Ancient Philosophy*, 158.

14. O'Brien, *Colossians-Philemon*, 109.

15. Josephus, *Antiquities* 18.11 and *Against Apion* 1.54 in *New Complete Works*.

16. Lohse, "Pauline Theology," 211.

> See to it that no one takes you captive through philosophy and empty
> deceit,
>> *according* to the tradition of men,
>> *according* to the elemental forces of the world,
>> and *not according* to Christ

Paul parallels philosophy with κενῆς ἀπάτης (empty deceit), which shows that he thinks it is without value and leads one down the wrong path. However, what is more interesting than *what* he thinks of it is *why* he thinks what he thinks. The structure in v. 8 is no accident; it is being used to compare the foci of the two worldviews—the Christian worldview and the alternative philosophy. What Paul is doing with the word κατά (according to) is placing the two worldviews side by side and describing how they function. The philosophy functions according to human tradition and according to the elemental forces of the world. Christianity functions according Christ. This is what Paul sees as the essential difference between the two worldviews, and it explains why he rejects the philosophy.

Now, if what Armstrong said about ancient philosophy is correct, if it was an attempt to arrive at an account of reality by the use of human reason with no assistance from anything other than human sources,[17] then this explains why Paul was criticizing the Colossian philosophy and saying it was inferior to Christianity. This philosophy was a *man-made* attempt to understand the nature of reality and guide one's life; it was "according to human tradition." Paul says that the *God-given* understanding of the nature of reality and the way God says a person should live his life is better—it is "according to Christ." In Christ, the Colossians have the true understanding, so why would they leave what is good for what is not? The one who created and is reconciling the world (1:15–20) is in a better position to explain reality and guide one's existence. This is why Paul warns the Colossians not to be taken captive (συλαγωγῶν) by this philosophy. No matter how convincing it might appear, it is inferior to the way of Christ.

The assertion that the alternative philosophy is based on human tradition is placed in parallel to the phrase τὰ στοιχεῖα τοῦ κόσμου (the elemental forces of the world). This is the other thing that the philosophy is "according to." But, what does it mean?

Wolter says that "with Plato one first encounters the idea of the στοιχεῖα (elemental forces) as the primordial physical elements out of which the universe is composed."[18] Schweizer says, "Philological evidence shows that up to the second century A.D. τὰ στοιχεῖα was used only in contexts in which

---

17. Armstrong, *Introduction to Ancient Philosophy*, 158.
18. Wolter, *Brief an die Kolosser*, 123.

it means 'letters,' 'fundamental principles,' or 'elements.' The term most frequently meant 'elements,' and this is the exclusive meaning of the term with the addition of τοῦ κόσμου [of the world]. These 'elements' included the basic four (earth, water, air, fire) but sometimes ether was included as a fifth element representing the 'heaven.'"[19]

However, τὰ στοιχεῖα τοῦ κόσμου (the elemental forces of the world) were not merely inactive parts of creation. They were entities that could affect the lives of individuals. Bruce says that, in some mystery religions, "security was sought from cosmic intimidation—from the terrors of existence in a world which was directed by hostile and implacable powers. Those powers are referred to in this letter as στοιχεῖα—'elements' or 'elemental forces.'"[20] In his view, humans could either worship the elements or entrust themselves to a higher power that had authority over them. "It appears that the Colossian Christians were disposed to embrace the former, while Paul commends the latter: faith in the heavenly Lord, who is not only creator of the cosmic powers but has proved himself their master by his victory on the cross."[21]

Similar to this, Schweizer says:

> I think that the power of the elements is close to what we call "the power of the world." People in the first century A.D. did "believe in the Cosmos!" Like the power of the law, it was a real power, and yet not a demonic being or group of demons. It was feared, but not worshipped by the Colossians, who tried to free themselves from the worldly contagion by abstinence . . . . To be sure, it is difficult to draw a clear line between these views and a belief in personal demonic beings, and what I suggest remains a hypothesis.[22]

Unfortunately, with the information available, it is not possible to determine precisely what was meant by τὰ στοιχεῖα τοῦ κόσμου (the elemental forces of the world) to those at Colossae. However, what is certain is that, in the view of the Colossian philosophers, these τὰ στοιχεῖα τοῦ κόσμου (the elemental forces of the world) were powerful forces one could not simply ignore. And this is the key meaning.

It is at this point that one should recall that the phrase τὰ στοιχεῖα τοῦ κόσμου (the elemental forces of the world) is placed in parallel with

---

19. Schweizer, "Slaves of the Elements," 455.

20. Bruce, *Epistles to the Colossians*, 95.

21. Bruce, *The Epistles to the Colossians*, 95.

22. Schweizer, "Slaves of the Elements," 468, and Wolter, *Brief an die Kolosser*, 123.

τὴν παράδοσιν τῶν ἀνθρώπων (the tradition of men). Sappington says the following:

> [Both phrases] attack the claims of the error in parallel fashion: in spite of its claims to superior, heavenly revelation, it actually reflects 'the traditions of men'; in spite of its claims to lift the 'worshippers of angels' to a higher level of spirituality and blessing, the 'philosophy' of the errorists is really nothing more than 'the elementary principles of the world'—in other words, the religious ABCs of this world. The Colossian error, therefore, rather than leading believers toward maturity, was actually a step backward toward spiritual infancy.[23]

In Sappington's view, the case Paul is making attempts to keep the Colossians from returning to a more primitive form of religion. In Paul's view, this philosophy is nothing more than an attempt by *man* to understand the world around him and how he should interact with it. The Colossians, on the other hand, have the true religion: the religion given to them by the one who created the cosmos and has reconciled them to their creator. How could they possibly leave the God-given truth for a man-made *attempt* at truth? This argument is part of the overall strategy of Paul in this letter to get the Colossians to focus on the things above rather than on the things on earth (3.1–4).

There is no power in the entire cosmos, whether human, demonic, personal, or impersonal that could ever be as great as that of Christ (1.15–20). Therefore, no allegiance or attention should be given to lesser forces. Everything should be κατὰ Χριστόν (according to Christ) and not according to anyone or anything else.

2:9-10

> ὅτι ἐν αὐτῷ κατοικεῖ πᾶν τὸ πλήρωμα τῆς θεότητος σωματικῶς
> καὶ ἐστὲ ἐν αὐτῷ πεπληρωμένοι ὅς ἐστιν ἡ κεφαλὴ πάσης ἀρχῆς
> καὶ ἐξουσίας
>
> because in him all the fullness of deity dwells bodily, and you
> have been filled in him who is the head of all rule and authority

These verses begin with a ὅτι (because). Here, Paul begins to explain his reasoning behind v. 8, namely, that the Colossians should follow the way of Christ and not that of the philosophy. Everything from v. 9 through the end

---

23. Sappington, *Revelation and Redemption*, 169.

of ch. 2 answers the question the Colossians would ask at this point: "Why should one follow Christ and not the philosophy?"

The first part of Paul's answer has to do with τὸ πλήρωμα (the fullness), and it is almost identical with part of the hymn. Look at 1:19 and 2:9 side by side:

> 1:19—ὅτι ἐν αὐτῷ εὐδόκησεν πᾶν τὸ πλήρωμα κατοικῆσαι
>   because in him all the fullness was pleased to dwell[24]

> 2:9—ὅτι ἐν αὐτῷ κατοικεῖ πᾶν τὸ πλήρωμα τῆς θεότητος σωματικῶς
>   because in him all the fullness of deity dwells bodily

Given that the hymn was material Paul inserted into the letter and that these verses resemble each other so closely, 2:9 is probably Paul's commentary on or further explanation of 1:19. The question is, "What difference do Paul's additions make?"

The main focus of 2:9 is the word πλήρωμα (fullness).[25] In 1:19, the hymn used the word πλήρωμα (fullness) to mean God in all his fullness. There, the context made it clear that the fullness was God's via the verb εὐδόκησεν (was pleased). Here, that verb is not present, but Paul explains the meaning of πλήρωμα (fullness) further by using τῆς θεότητος (of deity). This is the first of Paul's additions.

Sumney says that, "The choice of the word *theotetos* over *theiotes* . . . indicates that the writer employs the most exalted language available to speak of the fullness that dwells in Christ. *Theiotes* could refer to many kinds of beings and powers in the spirit world, but *theotetos*, the word Colossians used here, could apply only to those recognized as gods."[26] With the addition of τῆς θεότητος (theotetos, of deity), πλήρωμα (fullness) is simply

---

24. The English translation for this verse is different than the investigation into v. 19 decided it should be. There it was "because God in all his fullness was pleased to dwell in him." It has been translated differently here in order to bring out the similarities between the two verses. For more information on how the Greek is similar, see the footnote on 1:19 where these two verses are compared.

25. Some who have looked at Colossians have thought that πλήρωμα (fullness) was being used as a technical term from proto-gnostic thought. However, in the discussion of the hymn (see the excursus on Gnosticism in 1:19), it was shown that it was unlikely that πλήρωμα (fullness) was being used in that way in Colossians. Furthermore, if πλήρωμα (fullness) were being used as a technical term, there would be no need for τῆς θεότητος (of deity). It would be enough to say that the πλήρωμα (fullness) dwelled in Christ, and the Colossians would know what that meant. C.F.D. Moule says, "It appears that the most commonsense, non-technical interpretation [of πλήρωμα] may be nearest to the truth: we shall not go far astray if we keep close to the simple, basic idea of 'filling'" ("'Fulness' and 'Fill,'" 86).

26. Sumney, *Colossians*, 132–33.

being used to mean "fullness" or "all of," and τῆς θεότητος (theotetos, of deity) is that which there is "all of." The focus here is on deity rather than fullness, and it is in Christ that one finds the fullness of deity. Thompson explains, "When Paul writes that the 'fullness of deity' dwells in Christ, he means that the very fullness of the one true God is to be found in Christ. It is not as if Christ has a portion of deity, as if deity were a substance or characteristic that could be divided among many number of entities."[27] πλήρωμα (fullness) here is simply being used to explain that it is not a portion of God that is found in Christ. All of God, in an abundant, overflowing manner, dwells in Christ.

The second addition that Paul makes is to say that the fullness of deity dwells σωματικῶς (bodily) in Christ.[28] While some have attempted to define σωματικῶς (bodily) as something other than "in a body," many commentators think that the obvious definition makes the best sense.[29] While it is possible that σωματικῶς (bodily) could mean something to the Colossians other than its normal sense (perhaps related to the philosophy), there is no indication in the letter to suggest such a meaning. And, just as there is no need to invent a meaning for πλήρωμα (fullness) beyond the simple act of filling (unless the context warrants it),[30] neither should a meaning be invented for σωματικῶς (bodily) (unless the context warrants it).

Rather, what seems most likely is that 2:9 is an explanation and application of 1:19, and σωματικῶς (bodily) makes it clear that the indwelling described in 2:9 was *bodily*, just as the reference to the blood of his cross in 1:20 made it clear that Jesus of Nazareth was the one in whom God's fullness was pleased to dwell (1:19). In both places, the author ties the πλήρωμα (fullness) to the Jesus of history.

With the use of ὅτι (because) in v. 9, the Colossians are being told why they should follow the way of Christ rather than the way of the philosophers, as well as why the way of Christ is from above and the way of the philosophers is of the earth. Thompson explains, "The addition of the adverb 'bodily' drives home the point: God's presence and fullness are known

27. Thompson, *Colossians and Philemon*, 55. This point is emphasized by the use of πᾶν (all). In case πλήρωμα (fullness) was not clear enough, or the Colossians could somehow think that *part* of the fullness could dwell in Christ (which doesn't even make sense), Paul makes it clear that *all* the fullness dwells in Christ by redundantly pointing it out: πᾶν τὸ πλήρωμα (all the fullness).

28. The "dwelling" will be addressed after looking at σωματικῶς (bodily).

29. For example, C.F.D. Moule says, "And as for 'bodily' in the Colossians phrase— attractive though it is to interpret it as 'organized in one personality,' it seems more probable that it means 'in a bodily person—in the Jesus of history'" ("'Fulness' and 'Fill,'" 80). See also Overfield, "Pleroma," 392.

30. See discussion on 1:19.

through and in the particular historical figure of Jesus, leaving no room for anyone who names Jesus as Lord to seek access to God along other paths."[31]

Similar to Thompson, Dunn says, "σωματικῶς [bodily] reinforces the encounterable reality of the indwelling: as the human σῶμα [body] is what enables a person to be in relationship with other persons, so the somatic character of this indwelling meant that God could be encountered directly in and through this particular human being, Christ."[32] Both Thompson and Dunn are making the point that σωματικῶς (bodily) points toward the historical person, Jesus of Nazareth, as the place in which one can expect to encounter *all the fullness of God*. This is the foundation of Paul's polemic against the philosophers. If God is to be encountered through Jesus, then quite literally the God-given way of encountering him is *through Jesus*. Anything the philosophers might offer is going to be man-made at best, because it is not the God-made way. This is why Paul says their philosophy is "according to human tradition."

Now, when one looks at the verb κατοικεῖ (dwells), it becomes clear why some interpreters have a problem with a straightforward rendering of σωματικῶς as "bodily." Because κατοικεῖ (dwells) is in the present tense, it indicates that the dwelling is ongoing—even though Christ has already died. In other words, "The passage appears to affirm a continuing bodily existence for the risen Christ."[33] The verb κατοικεῖ (dwells) serves to remind the Colossians that the fullness of deity can be seen completely in the historical person Jesus of Nazareth and that the fullness of deity remained in him even after his death and resurrection.

Now, it would probably be too much on the basis of the tense of this verb alone to come to the conclusion that a bodily resurrection was in view here. However, much of the weight is taken off the verb if one remembers

---

31. Thompson, *Colossians and Philemon*, 54. She continues, "While some philosophers of religion label (and also reject) as 'exclusivist' this claim of Christian faith, others have pointed out that it is properly called 'particularist.' That is, the primary claim of the Christian faith is a positive one, namely, that God has become manifest in the *particular* person of Jesus of Nazareth and is therefore known in the *particular* narrative of this man's life, death, and resurrection. Therefore a Christian understanding of the identity and character of God is inseparably linked to and with this particular human being and his story." As was said previously, God's fullness dwelling (bodily) in Christ does not mean that there cannot be partial glimpses of truth elsewhere (which will be seen again in 2:17). The claim here is that there is only one place to find complete revelation: in Jesus of Nazareth. Paul's argument is, therefore, that it makes no sense to ignore full revelation in favor of partial revelation. And, as he will soon make clear, it is not just revelation that is important. Forgiveness and freedom can be found only in Christ—things the philosophers cannot offer.

32. Dunn, *Epistles to the Colossians*, 152.

33. Sumney, *Colossians*, 133.

that the Jewish idea of resurrection was the one used in the hymn (which, unlike the Greek view, was a bodily resurrection). κατοικεῖ (dwells), therefore, does not need to make the case for a bodily resurrection. All it has to do is to remind the Colossians that the Jewish view of resurrection is in view in this letter. This verb emphasizes that not only is God in all his fullness seen in Jesus, but this fullness remains in him even after his death and resurrection.

Verse 10 connects the Colossians to Christ through the πλήρωμα (fullness) theme. Just as in him all the fullness of deity dwells bodily, so also ἐστὲ ἐν αὐτῷ πεπληρωμένοι (you have been filled in him). "It is no accident that the noun πλήρωμα [fullness] and the participle πεπληρωμένοι [you have been filled] occur in succession in these two verses. For it is only because 'all the fullness of deity' dwells in Christ that Christians can be certain that they are 'made full' or 'made complete' in him. They lack nothing because he lacks nothing. The fullness that resides in Christ is, in a sense, imparted to those who are 'in him.'"[34] Paul makes it clear that the fullness found in Christ can be experienced only by being connected to Christ.

This phrase, "and you have been filled in him," leaves the reader wondering what the fullness that the Colossians experience might be. However, it will not be long until Paul explains what this means. Verses 11–15 answer that question in detail.

At the end of 2:10, Christ is said to be ὅς ἐστιν ἡ κεφαλὴ πάσης ἀρχῆς καὶ ἐξουσίας (who is the head of all rule and authority). The first thing to note is that the rulers and authorities are not referred to as the "body" like the church is in 1:18. Christ is simply their head; they are not his body. Second, in combination with the first part of v. 10, Paul is preparing the Colossians for what is to come. He is reminding them that Christ is the uncreated creator, and all rulers and authorities are under him. Like the first part of v. 10, this will be discussed further in vv. 11–15.

2:11–15

In vv. 11–15, Paul explains the relationship the Colossians have with Christ in more detail through a series of five metaphors: circumcision, baptism, death and resurrection, cancellation of the record of debt, and disarming and triumph.

At this point, it is important to remember (as discussed above) that metaphors are meant to explain abstract concepts in a more easy-to-understand

---

34. Sappington, *Revelation and Redemption*, 204, and N.T. Wright, *Colossians and Philemon*, 103.

way. Paul is using these five metaphors to help explain the relationship the Colossians have with Christ (an abstract concept), using ideas that will be more familiar to them. Additionally, these metaphors are all linked to one another, yet they are also somewhat independent. It is like Paul is walking the Colossians around this thing that is their relationship with Christ and explaining to them what it looks like from all sides. He is giving them a multi-faceted view of what Christ has done for them.

Circumcision

ἐν ᾧ καὶ περιετμήθητε περιτομῇ ἀχειροποιήτῳ ἐν τῇ ἀπεκδύσει τοῦ σώματος τῆς σαρκός ἐν τῇ περιτομῇ τοῦ Χριστοῦ

in him also you were circumcised with a circumcision made without hands by putting off the body of the flesh, by the circumcision of Christ

The circumcision here almost certainly refers to Jewish circumcision. That is because circumcision had become so strongly identified with the Jewish people that it had become one of their identity markers, and in their eyes, "marked them as belonging to the covenant and as those obedient to the Law."[35]

However, there is more happening here than mere physical circumcision. The circumcision in this passage is made ἀχειροποιήτῳ (without hands), which intentionally differentiates it from the standard, physical circumcision. This alternate form of circumcision is not unheard of within Jewish theology, though. "In addition to the literal practice of circumcision, the Jewish Bible made frequent use of a metaphorical meaning for circumcision. The cutting off of the excess of the flesh was extended to a circumcision of the heart (Deuteronomy 10.16; 30.6; Jeremiah 4:4). Uncircumcision was applied to that which was not consecrated to God or unfit for his service—the heart (Leviticus 26.40; Jeremiah 9.26; Ezekiel 44:7, 9), lips (Exodus 6.30), or ears (Jeremiah 6.10)."[36]

Here in Colossians, one finds the same basic meaning, the removal of that which was not consecrated to God or was unfit for his service. However,

---

35. Thompson, *Colossians and Philemon*, 56. For this reason, Roberts says that "the author's references to circumcision (2:11–13) can be understood adequately only if the opponents were Jews" ("Jewish Mystical Experience," 169). It should be remembered, however, that whatever the exact nature of the philosophy was, it was not traditional Judaism.

36. Ferguson, "Spiritual Circumcision," 485–86.

in Col 2:11, that which is unfit for service is the entire body of flesh. Paul is making a statement using opposing imagery—flesh vs. spirit. That which is removed is the body of flesh, which signifies the earthly, sinful part of man. However, the circumcision that takes places is not the usual, earthly circumcision; rather, it is a circumcision made without hands, i.e., a spiritual circumcision performed by God. The removal of the earthly/physical/sinful part of man by God suggests translation of the Colossians from one sphere/kingdom/realm to another (earth/domain of darkness to heaven/Christ's kingdom).[37] They are no longer to be the sinful beings that live for this world. Rather, they have been consecrated by God (as the Old Testament spiritual circumcision implies), and they are to live their lives for him.

This spiritual circumcision has been accomplished by means of the circumcision of Christ. Some commentators take this as the actual circumcision of Jesus,[38] but this is to ignore the following verse. Verse 12 gives an explanation of the circumcision of Christ as "having been buried with him in baptism . . . ." For this reason, most commentators see the circumcision of Christ as a reference to his death rather than to his circumcision. If this is true, then Christ's circumcision here would not be a literal circumcision but rather a metaphorical or spiritual one. This fits well with the first part of v. 11 that says that the Colossians' circumcision is one made without hands (i.e., spiritual—as the Old Testament background implies).

Finally, both physical and spiritual circumcision signify the identification of the recipient into a new people. Physical circumcision meant the child had become part of the nation of Israel, the people of God. Spiritual circumcision means the believer has become part of the *new* people of God, the church. The circumcision of Christ is the beginning of this new people of God, and when believers are spiritually circumcised, they become part of this new people of God. This spiritual circumcision occurs via the death of Christ, but v. 11 does not describe how that is applied to the believer. For that, one must look to v. 12 and baptism.

Baptism

συνταφέντες αὐτῷ ἐν τῷ βαπτισμῷ ἐν ᾧ καὶ συνηγέρθητε διὰ τῆς πίστεως τῆς ἐνεργείας τοῦ θεοῦ τοῦ ἐγείραντος αὐτὸν ἐκ νεκρῶν

37. Sumney points out, "Rejection of 'the flesh' does not constitute a judgment against material existence or embodiment as a mode of existence. Rather, here sarx [flesh] refers to that element of our humanity that is dominated by evil" (*Colossians*, 137).

38. For example, Jacobs, *Christ Circumcised*, 142.

> having been buried with him in baptism, in which you were also
> raised with him through faith in the powerful working of God,
> who raised him from the dead

Most commentators see the baptism in v. 12 as a further explanation of the circumcision in v. 11.[39] This makes sense when one considers that v. 12 begins with συνταφέντες αὐτῷ (having been buried with him. . .). In other words, Paul is saying the spiritual circumcision he was talking about in v. 11 happened to the Colossians in baptism (v. 12). The question that needs to be answered is: "How does baptism explain spiritual circumcision?"

Moo says, "Paul's logic runs like this: you have been spiritually 'circumcised.' This 'circumcision' took place when you were buried with Christ and raised with him. And this burial and resurrection with Christ happened when you were baptized."[40] Ferguson says, "Baptism seems to be the occasion or to be connected in time or in thought with the spiritual circumcision."[41] In some way, then, baptism is related to the point at which the Colossians became spiritually circumcised.[42]

As discussed above, spiritual circumcision (like physical circumcision) represents the identification of the recipient with a new people. This does not mean that Gentile Christians have now become part of Israel;[43] rather, the Colossians have become identified with the new people of God, the church, through their burial and resurrection with Christ. The flow of logic of these two verses is as follows:

> v. 11—In Christ, you (Colossians) have experienced the spiritual circumcision foretold in the Old Testament. This new circumcision was performed by God rather than men and has removed your entire sinful nature rather than a piece of flesh. You now can serve God with a pure heart and leave behind all the things of this world.[44]

---

39. Including Bruce, "Colossian Problems: Part 3," 197; Ferguson, "Spiritual Circumcision," 491; Gundry, *Soma in Biblical Theology*, 41; MacDonald, *Colossians and Ephesians*, 99; Moo, *Letters to the Colossians*, 202; Perrin, "Sacraments and Sacramentality," 60; Rese, "Church and Israel," 30; Sumney, *Colossians*, 135; and Thompson, *Colossians and Philemon*, 56–57.

40. Moo, *Letters to the Colossians*, 202.

41. Ferguson, "Spiritual Circumcision," 491.

42. However, no further questions about baptism (such as, "Should children be baptized?") are answerable from this passage.

43. Rese, "Church and Israel," 30.

44. It is necessary to reiterate that Paul is not saying the physical world is evil. Rather, this world is representative of sin and death, and those are what the Colossians are leaving behind.

v. 12—In the Old Testament, the people of God were identified by physical circumcision. Now, people are identified into the new people
of God by spiritual circumcision. This new circumcision begins at
and is represented by baptism.

Baptism is the "place" in which the burial and resurrection with Christ
occur,[45] and there are three reasons why burial and resurrection are important to the Colossians. First, the burial points towards the fact that the old
life is a thing of the past. Paul is telling the believers: "Now that you have
been buried with Christ, everything you have done and everything you were
is behind you." Burial points towards believers leaving their old lives behind
them.

Second, the fact that believers are already raised with Christ is what
allows them to live the new life.[46] Just as their burial with Christ points
towards their old life being behind them, so their being raised with Christ
points towards a new life being in front of them. If only the burial occurred,
there would be no future and no hope for the Colossians. The resurrection
with Christ speaks to a way forward for the Colossians.[47]

Finally, the fact that both the burial and resurrection happen *with*
Christ emphasizes that this leaving the old life behind and beginning a new
life can occur only in Christ. The hymn explained how Christ could accomplish this (firstborn over all creation, firstborn from the dead, etc.). In
2.16–23, Paul will respond directly to the claims of the alternative philosophy, and this point prepares the audience for that response. Only in Christ

45. In modern Christian churches, baptism (burial with Christ) is enough to make
a full symbol. Most people understand that burial with Christ implies resurrection
(whether they believe it or not; it's just part of the Christian message). However, according to Dunn, "the problem is that the term 'baptism' did not yet denote the whole
action, but properly speaking only the act of immersion as such" (*Epistles to the Colossians*, 160). If he is correct, it would have been necessary to pair the burial with the
resurrection in order to represent both parts of dying and rising with Christ. Others,
like Petersen ("Pauline Baptism," 218) and Sumney (*Colossians*, 138), disagree with
Dunn and think that baptism refers to the entire process. It does seem that baptism
would refer to both burial and resurrection here, since Paul says ἐν ᾧ καὶ συνηγέρθητε
(in which you were also raised with him). This seems to indicate that the Colossians'
resurrection happened in the baptism as well. In either case, Paul includes rising with
Christ when he talks about dying with Christ, so the whole process is in view here.

46. συνηγέρθητε (you were raised with him) points towards an action in the past,
which means that the Colossians have already been raised.

47. Petersen says, "While Pauline baptism marks the believers' separation from
worldly society, it more importantly signifies the beginning of the believers' transition
to the new society of the kingdom of God. It is a rite of initiation into a transitional
process" ("Pauline Baptism," 225).

can one leave the old life behind and have new life. This is something that the philosophy cannot offer.

Before moving on to the next metaphor, it should be noted that the way that the Colossians were raised with Christ was through faith in the powerful working of God, who raised Christ from the dead. In other words, it is through God that all of this has happened. Paul's primary critique of the philosophy was and will be that it is according to human tradition. The philosophers were trying to build or work their way up to God. Paul is saying here that it is only by faith in God and trusting in his path that you (Colossians) have been raised from the dead.

Death and Resurrection

> καὶ ὑμᾶς νεκροὺς ὄντας ἐν τοῖς παραπτώμασιν καὶ τῇ ἀκροβυστίᾳ τῆς σαρκὸς ὑμῶν συνεζωοποίησεν ὑμᾶς σὺν αὐτῷ χαρισάμενος ἡμῖν πάντα τὰ παραπτώματα
>
> and you, who were dead in your trespasses and the uncircumcision of your flesh, he made alive together with him, having forgiven us all our trespasses

The themes in this verse (v. 13) connect strongly with the themes from the surrounding verses. Circumcision was the theme in v. 11, burial and resurrection in v. 12, and forgiveness from one's trespasses here in v. 13 will be explained further by the cancelling of the record of debt in v. 14. None of this should come as a surprise, because Paul is walking his audience around the thing that is their relationship with Christ, and he is showing them what it looks like from all sides. There is some overlap between metaphors, but this is to be expected. The question is, what does this third metaphor (death and resurrection) mean?

Understanding this verse really comes down to understanding what παραπτώμασιν (trespasses) and ἀκροβυστίᾳ (uncircumcision) mean and how they interact. Perhaps the most important thing to notice is that Paul uses different pronouns in connection with each term. It is the uncircumcision of *your* flesh, yet *our* trespasses were forgiven. Paul is making a distinction Jews and Gentiles. His audience consisted primarily of Gentile converts (who were, of course, uncircumcised), while Paul was a Jew (who was, of course, circumcised).[48] It is *you* (Gentiles) who were dead in your 1) trespasses and 2) uncircumcision of your flesh. However, it is the forgiveness

---

48. MacDonald, *Colossians and Ephesians*, 101, and Sumney, *Colossians*, 143.

of *our* (Jews and Gentiles') trespasses, which means that this combined group was 1) dead in their trespasses but 2) may or may not have been uncircumcised.[49]

This distinction Paul makes between the two groups seems best explained by the fact that the Jews were already part of the people of God through physical circumcision, although they were still dead in their trespasses. This means that they only had to be forgiven their trespasses, because they were not outside the people of God as the Gentiles were. The Gentiles were both outside the people of God and were dead in their trespasses, so both issues were relevant for them.

Much of the confusion over this issue can be avoided if one views physical circumcision as a category of relationship rather than as a moral category. To view physical circumcision as a moral category, one would have to say that there was some additional kind of sin of which the Gentiles were guilty but that the Jews were not. If there were some additional kind of sin, Paul does not discuss it here. Instead, Paul describes the trespasses only as the moral category, so it is only these that need to be forgiven and not the uncircumcision.

Because of this, it looks like Paul is not connecting circumcision and sin. Rather, the use of circumcision here, as well as in v. 11, points toward circumcision as a category of relationship. In v. 11, the background for circumcision made without hands (spiritual circumcision) was Old Testament physical circumcision, which identified a person as belonging to the people of God. Verse 11 said that spiritual circumcision is what identified the believer as part of the *new* people of God. So, while the term ἀκροβυστία (uncircumcision) may or may not carry connotations of sin and disobedience elsewhere, here it simply means that a person is outside the people of God. It is a category of relationship.

So, in this passage, circumcision/uncircumcision represents a category of relationship; it is about belonging to a group of people, specifically, the people of God. It is not, inherently, a moral category. Any moral meaning would be added after the fact. However, the need for forgiveness was shared by Jews and Gentiles (moral category), because it is not something that was specific to one people group. All humans are guilty of trespasses and need to be forgiven. As a result, v. 13 contains two separate categories. Circumcision/uncircumcision relates to the relationship of a person to the people of God, and trespasses relates to the moral culpability of a person before God. There are, then, two categories: the moral and the relational.

49. The "our" must refer to both Jews and Gentiles and not Jews alone, because otherwise Paul would be saying that the Colossians had not been forgiven. Since they were already in Christ, then they were already forgiven (see also 1:14).

How should one understand this verse? As mentioned above, this verse builds on the previous two. The theme of dying and rising with Christ continues into this verse, and Paul says that there is life and forgiveness for those who are in Christ, while there is death and (by implication) condemnation for those outside Christ. His reasoning for this is based on two points. First, there are transgressions from which every person, Jew or Gentile, needs forgiveness. This is a state of spiritual deadness in which one lives in hostility toward God, doing evil deeds (1:21).

Second, the categories that were previously separate (relational and moral) have been combined in Christ. Those who are in Christ are spiritually circumcised, and it is they who have received forgiveness.[50] Before Christ, it was possible to be circumcised and still be guilty of trespasses. That time has passed. If one in is Christ, he is both spiritually circumcised *and* no longer guilty of trespasses. However, since forgiveness is only in Christ, the converse is also true. If one is outside Christ, he still is guilty of trespasses, since forgiveness is only in Christ. Now that Christ has come, the categories of relationship and morality have been combined. In Christ, one has a good relationship with God and is forgiven; outside Christ, one has a bad relationship with God and is not forgiven.

This point represents a strong argument against the Colossian philosophers. If forgiveness is to be found only in Christ, then one can be forgiven only by belonging to Christ. It is not possible to be forgiven by any other means. Furthermore, Paul says that even we Jews were in our trespasses, which means that the Old Testament laws (including sacrifices) were not sufficient for clearing the guilt away from someone who already belonged to the people of God. Therefore, Paul says, you Colossians have only one choice: "as you have received Christ, so walk in him." By dying and rising with Christ through baptism, one becomes part of the new people of God, and it is here and only here that one finds forgiveness.

Cancellation of the Record of Debt

ἐξαλείψας τὸ καθ᾽ ἡμῶν χειρόγραφον τοῖς δόγμασιν ὃ ἦν ὑπεναντίον ἡμῖν καὶ αὐτὸ ἦρκεν ἐκ τοῦ μέσου προσηλώσας αὐτὸ τῷ σταυρῷ

---

50. Even though Jews had already been physically circumcised, they still receive spiritual circumcision when they become "in Christ." It is not as though they need a new circumcision; rather, it seems that their state of circumcision continues into their relationship with Christ.

by cancelling the record of debt that stood against us with its legal demands. This he set aside, nailing it to the cross.

Verse 13 ended with saying that Christ has "forgiven us all our trespasses." But, how did he do that? The answer comes in this verse. Christ cancelled "the record of debt that stood against us with its legal demands."

The meaning of this verse centers entirely around the interpretation of χειρόγραφον τοῖς δόγμασιν (the record of debt). There are two main theories as to what this phrase means.[51] The first theory is that it refers to the Mosaic law. Given the previous discussion about circumcision as an identity marker signifying that someone is a part of the people of God, it is difficult to accept the view that χειρόγραφον τοῖς δόγμασιν (the record of debt) refers to the Mosaic law. The problem is that the Gentiles were uncircumcised and not under the law, and therefore it is hard to see how the regulations of the law could be applied to them.[52]

The second main theory about how to interpret this phrase is that χειρόγραφον τοῖς δόγμασιν (the record of debt) refers to a more general record of debt.[53] O'Brien says:

> Our preference is to understand χειρόγραφον as the signed acknowledgement of our indebtedness before God. Like an IOU it contained penalty clauses. The Jews had contracted to obey the Law, and in their case the penalty for breach of this contract meant death. Paul assumes that the Gentiles were committed,

51. Sappington also suggests it is possible that δόγμασιν (debt) "refers to the regulations of the errorists at Colossae that find their basis in the Jewish law" (*Revelation and Redemption*, 219). However, it seems doubtful that Paul would view the regulations of the errorists as standing against the Colossians given that 1) they were Gentiles, so the Jewish law wouldn't apply to them, and 2) the regulations of the errorists were nothing more than human inventions and thereby carried no real weight.

52. N.T. Wright attempts to say that the law condemned all men, only it worked differently against Jews and Gentiles (*Colossians and Philemon*, 113). However, Paul said that the χειρόγραφον τοῖς δόγμασιν (record of debt) stood against everyone without suggesting it was different for Jews and Gentiles. Rather, Paul said it stood καθ' ἡμῶν (against us), which sounds like he was putting both Jews and Gentiles into the same group. If the record of debt stood against the two groups in different ways, it would be more likely Paul would differentiate them here, as he did in the last verse with the discussion of circumcision and trespasses. Rather, given the use of καθ' ἡμῶν (against us), it sounds like here there is only one "something" (whatever it may be) that stands against all men in the same way, regardless of national identity. Suggesting that the χειρόγραφον τοῖς δόγμασιν (record of debt) is the Mosaic law does not work very well, since Jews and Gentiles have different relationships to the law but not the χειρόγραφον τοῖς δόγμασιν (record of debt).

53. Sumney says that χειρόγραφον (record) often designated a record of debt in the first century (*Colossians*, 144).

through their consciences, to a similar obligation, to the moral law in as much as they understood it. Since the obligation had not been discharged by either group the 'bond' remained against us (καθ' ἡμῶν).[54]

O'Brien speaks of the indebtedness of all humanity before God, although the means of indebtedness was different for Jews (the Mosaic law) and Gentiles (their consciences). On this view, the actual χειρόγραφον τοῖς δόγμασιν (record of debt) that stands against all humanity would not be the Mosaic law but something that stands *above* it (otherwise it could not apply to both Jews and Gentiles). There is only one thing that could possibly stand *above* the Mosaic law, and that is the moral law itself.

The moral law is the unchanging standards of right and wrong that are based on God's own nature.[55] The Mosaic law is a particular application of the moral law to a particular people at a particular time. The more limited understanding of right and wrong that the Gentiles had (O'Brien would say the Gentiles' consciences) would also be pointing in the direction of God's moral law, although Paul would have considered this to be more primitive than the Mosaic law.

Verse 14 requires there to be something that could apply equally to both Jews and Gentiles that would result in their indebtedness to God because of their trespasses against it. That "something" is the moral law. While the Jews and Gentiles would have known the moral law in different ways (with varying degrees of limitation), Paul says both groups have known it and have trespassed against it. The χειρόγραφον τοῖς δόγμασιν (the record of debt) might, therefore, be best explained as the record of each person's actions in response to the moral law (taking into account that some people had a more complete understanding of it than others).[56] And, it was against them, because they had not lived perfectly.

The death of Christ on the cross had the effect of removing the χειρόγραφον τοῖς δόγμασιν (the record of debt). All humanity stands guilty before God of having broken the moral law, but those who become part of the new family of God have their trespasses forgiven. This is possible because Christ cancelled the χειρόγραφον τοῖς δόγμασιν (the record of debt)

---

54. O'Brien, *Colossians-Philemon*, 126, and Moo, *Letters to the Colossians*, 209.

55. Philosophers refer to the content of such a law as objective moral values and duties.

56. Some, like Sappington, view the record as a set of heavenly books which are opened and then used to judge mankind in an apocalyptic judgment scene (*Revelation and Redemption*, 219).

by nailing it to the cross. This is something that can be found only in Christ and nowhere else.

Disarming and Triumph

ἀπεκδυσάμενος τὰς ἀρχὰς καὶ τὰς ἐξουσίας ἐδειγμάτισεν ἐν παρρησίᾳ θριαμβεύσας αὐτοὺς ἐν αὐτῷ

He disarmed the rulers and authorities and disgraced them in public, by triumphing over them in him

There has been a lot of discussion about the meaning of 2:15, most of which centers around the word ἀπεκδυσάμενος (stripped off). Moo says, "The form in which the verb [ἀπεκδυσάμενος] occurs here (the middle voice) would normally convey a reflexive idea—'he stripped off from himself the powers and authorities.'"[57] The problem is that this is a little awkward. What could it mean for Christ to strip off the powers and authorities from himself like one would take off clothes? What were they doing on him in the first place?

Because of this, others take ἀπεκδυσάμενος (stripped off) to mean "disarmed." Rather, than stripping them off himself like one would strip off ruined garments, Christ has disarmed them by taking away their weapon, the χειρόγραφον τοῖς δόγμασιν (the record of debt).[58] The problem with this view is that it interprets ἀπεκδυσάμενος (stripped off/disarmed) as if it were in the active voice, which it is not. While Koine Greek was in transition and this would eventually become grammatically possible, this meaning would not be attested for some time.[59]

It might be best not to try to push the grammatical meaning of ἀπεκδυσάμενος (stripped off/disarmed) too far, and instead "simply allow the powerful imagery of old and wasted garments being discarded to work its effect. For the Colossians at any rate the point would be clear: the spiritual powers, including the elemental forces (2:8), should be counted as of no grater value and significance than a bunch of old rags."[60] This means that Christ has removed the "power or authority which the principalities

---

57. Moo, *Letters to the Colossians*, 212.

58. The difference between the views described by Moo and Sappington is whether the action is done to Christ or to the powers and authorities. In the former case, it makes better sense to render it as "stripped off," in the latter, "disarmed."

59. Dunn, *Epistles to the Colossians*, 167.

60. Dunn, *Epistles to the Colossians*, 168.

exercised over the lives of men by holding the certificate of indebtedness in their grip."[61] The Colossians are now free through Christ.

However, there is one potential problem. Suppose ἀπεκδυσάμενος (stripped off/disarmed) is interpreted in a neutral sense, and it means something like: "Christ removed the spiritual powers' authority so they are no longer of any consequence." Even though this makes grammatical sense, nothing in the immediate context explicitly says that the spiritual powers are evil, which this interpretation implies. How is it possible to say that the spiritual powers are evil? It may be possible to answer that question by looking at the phrase ἐδειγμάτισεν ἐν παρρησίᾳ (disgraced them in public).

The word ἐδειγμάτισεν (disgraced) is not a commonly used word, but it may help to shed some light on the issue. The term does not mean "to make an example of them" but rather to "'show them in their true character.' By putting them on public display God exposed the principalities and powers to ridicule."[62] The point Paul is making is not that the rulers and authorities are being actively shamed (as one might think from the way this word is often translated into English). Rather, they are being exposed for what they truly are, and because of what they are, shaming results.

The only other NT use of ἐδειγμάτισεν (disgraced) in the New Testament helps to show the nuance that doesn't find its way into English. It occurs in Matt 1:19 when Joseph refused to "make an example" (δειγματίσαι) of Mary. Similar to Col 2:15, if Joseph had exposed Mary, he would not have been actively shaming her or saying hurtful things about her in public. He would merely have been exposing her for what (he thought) she was—an adulteress. The shaming by the community would have happened on its own because of how what she had (supposedly) done would have been viewed by the community.

Additionally, it is worth noting that δειγματίζω (disgraced) is used solely in a negative context outside the New Testament.[63] Certainly, it is hard to see how being disgraced could be a positive thing. But the point is that if this word carries with it an understanding that those who are being exposed have done wrong (as it seems it does), then the use of δειγματίζω (disgraced) in 2:15 is an implicit reference to the powers and authorities being malevolent, and it points towards what their end will be: disgrace.

---

61. O'Brien, *Colossians-Philemon*, 127.

62. O'Brien, *Colossians-Philemon*, 128.

63. Bauer et al. define it as "expose, make an example of, disgrace" and list other examples where the person exposed experiences negative results (δειγματίζω, *Greek English Lexicon*, 214). No positive examples are given.

Finally, moving on to θριαμβεύσας (triumphing), there is discussion over whether this verb needs to be interpreted as a Roman triumph or not.[64] After all, it could simply mean "to manifest, reveal, or make known."[65] However, even though it is a common subject for discussion, it does not make much difference to the meaning whether the imagery of a specifically Roman triumph lies behind this word or not. Assuming the powers in Colossians 2 are malevolent (as the above argument suggests), the imagery of a triumph would add nothing new to what can be learned otherwise.

In a Roman triumph, the captured forces were led in public humiliation by their victor after they had been defeated in battle. ἀπεκδυσάμενος (disarmed) shows that the powers had been disarmed and ἐδειγμάτισεν (disgraced) shows them as being put to public shame. So, if the imagery of a triumph does not lie behind θριαμβεύσας (triumphing), then the word is simply being used to show Christ's conquering of the evil powers. If the imagery is there, then it adds additional (and redundant) imagery to what has already been said to increase its rhetorical effect. Either way, the meaning remains unchanged.

So, pulling all the threads together, the powers and authorities are malevolent and stand in opposition to the Colossian Christians. In the powers' fight against the Colossians, their weapon of choice was the χειρόγραφον τοῖς δόγμασιν (record of debt)—the record of each person's actions in response to the moral law. When Christ died on the cross, the Colossian believers were forgiven all their sins, the χειρόγραφον τοῖς δόγμασιν (record of debt) no longer stood against them, and so the enemy lost its only weapon. Christ exposes them (the rulers and authorities) for what they are, and as a result, they are shamed publicly as he triumphs over them in victory.

Finally, it is necessary to ask the question, "Who are the evil powers?" Wright thinks they are the rulers and authorities of Israel who conspired to put Jesus on the cross.[66] This is an interesting theory, but if the χειρόγραφον τοῖς δόγμασιν (record of debt) were the weapon of the evil powers, this would not make sense. Rome and Israel could not have wielded the record of human misdeeds. On the other hand, if one takes the powers and authorities as forces beyond the rulers of this world, such as malevolent angelic

---

64. Yates says a Roman triumph was a celebration for a military commander who had led Roman forces to victory in the service of the state. It resembled something like a modern parade and was celebrated only in Rome. The military commander rode in a chariot. Preceding the chariot were prisoners captured in battle, while following the chariot were "those Romans who had been liberated from slavery, along with dancers, chorus and rejoicing crowds" ("Colossians 2:15," 579ff.).

65. Sappington, *Revelation and Redemption*, 221.

66. N.T. Wright, *Colossians and Philemon*, 116.

forces, the use of the record of debt as a weapon of accusation before God makes more sense. The real point that Paul is making is that there is no need to worry about any evil forces who would wish to do believers harm. Christ has triumphed over them and will put them to an open shame.

Summary of the Five Metaphors

It was said previously that "abstract concepts are not defined by necessary and sufficient conditions. Instead they are defined by clusters of metaphors. Each metaphor gives a partial definition."[67] It now time to pull together the meanings of the five metaphors.

1. *Circumcision* (2:11)—This refers to spiritual circumcision. Like physical circumcision, spiritual circumcision signifies the identification of the recipient into a new people. The believer has become part of the church and the new people of God.

2. *Baptism* (2:12)—Baptism is the initiation rite for the Colossians' spiritual circumcision and their entrance into the new people of God, the church. Additionally, baptism is representative of being buried and raised with Christ. Their old life is behind them, and their new life is in front of them.

3. *Death and Resurrection* (2:13)—The death and resurrection of the Colossians with Christ has provided forgiveness from their moral transgressions. Because forgiveness is found in Christ and only in Christ, the categories of relationship and forgiveness are now combined.

4. *Cancellation of the Record of Debt* (2:14)—The "something" that stood against both Jews and Gentiles equally was the moral law. The χειρόγραφον τοῖς δόγμασιν (record of debt) is the record of each person's actions in response to the moral law (although some had a more full understanding of it than others). In Christ, the Colossians are now free from accusation via this record of debt.

5. *Disarming and Triumph* (2:15)—The χειρόγραφον τοῖς δόγμασιν (record of debt) was the weapon the evil powers used against the Colossian believers. Christ took this away, thereby disarming them. Via Christ's victory on the cross, the powers have now been exposed for what they truly are, which results in their public shame.

---

67. Lackhoff and Johnson, "Metaphorical Structure," 200.

While the metaphors in 2:11–15 appear a little disjunct at first glance, their meanings provide a unified picture. In Christ, the Colossian believers gain: 1) entrance into the new people of God (circumcision plus baptism), 2) forgiveness from moral transgressions (death and resurrection plus cancellation of the record of debt), and 3) freedom from the powers who stood against them (disarming and triumph). In Christ, and only in Christ, the Colossians have been transferred from their old existence as part of the world, subject to its powers, into a new people, the new people of God. In Christ, and only in Christ, the Colossians have received forgiveness. All of this is made possible through Christ's death on the cross and subsequent resurrection.

Therefore, because Christ is who he is (1:15–20), and because this new life comes through his death and resurrection, it is not possible that anyone else could have provided this new life for the Colossians. Even if someone else died on a cross in an attempt to do what Christ did, that person would still not have been the image of the invisible God, the uncreated creator, etc.[68] Christ's death and resurrection are unique and cannot be replicated. If the Colossians want new life as part of the new people of God, they must find it in Christ. They cannot achieve even a single thing apart from Christ (forgiveness, freedom, etc.), because all the benefits Paul lays out in this passage are only possible through Christ's work.[69] The Colossians have been made full/complete in Christ (2:9–10),[70] and as they have received him, so they should walk in him (2:6–7). Nothing the philosophers offer could come close.

2:16–19

μὴ οὖν τις ὑμᾶς κρινέτω ἐν βρώσει καὶ ἐν πόσει ἢ ἐν μέρει
ἑορτῆς ἢ νεομηνίας ἢ σαββάτων ἅ ἐστιν σκιὰ τῶν μελλόντων
τὸ δὲ σῶμα τοῦ Χριστοῦ μηδεὶς ὑμᾶς καταβραβευέτω θέλων
ἐν ταπεινοφροσύνῃ καὶ θρησκείᾳ τῶν ἀγγέλων ἃ ἑόρακεν
ἐμβατεύων εἰκῇ φυσιούμενος ὑπὸ τοῦ νοὸς τῆς σαρκὸς αὐτοῦ
καὶ οὐ κρατῶν τὴν κεφαλήν ἐξ οὗ πᾶν τὸ σῶμα διὰ τῶν ἀφῶν

---

68. That also means the subsequent resurrection probably would not have happened.

69. For the sufficiency of Christ, see Dettwiler, "La Lettre aux Cosossiens," 118; Lohse, "Christusherrschaft und Kirche," 203; Sumney, *Colossians*, 148; and Thompson, *Colossians and Philemon*, 60.

70. Moo, *Letters to the Colossians*, 212, and Sappington, *Revelation and Redemption*, 205.

καὶ συνδέσμων ἐπιχορηγούμενον καὶ συμβιβαζόμενον αὔξει
τὴν αὔξησιν τοῦ θεοῦ

Therefore let no one pass judgment on you in questions of food and drink or with regard to a festival or a new moon or a Sabbath. These are a shadow of the things to come, but the substance belongs to Christ. Let no one disqualify you, insisting on asceticism and worship with angels, going on in detail about visions, puffed up without reason by his mind of flesh, and not holding fast to the head, from whom the whole body, nourished and knit together through its joints and ligaments, grows with a growth that is from God.

The οὖν (therefore) in v. 16 serves to contrast the description of Christianity in vv. 9–15 with the description of certain elements of the philosophy in vv. 16–23. That probably means Paul will be presenting some things that he thinks are deficient in the philosophy.[71] Also, in 2:16–19, there are some very direct statements which seem to indicate at least some of the content of the philosophy—likely the most objectionable parts. Since Paul never explicitly stated what the alternative philosophy in Colossae was (and probably did not need to, since the Colossians would already have been familiar with it), most of what can be known about it has to be pieced together from scattered references.[72] However, from these verses it should be possible to gain at least a rough idea of what it was about this philosophy that Paul found objectionable.

Immediately in v. 16, Paul brings up some very specific issues: food and drink, festivals, new moons, and Sabbaths. The fact that Sabbaths are in this list points toward at least some level of Jewish influence in this philosophy, because "festivals and new moons were observed by non-Jews as well as Jews, but Sabbaths were distinctively Jewish."[73] However, Dunn thinks that Sabbaths were so distinctively Jewish that the whole sequence should be read as Jewish. He says, "But if sabbath is so clearly a distinctively Jewish festival, then the probability is that the 'festival' and 'new moon' also refer to

---

71. Sappington says that because the οὖν (therefore) of v. 16 connects what follows with v. 15, "the ὅτι [because] of v. 9 suggests that the whole of 2:9–15 is foundational not only for vv. 16–23 but also for the warning of v. 8" (*Revelation and Redemption*, 205).

72. While some might question the accuracy of the representation of an opponent's position found in a polemic such as this, Martin pushes back against that idea. He says, "Although the author discounts the opponents' positions in favor of his Christian tradition, he must describe the opposition accurately because his readers are familiar with it. If the author inaccurately presents the opponents, his readers will not be convinced by his rebuttal of the opposition's positions" (Troy Martin, *By Philosophy*, 36).

73. Bruce, "Colossian Problems: Part 3," 197.

the Jewish versions of those celebrations. The point is beyond dispute when we note that the three terms together, 'sabbaths, new moons, and feasts,' was in fact a regular Jewish way of speaking of the main festivals of Jewish religion."[74]

In v. 17, the Colossians are told not to let people pass judgment on them because these things "are a shadow of the things to come, but the substance belongs to Christ." In other words, the problem is that these things are not as good as the alternative. Wright says the following:

> The phrase "of the things that were to come," which qualifies "shadow," shows that the proper contrast is between the old age and the new. Christ has inaugurated the "age to come." The regulations of Judaism were designed for the period when the people of God consisted of one racial, cultural and geographical unit, and are simply put out of date now that this people is becoming a world-wide family. They were the "shadows" that the approaching new age casts before it. Now that the reality is come, there is no point clinging to the shadows. The reality belongs to Christ.[75]

The age to come is not described in the immediate context, but the "things to come" are mentioned, and this agrees with the thought elsewhere in Colossians. Paul says that the work of Christ involves the reconciliation of all things and the renewal of those who follow him. The objection here could be simply that the Colossians were allowing people to persuade them to follow the old ways. It would be enough to object to the old ways because they were meant simply as a warm-up to prepare people for the real thing. Now that the movie is playing, there is no point in continuing to watch the trailer.

However, the question to ask is "If the things in this list were simply part of the Jewish religion, why would Paul object?" After all, in the christological hymn (which represents the foundation of the theology of the letter), Paul assumes the Jewish narrative of the creator God and the Jewish view of resurrection (although adding the distinctly Christian element that resurrection has already occurred in Christ). If the other group at Colossae were trying to lead the Christians astray with traditional Judaism, one would expect to find a letter that focuses more on why Christianity is superior to Judaism. This is not what Colossians looks like.

It seems there was more going on with this philosophy than simply continuing with things as they have always been and ignoring the update

---

74. Dunn, *Epistles to the Colossians*, 171.

75. N.T. Wright, *Colossians and Philemon*, 120.

via Christ. Very probably, the false teaching (especially as described in v. 18) involved ascetic practices in an attempt to be able to worship *with* the angels. For example, Lane says, "The expression 'worship of angels' in Col 2:18 signifies not the veneration of angelic creatures by men but the worship directed toward God by the angels. By rigorous asceticism and extended fasting, the false teachers contended, men could experience visionary ascent and witness the angelic service into which even they might enter."[76]

This interpretation is supported by the meaning of the word ταπεινοφροσύνη (asceticism). Lane says, "ταπεινοφροσύνη [asceticism] is a technical term for fasting with the intention of inducing visions and visionary ascent into the heavenly realm."[77] Dunn thinks, "It is quite possible, therefore, to envisage a Jewish (or Christian Jewish) synagogue in Colossae which was influenced by such ideas and which delighted in their worship sabbath by sabbath as a participation in the worship of the angels in heaven. In this case the 'humility' associated with this worship could very well denote the spiritual discipline and mortification (particularly, but not only, fasting) regarded as essential to maintain the holiness required to participate with the holy ones and the holy angels."[78]

If this is what was going on, then Paul objected to it because the teachers of the Colossian philosophy would have been telling the Christians that if they did not participate in these practices they would be "disqualified" (v. 18). This is an important choice of words, because in 1:12, Paul said that God has "qualified" the Colossians to share in the inheritance of the saints in light. Here, Paul is making an implied comparison between the God who qualifies and the men who disqualify. The unspoken question behind this is "If God qualified you, how could man possibly disqualify you?"

The Colossians should recognize that since they have already been qualified by God through Christ, then it does not matter what anyone else says. They have already been given entrance into the new people of God, forgiveness from moral transgressions, and freedom from the powers who stand against them. The philosophers cannot provide these things, nor can they take what the Colossians already have. "The problem with the teaching is its insistence on further rites [2:16] and experiences [2:18] in order to embrace the fullness of religion. It is this aspect which Paul finds so unhealthy."[79] As 2:9–15 made clear, connection to Christ is not only a

---

76. Lane, "Creed and Theology," 217; Roberts, "Jewish Mystical Experience," 171; and Rowland, "Apocalyptic Visions," 75.

77. Lane, "Creed and Theology," 217.

78. Dunn, *Epistles to the Colossians*, 181.

79. Rowland, "Apocalyptic Visions," 77.

necessary condition to experience God's fullness, it is a *sufficient* condition. There is nothing else one needs, whether rites, experiences, or the approval of men, to have a restored relationship with God and to be made perfect. And, it is only in Christ that those things are possible.

Concerning the final phrase of v. 18, there is an implied critique which invalidates the philosophy's entire foundation for argument. Dunn says:

> The most stinging part of the rebuke, however, would have been the final phrase, "by his mind of flesh." For in a Hellenistic context,[80] as Philo again well illustrates, it was precisely the "mind" which would have been the medium by means of which the person could enter the higher realms, the *logos* of human rationality, itself part of the medium of the divine Logos that interpenetrated the cosmos. In such a scheme "mind" and "flesh" were quite antithetical since it was impossible for the divine substance to mingle with the material. To speak of "the mind of flesh," was therefore in effect to deny that this Colossian worshipper with angels could ever have "lifted off" from earth: even his mind was "flesh," fast bound to earth.[81]

Since Paul was saying that there is no way that a mind of flesh could ever ascend to heaven, it makes perfect sense that he would say these teachers are puffed up and without reason. Not only could the Colossians never have anything taken away from them that Christ had given them (i.e., be disqualified), neither do these teachers actually have anything that they claim to have. They are teachers who make claims but cannot deliver on their promises.

Furthermore, not only can the philosophers not deliver on their promises, their entire project is ill-founded. Paul's original critique of them in v. 8 is that they were acting according to human tradition rather than according to Christ. In other words, they were trying to build their way up to God rather than accepting the way that God has sent down to them, Christ. A mind of flesh is good for many things, but, according to Paul, it is simply not able to ascend to God. Humanity cannot reach up to God. It must accept God's hand when it reaches down.

---

80. This assumes that the mysticism was Hellenistic. While it's not possible to be one hundred percent certain what the exact nature of the philosophy was, there seem to be both Jewish and Greek elements to it. This is why it is common for scholars to consider the philosophy to be some sort of Jewish mysticism (with a Greek flavor).

81. Dunn, *Epistles to the Colossians*, 184–85. O'Brien says, "Perhaps the opponents boasted (εἰκῇ means 'without cause') [that] they were directed by the mind (ὑπὸ τοῦ νοὸς); Paul's answer is, yes. But a mind of the flesh! (τῆς σαρκὸς is a possessive or characterizing genitive)" (*Colossians-Philemon*, 146).

Moving to v. 19,[82] the emphasis shifts from the bankruptcy of the philosophy's claims to Paul's warning to the Colossians not to leave the very thing that has made them grow. The philosophy is criticized for being bankrupt and unable to deliver on its promises, and the Colossians are warned against turning away from the only person who can actually deliver on his promises. The point Paul is making is that if the Colossians really believe that Christ is who the hymn says he is, why would they leave him for anything else? In Christ, they have been made part of the new people of God, they have been forgiven for their sins, and they have freedom from the powers that would do them harm.

There is something greater in what Christ has to offer than can be found anywhere else. Christ does not simply give people a way to get through their daily lives. He rescues them from the domain of darkness and transfers them into his kingdom, where they have redemption, the forgiveness of sins. Paul said this back in 1:13–14, but he gives the reasoning here in 2:9–15. Furthermore, true fullness exists only in Christ, because the fullness of deity dwells only in him. Because the Colossians share in Christ's death and resurrection, they are able to share in his transcendence of death and receive the forgiveness of sins. This is something the alternate philosophy cannot offer. The irony is that the philosophers are threatening to exclude the Colossians from membership in God's people, but in reality, it is they who are in danger of being excluded.[83]

2:20–23

εἰ ἀπεθάνετε σὺν Χριστῷ ἀπὸ τῶν στοιχείων τοῦ κόσμου τί ὡς ζῶντες ἐν κόσμῳ δογματίζεσθε μὴ ἅψῃ μηδὲ γεύσῃ μηδὲ θίγῃς ἅ ἐστιν πάντα εἰς φθορὰν τῇ ἀποχρήσει κατὰ τὰ ἐντάλματα καὶ διδασκαλίας τῶν ἀνθρώπων ἅτινά ἐστιν λόγον μὲν ἔχοντα σοφίας ἐν ἐθελοθρησκίᾳ καὶ ταπεινοφροσύνῃ καὶ ἀφειδίᾳ σώματος οὐκ ἐν τιμῇ τινι πρὸς πλησμονὴν τῆς σαρκός

If you died with Christ to the elemental forces of the world, why, as if you were still alive in the world, do you submit to regulations—"do not handle, do not taste, do not touch" (referring to things that all perish as they are used)—according to

82. καὶ οὐ κρατῶν τὴν κεφαλὴν ἐξ οὗ πᾶν τὸ σῶμα διὰ τῶν ἁφῶν καὶ συνδέσμων ἐπιχορηγούμενον καὶ συμβιβαζόμενον αὔξει τὴν αὔξησιν τοῦ θεοῦ (and not holding fast to the head, from whom the whole body, nourished and knit together through its joints and ligaments, grows with a growth that is from God).

83. N.T. Wright, *Colossians and Philemon*, 124.

> human precepts and teachings? These indeed have an appear-
> ance of wisdom in promoting self-made religion and asceticism
> and severity to the body, but they are of no value in stopping the
> indulgence of the flesh.

In these verses, Paul reminds the Colossians that they have died with Christ, which has produced a radical shift in their lives. "Here the argument presented to the Colossian Christians is that, as death severs the bond which bound them to the service of the principalities and powers, why then should they go on submitting to the rules imposed by those powers?"[84] The argument that Paul makes in v. 20 seems to be that as long as one is in this world, he is under the control of the powers of this world. Death ends that, because with death, a person leaves this world. He then says that since the Colossians have died with Christ, they are no longer under the control of the world's powers.

There are two obvious issues with this. First, the Colossians have not died (at least in the normal sense), and second, the world's powers clearly still have an impact on those who have "died with Christ." After all, the letter says that Paul is writing this from prison, so the letter itself acknowledges that the impact the world's powers can have is real. This can be resolved, however, if one considers the difference between physical death and spiritual death. Obviously, the Colossians did not physically die with Christ. That means that their death must have been a spiritual death.[85]

In this case, because the Colossians have died spiritually with Christ, they have a new future reality.[86] Yet, because they still live in this world physically, the world's powers still have an impact on them.[87] What is significant is that while those powers can have an impact on those who are in Christ, they cannot *control* them. To be in Christ is to have freedom from the rulers and authorities (2:15). By no longer being under the control of the earthly powers and authorities, the reference point for one's life changes. For those who follow Christ, the death of Christ and their dying with him means that "they are no longer to live under the authority of 'the elemental forces' which rule 'the world,' living lives determined by reference to those forces, living as though the world itself was ultimately determined by such

---

84. Bruce, *Epistles to the Colossians*, 125–26.

85. Think back to the Colossians' spiritual circumcision.

86. Chapter 1 and especially the discussion of the word "hope" pointed towards this. There will be more on this subject at the beginning of ch. 3.

87. Again, think of Paul's suffering and imprisonment as a follower of Christ.

factors, as though the values and conduct which they stood for were what really counted in daily life."[88]

Here, τῶν στοιχείων τοῦ κόσμου (the elemental forces of this world) make another appearance. However, it is not their identity that is so important as their effect—or, rather, lack thereof. Think back to Paul's statement about disarming the rulers and authorities in 2:15. Paul was and is speaking of the freedom of Christians from any ruling authorities other than Christ. There are several concepts throughout the letter that tie in together here.

First, there is τῶν στοιχείων τοῦ κόσμου (the elemental forces of this world). Whether one thinks of this as "the powers that be," a sort of "fate/destiny," or demonic forces, the philosophers in Colossae obviously thought this was something to which people had to pay attention. Second, there are the rulers and authorities that were disarmed in 2:15. Finally, there is the domain of darkness in 1:13. Paul does not give a lot of details about any of these. However, given that there are only two kingdoms, this means that everyone is either in the kingdom of Christ or the domain of darkness.

So, if the τῶν στοιχείων τοῦ κόσμου (the elemental forces of this world) and the rulers and authorities are part of the domain of darkness, then the Colossians do not need to worry about them. But, if these groups are part of the kingdom of Christ, then they still serve Christ. Paul's argument is that everyone is subject to Christ,[89] so the only real power that anyone should be concerned about is Christ. Everyone either already serves him, or they work against him but will ultimately be put back in their creational order, even if they don't want to be. Granted, evil rulers can still impact the Colossians' lives, much like the enemy can impact a soldier's life on the battlefield. However, that does not mean that the soldier must take orders from those rulers. He is part of a different kingdom and lives in a different camp.

All of this has a direct impact on the Colossians' daily lives. In v. 20, Paul says the Colossians are no longer alive ἐν κόσμῳ (in the world). In the following two verses (vv. 21–22), he references what must be characteristic teachings of the philosophy, "Do not handle, do not taste, do not touch." In v. 23, he says that these exercises are aimed at stopping the indulgence of the flesh, although he denies that they are effective. When what is said about the philosophy in these verses is compared to what Paul says about Christianity in 2:9–15, one sees two very different pictures of spirituality.

The primary differences between the two paths are their source of knowledge and what they are doing with that knowledge. According to

---

88. Dunn, *Epistles to the Colossians*, 189, and Wolter, *Brief an die Kolosser*, 151.

89. Even if Christ is allowing them to work against him for the time being, Christ's resurrection has already made the end certain.

Paul, Christianity is based on the revelation of God to man, and the proper response of man is to follow the path that God has put in front of him. With the philosophy, everything is backwards. One sees a focus on the things of this world and an attempt to gain mastery over them through asceticism and severity to the body (2:23, as well as 2:18). It is almost as if the philosophers are trying to gain freedom from the same things as the Colossians, but instead of letting God do the work through Christ, they are trying to become tough enough to resist those things on their own strength. They fast so that they don't become dependent on food and can gain mastery over their bodies. They are trying to reach up to heaven by becoming less dependent on and less attached to earthly things.

In Paul's view, this will never work. Separating oneself from the earth will never lift one up to heaven. As ch. 1 made clear, God is transcendent, and there is no way that a mere human could reach up to him. So, even though the path that the philosophers recommend has the appearance of wisdom and sounds reasonable (2:4), ultimately, it is just empty deceit (2:8), even if the philosophers mean well. Through his arguments, Paul is telling the Colossians, "Don't you think that God would know the best way to God? Why don't you just follow the path he gave you instead of trying to follow one that humans made (which won't work, by the way)?"

Because this philosophy leads people away from the true path, Paul portrays it as dangerous in v. 22. O'Brien says the following:

> "Behind the phrase lies the wording of Isaiah 29:13 (LXX) which reads: 'But in vain do they worship me teaching the commands and doctrines of men' (ἐντάλματα ἀνθρώπων καὶ διδασκαλίας). In the original context the prophet complains that Israel's religion is not a personal knowledge of God but a set of conventional rules learned by rote. The text was cited by Jesus in the Gospels (Mark 7:7; cf Matt 15:9) in his dispute with the Pharisees and scribes about the 'tradition of men' (ἡ παράδοσις τῶν ἀνθρώπων), by which the Jews had nullified the word of God."[90]

The root of the issue appears to be a mistaken order of importance. God is the highest authority, and his commandments should come first.

---

90. O'Brien, *Colossians-Philemon*, 151. On the issue of rule-following, Henderson says, "Indeed, the writer goes so far as to ascribe 'rule-following' to the realm of the *stoicheia* [elemental forces]. . . . This question [2:20] sounds a clear hermeneutical warning: life in Christ precludes the possibility of viewing any human tradition in dogmatic terms. To place oneself under the lordship of Christ is to submit not to regulations that divide and distinguish but to the power of God that works to reconcile the world" ("Taking Liberties," 426).

However, by referencing the rebuke of Isaiah, Paul is saying that this philosophy is placing the commandments of men *above* the commandments of
God, when they should come *below* those of God.

Paul's final point is that these commandments do not even achieve
their desired goal, stopping the indulgence of the flesh. The adherents of
the philosophy are trying hard to make themselves more holy. And, hon-
estly, what they suggest sounds reasonable,[91] which is why Paul said that it
has the appearance of wisdom. However, the only thing they are accomplishing is making themselves *feel* holy because of their efforts. In Paul's
view, the only way which will actually stop the indulgence of the flesh is
to die to the things of this world and become alive to the things of the
next world. This was his argument in this chapter, and he will continue this
argument in the next chapter. This is something that Christ can provide but
the philosophers cannot.

SIGNIFICANCE

In 2:6–23, Paul aims to show that the philosophy does not measure up to
Christianity in either its theology or its practical results. While there is no
direct explanation of what the Colossian philosophy is, there does not really
need to be. The statements Paul makes in this chapter are sufficient to show
why Christianity is superior to any other philosophy or religion. Everything
that Paul says the Colossians have received is to be found in Christ and in
Christ alone (2:9–15). In Christ, the Colossians have received entrance into
the new people of God, forgiveness from moral transgressions as part of this
new relationship, and freedom from the powers that stand against them.
Through dying and rising with Christ, the Colossians are no longer part of
the earthly world, even though they continue to live in it.[92] All of this has
come about through the person and work of Christ, which means there is
no point in trying to find something better outside of Christ. No one else is
in a position to provide more, and there is nothing more to be had anyway.

91. As discussed above, the philosophers are basically trying to make themselves
less reliant on the things of the world by disciplining themselves strictly and treating
their bodies harshly. At first glance, this does seem like it would improve one's ability to
resist the temptations of the world. However, Paul does not think that it actually works.

92. In the next chapter, Paul will say that the Colossians should set their minds on
the things above, because that's where they're headed. Ironically, the philosophers tried
to separate themselves from the flesh so they could set their minds on the things above,
so they could head in that direction: towards God. Of course, Paul says their efforts
failed.

On the practical side, the philosophy is little more than empty promises. Paul says that despite the philosophers' claims to provide access to the heavenly realm and to make the adherents more spiritual, they cannot deliver. The philosophers try their best to create a manmade path to God, but their teachings are just a shadow of the things to come at best (2:17) and are of no value at worst (2:23). Christianity, on the other hand, is the path created by God, and as such, it is certain to work.

One of the main themes in Colossians is the person and work of Christ. In 1:15–20, Paul focuses on the person of Christ. In 2:11–15, he looks closely at the work of Christ and how it affects Christian believers. Together, these two passages work to explain both Christ's supremacy and his sufficiency. In 2:11–15, the emphasis is on the Colossians' relationship *to* him and what he has done *for* them.

All of this is meant to show why the Colossians should live their lives κατὰ Χριστόν (according to Christ). Living κατὰ τὴν παράδοσιν τῶν ἀνθρώπων (according to human tradition) is living according to the way that man thinks is best. It is about trying to build one's own way up instead of following God's path. Living κατὰ τὰ στοιχεῖα τοῦ κόσμου (according to the elemental forces of the world) is living in fear of anything that can harm you. It is taking whatever path forward promises to cause the least amount of resistance right now. Instead, everyone should live κατὰ Χριστόν (according to Christ), because this is the path that God has given to humanity, and it is the true path.

Any philosophical or religious system can provide a code of conduct by which one can order his or her life. But, it is only in Christ that people are rescued from the domain of darkness and transferred into the kingdom of God's beloved Son, in whom they have redemption, the forgiveness of sins (1:13–14). In 2:11–15, Paul explains how 1:13–14 work out in the lives of believers. Through Christ's death and resurrection and the entrance of believers into the new people of God, people are able to share in Christ's victory. Because it is only *Christ* who is the creator and redeemer of mankind, it is only *in Christ* that redemption is possible. Without the work of Christ and the believers' relationship to him, the new life would not be possible.

11

The Christian Life
(3:1–4:6, minus 3:18–4:1)

INTRODUCTION

In 1:3–2:5, Paul explained the theology of the Christian worldview. In 2:6–23, he showed how the Christian worldview was superior to the alternative philosophy (and every other worldview). In 3:1–4:6, Paul will explain to the Colossians how everything he has just talked about applies to their everyday lives. He begins by explaining what the goal or focus of a Christian should be, moves through what the life of someone who follows Christ looks like, shows how this will impact their community, and ends with how they should act towards others outside their community (non-Christians).

Near the end of this section, Paul inserts a preformed piece of material—much like he did with the hymn in 1:15–20. The section 3:18–4:1 is what is known as the household code. It is a short explanation of how all the basic relationships in a household should function (husbands/wives, parents/children, and masters/slaves). The household code will be addressed in its own chapter for two reasons. First, how a household should function was a topic that had been discussed for hundreds of years by the time Paul gave his opinion. Understanding it involves entering into that centuries-old discussion. Second, the household code was meant to be a concrete example of everything else Paul says in 3:1–4:6. It is Paul's idea of how the things he talks about in this section should be lived out in real-life situations. For both these reasons, the household code will get its own chapter.

Much of the letter up till now has focused on what Christ has done and how that has impacted the Colossians. This part of the letter more heavily emphasizes what the Colossians should do in response to Christ's actions. Of particular importance to this study will be Paul's reasoning in this section. The way he argues will reveal a lot about how he thinks, but it will also do something further. The way Paul argues will answer a lot of the "Why?" questions people often have about the Christian life, such as "Why does God care what we do at all?" and "Why does God command these particular actions?"

Before looking at the text, there are three things that should be remembered. First, while 3:1 begins the section on the Christian life, there are very strong ties to the material that comes before it, and it is somewhat artificial to separate the two. Col 3:1, εἰ οὖν συνηγέρθητε τῷ Χριστῷ . . . (If then you have been raised with Christ . . .), provides the counterbalance to 2:20, εἰ ἀπεθάνετε σὺν Χριστῷ . . . (If you died with Christ . . .). Just as the Colossians have died to the world and should put worldly things behind them (2:20ff.), so they should live for the world above and seek heavenly things (3:1ff.).

Next, while 3:1 begins a new theme (how to live a Christian life), one is really looking at the logical result of a theme rather than at a new and separate theme. How to live is based on who Christ is and what he has done. The thematic statement in 2:6–7 said, ὡς οὖν παρελάβετε τὸν Χριστὸν Ἰησοῦν τὸν κύριον ἐν αὐτῷ περιπατεῖτε (Therefore, as you have received Christ Jesus the Lord, so walk in him). Beliefs and actions are strongly connected throughout this letter and are not separate from one another. It will become clear in this chapter that the Christian life cannot be separated from its theological foundation.

Finally, there is a strong connection with the last section of ch. 2 through Paul's comparison of Christianity with the philosophy. He just finished making a critique of how the philosophy has both bad theology (what one believes) and bad praxis (how one lives). In 2:9–15, Paul explained the good theology of Christianity, but he has yet to explain its good praxis. He does that here, so while this is a new section, it really should be considered an extension of all the themes up to this point.

3:1–4

εἰ οὖν συνηγέρθητε τῷ Χριστῷ τὰ ἄνω ζητεῖτε οὗ ὁ Χριστός
ἐστιν ἐν δεξιᾷ τοῦ θεοῦ καθήμενος τὰ ἄνω φρονεῖτε μὴ τὰ
ἐπὶ τῆς γῆς ἀπεθάνετε γάρ καὶ ἡ ζωὴ ὑμῶν κέκρυπται σὺν τῷ
Χριστῷ ἐν τῷ θεῷ ὅταν ὁ Χριστὸς φανερωθῇ ἡ ζωὴ ὑμῶν τότε
καὶ ὑμεῖς σὺν αὐτῷ φανερωθήσεσθε ἐν δόξῃ

If then you have been raised with Christ, seek the things above,
where Christ is, seated at the right hand of God. Set your mind
on things that are above, not on things that are on earth. For
you have died, and your life is hidden with Christ in God. When
Christ who is your life appears, then you also will appear with
him in glory.

In these verses, Paul gives the Colossians two reasons why they should "seek/
set their minds on the things above." Verse 1 starts with εἰ οὖν συνηγέρθητε
τῷ Χριστῷ (If then you have been raised with Christ). This is meant to connect to everything Paul has said up to this point about the Colossians having
been raised with Christ and then to add the logical conclusion. "If then you
have been raised with Christ," you should "seek the things above." Verse 3
starts with ἀπεθάνετε γάρ (For you have died). Here, Paul is about to give
the reason for what comes before v. 3, "Set your minds on things that are
above . . ." (v. 2). The way Paul starts both of these sentences shows that he is
explaining his reasoning. Why, then, does Paul think they should "seek/set
their minds on the things above"?

Verse 1 says that the Colossians are on their way to the world above,
because they have been raised with Christ. Paul's reasoning behind this
is very straightforward: "Since you are going to be with Christ (who is at
the right hand of God), then start acting like it now. Get ready for what's
coming."

Paul's reasoning in vv. 3–4 looks a little more complicated. The first
part of the logic in these two verses is "because you have died with Christ,
your life and future are now tied to Christ's life and future." This takes the
reader back to 1:18. Christ is the founder of a new group of people, the
church. One becomes a part of the church by dying and rising with Christ.
Everything that happens to the Christian happens because he/she has followed Christ and is "in Christ," i.e., on Christ's team. Where Christ goes, the
church follows. The second part of Paul's logic is "Christ will appear one day,
in glory," and because of part one, "then you will appear in glory with him."

Truthfully, though, Paul's reasoning in v. 1 and vv. 3–4 is almost the
same. It's basically two different ways of saying the same thing. In v. 1, he

focuses on the place and tells them that they are headed to the place above, so they should get ready. In vv. 3–4, Paul focuses on the person and says that they are going to be with Christ, and since Christ is going to appear in glory, then they will, too. He gives this as the reason why the Colossians should set their minds on the things that are above (v. 2).

What Paul is trying to communicate in these four verses is pretty straightforward: he wants the Colossians to focus on the things above rather than the things on the earth. Here, Paul lays the foundation for the directions he will be giving the Colossians through the rest of the Christian living section (3:1–4:6). To live in a heavenly manner, one must first set his mind on heavenly things. This means a change in orientation for the Colossians; they are to be focused on the heavenly rather than the earthly. In these verses, Paul begins to bridge the gap between Christian theology and the moral life.

However, beginning with v. 5, Paul will exhort the Colossians to live moral lives. Moule says, "In a nutshell, the Christian command is a perplexing one: 'Become what you are!'"[1] At this point, one really wants to ask, "Why is this necessary at all? Why would the Colossians have to focus their minds on the things above and exert moral effort? Shouldn't their death and resurrection with Christ have accomplished that?"

With all of Paul's talk in the first two chapters about what an enormous change has happened as a result of what God has done for the Colossians through Christ, one would almost expect something more than mere moral exhortation. Certainly, the fact that a moral exhortation section exists at all shows that Paul thought the Colossians needed to be encouraged to follow the moral life. And yet, this does seem a bit odd considering the way Paul says the Colossians have *already* been rescued and transferred into Christ's kingdom and the way they have *already* died and been raised with Christ.

Part of the reason Paul thinks it is necessary to encourage the Colossians to follow the moral life can be found in their situation. The Colossians have died and been raised with Christ, but they are not yet perfected as Paul said he wished them to be in 1:22 and 1:28. It would appear that something was begun at their conversion that will result in their perfection, but this something is more of a process than it is a single, momentary act.[2]

This should not be surprising, though. After all, Paul did describe the Colossians' relationship with God as a "walk" in ch. 1. This walk with God,

1. C.F.D. Moule, "New Life," 481.

2. Even if the process might have begun with a single, momentary act, from the moment that it began, its completion was certain. Of course, this raises the question, "If perfection in the next life is certain, why bother with it in this life?" That question will be addressed later in this chapter.

or upward spiral, moves them towards their perfection, but it will not be completed during this life. Glory happens in the next life (3:4).[3] The idea that a process is what the Colossians are undergoing will return in 3:9–10. The Colossians began that process at their conversion, but it is not complete. They have *already* died and been raised with Christ, but *not yet* have they been perfected.

Another part to this answer might be the fact that Christ does not simply do everything in this world himself. The hymn said that Christ is working in this world through the church. Given that he created everything in existence and took the necessary steps to return everything to its original creational order, it does not seem too big of a task for Christ to take creation from its current state to its final state all on his own. For whatever reason, though, he chose to use humans to help him in this task. Unfortunately, the text does not say *why* Christ chose to use humans to help him, but if he is going to use humans' effort to repair creation, then it is at least consistent to use humans' effort to repair humans themselves. After all, humans are part of creation.

The process to repair humans begins with the work of Christ, but every human has two steps to take after that. The first step involves setting one's mind on the things above. Essentially, this is a reorientation towards heavenly things rather than earthly things. It is not enough, however, to just set one's mind on the things above. This is the first step, but it must lead to a second step: living in a heavenly manner. Setting one's mind on heavenly things is meant to lead to heavenly actions.

Resurrection with Christ is not meant to communicate that everything has been done for Christians. It does not mean they can now sit back and enjoy the ride. Rather, resurrection with Christ changes the future for Christians and is meant to inspire action in the present. Paul is saying something more along the lines of "because of what Christ has done, your future is different. As a result, you have the opportunity (and obligation) to live it here and now as well as share it with others."[4] In this chapter, Paul explains what living as someone who has been raised with Christ looks like, and in these verses (3:1–4), he says that this life begins with focusing on and seeking after the things above.

---

3. This is presumably the point at which they are presented holy, blameless, and above reproach before him (1:22, also 1:28).

4. Think back to ch. 1 and the role of the church. The church is how Christ is working in the world now. "Christ in you" means Christ working in and through the believer. Part of this is the receiving of revelation from God and sharing that revelation with others. However, there is one other part, receiving and sharing renewal, that has not yet been discussed. This is the focus of 3:1–4:6.

Finally, one should remember that the moral life is not something the Colossians can (or are expected to) do on their own. In 1:10–12, Paul used four participles to describe what walking in a manner worthy of the Lord looks like. Especially relevant here is the third participle, which said that Christians are "strengthened with all power, according to His glorious might, for all endurance and patience."[5] If the Colossians are going to be able to live the life that Paul is about to explain to them, they will need to seek the things above. But, they will also need to be strengthened by God.

3:5–11

νεκρώσατε οὖν τὰ μέλη τὰ ἐπὶ τῆς γῆς πορνείαν ἀκαθαρσίαν πάθος ἐπιθυμίαν κακήν καὶ τὴν πλεονεξίαν ἥτις ἐστὶν εἰδωλολατρία δι᾽ ἃ ἔρχεται ἡ ὀργὴ τοῦ θεοῦ ἐν οἷς καὶ ὑμεῖς περιεπατήσατέ ποτε ὅτε ἐζῆτε ἐν τούτοις νυνὶ δὲ ἀπόθεσθε καὶ ὑμεῖς τὰ πάντα ὀργήν θυμόν κακίαν βλασφημίαν αἰσχρολογίαν ἐκ τοῦ στόματος ὑμῶν μὴ ψεύδεσθε εἰς ἀλλήλους ἀπεκδυσάμενοι τὸν παλαιὸν ἄνθρωπον σὺν ταῖς πράξεσιν αὐτοῦ καὶ ἐνδυσάμενοι τὸν νέον τὸν ἀνακαινούμενον εἰς ἐπίγνωσιν κατ᾽ εἰκόνα τοῦ κτίσαντος αὐτόν ὅπου οὐκ ἔνι Ἕλλην καὶ Ἰουδαῖος περιτομὴ καὶ ἀκροβυστία βάρβαρος Σκύθης δοῦλος ἐλεύθερος ἀλλὰ τὰ πάντα καὶ ἐν πᾶσιν Χριστός

Put to death, therefore, what is earthly in you: sexual immorality, impurity, passion, evil desire, and greed, which is idolatry. Because of these, the wrath of God is coming. In these you too once walked, when you were living in them. But now, you must put them all away: anger, wrath, malice, slander, and obscene talk from your mouth. Do not lie to one another, since you have taken off the old man with its practices and have put on the new man, which is being renewed in knowledge after the image of its creator. Here, there is not Greek and Jew, circumcised and uncircumcised, barbarian, Scythian, slave, free; but Christ is all and in all.

In 3:1–4, the Colossians were told to set their minds on the things above and not on τὰ ἐπὶ τῆς γῆς (the things on the earth). In 3:5, Paul says, Put to death, therefore τὰ μέλη τὰ ἐπὶ τῆς γῆς (what is earthly in you), which probably is an intentional use of the same basic phrase from 3:2, as well as a contrast with τὰ ἄνω (the things that are above). With v. 3:5ff., Paul moves

---

5. "With joy" probably is attached to "giving thanks" (the fourth participle), but it would not be out of place attached to this third participle.

from telling the Colossians to focus on the things above to telling them how to make that happen in real life. Living out this new heaven-focused life begins by putting to death the members that are on the earth. The result of a change in focus should be a change in lifestyle.

With the words "put to death what is earthly in you," it can look like Paul is advocating a form of asceticism. However, given that in 2:20–23 he argued against such a plan for spiritual improvement, he is probably not promoting asceticism in 3:5ff.[6] Instead, he is saying something more like "every Christian has the responsibility, before God, to investigate the life-lines of whatever sins are defeating him personally, and to cut them off without pity."[7] Getting rid of the bad/earthly parts of their lives is one part of what the Colossians need to do to live out their focus on the things above.[8] In other words, they cannot play for two teams at the same time; they must choose a side. Since they have chosen to play for Christ's team, they must cut all ties with their previous, earthly team. In the following verses, Paul gives them two lists that spell out in concrete terms what this looks like in their day-to-day lives.

> Some have suggested that the lists of virtues and vices in Co-
> lossians were taken from either Greco-Roman or Jewish ideas.[9]
> For example, Maier says, "The ideals of moral transformation
> the author holds up for his readers (Col 3:5–11) are at home in
> imperial ethical ideals, especially in the representation of once
> unruly peoples brought into subjection to Roman morals."[10]
> Others are willing to accept borrowing from other schools of
> thought—but with modification. Witherington and Wessels

6. O'Brien says, "Putting to death those members which partake of the old nature is not the same as 'mortification of the flesh' traditionally understood . . . this latter phrase during its long history has acquired certain associations, often standing for self-inflicted bodily pain through flagellation as practiced by ascetics, or for 'self-denial' in the form of abstaining from what one enjoys so as to gain control over the body or acquire merit. But true 'mortification' in the context of Colossians 3:5 has to do with a transformation of the will, a new attitude for the mind, a radical shifting of the very centre of the personality from self to Christ, such that 'death' to selfishness is by no means too strong a description" (*Colossians-Philemon*, 178).

7. N.T. Wright, *Colossians and Philemon*, 135.

8. Paul will talk about the other parts later in the moral exhortation section.

9. Aune says, "Paraenesis [moral exhortation] is really an indirect way of addressing a behavioral problem. Since the content of paraenesis is generally approved by society, it provides a basis of agreement in situations that are potentially divisive" (*New Testament*, 191). In this case, Paul would be casting a wide net with these lists and drawing from prevailing thought patterns outside of Christianity, in addition to specifically Christian thought.

10. Maier, "Roman Imperial Iconography," 214.

say, "Paul adapts various early Jewish and Old Testament vice and virtue lists and uses them for his own purposes, most often to stress the contrast between what the believer once was and ought to be now."[11]

Meeks, on the other hand, thinks the attempt to find parallels is not as fruitful as others might suggest. He says, "A century of study by historians of religions has demonstrated that there is hardly a belief in the New Testament for which some parallel cannot be found somewhere in its environments or antecedents. But on balance these studies have also shown that these parallels, though often immensely illuminating, rarely explain the meaning and function of the given beliefs in their Christian contexts."[12] On Stoicism, for example, O'Brien says, "Christian borrowing from Stoicism was limited . . . . [T]he four cardinal virtues (wisdom, manliness, self-control, righteousness) and corresponding vices (folly, cowardice, intemperance, injustice) are not present in the NT catalogues; and several of the so-called virtues in the NT lists were regarded as vices in Stoicism."[13]

It is probably best, then, to consider these lists as having been influenced by existing ideas to some degree but not wholly dependent on them. Paul was aware of other ethical schools of thought and likely borrowed from them, but as Meeks said above, research into this topic has not been able to show that the early Christians simply copied external ethical thought and imported it into their practices or documents wholesale. The best course of action, then, is to evaluate these lists as they stand and try to understand how Paul thought these particular virtues and vices are connected to and flow from the theology of the last two chapters.

The first list of behaviors (v. 5) which the Colossians are to avoid begins with four examples of sexual vices.[14] The fourth behavior in the list, ἐπιθυμίαν (desire), is qualified with the word κακήν (evil), because the word

11. Witherington and Wessels, "Do Everything," 311.

12. Meeks, *First Urban Christians*, 91.

13. O'Brien, *Colossians-Philemon*, 179. Humility (ταπεινοφροσύνη) is one example he gives of a NT virtue that would have been considered a vice in Stoicism.

14. Witherington and Wessels, "Do Everything," 310. MacDonald says, "The ethical guidelines of 3:5–17 begin with a list of four vices that probably all have sexual connotation (immorality, impurity, passion and evil desire) and set a high moral standard. Here, the author of Colossians is laying out the vices of the Gentile unbelieving world and it is not possible for us to determine which precise activities are intended" ("Slavery, Sexuality," 101).

"desire" by itself could be used in a neutral sense.[15] And, the fifth item in the list, πλεονεξίαν[16] (greed), seems a little different from the others at first glance.

However, it is possible that this is not simply a random listing of vices; rather, it could be moving in a specific direction. It could be that the first catalogue of vices represents "a movement from the outward manifestations of sin to the inward cravings of the heart, the acts of immorality and uncleanness to their inner springs."[17] If this is correct, then the list would represent a movement from the external "immorality" (πορνεία is unlawful sexual intercourse and often rendered as "fornication")[18] to the internal "evil desire." Greed, then, would be an extension of the list to a non-sexual act that belongs on the same spectrum of immorality.

The key to understanding this list is the final phrase, ἥτις ἐστὶν εἰδωλολατρία (which is idolatry). This phrase does not stand on its own; rather, it modifies the final term, "greed." Now, up to this point, it seems like the moral commands do not connect to the letter's theology. Given the focus in the first two chapters on the person and work of Christ, it is a little difficult to see how sexual immorality and greed are related to this. There might be a way, though.

What if this list were considered in reverse order? Instead of starting with sexual sins and ending with idolatry as a description of greed, it might make more sense to start with idolatry as the connecting point between theology and practice and then work backwards. For something to be idolatry, one must put something besides God in God's place. Another way to describe idolatry might be to say that it is anything that disrupts the proper order of importance: God first, humanity (and anything else) second. In that case, it would be correct to call the placing of oneself and one's own desires above God and his desires[19] idolatry, because it is putting one's own self in God's place.

Suppose for a moment that idolatry is really the main issue here. How would that apply to the rest of the list? The place to start is with greed, because the letter itself says that greed is a form of idolatry: . . . πλεονεξίαν ἥτις ἐστὶν εἰδωλολατρία (. . . greed, which is idolatry). But the question is

15. N.T. Wright, *Colossians and Philemon*, 134. Dunn says it could even be used in a positive sense (*Epistles to the Colossians*, 215).

16. Bauer et al. define πλεονεξία as "the state of desiring to have more than one's due, *greediness insatiableness, avarice, covetousness*" (πλεονεξία, *Greek English Lexicon*, 824).

17. O'Brien, *Colossians-Philemon*, 175.

18. Bauer et al., πορνεία, *Greek English Lexicon*, 854.

19. God's desires likely include directions for how man should live.

"Why is greed a form of idolatry?" Dunn says, "'Greed' is a form of idolatry because it projects acquisitiveness and personal satisfaction as objective go(o)ds to be praised and served."[20] In other words, greed is a disruption of the order of importance. Man is placing himself and his own desires above God and his desires. Greed is making oneself the center of the universe. The person who is greedy is replacing God with himself.

Saying greed is a form of idolatry seems to make sense, but what about sexual sins? How are they a form of greed? It might be possible to say that sexual sins and greed are related because they are on the same spectrum. Whether it is a physical act or an inward (evil) desire, both seek to gratify a perceived need in an inappropriate manner. If God placed limits on the sexual interaction humans should have with one another,[21] then to ignore those limits is to ignore God. To commit sexual sin, then, would be to place one's own desires above God's desires. This results in idolatry by replacing God with one's own self.

However, besides the issue of ignoring boundaries that God has set, there may be something in some forms of sexual relations that is inherently idolatrous. Immediately, that seems like a leap, but if one considers this in the context of the proper order of importance, it may not be that large of a leap. The place to start is with the sexual relations themselves and then come back to address the question of idolatry.

Consider, for a moment, two kinds of (consensual) sexual relationships. The first is one in which both people are primarily interested in having a good time, and there is no commitment or expectation beyond what each person gets out of it. The second is one in which sex happens within a committed relationship that seeks the good of the other person.

In the first relationship, each person is having sex with the other primarily to please his or her own self. This makes the sex inherently selfish. Each person is primarily interested in having a good time; neither is seeking the good of the other. This could be why Paul places sexual sins on the same spectrum with greed.[22] From a practical standpoint, each person's focus is on looking out for himself or herself. There is no inherent concern for the other. However, sexual relations in the second relationship are different, because while each person is no doubt interested in his or her own pleasure,

---

20. Dunn, *Epistles to the Colossians*, 216.

21. The question, "Why do people have to live in a particular way?" will be addressed in the discussion of v. 8.

22. Paul may have chosen to highlight sexual sins as opposed to some other kind of sin because it was a problem at Colossae. Unfortunately, it is not possible to know for certain.

the sex still occurs within a relationship that seeks the good of the other person.

The sexual relations in the first relationship are inherently selfish, while those in the second are not. Because of this, it seems at least reasonable to suggest that sex outside of a relationship that seeks the good of the other person can be placed on the same spectrum as greed. By having sex without concern for the good of the partner, a person is placing himself or herself above the partner (self first, sexual partner second). This has the effect of making the person a tool rather than a real partner. One person is *using* the other person as a means to an end, because it is not the other person they want. They want the sexual experience; the other person is merely the required apparatus for that experience. This is both selfish and greedy—even if both people accept the arrangement. The fact that two people agree to be selfish and greedy together does not change the nature of their relationship.

Paul called greed idolatry.[23] It seems pretty straightforward to call greed idolatry if a person is putting himself or herself above God in the order of importance. After all, that person is putting himself or herself in God's place. However, it probably still applies if a person is putting his or her own needs and desires above everyone else's. If a person is setting up his or her own desires as the things which are to be fulfilled above everyone and everything else, that person has (practically speaking) become his or her own god.

He or she is like the authoritarian and self-centered king who treats his subjects as if they exist only for his own pleasure. Whether the king claims divinity or not, by placing himself above everyone else and using his power to get what he wants at others' expense, he has become his own god. The person who puts his or her own desires above everyone else's may not go to the extreme that some kings have, but the idea is the same. If a person places himself or herself above everyone else, he or she has in effect become his or her own god. And this is idolatry.

Malherbe speaks of "the general conviction that philosophy educates one away from the passions toward self-control or the sober life. It was a common notion among philosophers that the king should embody the ideal human qualities."[24] The person who is in control of the fate of others needs to live a life that is centered on others rather than on self. The king was the special focus of this moral exhortation, no doubt because of the effects of his actions on others. In like manner, if Christians are responsible for revealing Christ to the world, they are in a position of even greater responsibility than

23. . . . πλεονεξίαν ἥτις ἐστὶν εἰδωλολατρία (. . . greed, which is idolatry).

24. Malherbe, *Moral Exhortation*, 31.

an earthly king, because they are working for something greater than an earthly kingdom. If they live self-centered lives, not only will they be unable to accomplish their task, but they will likely cause harm (and possibly even great harm).

In v. 5, Paul is showing the Colossians how a particular set of sins (which were likely an issue at Colossae)[25] relate back to the theology that has been the focus of the letter so far. However, Paul is not merely telling the Colossians that "God said you shouldn't do X, therefore, you shouldn't do X." He is explaining *how* their specific sins and sin in general relate back to theology. He is essentially saying, "By ignoring God's commands, you are committing idolatry. And, by putting yourselves above everyone else, you are making yourselves into your own gods. You have replaced God and his way with yourselves and your own way." The section of 3:9–10 will explain more about why that is a problem.

Paul describes the whole list of sins as idolatry; however, the root sin here might better be described as selfishness rather than idolatry. Idolatry is the general category; selfishness is a specific kind of idolatry. Idolatry is putting anything but God in God's place. The actions in this list do not describe merely putting *something* in God's place; they describe people putting *themselves* in God's place. Selfishness is placing *oneself* above God and everyone else.[26]

Idolatry is the way Paul is connecting beliefs and actions. Because of who Christ is, no one but Christ belongs in first place.[27] However, Paul is not merely letting things rest with the general category of idolatry. Rather, he focuses on what he thinks is the precise form of idolatry that is the real problem: selfishness. By acting in these ways, people are placing themselves above God and above others and turning themselves into their own little gods. They have turned the proper order of importance upside down and placed themselves, rather than Christ, at the top.

25. Dunn says, "'Catalogues of vice' were standard items in ethical teaching of the time. They were particularly popular among the Stoics, but common also in Judaism . . . . Nevertheless, such lists are never merely formal and always contain distinctive elements, presumably judged appropriate to the particular occasion" (*Epistles to the Colossians*, 213).

26. Witherington and Wessels say, "The root sin of all sins is ultimately self-centeredness and selfishness, and greed is one of the more obvious forms of this orientation in life. Self-centeredness is called idolatry in early Jewish and Christian contexts because it amounts to a form of self-worship, rather than giving God his due" ("Do Everything," 310).

27. Think back to the hymn.

Moving on to v. 6, Paul says that the actions he just listed result in the wrath of God (v. 6).[28] There are two possibilities for what this could mean. Wrath could be the consequences that follow from a failure to acknowledge and worship God as God. "In that case the wrath takes the form of God giving or allowing his human creatures what they want, leaving them to their own devices—the continuing avarice and abuse of sexual relations being its own reward."[29]

This does not sound like "the wrath of God" as much as it sounds like simple cause and effect. It sounds more like "if you do something the human machine was not designed to do, don't be surprised if something breaks." This could still be described as the wrath of God; however, the more common way of thinking of God's wrath is judgment. In that view, "the wrath of God" is the justice of a holy God that he brings down on everyone who does evil.

It may not be necessary to think of these as separate ideas. Consequences that happen in this life and judgment by God in the next life are not mutually exclusive. Unfortunately, Paul does not discuss what happens to those who are not in Christ, so it's impossible to know what he thinks for certain (at least from this letter). It might be possible, though, to get an idea of what happens to those who are not in Christ after this life by looking at what happens to those who are in Christ and then simply flipping it. This will be considered after v. 11.

Verse 7 describes the previous life of the Colossians, and v. 8 gives another list of actions that they need to put off or lay aside. Verses 7–8 say, ἐν οἷς καὶ ὑμεῖς περιεπατήσατέ ποτε ὅτε ἐζῆτε ἐν τούτοις (In these you too once walked, when you were living in them). Verse 8 says, νυνὶ δὲ ἀπόθεσθε καὶ ὑμεῖς τὰ πάντα ὀργήν θυμόν κακίαν βλασφημίαν αἰσχρολογίαν ἐκ τοῦ στόματος ὑμῶν (But now, you must put them all away: anger, wrath, malice, slander, and obscene talk from your mouth).

The first verb, περιεπατήσατέ (walked), points to a single event in the past, but because that verb is "to walk," it speaks to the ongoing lives they lived. The meaning of the word itself points toward an ongoing life, and the

---

28. Verse 6 says, δι' ἃ ἔρχεται ἡ ὀργὴ τοῦ θεοῦ (because of these, the wrath of God is coming). There is a textual variant that adds ἐπὶ τοὺς υἱοὺς τῆς ἀπειθείας (on the sons of disobedience) to the end of the verse. There is debate over whether these words were original or not; however, the meaning of the passage is not changed by either their presence or absence. ἐπὶ τοὺς υἱοὺς τῆς ἀπειθείας (on the sons of disobedience) would simply clarify who is receiving the wrath of God, but that is not really in question in the passage. The first part of the verse, δι' ἃ ἔρχεται ἡ ὀργὴ τοῦ θεοῦ (because of these, the wrath of God is coming), already points at the sins listed in v. 5 as the reason for God's wrath. Presumably, God would be angry at the people who do them.

29. Dunn, *Epistles to the Colossians*, 216.

tense of the verb indicates that that ongoing life is now behind them. The second verb, ἐζῆτε (were living) reemphasizes that the way the Colossians lived previously was ongoing. These two verbs work together to impress upon the Colossians that they used to have another pattern of life, but that life is now behind them.[30] Then, in case his point wasn't clear enough, in vv. 7–8, Paul uses the common ποτε . . . νυνὶ δὲ (once . . . but now) construction to highlight the contrast between what once was and what now is. You Colossians *once* lived differently, *but now* you must put those things behind you.[31]

It is important to understand that vv. 7–8 do not stand alone. They are based on Paul's command to seek the things that are above. In turn, that command is based on the fact that the Colossians have been raised from the dead with and by Christ. Verses 7–8, then, describe not merely what the Colossians need to do but what they need to do in response to what has been done on their behalf.

The thought behind this section is essentially the same as the thought behind the four participles in 1:10–12 and 2:7, only it emphasizes the Colossians' responsibility. In both 1:10–12 and 2:7, the emphasis was more on the X side of the formula: "God has done X for you through Christ, therefore you should do Y." In other words, it was more focused on God's actions than on Christians' response, even though both were present. The moral exhortation section (3:1–4:6) focuses more on the Y side of the formula; it is more about how Christians should respond to what God has done. However, even though some verses focus more on the X side and others on the Y side, the formula itself does not change. It is still "God has done X for you through Christ, therefore you should do Y."

God has acted through Christ to do something for the Colossians. Their response should be to be thankful. Presumably, they show their thankfulness not merely by thanking God in prayer (which is certainly included) but also by living in a manner that honors His work and reflects what is heavenly—thereby *showing* their thankfulness.

The second list of sins is: ὀργήν θυμόν κακίαν βλασφημίαν αἰσχρολογίαν (anger, wrath, malice, slander, and obscene talk). These are not as complicated to understand as the first list (v. 5), nor do they have a

---

30. Dunn says, "The aorist tense of the first verb sums up that previous behavior as a single event now past; the imperfect tense of the second verb, in contrast, indicates a sustained way of life" (*Epistles to the Colossians*, 217).

31. However, this new life is not something that merely happens to them passively; this is something they must work towards. O'Brien says, "The past behavior is characterized by the indicative mood, but instead of following this with another indicative to describe their present standing the apostle employs an imperative 'put away' (v. 8) to spell out their new responsibilities in Christ" (*Colossians-Philemon*, 185–86).

summary term. They are primarily about personal relationships within the Christian community.[32]

This second list of sins continues Paul's contrast between the heavenly way and the earthly way with which he began the first list. Those who are part of Christ's kingdom (i.e., in Christ) should live according to the pattern of life that corresponds to that kingdom. This is different from the pattern of life one is used to—the earthly way that corresponds with the domain of darkness.

Now, the first list (sexual sins, greed, and idolatry) is primarily internal. Its emphasis is on the problems within a person. Granted, some of the sexual sins involve other people, but the effect on other people is not the point of the list. The point of the list is that the people who do these things have their order of importance upside down. They are placing themselves in the top spot, when it is really God who belongs there. The proper order of importance is God first, everyone/everything else second. Their upside down list is self first, God/others second.

The second of Paul's lists is primarily (though not exclusively) external. It focuses on the things people do that are destructive of relationships with other people. Anger, wrath, malice, slander, and obscene talk are all harmful to healthy social relations. Certainly, one could argue that the first list of sins is harmful to social relations (external), and the second list also affects the individual who does them (internal). This would be correct. However, the internal/external distinction is only meant to point towards the primary emphasis of each list of sins. Both lists have both internal and external elements.

It might be possible to look at this second list in a way similar to the first list. There, the primary characteristic of an earthly life was idolatry. However, it was a specific kind of idolatry: selfishness. In a way, the second list is also very self-centered. The actions and attitudes that Paul describes point towards a preoccupation with how external events affect one's own self.[33] The Colossians might respond, "But, what is the problem with focusing on how things affect you? Isn't that natural?" One could easily hear Paul saying, "Yes, it is absolutely natural. But what is natural is the earthly way. You are followers of Christ, and as such, you should live in a heavenly way."

Like the first list of sins, the second list reveals an upside down order of importance. Anger, wrath, and malice likely show that a person thinks quite highly of himself or herself—as if his or her happiness and comfort

32. Dunn, *Epistles to the Colossians*, 218.

33. The precise cause(s) of anger, wrath, malice, and slander is not given. The only thing that can be known is that something about what the other party/parties did was upsetting.

were of supreme importance. However, the hymn said that Christ is "the head of the body, the church." The way Christ is working in the world is through those who are part of the church. That means the primary task with which a person should be occupied is the work of Christ. After all, who is greater than Christ? Doesn't Christ belong in the top spot rather than the Christian? Wouldn't anything else be idolatry?

Similarly, slander and obscene talk could very well arise out of anger, wrath, and malice. In this case, they would be external manifestations of internal sinful attitudes. However, even if slander and obscene talk do not arise out of anger, wrath, and malice, they are still both selfish. Slander raises a person up by putting others down, which is the same as placing yourself in a position above others. Obscene talk could also be translated as dirty talk, and it is essentially talking about sexual sins in public.[34] While there are different reasons a person might have for engaging in this kind of talk, that person is using (talk of) sinful actions for his or her own purposes. He or she is placing his or her purposes/desires above that which is right—what God said a person should or should not do.

Even though these two lists appear to be very different on the surface, there are strong connections between them. In both lists, the offender lives in an earthly manner, and while that may be common enough, Christians are called to live in a heavenly manner. This earthly/heavenly distinction is central to Paul's exhortations. Christians should live for where they're headed. They should live in a heavenly manner.

Beyond this, the actions and attitudes in both lists are characterized by selfishness. Selfishness is not merely a childish attitude that some people have not grown out of. Rather, Paul says selfishness is the specific form of idolatry that characterizes evil actions. The people who do these things are placing themselves above God and others in the order of importance. They are like tyrannical kings who view their subjects only as a means to an end, *their* own ends. They have become like little gods with their own tiny worlds who expect everyone to bow down to them and serve their needs. They view people as tools who can be used for whatever they want, and those who refuse to be tools will be met with anger, wrath, malice, and slander.

Because of the importance placed on not being selfish, it is possible to add a third party/group to the hierarchy of importance: other people. Those who follow Christ are not to act in selfish ways towards other people. Previously, the order of importance was God first, self second. Now, it is

---

34. Bauer et al. definesthis word as "speech of a kind that is generally considered in poor taste, *obscene speech, dirty talk.*" It "might properly be defined as story-telling involving such unseemly deeds as adultery or pederasty." Also, "obscene expressions would also be used to flavor derogatory remarks" (αἰσχρολογία, *Greek English Lexicon*, 29).

God first, then self and others after that. It is not yet been discussed whether "others" should be placed above "self," i.e., whether one should intentionally act in a selfless manner towards them. However, what has been said is that one should not act selfishly towards others. So, this brings others up to at least a neutral position in relation to oneself. It is not possible to say more now, because all that Paul has discussed is what things a Christian should *not* do. Soon, he will discuss what things a Christian *should* do.

This hierarchy shows why getting one's theology correct is so important. If one knows for certain that Christ really is the image of the invisible God, the uncreated creator, etc., then it is impossible to think that the top spot can be occupied by anyone but him. It is Christ's spot. And, if a person has a correct order of importance (Christ first, everyone/everything else after Christ), then all of the actions in these lists are at odds with what one knows to be true about the world.

At this point, two questions present themselves: "Why should people act in a particular manner?" and "Why is it the way of Christ that one should follow?"[35] Certainly, if God commanded something, then it should be done. However, the text does not actually point to any command from God. Paul says the wrath of God is coming because people are living according to the things they should put away (v. 6), but, there is no mention of a command. Paul's reasoning is not simply, "God told you not to do X, so you had better not do X."

The reasoning Paul is using is more basic than following a command from God. It is about functioning properly in one's environment. It makes no sense to try to run underwater; the action isn't suited to its environment. Running is for the land. If one is in the water, it makes better sense to swim. It makes a difference who created the world and who is in charge, because whoever that is will have shaped the world in a particular way and set it up to operate in a particular way. Getting along well in the world means swimming in the water and running on land. Confusing the two will result in actions that are inefficient at best (running in the water) and deadly at worst (breathing underwater). If Christ is the creator and ruler of the cosmos, then things will be one way. If someone else (or no one else) is in charge, things will be another way.

The answer to the first question, "Why should people act in a particular manner?," is that one's actions should be suited to one's environment. This is something that holds true for everyone and not just for Christians. One's actions, whether Christian or not, should be suited to one's environment.

35. There is a third question that presents itself: "Why are Christians told to live in *this* particular way instead of some other way?" That question will be addressed later in this chapter.

Now, to the second question, "Why is it the way of Christ (instead of another way) that one should follow?" The answer is that Christ is the one who created the world and is reconciling it (1:15–20). Christ is the ruler over the rulers of the domain of darkness, and one day, the domain of darkness will be reconciled (put back in its creational order). On that day, everything will function according to the pattern of life one finds in Christ's kingdom. There is no point in following sub-rulers and living according to the rules of a kingdom that will ultimately pass away. Paul is telling the Colossians they should follow the supreme ruler and live according to the environment he is setting up.

Like the answer to the first question, though, it is not just the Colossians who should follow the way of Christ. If what Paul says is true, then all humans should follow the way of Christ, because what Christ is doing is something that will affect all humans, not just Christians.

Two questions about this way of life have just been answered. Now it is time to look at 3:9–10 for the answer to a third question: "Why are Christians told to live in *this* particular way instead of some other way?" In other words, why does the prescribed Christian life look the way it does?

Verses 9–10 say: μὴ ψεύδεσθε εἰς ἀλλήλους ἀπεκδυσάμενοι τὸν παλαιὸν ἄνθρωπον σὺν ταῖς πράξεσιν αὐτοῦ καὶ ἐνδυσάμενοι τὸν νέον τὸν ἀνακαινούμενον εἰς ἐπίγνωσιν κατ᾽ εἰκόνα τοῦ κτίσαντος αὐτόν (Do not lie to one another, since you have taken off the old man with its practices and have put on the new man, which is being renewed in knowledge after the image of its creator).

The key to understanding the meaning of vv. 9–10 is the word εἰκὼν (image). In ch. 1, Christ was described as the εἰκὼν τοῦ θεοῦ τοῦ ἀοράτου (image of the invisible God). Christ is the representation and representative of the invisible God. In other words, if one wants to know more about God, he or she needs to look at Christ. Here, in ch. 3, the Colossians are to put on the "new man" which is being renewed in knowledge κατ᾽ εἰκόνα τοῦ κτίσαντος αὐτόν (after the image of its creator). The Colossians are to reflect and represent Christ, just as Christ reflects and represents God.[36] This an-

---

36. In religions contemporary to early Christianity, symbolism via an image of a god/goddess was the norm. The way in which a particular deity was represented told the worshipper something about that deity. As an example, consider the images/statues of Artemis of Ephesia. Rogers says, "All the statues of Artemis Ephesia found by Miltner in the prytaneion have distinct iconographic features and can be interpreted individually as evoking Artemis's different functions and spheres of power. Yet we should not overlook the fact that all of the statues share certain features in common, most suggestively the pendants on Artemis's chest and bees on the sides of her skirt" (*Mysteries of Artemis*, 181). Rogers does point out that scholars argue over the meaning of the pendants, whether they were "the scrota of bulls, rows of the Hittite leather bag known

swers the third question, "Why are Christians told to live in *this* particular way instead of some other way?" Paul's answer is that Christian morality looks the way it does because Christians are meant to reflect Christ.[37] In order to reflect Christ to the world, the Colossians must act in a manner that accurately reflects his nature. As such, they need to change their way of life. Some things will need to be "put to death" (v. 5) or "put off" (v. 9), and some things will need to be "put on" (vv. 12, 14).

In several places in this letter, Paul spoke of the need to be thankful. Thanksgiving is Paul's response to the believer's question "Why would I want to live as God tells me to?" Paul would respond, "Because of all the things he has done for you through Christ." Here, Paul is answering the follow-up question "Why am I supposed to live in this particular manner?" Paul's answer is not that God wants to curtail the Colossians' fun or that God or Paul has any desire to make their lives unpleasant. Paul does not even make the argument that following God's commandments will (in the end) lead to a more pleasant life than another way of life (which may or may not be true anyway; remember, the letter says Paul is writing from prison). Rather, the argument he is making is that the Colossians have signed up for the job of revealing Christ to the world as his images.[38] The moral commands are what they are so that if the Colossians follow them, then they will be accurately reflecting Christ (and, by extension, God).

Understandably, for the Colossians to represent Christ to the world, some changes need to take place. Paul tells them they need to "put off the old man with its practices" and "put on the new man." The word he uses to

---

as 'kursa,' hilltops, or amber pendants that were attached to the original wooden statue of the goddess in the Artemision" (*Mysteries of Artemis*, 180–81). However, while there is not agreement over the meaning of the pendants, there is no disagreement that the pendants stood for something. The point is that the image of a deity is not meant to describe what that deity actually looked like, but rather the image was meant to symbolize things about the character and nature of the deity. As images of Christ, Christians are supposed to symbolize Christ and (since they are living beings) be his representatives.

37. Indirectly, the Colossians are actually reflecting God. Christ represents God, because he is the image of the invisible God. Those humans who are being renewed in the image of their creator, Christ, are representing Christ. By the transitive relation, the Colossians are actually representing God to the world. In mathematics, one might represent the transitive relation as "if A = B and B = C, then A = C" or "if A > B and B > C, then A > C." While the representation of another being is not a mathematical equation, nevertheless this illustrates the point being made. If the Colossians are representing Christ, who is representing God, then they are essentially representing God. Obviously, though, they are not representing God in the same capacity as Christ.

38. Now that they are part of the body of Christ, Christ is working in the world through them ("Christ in you"). To be in Christ (in the body of Christ/in Christ's kingdom) is to accept the responsibility of having Christ work in the world through you. This means reflecting him and representing him as his images.

describe this, ἀπεκδυσάμενοι (since you have taken off), carries with it the connotation of taking off clothes. This "does not mean simply the making of good resolutions or promises to behave differently. It is the action—itself the reflex, in human experience, of God's action in grace by the Spirit—of leaving one family, or household and moving lock, stock and barrel into another, where a different rule of life obtains."[39] In other words, the new life is not the half-hearted attempt to change one or two things and then expecting everything to be fine. Rather, "in committing themselves to Christ in baptism they had stepped completely out of one whole life, equivalent to the 'losing of life' that Jesus himself had demanded of his disciples (Mark 10:34–35). This event was the decisive starting point of all subsequent exhortation and moral seriousness."[40]

The same idea is communicated with what the Colossians are to take off/put off. The "old man" the Colossians are to put off (3:9) points to their former life when they lived in hostility towards God (1:21). Paul is speaking here of the need for the Colossians to step completely out of their old life (3:9) and step into a new one (3:10). However, this is not merely a one-time decision that the Colossians can make and then forget about. "The aorist event of the conversion-initiation past is qualified by an ongoing present: the new self is in process of being renewed (ἀνακαινούμενον)."[41] While the decision to become a Christian might take place at a single point in time, the process of renewal is ongoing, and moral effort will be required.[42]

39. N.T. Wright, *Colossians and Philemon*, 138. Maier says, "The image of putting on and putting off clothing may refer to the literal stripping and re-robing we know from later sources to be a key component to Christian baptism" (*Picturing Paul in Empire*, 66). This would have the symbolic effect of the experience Wright was talking about—leaving one's family or household for a new one where a different rule of life applies.

40. Dunn, *Epistles to the Colossians*, 220.

41. Dunn, *Epistles to the Colossians*, 221.

42. Related to this, one might ask the question, "Why doesn't God just change people instantly? Why does there need to be a process at all?" Unfortunately, the text doesn't give an answer; but between what life as a Christian is supposed to be like, in combination with what the goal of a Christian is supposed to be, there may be a possible answer. The Christian life is described as a walk, which means that it is a journey and not a single momentary change. (Even though one's future is changed in a moment, one's life is not. The goal has changed, and so the direction has changed, but a person is still standing in the same place he/she was before.) The Christian is supposed to both receive revelation and renewal, as well as to share it. It is possible that one reason a Christian is not changed instantly is that others may be able to see God better by watching the Christian become renewed day by day rather than seeing all the change happen at once. Additionally, there are other elements (like faith and patience) that are learned in the process of following God. Certainly, God helps a believer with these things (1:11); however, it may be that the process is required. Unfortunately, the text does not seem to answer this question, so there is no way to know for sure (at least from Colossians).

No doubt, Paul viewed Christ's death on the cross (1:20), as well as his own sufferings (1:24ff.), as symbolic of the life the Christian is called to lead. He likely expected these to inspire or at least guide the Colossians in a way that caused them to act differently—more selflessly. Symbols are both carriers of vital information[43] and stimulators of action.[44] Christ and Paul were both symbols to the Colossians that they (the Colossians) should view as examples of the symbols they themselves were to be to the rest of the world.

The natural result of the connection with Christ and the renewal of the individuals who are part of the body of Christ is a renewal of the Christian community. Verse 11 says, ὅπου οὐκ ἔνι Ἕλλην καὶ Ἰουδαῖος περιτομὴ καὶ ἀκροβυστία βάρβαρος Σκύθης δοῦλος ἐλεύθερος ἀλλὰ τὰ πάντα καὶ ἐν πᾶσιν Χριστός (Here, there is not Greek and Jew, circumcised and uncircumcised, barbarian, Scythian, slave, free; but Christ is all and in all).

"Verse 11 with its statements about the abolition of racial, religious, cultural and social barriers underscores this corporate aspect. The renewal refers not simply to an individual change of character but also to a corporate recreation of humanity in the creator's image."[45] If the individuals are renewed, it would only make sense that the interactions between individuals also become new. But, why is it that the renewal of the community means the breaking down of barriers between people?

The answer actually comes from the hymn in ch. 1. In 1:20, the hymn said that all things had been reconciled to God through Christ. Since all people are reconciled to God through Christ, everyone comes to God the same way. Because of the way God and humanity are reconciled, men and women of different backgrounds are now brothers and sisters. They now share

---

43. Mach says, "A symbolic message is usually of such great importance to a sender that it is repeated over and over again in order to ensure that the receiver does not miss or misunderstand it. Such a phenomenon, known as redundancy, is particularly well-known from the analysis of myth, where the same, sometimes simple but vital information is repeated through different combinations of symbols in order to make sure that it will be received and properly understood" (*Symbols*, 35–36). Paul explains how the Colossians are to live in propositional language, but in the examples of both Christ and himself, he shows them symbolically. When both methods of communication of information are considered, one can see that Paul quite frequently repeats the content about the life the Colossians should live as the representatives of God.

44. Mach says symbolic communication "has another, very practical function, namely, it stimulates action. By stirring emotions and directing them round certain ideas and values, a symbolic message can push and direct people to action in pursuit of particular goals or, as often in the political context, against other people" (*Symbols*, 36). The Colossians are to be symbols for the rest of the world in the same way that Christ and Paul are symbols for them.

45. O'Brien, *Colossians-Philemon*, 190–91.

a relationship to each other because they share a relationship to Christ. They are now all part of one body, the church, of which Christ is the head (1:18).

Now, not only should the boundaries between people groups be broken down, but the way people are to treat one another is to be transformed. Both lists of negative actions (vices) the Colossians were to put off (especially the second one) contained a heavy social element. In other words, they were not supposed to just have private "God time" and then carry on living the way they always did. Their actions towards others were supposed to be transformed as well. Whether it was the ignoring of others in favor of self-gratification (first list of sins) or the outright attack on the social structure by putting one's needs and desires above others (second list of sins), the new man is characterized by the termination of selfishness that was so much a part of the old man. The renewal of humanity involves the ending of selfishness and the breaking down of racial, religious,[46] cultural, and social barriers.[47] Not only are Christian individuals supposed to reveal God to the world through their lives, but the church as a community is to reveal God to the world through its life.

That is, strictly speaking, the end of the investigation of 3:5–11. However, before moving on, there is another question that was mentioned earlier and is worth asking, even though it is not easy to answer: "What happens to those who reject God?" Paul does not give a direct answer to the question in the letter; however, it might be possible to suggest an answer (even if it is a bit speculative) by asking the question: "What would it look like if what happens to those who reject Christ were simply the opposite of what happens to those who accept him?" Three things would characterize that state of affairs.

First, if those in Christ experience a progressively better knowledge of God (revelation), then those outside of Christ would experience a progressively worse knowledge of God. Those who are in Christ are on an upward spiral in which their knowledge of God and their actions based on that

46. That is not to say that all religions provide a path to God (Paul certainly would not agree with that). Rather, the breaking down of religious barriers refers to the background of the religion out of which one comes. The point is not that religion doesn't matter, rather that, in Christ, there is now no distinction between peoples.

47. Campbell thinks that just as there is a chiastic structure between Ἕλλην καὶ Ἰουδαῖος περιτομὴ καὶ ἀκροβυστία (Greek and Jew, circumcised, and uncircumcised), so is there also one between βάρβαρος Σκύθης δοῦλος ἐλεύθερος (barbarian, Scythian, slave, free). He says, "The author's (relatively simple) point would be that, just as baptism abolishes the broad antithesis between circumcised Jew and uncircumcised Greek, so it does for that between free barbarian and Scythian slave" ("Unravelling Colossians 3:11b," 128). However, even if he is incorrect about the chiasm, the point will still stand. Not only are the racial boundaries between Jew and Greek broken down, but so are the boundaries between slave and free. This statement prepares the audience for the statements about slavery to be made in the household code.

knowledge work together in a way that produces a progressively clearer understanding of and relationship with their creator. By contrast, those outside Christ would be on a downward spiral in which their refusal to receive knowledge of God or act on that knowledge progressively dulls their senses and causes their relationship with their creator to deteriorate.

It is as if they are shutting their eyes and putting their hands over their ears so they can neither see nor hear God. Unless God overrides their decision to reject knowledge of him, then they will see and hear less of God. By rejecting any new input from God and ignoring the input they have already received, the percentage of their thoughts that is occupied with God's input continually decreases (as they get new thoughts in from other sources). That means that their knowledge will be ever decreasing, and their actions (which are based on knowledge/beliefs) will be less and less based on what God has revealed to them. Both their thoughts and actions will be quite literally less godly. So, while the knowledge of God with which believers start will be increased in their walk toward God, the knowledge of God with which unbelievers start will be reduced in their walk away from God.

The second thing that would happen to those who reject God has to do with the image of Christ. Those who are in Christ are continually being renewed into the image of Christ. Now, if humanity is being renewed into the image of Christ, then humanity's original state (pre-fall) probably either was the image of Christ or something like it. Additionally, the final state of those humans who are in Christ will also be the image of Christ, because that is what they are being renewed into (3:9–10), and they will one day be made perfect (1:22, 28). One could say, therefore, that humanity was meant to be in the image of Christ, and some portion of humanity will be in the image of Christ again. Given that humanity was created in (or near to) the image of Christ and that Christ has been working to renew humanity into his image, it seems at least reasonable to conclude that to be in the image of Christ is to be human.

If this is true, then those who are being renewed into the image of Christ are being renewed into true humanity. Consequently, for a person to lose the image of Christ in himself or herself is for that person to lose his or her humanity. So, by following God, the believer becomes more human, and by rejecting God, the unbeliever becomes less human. Whereas the believer experiences a renewal of self, the unbeliever experiences a destruction of self—that which makes a person human progressively falls away as one lives in disobedience and hostility to God. The person in Christ will experience a complete renewal of self at the end of his or her life and become truly human as the process that began in this life is completed. The person outside

Christ will finally lose his or her last shred of humanity as the dehumanizing process that began in this life is finally completed.[48]

Finally, whereas believers will be revealed with Christ in glory, the unbelievers will receive the opposite. This is harder to picture since the statement about what happens to believers appears in only one place (3:4) and isn't described in detail. It is worth including, though, because this is something that happens at the end of the believer's journey. Presumably, unbelievers would experience the opposite of being revealed in glory—perhaps being exposed in shame in a way similar to the powers and authorities (2:15), as well as experiencing God's wrath (3:6).

It is not possible to be too dogmatic about these points, because Paul does not explicitly say anything about what happens to unbelievers in the letter. However, it seems like a reasonable picture of the alternative to believing in Christ, based on mirroring what Paul says happens to believers.

3:12-17

ἐνδύσασθε οὖν ὡς ἐκλεκτοὶ τοῦ θεοῦ ἅγιοι καὶ ἠγαπημένοι
σπλάγχνα οἰκτιρμοῦ χρηστότητα ταπεινοφροσύνην πραΰτητα
μακροθυμίαν ἀνεχόμενοι ἀλλήλων καὶ χαριζόμενοι ἑαυτοῖς
ἐάν τις πρός τινα ἔχῃ μομφήν καθὼς καὶ ὁ κύριος ἐχαρίσατο
ὑμῖν οὕτως καὶ ὑμεῖς ἐπὶ πᾶσιν δὲ τούτοις τὴν ἀγάπην ὅ
ἐστιν σύνδεσμος τῆς τελειότητος καὶ ἡ εἰρήνη τοῦ Χριστοῦ
βραβευέτω ἐν ταῖς καρδίαις ὑμῶν εἰς ἣν καὶ ἐκλήθητε ἐν
ἑνὶ σώματι καὶ εὐχάριστοι γίνεσθε ὁ λόγος τοῦ Χριστοῦ
ἐνοικείτω ἐν ὑμῖν πλουσίως ἐν πάσῃ σοφίᾳ διδάσκοντες καὶ
νουθετοῦντες ἑαυτοὺς ψαλμοῖς ὕμνοις ᾠδαῖς πνευματικαῖς ἐν
τῇ χάριτι ᾄδοντες ἐν ταῖς καρδίαις ὑμῶν τῷ θεῷ καὶ πᾶν ὅ τι
ἐὰν ποιῆτε ἐν λόγῳ ἢ ἐν ἔργῳ πάντα ἐν ὀνόματι κυρίου Ἰησοῦ
εὐχαριστοῦντες τῷ θεῷ πατρὶ δι' αὐτοῦ

Put on, then, as God's chosen ones, holy and beloved, compassionate hearts, kindness, humility, meekness, and patience, bearing with one another and, if one has a complaint against one another, forgiving each other; as the Lord has forgiven you, so you also must forgive. And above all these put on love, which binds everything together in perfect harmony. And let the peace of Christ rule in your hearts, to which indeed you were called in

---

48. In 3:5–11, Paul's main focus has been to describe what actions are part of the dehumanizing process. In the next section, he will start to talk about the actions that lead to one becoming more truly human.

one body. And be thankful. Let the word of Christ dwell in you richly, teaching and admonishing one another in all wisdom, singing psalms and hymns and spiritual songs, with thankfulness in your hearts to God. And whatever you do, in word or deed, do everything in the name of the Lord Jesus, giving thanks to God the Father through him.

As the Colossians are being told to put on certain attitudes, they are called ἐκλεκτοὶ τοῦ θεοῦ ἅγιοι καὶ ἠγαπημένοι (God's chosen ones, holy and beloved). Very probably, this is "an echo of the classic covenant text, Deut. 7:6–7 . . . . More clearly than anywhere else in Colossians it is evident that the Gentile recipients of the letter were being invited to consider themselves full participants in the people and heritage of Israel."[49] The question of the church's relationship to Israel is beyond the scope of this study, but it is important to notice the language used here. The same sort of language that was used of Israel and her intimate relationship with God is now being applied to the Colossians and the new people of God, the church. Those who are "in Christ" are chosen, holy, and beloved; and Paul is telling them that their lives should reflect that fact.

In looking at the list of things which the Colossians are to "put on," one finds that it is not a set of actions that they are to do or deeds they are to perform. Barram says:

> Many items in these catalogues are most appropriately understood as qualities or overarching characteristics. Conduct informed by the resurrection is identifiable, but it is not narrowly restricted to a set of specific actions. Resurrection behavior— regardless of the circumstances—will be devoid of wrath, rage, and other vices. At the same time, those conducting themselves in light of "the things above" will be recognizably compassionate, kind, gentle, and so forth.[50]

Paul does not view Christian morality as a mere list of rules. There is considerable freedom in *how* the Colossians are allowed to act; however, these actions are to be pointed in a specific direction—a heavenly direction. Compassion, kindness, humility, meekness . . . are expected of the Colossians. How they choose to live these out is up to them.

Nevertheless, while Christian morality is not a mere list of rules, it does actually involve actions. One cannot merely *agree* that being kind is good. One must actually *practice* being kind. And as the Colossians practice

49. Dunn, *Epistles to the Colossians*, 228.
50. Barram, *Colossians 3:1–17*, 189.

compassion, kindness, humility, and all the other things Paul tells them to put on, they will spiral upward in their knowledge of and walk with God.[51] They will continually know more about God, begin to act more like him, and in the process, increase in their knowledge of God himself.

So, by practicing the things that help one reflect God, one starts to actually *look* more like God.[52] The more one starts to look and act like God, the less one will have to simply *do* kind things in an awkward kind of way. There will be less need to think things like, "I should do something kind for someone today." Rather, as the Christian starts to look more like God, he or she will actually *become* a kind person—and so, his or her pattern of life in this world will be characterized by kindness.

In the end, the lists of things that Christians are *not to do* and the lists of things Christian are *to do* are not about following some rigid set of actions dictated to them by God or some earthly leader. These lists are meant to show people what it looks like to live for oneself and compare it with what it looks like to live as a representative of God. And because of the upward/downward spiral and what happens as a person either accepts or rejects knowledge of God and either lives or doesn't live in light of that knowledge, how one acts is who one becomes. The actions that a person performs lead to the person they will be in the future. Paul is telling them that to reflect Christ, they need to live in this particular way. Then, they will be kind, compassionate, and humble people who will be able to reflect and represent Christ in each of their unique situations. Again, it is not about making people follow some arbitrary list of rules. It is about reshaping people into the image of their creator, so they can be his representatives on earth.

Importantly, the focus of this morality is reversed from that of the Colossian philosophy. "The philosophy has a wisdom that takes its starting point from below and moves to the above by means of ascetic rigor and visionary experiences involving angels. The wisdom of the Christian gospel, he asserts, is that believers are already related to the above through union with Christ and that this relationship is to be worked out on earth."[53] The Colossians' new life is to reflect its heavenly focus through compassion, kindness, humility, meekness, patience, forgiveness, and, above all, love. This new way of life is based on something they have been given from God rather than the best way they could come up with to reach God.

---

51. For more information on what it means to spiral upward, see the discussion on 1:9–12.

52. This is what humans were always meant to do. See discussion after the end of 3:11.

53. Lincoln, "Household Code," 108.

In 3:14, Paul pays special attention to the role of ἀγάπη (agape/love). As was discussed when looking at 1:4, ἀγάπη (agape/love) was rarely used in non-biblical Greek before the second or third century AD. Christians basically took this word and gave it their own meaning. That means that the best way to understand what Paul meant by ἀγάπη (agape/love) is to look at how he uses it in the letter.

Now, Paul says that love is the characteristic which binds everything together in perfect harmony. It it often suggested that "everything" is a reference to the other virtues, which would mean that love is what binds all the virtues together. Some object to this interpretation. Instead, they think that love is the characteristic which binds together the members of the congregation as the church. However, there may be another way to look at the role of love.

What if love were considered the foundational virtue in the same way that selfishness was considered the foundational vice? Given that all of the other vices (such as greed and sexual sins) flow from or are manifestations of selfishness, there may be something to this. What would be the opposite of selfishness if not love?[54] Instead of putting oneself above others, love demonstrates that a person considers others to be more important than himself or herself. All the other virtues in these verses point in the same direction. To be compassionate, kind, humble, meek, patient, or forgiving—all result in a denial of self and a focus on others. Love is the most important virtue of all of them. It is the foundation of all these other virtues, and it is what holds them all together.[55]

This brings the hierarchy of importance from 3:5–11 to a final form. Previously, it was 1) Christ and 2) self/others. From the discussion of the vices, it was only possible to bring others up to the same level as oneself. It was only possible to say that one should act in a neutral way towards them, since all that Paul had said by that point was that one should abstain from doing anything bad to them. However, with the discussion of virtues, that has changed. To be kind, for example, involves actually doing something positive for other people instead of merely leaving them alone. Paul is telling the Colossians to place a higher level of importance on others than on

54. Remember, selfishness is essentially idolatry, because it places oneself at the center of the universe instead of Christ, who actually belongs there.

55. Du Toit says, "It speaks volumes for the quality of early Christian ethics that, following Jesus and the Jesus tradition, it did not create a new code of law. Instead, as the decisive criterion for ethical behavior, a disposition such as love was singled out, to touch the innermost nerve of human existence and flow from the heart in response to God's love . . . going radically against the grain of the self-assertive σάρξ [flesh]" ("Shaping a Christian Lifestyle," 176).

oneself. The final form of the hierarchy of importance, then, is 1) Christ, 2) others, and 3) self.

All these virtues are meant to give Paul's audience a picture of what it looks like to live out this hierarchy. The Colossians are not merely to leave others alone and go on about their own lives. Rather, the Colossians are to actually *act* selflessly. They are to step out of their normal pattern of life and/or do things that are against what they might want to do as individuals in order to do good for others. The ἀγάπη (agape/love) Paul is telling them to have here is essentially selflessness. However, it is not a passive selflessness in which one leaves everyone else alone. Rather, ἀγάπη (agape/love) is an active selflessness in which one lives in service of others. Love/acting selflessly is the central element in the virtuous life of a Christian. The other virtues are examples that spell out in more concrete terms what acting selflessly should look like.

The end result of this is that Christian morals are centered on a single question: "Are one's actions focused on self or others?" Do the Colossians put themselves at the center of the universe, or do they have their hierarchy in the proper order: 1) Christ, 2) others, and 3) self? Paul's morals follow directly from his theology. Christ is in the first place, because of who he is. Others are to be placed before self, because this is what it takes for the Christian to reflect Christ. Christ placed others before himself (remember, he died for them while they were actively hostile to him, 1:21–22), so living like Christ means putting others above self. One's beliefs show up in how one lives, and how one lives reflects what one believes.

To return to the question of love as the binding element, it is probably not necessary to make too fine a separation between binding together the virtues and binding together the members of the church. Perhaps more than one meaning was intended. Love/selflessness is the chief moral virtue and all the other virtues (compassion, kindness, forgiveness, and so forth) are based on putting others before oneself. And, if the Colossians live by these virtues, the result will be peace (v. 15).

This "peace" that Paul talks about in v. 15 is probably not the "inward, individual peace of mind which accompanies humble, confident trust in God's love, but a peace which characterizes the community, the 'body,' as a whole."[56] Paul is probably referring to "the concept of *shalom*, well-being and wholeness. Nothing should be allowed to interfere with the well-being of the body of Christ. Peace must be the ruling principle. In an antagonistic culture where rivalry and competition for honor was a part of everyday

---

56. N.T. Wright, *Colossians and Philemon*, 143.

life, the audience must be reminded that they are called to peace."[57] If the Colossians' lives are ruled by love, by doing the best they could for the other person instead of themselves, then peace should rule the community.

This new community, marked by peace among its members, is to be centered around the word and wisdom of Christ (v. 16). Importantly, the means by which the Colossians are to teach and admonish one another in all wisdom is through the use of psalms, hymns, and spiritual songs. How convenient is it that the letter to the Colossians contains a hymn?[58] As if Paul is leading by example, the hymn forms the foundation of theological thought, which in turn forms the foundation for ethical action. So, it should be no surprise that in the middle of Paul's ethical commands, one finds a command to go back to the hymn. Paul is reminding the Colossians that their actions should be based on their theology. Beliefs imply actions; Christian theology implies Christian living.

Everything in the theology of the letter is centered around the person and work of Christ. Interestingly, the next part of v. 16, the verb ἐνοικείτω (let dwell), actually highlights the importance of Christ. "As the rabbis later pointed out, he who dwells in a house is the master of the house, not just a passing guest."[59] Here, Paul is telling the Colossians to let Christ, who is supreme, reign in their lives. They should let him dwell among them as the master of the house, not simply as a guest who is passing through. He is telling them that if they truly believe Christ is who he has been described as in this letter, then they should act on those beliefs. "Let him rule your house."[60]

Also, there is almost certainly a strong echo here of 1:28, the point of which is to present everyone mature in Christ.[61] Furthermore, because the Colossians are to teach and admonish *one another*, there is a communal aspect here, whereby not only are the Colossians to let Christ dwell as master among them, but they are to build up one another through the message that

57. Witherington and Wessels, "Do Everything," 314.

58. As mentioned in the investigation of the hymn, hymns were a lot like creeds. They were not primarily songs (as one might think of modern hymns); rather, they were densely packed, highly structured pieces of theological material. Because of that, hymns are ideal for teaching and admonishing one another (v. 16). Additionally, it was discussed there that there have been many attempts to separate psalms, hymns, and spiritual songs into distinct categories, but there has not been agreement among scholars on what those categories might look like. It is probably best to simply take all three together as one large category.

59. Dunn, *Epistles to the Colossians*, 236.

60. This also points the reader to the household code, which is coming up in two verses.

61. Dunn, *Epistles to the Colossians*, 237; Moo, *Letters to the Colossians*, 289; Sumney, *Colossians*, 224; and Thompson, *Colossians and Philemon*, 86.

proclaims Christ. In Paul's view, the Colossians will not magically become good representations of Christ or somehow be made perfect the instant they become Christians. The end is certain, but that does not mean it has happened yet. The Colossians have a lot of growing to do before they actually look like images of Christ. This is why Paul exhorts them to let the word Christ dwell among them and to teach and admonish one another.

Finally, this worship should be contrasted with the worship of those who follow the alternate philosophy, because the two worldviews couldn't be more different. "It is the worship addressed to God with grateful hearts, from a community bound together by love and shaped by Christ's peace, and not the 'angelic worship' that prides itself on visions of the heavenly realm, which God desires."[62] The philosophers in Colossae were performing their worship for something they might receive (such as a heavenly vision) and were doing it out of pride ("puffed up without reason by their minds of flesh," 2:18).[63] Paul tells the Colossians, that worship is to be to God, and as a result it will be centered on him rather than on them.[64] This focus on putting God at the center of one's worship and letting Christ dwell as master among the Colossian congregation leads directly into the sort of ethical summary statement one finds in the next verse.

Verse 17 summarizes perhaps the most important point to remember when considering whether a particular action is in line with Christian ethical teaching or not: "And whatever you do in word or deed, do everything in the name of the Lord Jesus, giving thanks to God the Father through him." All of the Colossians' actions are to be done in the name of the Lord Jesus; they are not to be done in their own names or for their own purposes. "Whatever you do in word or deed" is more about walking with Christ than it is about following rules. The lists which Paul presents to the Colossians are not, strictly speaking, rules. Rather, they describe how to be good representatives of Christ and explain what should be going on in their hearts as they live their lives. Paul tells them to think about each of their actions and ask, "Am I doing it for Christ, or for myself?"

This verse is important for the reader of Colossians to keep in mind, because it will be critical for understanding the verses to follow. "Colossians

---

62. Thompson, *Colossians and Philemon*, 87.

63. Sumney also points out that the teaching and admonition of one another was to be undertaken by the whole congregation and not just a select few. "This suggests a mutuality rather than a strict hierarchical structure within the church. There is no one group responsible for teaching, warning, and encouraging; instead, all have the commission to engage in these tasks" (*Colossians*, 224).

64. Sumney says, "Singing in worship has an important communal function, but its ultimate goal is to honor God" (*Colossians*, 227).

3:1–17, especially as it culminates in Col 3:17, frames the ensuing discussion by emphasizing not the specific conduct itself ('whatever you do') but the manner and spirit in which the conduct is performed ('in word or deed, do everything in the name of the Lord Jesus')."[65] This verse will be important for understanding the household code in 3:18–4:1, because the idea of the spirit behind a person's actions impacts the meaning of those verses.

The household code in 3:18–4:1 is a section that requires a lot of thought to understand. It will be treated in its own chapter and, therefore, temporarily skipped. Furthermore, as that chapter will make clear, the household code is an insertion into the letter, and it functions like an excursus in Paul's thought.[66] Because of this, one will find that the themes from 3:1–17 continue directly into 4:2–6. That means that, thematically, 4:2 follows 3:17. That is why the next section begins with 4:2 and the household code has been skipped. The entire next chapter will be spent looking at the code in detail.

4:2–6

τῇ προσευχῇ προσκαρτερεῖτε γρηγοροῦντες ἐν αὐτῇ ἐν εὐχαριστίᾳ προσευχόμενοι ἅμα καὶ περὶ ἡμῶν ἵνα ὁ θεὸς ἀνοίξῃ ἡμῖν θύραν τοῦ λόγου λαλῆσαι τὸ μυστήριον τοῦ Χριστοῦ δι' ὃ καὶ δέδεμαι ἵνα φανερώσω αὐτὸ ὡς δεῖ με λαλῆσαι ἐν σοφίᾳ περιπατεῖτε πρὸς τοὺς ἔξω τὸν καιρὸν ἐξαγοραζόμενοι ὁ λόγος ὑμῶν πάντοτε ἐν χάριτι ἅλατι ἠρτυμένος εἰδέναι πῶς δεῖ ὑμᾶς ἑνὶ ἑκάστῳ ἀποκρίνεσθαι

Continue steadfastly in prayer, being watchful in it with thanksgiving. At the same time, pray also for us, that God may open to us a door for the word, to declare the mystery of Christ, on account of which I am in prison, that I may make it clear, which is how I ought to speak. Walk in wisdom toward outsiders, making the best use of the time. Let your speech always be gracious, seasoned with salt, so that you may know how to answer each person.

The theme of prayer makes a return in 4:2–3. Paul began the letter by praying for the Colossians (1:3, 9). In 4:2, Paul tells the Colossians to continue in prayer, and in 4:3, he tells them to pray for him and his companions

---

65. Henderson, "Taking Liberties," 428.

66. The section itself functions like an excursus in that it is an insertion into the flow of thought that could be deleted, and no one reading the letter for the first time would notice. However, the content of the section functions like a case study for everything Paul has been saying about the Christian life. Again, that will be discussed in the next chapter.

as well. The content of the prayers for Paul is for the success of his mission—to declare the mystery of Christ. When the prayer from ch. 1 is placed next to this one, one finds two things that make up the prayers made by and for Paul: spiritual growth and Christian mission. To grow in the knowledge of God, walk more closely with God, and accomplish God's work, one is going to need God's help.

At the end of v. 2, thanksgiving makes a reappearance, only this time it is paired with watchfulness. Here, thankfulness provides "an important balance to the call for watchfulness: they are to keep alert, not in a spirit of fear or anxiety, but with the confidence and assurance that their resources (in Christ) are more than equal to the potential challenges."[67] At the same time that they are to be alert, the Colossians are to remember what Christ has done for them. Throughout this letter, thankfulness has been described as the reason believers live the life they do. The Colossians should want to work for Christ and engage in mission for him, because of what he has done for them. Here, Paul speaks to them of mission, which will be the theme for the rest of the section.

The spreading of the gospel is emphasized in 4:3, "that God may open to us a door for the word." What is interesting is that this is the first place in the letter that Paul really looks at how the Colossians are to apply their faith toward outsiders. Throughout the rest of the letter, the mention of non-Christians has been limited to the Colossians' past life as unbelievers (which was evil and needed to be put to death) and the errors of the philosophers (who taught according to the traditions of men and whose teaching should be rejected). Here, however, the tone is different.

Before looking at how Paul expects the Colossians to act towards non-Christians, it is worth noticing where his thoughts on this subject occur in the letter. For three full chapters, Paul has been speaking to the Colossians about correct theology and proper living. Now, in the last five verses of the letter body, he turns to the subject of interaction with outsiders. There is probably an implication that before one attempts to engage in missions and reach those on the outside for Christ, one needs to make sure one is actually able to do so. Christians are to be representatives of Christ to the outside world. That means that, in order to represent Christ accurately, the Christian must actually look like Christ. That means both communicating truth *and* living in a manner that reflects Christ's characteristics.

The focus of the last two verses in this section is on *how* to communicate truth. Paul tells them to "walk in wisdom toward outsiders." "The exhortation to 'walk in wisdom' [4:5] (ἐν σοφίᾳ περιπατεῖτε) is an effective

---

67. Dunn, *Epistles to the Colossians*, 262.

summary of one of the main emphases of the letter, forming an *inclusio* with both 1:9–10 (ἐν πάσῃ σοφίᾳ . . . περιπατῆσαι) [in all wisdom . . . walk] and 2:6–7 (ἐν αὐτῷ περιπατεῖτε) [walk in him], with the theme of wisdom prominent also in 1:28; 2:3, 23; and 3:16. As in 1:28 and 2:3 in particular, the wisdom is related to the revelation of the mystery. It is just the same wisdom, with its double sense of God-given but also pragmatic wisdom, which should be expressed in all their dealings with outsiders."[68] Additionally, "[t]he wisdom which the apostle sets forth is fundamentally different from that propounded by the false teachers. The latter is but an empty show of wisdom (2:23). Here 'wisdom,' which has to do with a knowledge of God's will (1:9) and walking worthily of the Lord (1:10), is essentially practical and realistic."[69]

The phrase "walk in wisdom" combines the various uses of wisdom in the letter into a single, statement. Christians are to walk in wisdom toward outsiders (both theologically/intellectually and practically/morally), making the most of every opportunity.[70] "Here the injunction to 'redeem the time' seems to have special application to their duty to unbelieving neighbors. Paul wishes to emphasize that, while he has an exceptional opportunity of witness-bearing at the heart of the [Roman] empire, each Christian has a special opportunity for witness and should make the most of it while it lasts."[71]

Verse 6 speaks to the manner in which the Colossians should interact with their non-Christian neighbors. "Here the last term certainly echoes the normal usage of χάρις [grace] in relation to speech, that is, 'graciousness, attractiveness,' that which delights and charms, though no Paulinist would intend such a usage to be independent of the χάρις [grace] manifested in Christ and fundamental to the Pauline gospel."[72] This point is reemphasized by the phrase "seasoned with salt." There is disagreement on the exact background of this phrase,[73] but the basic meaning includes such ideas as

68. Dunn, *Epistles to the Colossians*, 265.

69. O'Brien, *Colossians-Philemon*, 241.

70. O'Brien says, "Once again the participle has been regarded as having the force of an imperative; on the other hand, it is quite natural to take the participle as specifying the means by which the command for the readers to conduct themselves wisely is to be carried out, that is, by 'snapping up every opportunity that comes'" (*Colossians-Philemon*, 241).

71. Bruce, *Epistles to the Colossians*, 174.

72. Dunn, *Epistles to the Colossians*, 266.

73. O'Brien says, "This could be taken to mean 'witty' since salt had this significance in pagan usage or 'winsome,' so that the Colossians' speaking was to exercise a wholesome influence in conversation which might otherwise become debased or crude. However, attention has been drawn to rabbinic parallels for a metaphorical use of salt

being witty and interesting, as well as appropriate to both the person and the time. "It remains true that the reputation of the gospel is bound up with the behavior of those who claim to have experienced its saving power. People who do not read the Bible for themselves or listen to the preaching of the word of God can see the lives of those who do, and can form their judgment accordingly. Let Christians make full use, then, of the present season of opportunity."[74]

Here, the two themes of missions and walking in wisdom come together. "In the end, the letter's thrust is not inward and protective but outward and interactive. The writer encourages the community to mediate the gospel claims through gracious speech (Col 4:6), thus bearing the distinctive mark of their faith."[75] The church is God's agent of change here on earth with the mission to reach the world—just as Paul is doing. This cannot be done without walking in wisdom. Change in others will not occur unless it occurs in oneself first.[76] Furthermore, the point in telling the Colossians to walk in wisdom is not simply so that they will be better people themselves; the point is to be a witness to others. To give revelation of God to others and to take part in the renewal of the world, the Colossians must first experience both revelation and renewal themselves; only then can they move outward.

SIGNIFICANCE

Paul connects Christian theology to the Christian life in a way that reveals a lot about his thinking. To begin with, he heavily uses a theme here that has been present throughout the letter up to this point: belief implies action. *Thinking* is not enough; one must also *do*. The pattern of life that Christians are to live is based directly on the fact that Christ is supreme and that they are to reflect his character in their actions.

---

as wisdom, while in Hellenistic contexts as well as rabbinic ones salt could describe the appropriate word used in speech. Here, Paul's statement has particular reference to Christians responding with the right word to those who ask questions of the community, perhaps in connection with their beliefs and behavior. So not only must the addressees' conversation be opportune as regards the time; it must also be appropriate as regards the person. They are, in the words of Peter, 'always [to] be prepared to give an answer to everyone who asks you to give the reason for the hope that you have' (1 Peter 3:15)" (*Colossians-Philemon*, 243).

74. Bruce, *Epistles to the Colossians*," 174.

75. Henderson, "Taking Liberties," 429.

76. This is much like Jesus' command to remove the log from your own eye before trying to remove the speck from your brother's eye.

Something else that Paul makes clear is that the Christian life is not completed in a single act. It is a process of renewal that begins at a point in time, but it is something that needs to be pursued throughout a person's life and will require moral effort. Paul's commands to the Colossians to "*seek the things above*" and "*set your minds* on the things above" demonstrate that this process is active and not passive. There would be no need to "seek" or "set" if Christ were going to do the work for them, without the Colossians' involvement. They are to focus on living for the world above and actively pursue a life that reflects that world.

The actual commands that Paul gives are basically descriptions of the actions and attitudes that should or should not characterize the Christian life. He does not give them a rigid list of rules they have to follow. Rather, he points back to the supremacy of Christ by telling them that the path that puts themselves first is idolatry (3:5). What they should do instead is let Christ rule in their hearts (3:15) and dwell in them richly (3:16). How they live their lives (actions) demonstrates what they think about who really belongs at the center of their universe (beliefs). The wrong way to live is to place oneself above Christ and everyone else—thereby becoming one's own idol.

The central distinction between the virtues and vices is the issue of the self. Just as the chief vice is selfishness (idolatry of self), the chief virtue is selflessness (or love). There is an elegance and a simplicity to Paul's view on ethics that allows for both guidance of the Colossians' actions and a freedom that avoids the pitfall of legalism. This is best seen in how Paul reduces a wide spectrum of different actions and attitudes to either selflessness or selfishness—love or not love. This is very simple to remember and is the very antithesis to a cumbersome list of rules. Paul is essentially telling the Colossians to do unto others as you would have them do unto you. You would want people to be kind and compassionate to you, and you would not want them to take advantage of you for their personal gain. Therefore, go and do likewise. Living by this simple standard will result in peace among their community which will be noticed by those outside.

This lifestyle that Paul is promoting comes as a result of dying and rising with Christ. The Christian life is a walk or journey in which believers are more closely conformed to Christ's image. It is part of their process of renewal, part of their upward spiral,[77] so that one day they may be presented holy, blameless, and above reproach.

Another way to look at Christian morality is to ask what God wants of man. In Paul's view, God is not asking for man to obey a strict moral code. If this were the case, the letter would look different. Rather, in Paul's view,

---

77. For more on the upward spiral, see the discussion on 1:9–12.

God's desire for man is much more like the simple command of Jesus in the gospels, "Follow me." The life one lives is not payment either to get into heaven or to receive good things in this world. Good things may or may not even happen in this world (consider Paul's suffering). Rather, the reward is that the ones who follow Christ receive greater revelation of God, are more greatly renewed in the image of their creator,[78] and have the opportunity to spread both revelation and renewal to the rest of the world.

There is one additional implication of this view of morality that may not be immediately obvious. If the Colossians are going to put Christ at the center of their universe and displace themselves from that position, they will no longer be in charge of their own lives. From the point that they start following Christ, they will be expected to actually follow Christ—and not just do whatever they want.

Now, following Christ does not mean that Christians no longer have to make decisions. This is not a passive process, and the presence of moral exhortation should make that clear. It also does not mean that Christians will be able to avoid thinking through their choices (even a cursory look at the ethical section makes it clear that this is not an exhaustive list of rules). What it does mean is that they can no longer be the leaders of their own lives. One cannot follow Christ and still be the leader; to follow Christ is to become a follower. For the Colossians to try to still chart their own paths is to try to still be in control, i.e., to continue to put themselves at the center of the universe by doing things the way they want to. Paul is telling them that, as Christians, they must put Christ at the center and follow where he leads them and live the lives that he expects. This is the only way they will actually be able to represent Christ (3:9–10). Otherwise, they will just be representing themselves.

In practical terms, this means that when one of the Colossian believers wants to do a particular thing, he or she would no longer be allowed to do it if it were something contrary to what Christ wants.[79] The believer must ask, "What does Christ want me to do?" No doubt Paul would respond that they should "be filled with the knowledge of his will in all spiritual wisdom and

78. There are two options for what this could mean: 1) a person could become more "holy, blameless, and without reproach" than others during this life, but ultimately be equalized out to the same level as everyone else in the next life; 2) a person could reflect God to a greater degree than others will ever be able to (sort of like how Christ reflects God more than other humans can, although these humans would reflect God to a lesser extent than Christ). Which of these two options is not discussed in this letter; however, those who spiral up further in this life will reflect Christ more now. Whether their ultimate destiny is the same or different than others is a separate issue.

79. The opposite is also true. Christ might tell them to do something even if they previously had no plans to the contrary. The direction from Christ could be either positive (do a thing) or negative (don't do a thing).

understanding, so as to walk in a manner worthy of the Lord, fully pleasing to him, bearing fruit in every good work and increasing in the knowledge of God" (1:9–10). Putting Christ at the center of one's life means that the Colossians must pursue knowing him and walking in his path. They must be focused, therefore, on how Christ would want them to live, rather than on how they want to live. More so than any list of rules, Paul's view of the Christian life is founded on pursuing knowledge of Christ, following his leading, and treating others as one would want to be treated oneself.

The ethics presented in this letter are not merely a way of getting along with one's neighbor in hopes of having a stable society. The ethics here are about living a Christ-like life and acting as his images/representatives to the world. Peace in the community will result, but the ethics are not tailored to produce peace, as much as peace is the byproduct of the members of the Christian community living lives as true humans.

In the hymn, Christ was said to be the beginner of a new humanity.[80] The two things necessary to make this happen are revelation and renewal. Individuals must first receive revelation and then act on it. The previous chapters have spent more time discussing revelation; this chapter emphasizes renewal and what this looks like in an individual's life. Those who have died with Christ and been raised with him have begun this process. They are being renewed in the image of their creator, Christ. They are being renewed as part of the new humanity Christ began in the church.

As Paul explains in the last section, Christians are not just to receive revelation and renewal; they are to share them. As representatives of Christ, they are to perform the work of Christ in this world. While Christ will ultimately reconcile the world and people will no longer have a choice whether they will put Christ first or not, Christ calls humans to begin to live like that now. He is renewing those who are willing now, and he is using Christians as his agents on earth to help him in that task. However, before a person can share something with others, he or she must first possess it. Christians must first receive revelation and begin the renewal process before they can live as examples and share what they have been given with others.

---

80. This is based on Christ being the founder of the church and the fact that those in the church are being renewed into true humans.

12

The Household Code (3:18–4:1)

INTRODUCTION

In looking at the section on the Christian life, 3:18–4:1 was temporarily skipped both because investigation into its meaning will not be a brief endeavor and because it is a stand-alone unit. However, the household code is no mere digression.[1] Rather, "Col 3:18–4:1 functions as a practical application of the verse that it follows: 'Whatever you do, in word or deed, do everything in the name of the Lord Jesus' (Col 3:17)."[2] This section explains how the Christian life that Paul has been talking about in 3:1–17 applies to a real-life situation. It functions therefore as a sort of case study on the application of Christian ethics. So, what does that actually look like?

There are two main parts to 3:17, and they correspond to the two main issues to investigate in the code. "Whatever you do in word or deed" is about

1. Witherington and Wessels say, "For good reasons scholars have often suggested that 3:18–4:1 is a pre-set piece which has been inserted into its present context. Of course what some scholars fail to take into account is that this is precisely how a rhetorical digression is meant to work. It is a self contained unit after which the author returns to the subject he left behind and the outset of the digression" ("Do Everything," 315). Were this section not in the letter, 4:2 would have followed 3:17, and no one might have noticed the absence of the code.

2. Henderson, "Taking Liberties," 421, and O'Brien, *Colossians-Philemon*, 233.

how one lives one's life—all the things that one actually says and does. "Do everything in the name of the Lord Jesus" is about the motivation behind what one says and does—*why* one lives in this particular way.

Understanding the household code would probably not have been difficult for the Colossians. Living it might very well have been difficult, but understanding it probably would not have been. After all, it was directed to them in their own situation. Understanding what the code means and how it should be interpreted is far more complicated for a modern audience. One reason for this is because ancient households functioned much differently than modern households. For example, it is not nearly as common today for households to include slaves. And yet, the largest part of the household code in Colossians is directed to slaves.

The other reason it is so difficult for modern people to understand something like the household code is because many things in it are objectionable to them. In addition to slavery, there is also the way women are treated. Wives are told to submit to their husbands, which makes them sound inferior and unequal to men. It is really hard for modern people to get past their revulsion at these ideas long enough to examine the text in-depth. In church, it is extremely common to simply skip these passages, because no one knows what to do with them. Or, if they are addressed, it is often very briefly and includes the caveat, "That is how things were back then. But they're (thankfully) different now."

In order for modern readers of Colossians to understand what Paul was trying to do with this letter, there will need to be a lot of focus on the ancient context. What did the ancient world in general think about issue X? How are Paul's views about X the same? How are his views about X different? This will help make it possible to look at Paul's motivation. Why did he command the particular things that he commanded? What was he trying to accomplish?

As the last chapter described, the Colossians are in a difficult situation. They live in this world that has one pattern of life. Yet, they are headed for a heavenly world that has a very different pattern of life. The one world elevates self above everyone else, and members of this world do whatever they want. The other world elevates Christ above everyone else and expects its members to act selflessly towards others. In 3:5–17, Paul gave the Colossians some very general guidelines, but what does this actually look like in a real-life situation?

How are the Colossians to navigate a world that operates so differently? If they live too differently, then they're not really living in the world at all. They would essentially be forming their own communities and living apart from everyone else. They would really just be living *near* everyone else rather than *in* and *among* them. How would they be images of Christ then? On the other hand, if they live like everyone else, then they're no different from them. So, what's the point? They wouldn't be representing Christ at all then.[3]

So, how does a person live in and among people who live in a completely different way? How does a person act the same enough to be part of the group, and yet be different enough to point upwards—in a heavenly direction? This is a very difficult situation to navigate, and that is the exact situation the household code addresses. This is not merely a section with some antiquated and/or immoral[4] ideas that needs to be skipped over or explained away. Rather, this is one of the greatest theologians of all time showing a specific group of people how to live in the world but be better than the world, so that they can accomplish the work of God. This section should be studied in depth and with great care.

So, here is what the code actually looks like. Structurally, the household code consists of nine verses divided into commands directed to three reciprocal pairs of people: wives and husbands, children and parents, and slaves and masters, with the bulk of the material focused on the commands to slaves. The lesser party is addressed first in each of the pairs, which would have been unusual in the ancient world.[5] While there are many similarities to contemporaneous ideas on household management, some parts are very different.

With the household code, Paul was not creating a household morality from scratch. Rather, he was entering into a discussion that was centuries old. A list of the duties of each member of the household, like the one in Colossians, reflected "the tendency to reduce more extended discussions of common moral topics to lists which are evocative of such standard teaching."[6] Paul's unique take on the roles of members of the household shows his opinion of contemporary moral thought in relation to the household, as well as how Christians should live in a world that operates according to that thought.

---

3. And they wouldn't be on the path towards renewal themselves, either.

4. Such as the command for slaves to obey their masters.

5. It was unusual not only in that the lesser parties were addressed first, but that they were addressed at all. There will be more on this later.

6. Malherbe, *Moral Exhortation*, 135.

ANCIENT CONTEXT

It is important to understand that the concept of a household code was not a Christian invention. This code was a Christian comment on a discussion that had existed for some time in the ancient world. Lincoln says the following:

> [The household code] needs to be situated in the broader context of the discussion of household management in the ancient world that goes all the way back to the classical Greek philosophers. This broader tradition, which also treats husband-wife, parent-child and master-slave relationships and focuses on authority and subordination within the relationships, connects the topic of the household to the larger topic of the state and derives from the classical Greek philosophers (cf. Plato, Leges 3.690 A-D; 6.791E—7.824C; Aristotle, Pol. 1.1253b. 1259a). All the elements of their discussion are continued down into the later Roman period, and Philo (Hyp. 7.1–9) and Josephus (Apion 2.190–219) also adapted Aristotle's outline of household subordination in their interpretation and recommendation of Mosaic law.[7]

In order to make sense of Paul's thoughts on the household,[8] it is necessary first to understand some general thoughts concerning the household order in the ancient world. This tradition of organizing the household goes back at least as far as Aristotle, who classified the house into the same three pairs seen in Colossians: master and slave, husband and wife, father and children. Aristotle says:

> Now, it is obvious that the same principle applies generally, and therefore almost all things rule and are ruled according to nature. But the kind of rule differs; the freeman rules over the slave after another manner from that in which the male rules over the female, or the man over the child; although the parts of the soul are present in all of them, they are present in different degrees.

7. Lincoln, "Household Code," 100. Hull adds other possible parallels to those mentioned by Lincoln, which include Dionysius of Halicarnassus, *Roman Antiquities* 2.24:3–2.27.2; Seneca, *Epistle* 94:1; and Philo, *On the Decalogue* 165–7 ("Family of Flesh," 23–24).

8. Like the hymn in Colossians 1, the household code represents material inserted into the letter. Whether Paul composed the code, modified it, or simply included it as written is another question. However, by including it in the letter without commentary on any ways he thought it should be changed, he shows that he agrees with its content. Therefore, since he puts his stamp of approval on it by including it in the letter, the code will be considered as Paul's thought, even if it might not have originated from him.

> For the slave has no deliberative faculty at all; the woman has, but it is without authority, and the child has, but it is immature.[9]

Hull says that, in Aristotle's thought, "It is clear that for some to be ruled and others to be rulers is not simply an arbitrary decision or a matter of political convenience, but a determination by nature."[10] Furthermore, the idea of organizing the household was tied tightly to the organizing of society. Henderson says that for the ancient writer, "the household serves as a microcosm of society, and its members are encouraged to practice the relational standards established by the broader world within which they live."[11] Hull summarizes the general situation in the ancient world as follows:

> With certain local and temporal qualifications, in the first-century world of early Christianity, gender roles and concepts were roughly the same among Greeks, Romans, and Jews. Men were expected to be the guardians, women the guarded; men politically powerful, women powerful within the house; men well educated, women less well educated . . . . A person's social status (legal class, citizenship, wealth, pedigree) could affect the generalizations described above, but the idea that women were the equals of men would simply not have been entertained in the ancient world.[12]

The question is then how does this compare to the views presented in Colossians, and what, if any, changes to the household order did Paul make?

3:18–19 (WIVES AND HUSBANDS)

> αἱ γυναῖκες ὑποτάσσεσθε τοῖς ἀνδράσιν ὡς ἀνῆκεν ἐν κυρίῳ οἱ ἄνδρες ἀγαπᾶτε τὰς γυναῖκας καὶ μὴ πικραίνεσθε πρὸς αὐτάς

> Wives, submit to your husbands, as is fitting in the Lord. Husbands, love your wives, and do not be harsh with them.

The household code begins in 3:18 with the command for wives to ὑποτάσσεσθε (submit) to their husbands. Because there was such interest

---

9. Aristotle, *Politics* 1260a 8–14, in McKeon, ed., *Basic Works of Aristotle*, 1144.

10. Hull, "Family of Flesh," 24.

11. Henderson, "Taking Liberties," 423.

12. Hull, "Family of Flesh," 25. For a comparison of women's rights in the various cultures across the Mediterranean, see Witherington, *Women and the Genesis of Christianity*, 3–26.

in the ancient world on the proper ordering of the household,[13] it should come as no surprise that the word ὑποτάσσω (submit) was not *just* a word. It pointed toward a legal reality. ὑποτάσσω (submit)

> reflects the legal state of affairs, under Roman law at least, whereby the paterfamilias[14] had absolute power over the other members of the family. And while there were variations in Greek and Jewish law, the basic fact held true throughout the Mediterranean world that the household was essentially a patriarchal institution, with other members of the household subject to the authority of its male head.[15]

Because certain aspects of household management were so common in the world in which Paul and the Colossians lived, the casual (ancient) reader of Colossians would have seen the command for wives to ὑποτάσσω (submit) to their husbands and thought nothing of it. The assumption would have been simply that Paul's command was right in line with the rest of the Mediterranean world, that husbands are the rulers of the households and wives are to submit to them. Whether that is what Paul meant or not will be addressed shortly. But, the world in which Paul and the Colossians lived was in general agreement that husbands were in charge of the household, and their wives should submit to them.

Christian theology, however, has something important to say about the word ὑποτάσσω (submit). Witherington and Wessels say:

> Since this verb is also used of Christ's relationship to God the Father (1 Cor 15:28), and of believers to each other (Eph 5:21) it surely does not imply the ontological inferiority[16] of

---

13. Of course, what exactly makes a marriage or a family is a very hot topic today. So, it seems that even modern people are interested in the proper ordering of a household.

14. The paterfamilias is the male head of the household.

15. Dunn, *Epistles to the Colossians*, 247. Dunn also points out that, "It is important to note that it is wives and not women generally who are in view. Women who were single, widowed, or divorced and of independent means could evidently function as heads of their own households, as in the case of Lydia (Acts 16:14–15), Phoebe, the first named 'deacon' in Christian history and patron of the church at Cenchreae (Rom 16:1–2), Chloe (1 Cor. 1:11), and presumably Nympha in Colossae itself. The concern here is primarily for the household unit, with the implication that for Christians, too, its good ordering was fundamental to well-ordered human and social relationships. That wives are addressed first is presumably also a recognition that their relationship to their husbands was the linchpin of a stable and effective household" (*Christology*, 246–47).

16. Ontological inferiority means that one party is *actually* inferior to another. The contrast to this would be ontological equality in which both parties are *actually* equal to one another. In the latter case, it would be possible for one party to submit to another

the submitter to the one submitted to. Rather, it has to do with the relationship between two persons. It may also in fact have more to do with following the example of Christ who humbled himself and took a lower place. In other words, in a Christian context the verb has to do with humility and service as modeled by Christ who even served the lost as well as believers.[17]

The examples of Christ submitting to the Father and believers submitting to each others show that it is possible within early Christian thought for one party to submit to another without being inferior. In early Christian thought, then, it was at least possible for submission to be solely something one did for a purpose. Submission did not have to have anything to do with one's value, and it did not necessarily imply that the one who submitted was inferior to the one who did not. Whether Colossians points towards the equality of men and women or not is another question. But, it was at least possible in early Christian thought for one party to submit to another without being inferior.

Now, in Colossae (as well as the rest of the ancient world), women did not have the option to choose whether to submit themselves to their husbands or not. So, it cannot be said that their submissive position is a voluntary one. However, while that does complicate the issue somewhat, really it just adds another layer to the question. It doesn't change the core issue. The core issue is "How should a husband and wife relate to each other?" The additional layer is "How should a husband and wife relate to each other *given the cultural context in which they live?*"[18]

To start working towards answers to these questions, additional questions need to be asked. How does Paul's formulation of the relationship between the husband and wife compare to his contemporaries? Was Paul simply conforming to the standard thought of the ancient Mediterraneans? Did he believe something entirely different? Or, was his view more nuanced? Answering those questions will take two steps: 1) discovering what is unique about Paul's view and 2) thinking about what Paul's view would have looked like in practice. This will help paint a picture of Paul's view of marriage (or at least what can be discovered from this letter).

---

in order to achieve some goal. This would have the effect of the two parties working together yet still being equal. This is what Christian theology has traditionally said of Christ's relationship to God the Father. Christ has voluntarily submitted himself to God the Father in order to accomplish God's plan for humanity; however, he is still ontologically equal (actually equal) to the Father.

17. Witherington and Wessels, "Do Everything," 324.

18. This question will be especially important when discussing the master/slave relationship.

There are at least six ways in which Paul's directions to husbands and wives would have been unusual or unique in the ancient world. First, while the wives are commanded to submit to their husbands, it is both unusual and significant that the command is to the wives and not to the husbands. In addressing the wives directly, Paul is treating them as free agents who are responsible for their own actions. They are not mere property. This will be a common theme throughout the household code with each of the submissive parties.

Second, wives are told to submit *to their husbands*. They are not being told to submit to all men. Paul is not arguing for the submission of all women to all men. Maybe that's how he thinks things should be; maybe it's not. However, in Colossians, all Paul is talking about is the relationship between husbands and wives—*not* the relationship between men and women.

Third, this submission is not an unquestioning obedience in all things. It is a step down from that. There will be more discussion on this in the next section on fathers/parents and children, because children are told to obey their parents in an unquestioning way. Wives, however, are not told to do this. It is impossible to know from these verses alone what Paul means by this, but given that he does not mean unquestioning obedience but something less, it might be better to think of this as "wives, follow your husbands."[19]

Fourth, the wives are told to submit themselves to their husbands ὡς ἀνῆκεν ἐν κυρίῳ (as is fitting in the Lord). This phrase "in the Lord" is important in the household code, and it will show up in all three reciprocal pairs of relationships. There will be a whole section near the end of this chapter that discusses what this phrase means, but essentially, it does two things that change the nature of earthly relationships. It gives new motivation for why one should act in a particular way, and it points towards how one should live in this world while preparing for the next. Again, there will be a whole section near the end of this chapter that looks at this phrase specifically.

Fifth, the command for wives to submit to their husbands is balanced with a command for husbands to love their wives. Commonly in household codes, the more authoritative party would have been given directions on how to order his house. However, there would have been no mention of reciprocal duties. It would be more like "husbands, your wives should submit to you, so make sure that they do," rather than "husbands, remember you

---

19. There will be more on the linguistic differences between the command to wives and the command to children in the next section. That discussion will point towards this suggestion, that wives are to "follow" their husbands. However, even in the next section, there will not be enough data to say this translation is a necessary conclusion. From this context alone, it can only be said that it is somewhere between possible and likely that "follow" is the best way to translate Paul's intent.

have obligations to your wives just as much as they have obligations to you." The fact that husbands have responsibilities to their wives would have been unusual.

Sixth and finally, husbands are told to ἀγάπη (agape/love) their wives. The meaning and importance of ἀγάπη (agape/love) was featured in the last chapter. However, one should keep in mind that when reading the letter, 3:18–19 comes immediately after 3:12–17, which is where ἀγάπη (agape/love) was a central topic of discussion. So, for the Colossians, ἀγάπη (agape/love) would have been fresh in their minds as they were hearing 3:18–19.

As discussed in the last chapter, to show someone ἀγάπη (agape/love) means that one person is to act selflessly towards another person. It is not a passive way of behaving, whereby one person leaves another person alone and doesn't bother them. Rather, it means that one person is to actively seek the good of another person. This is what husbands are commanded to do towards their wives.

So, those are the main points of difference between Paul and contemporary thought. What does this mean for his views on marriage? What does Paul think a marriage should look like?

The place to start is with the husbands and the command for them to show ἀγάπη (agape/love) to their wives. In the last chapter, it was discovered that the chief moral vice is selfishness, and the chief moral virtue is acting selflessly. Acting selflessly is what Paul meant by the word ἀγάπη (agape/love). What is significant is that when husbands are told here to love their wives, they are told to ἀγάπη (agape/love) their wives.[20] This does not mean merely that they are to have positive emotional feelings for their wives while they continue to order them about. Rather, it means that they are to act in a selfless manner towards their wives.

This one point demolishes much of what is objectionable (to modern people) about the patriarchy. Probably the central modern objection to the ordering of men and women in this way is that is places the man over the woman and makes her subservient to him. But, look at what happens with this one word, ἀγάπη (agape/love). As discussed in the last chapter, when Person A loves Person B with ἀγάπη (agape/love), Person A is placing Person B in a more important position than Person A. On Paul's view, the correct order of importance is 1) God, 2) others, and 3) self. As discussed in the last chapter, the entire reason others are to be placed over self (instead of just being considered at the same level) is because of ἀγάπη (agape/love).

---

20. They are actually told to ἀγαπᾶτε (agape/love) their wives, but this is just the command form of ἀγάπη (agape/love).

Since one is supposed to act selflessly towards others, then one is supposed to place others higher in the order of importance than one's own self.

Here is what this means for Paul's view on the interaction between husbands and wives. Men are still in charge. Whether this is merely something he is doing to fit in at least somewhat with culture or he really believes this is how things should be, it is not possible to tell from this letter alone. However, what can be known and what is significant is what Paul thinks men should do with the authority they have: act selflessly towards their wives. Paul says that husbands should place their wives above themselves in their hierarchy of importance. They are to put their wives before and above themselves. So, do men still have the authority? Yes. But, in Paul's view, that authority is being used correctly only insofar as husbands ἀγάπη (agape/ love) their wives and act selflessly towards them. In Paul's view, the husband is not allowed to put himself first.

With the command for husbands to ἀγάπη (agape/love) their wives, it is really hard to make Paul's statements fit the ancient patriarchal model. It is just not possible to say the man can be an authoritarian master when he is supposed to serve his wife. Rather, the comparison that Paul would almost certainly make is between the husband and Christ. Christ is in the top position, but what did he do with that position? He was tortured to death on a cross in order to help others by reconciling God and humanity and making it possible for humans to become renewed, i.e., restore their humanity. Christ used his authority and position to die for others and help them. Paul is telling husbands to do likewise. This is the exact opposite of the ancient patriarchal model. With a single word, ἀγάπη (agape/love), Paul has broken that mold.[21]

So, what about the wives? The wives are to follow their husbands. As discussed above and as to be investigated in the next section on father/parents and children, this is not an unquestioning obedience. That is what a child is supposed to have for his or her father/parents. The wife's position towards her husband is a step down from that, and probably would be better translated as "wives, follow your husbands."

Combined with the command for husbands to ἀγάπη (agape/love) their wives, the command for wives to follow their husbands creates an interesting dynamic. The husband is to be the leader (not the commander) of the relationship and guide the two in their journey through life. The wife is to follow her husband, and presumably, help him in the journey the two of

---

21. Of course, Paul would probably say the ἀγάπη (agape/love) of Christ has broken the mold.

them are on.[22] The husband's actions are to be modeled after the way Christ used his position of authority: he sacrificed himself to help others. This is what it means to show ἀγάπη (agape/love) to someone. The wife's actions are be characterized by her service to the Lord. This is what it means when Paul says she should submit to her husband ὡς ἀνῆκεν ἐν κυρίῳ (as is fitting in the Lord). She is ultimately following a heavenly leader, Christ, and the way she follows her husband should reflect that.

If both husband and wife actually follow through on what each of them are supposed to do, then what will result could be described as a true partnership—but a partnership that is meant to accomplish something. It is hard to move forward without a leader. If decisions are made by committee, the results may be safe, but they are usually not impressive. More progress is usually made if there is a strong leader. However, leaders who are primarily concerned about making progress for themselves rather than for the group usually cause more harm than good.

But, what if the leader used Christ as his example and placed the needs of the group above his own needs? What if he considered others to be more important than himself? This would be the best of both worlds. The organization (or, in this case, the marriage) would have a strong leader who could move the group forward, but this leader would not cause harm by only or primarily seeking his own good.

If this is the kind of leader one has, then the best thing the other members of the organization (or, in this case, the only other member of the marriage) can do would be to follow. Attempting to 1) take control or 2) force equal decision-making opportunities would be to 1) remove a good leader from the leadership position[23] or 2) return to decision by committee.[24]

It is impossible to know for certain whether these are the sorts of ideas Paul had in mind when he was describing how a husband and wife should act towards one another. After all, there are only two short verses on the subject. However, given ancient ideas on how marriage should function and how Paul decided to modify those ideas to express his own, this seems like at

22. The text does not actually say she should "help," but it seems like a reasonable parallel to the leading/guiding the husband does. Perhaps this would connect with the statement in Genesis that the wife is to be a helper to her husband, or perhaps not. Since the text does not actually use this word, no parallel can be drawn. The idea that a wife should help her husband is not actually in the text here; it is simply speculation. But it does seem reasonable, given that the husband is supposed to lead and the wife is to follow.

23. Assuming one defines a good leader as someone who is in charge of the group while at the same time considering the needs of the group as more important than his own.

24. Which, again, may produce safe results, but not usually ones that are impressive.

least a reasonable interpretation of his meaning. Paul seems to move beyond the idea that marriage was merely a business arrangement or simply about family connections, the creation of heirs, or something of that nature. It sounds like Paul is describing a marriage that is meant for something more.

Unfortunately, it is not possible to paint a complete picture of Paul's views on marriage from this passage alone. There are still many large issues that these two verses don't even address. Here are just a few of the questions that are left unanswered by this passage and would probably take several books to answer:

- How do Paul's ideas of marriage work in the real world? For example, what if only one person fulfills his or her role?

- Why do women have to be the ones to submit rather than men?

- What is the relationship between men and women in general?

- How much of what Paul says is based on culture and would and should change with time?

- Is marriage between one man and one woman only?

In Colossians, Paul is addressing only a particular situation. He is telling the Colossians how to act in their unique environment in order to reveal Christ to others. Paul's commands do not cover every aspect of marriage. However, there are some good points here that will be useful in the larger discussion of marriage.

Ultimately, Paul's goal is to create peace/shalom in both individuals and the community (3:15) in order to represent Christ both inside and outside of the community (4:2–6). Paul is less concerned with changing the social structure than he is with representing Christ.[25] This is a concrete example for the Colossians on how to fulfill his command to them from 3:17: "And whatever you do, in word or deed, do everything in the name of the Lord Jesus, giving thanks to God the Father through him." Paul told the Colossians they should make sure to represent Christ in everything they do and make sure that the motivation behind what they do is to do everything for Christ. The household code shows them how they are to do that in their everyday lives.

---

25. This will be seen especially in the section on masters/slaves.

3:20–21 (CHILDREN AND PARENTS/FATHERS)

τὰ τέκνα ὑπακούετε τοῖς γονεῦσιν κατὰ πάντα τοῦτο γὰρ
εὐάρεστόν ἐστιν ἐν κυρίῳ οἱ πατέρες μὴ ἐρεθίζετε τὰ τέκνα
ὑμῶν ἵνα μὴ ἀθυμῶσιν

Children, obey your parents in everything, for this pleases the
Lord. Fathers, do not provoke your children, lest they become
discouraged.

The theme of obedience continues into the second reciprocal pair (children
and parents/fathers). However, it is a little different here from wives and
husbands. O'Brien says:

> The injunction to children, like that to slaves, is put rather more
> strongly than the one to wives. While the latter was expressed
> in the middle voice (ὑποτάσσομαι, 'be subordinate'), suggesting
> voluntary submission, the admonitions to children and slaves
> are in the active imperative denoting absolute obedience. The
> absoluteness of the commands is strengthened by the phrase
> 'in all things' (κατὰ πάντα, cf. v22). Also the verb ὑπακούω ('to
> obey') is employed rather than ὑποτάσσομαι ('be subordinate')
> which may only sometimes imply obedience.[26]

Children are to obey their parents in everything, and the way Paul tells
them to do this implies absolute obedience. This is a firmer type of obedience
than was commanded to wives. As O'Brien said, the command to children is
stronger in three ways: 1) children are commanded in the active imperative
(absolute obedience) rather than as wives were with the middle voice (suggesting voluntary submission); 2) children are commanded to obey κατὰ
πάντα (in all things), while wives were not; and 3) children are commanded
with the word ὑπακούω (obey) rather than the word ὑποτάσσομαι (submit
to/be subordinate to/follow). The command to children, then, is definitely
stronger than the one to wives.

This is not something that comes across easily in English translations.
"Obey" and "submit to" sound similar to modern ears, but based on the way
that Paul is describing the two relationships, what he means by "submit" is
less than what he means by "obey." The "obedience" children are to show
their parents is or borders on unquestioning obedience, and the "obedience"
a wife is to show her husband is much less intense than this. A better way to
describe what Paul wants the wife to do might be to say she should "follow"

---

26. O'Brien, *Colossians-Philemon*, 224, and Witherington and Wessels, "Do Everything," 325.

her husband. Even though the word "follow" is not what is used here, following is more of the effect that would result from what has been described in these two verses.

The wife is not commanded to obey her husband with unquestioning obedience like children are commanded to obey their parents. And, if her following is not of the unquestioning variety, then it sounds like questioning her husband's direction and pushing back on his ideas is a real possibility— as long as it is done within the context of following him. What it sounds like is that the wife is being told to recognize that her husband is in charge and not to challenge him for that position. She is to work with him and can disagree with him, but she should still follow him.

There are two more categories to consider when comparing children and wives in their relationships to the father/husband: 1) the comparison to ancient parallels (for the command to children) and 2) the treatment of the child/wife by the father/husband. Investigating these two categories will help to show how different these two types of relationships are. And doing that will help to clarify what each type of relationship is like and make the picture Paul is painting just a little bit clearer to modern audiences.

More so than the command for wives to submit to/follow their husbands, the command for children to obey their parents was similar to other ancient views. There are, however, two real differences. First, the reason children are to obey their parents is because "this pleases the Lord." As mentioned previously, the role of the Lord is important and unique among ancient household codes, but since it applies to all three reciprocal pairs, it will be discussed after the last one.

However, even without in-depth analysis on the meaning of this phrase, it shouldn't be too hard to see that Paul is telling children *why* they are to obey their parents—because "this pleases the Lord." And, since the reason they are to obey their parents is because "this pleases the Lord," Paul is pointing towards obeying the Lord as one's ultimate motivation. The obedience children are to have towards their parents is the practical fulfillment of the general command Paul gave only three verses earlier: "And whatever you do, in word or deed, do everything in the name of the Lord Jesus, giving thanks to God the Father through him" (3:17).

The second way the command for children to obey their parents differs from other ancient thought is that the command is actually *to the children*. Paul is addressing them directly. This suggests that children "are thought of as both present in the Christian meeting where the letter would be read out [loud] and as responsible agents despite their youth. Responsibility in

Christian relationships is not to be determined by legal standing."[27] In other words, the children are being treated like partial grown-ups. Yes, they are immature, and no, they are not ready to be fully responsible for themselves yet. But they are responsible for at least the small part of their lives they can control. They are responsible for how they respond to their parents. And Paul is addressing them as responsible individuals, capable of making their own choices.

This same concern for the personal responsibility of the individual was present in the section with wives, and will return again in the final section on slaves. Even if the individual has little or no legal standing, it is still his or her responsibility to act in an appropriate manner. This was not the normal way of doing things in the ancient world.

The last thing to consider is the comparison of how the father/husband is to treat the child/wife. Paul says in v. 21: "Fathers, do not provoke your children, lest they become discouraged." Contemporaneous household codes did not have a section that told the fathers about their duties to their children; the commands went only one way. As with the first reciprocal pair (wives/husbands), much of the authority, rights, and privileges are being taken from the authority figure, and the subordinate figure is being endowed with both value and responsibility. This represents something unique in Paul's thought.[28]

Additionally, the way Paul addresses fathers is different from the way Paul addresses husbands. Fathers are not to provoke their children, so they do not become discouraged. Basically, Paul is saying something like, "Don't push your children too hard. You want to bring them along and help them grow. You don't want to give them a task so big they'll never be able to accomplish it and get discouraged. Help them learn how to walk as you have learned how to walk." This is very different from the ἀγάπη (agape/love), the active selflessness, husbands are to show their wives.

The relationship between fathers and their children seems to be somewhat formal—or at least formal in comparison to the relationship between husbands and their wives. Fathers and children are somewhat like coach and athlete or teacher and student (though probably more personal than that). However, husbands and wives are completely intertwined. The wife follows the husband as her leader, and the husband puts his wife's needs and the needs of the couple above his own. Fathers are teachers and guides. Husbands are partners and selfless leaders.

27. Dunn, *Epistles to the Colossians*, 250.

28. This will be discussed further later, since this is something that applies to all three pairs in the code.

3:22–4:1 (SLAVES AND MASTERS)

οἱ δοῦλοι ὑπακούετε κατὰ πάντα τοῖς κατὰ σάρκα κυρίοις μὴ ἐν ὀφθαλμοδουλίᾳ ὡς ἀνθρωπάρεσκοι ἀλλ᾽ ἐν ἁπλότητι καρδίας φοβούμενοι τὸν κύριον ὃ ἐὰν ποιῆτε ἐκ ψυχῆς ἐργάζεσθε ὡς τῷ κυρίῳ καὶ οὐκ ἀνθρώποις εἰδότες ὅτι ἀπὸ κυρίου ἀπολήμψεσθε τὴν ἀνταπόδοσιν τῆς κληρονομίας τῷ κυρίῳ Χριστῷ δουλεύετε ὁ γὰρ ἀδικῶν κομίσεται ὃ ἠδίκησεν καὶ οὐκ ἔστιν προσωπολημψία οἱ κύριοι τὸ δίκαιον καὶ τὴν ἰσότητα τοῖς δούλοις παρέχεσθε εἰδότες ὅτι καὶ ὑμεῖς ἔχετε κύριον ἐν οὐρανῷ

Slaves, obey in all things those who are your earthly masters, not in eye-service, as people-pleasers, but with sincerity of heart, fearing the Lord. Whatever you do, work heartily, as for the Lord and not for men, knowing that from the Lord you will receive the inheritance as your reward. You are serving the Lord Christ. For the wrongdoer will be paid back for the wrong he has done, and there is no partiality. Masters, treat your slaves justly and fairly, knowing that you also have a Master in heaven.

In the household code, the section on the relation between slaves and masters is by far the longest, and it has a heavy emphasis on the duties of the slaves. It is very likely that at least part of the reason for this was that there were more slaves than masters in Colossae[29] (though this is likely not the entire reason).[30]

The situation in the Roman world (which would have included Colossae) was one in which slaves were considered to exist for whatever purposes their masters deemed fit. "According to Roman law, a slave, though recognized in a sense as a human being (*persona*), was a thing (*res*). Owners had the right to bind, torture, or kill their slaves."[31] Williams adds to this that slaves could be expected to fulfill their masters sexually as part of their duties. He says:

29. Dunn, *Epistles to the Colossians*, 253, and O'Brien, *Colossians-Philemon*, 231–32.

30. Lincoln suggests that, "It is worth entertaining the possibility, therefore, that a major reason for [slavery] receiving the most attention is that it serves as a paradigm for the motivation that should inform all members of the household, and that is summed up in the notion of fearing the Lord (3:22c) and its elaboration in the command of 3:24b—'Serve the Lord Christ.' The basic insight lying behind such a paradigm is of course indebted to Paul, since he held that all humans are under some power and had used slavery as a metaphor for this perspective. Humans are either slaves to sin or slaves to God (Rom 6.15–23), and even if Christian believers are free persons in social terms they are still slaves of Christ (1 Cor. 7.22)" ("Household Code," 106).

31. Dale Martin, *Slavery as Salvation*, xiii.

> In the eyes of the law slaves were property pure and simple, and
> in general neither the law nor popular morality had anything
> to say about how a man used his own property. Slaves' bodies
> were entirely at their masters' disposal, and from the earliest of
> times it seems to have been understood that among the services
> that Roman men might expect their slaves to perform was the
> satisfaction of their sexual desires.[32]

The point of this is that slaves had control over nothing, including their own
bodies. While some masters might have treated their slaves better, most
slaves were simply considered property.[33]

Most of this is nothing new, and both ancient and modern audiences
understand the concept of slavery. However, Paul's response to slavery can
be a little difficult to understand. In Col 3:11, Paul says that, in Christ, there
is neither slave nor free. Yet, in the household code, he tells slaves to obey
their masters. Not only are slaves just to obey their masters, they are to do
it μὴ ἐν ὀφθαλμοδουλίᾳ ὡς ἀνθρωπάρεσκοι ἀλλ᾽ ἐν ἁπλότητι καρδίας
φοβούμενοι τὸν κύριον (not in eye-service, as people-pleasers, but with
sincerity of heart, fearing the Lord). In other words, Paul is telling them that
they are to serve their masters like they are serving the Lord and to really
give their tasks their best effort.[34] At the same time, he is telling the Colossians that there is neither slave nor free. It is easy to see why this section has
confused people over the years.

The first thing to notice about this section is that, like with the commands to wives and children, the slaves are addressed directly. Balch says:

> What is most notable is not the subordination of the slaves, but
> that they are *addressed* in the codes. Many modern evaluations
> underestimate the integrating power of the early Christian
> congregation. These groups are addressed as members of the

32. Williams, *Roman Homosexuality*, 310. Williams goes on to say, "And, as we will
see both in the earliest contemporary sources and in later references to the distant past,
it seems always to have been assumed that the master would make such use of his slaves
of both sexes."

33. It is not clear whether slaves were treated any different at Colossae than they
were anywhere else, but the above are general statements concerning attitudes towards
slaves in the Roman world, and it is important to consider this as contextual background for the situation into which Paul was speaking. For a more in-depth treatment
of slavery, see Dale Martin's *Slavery as Salvation*.

34. O'Brien says, "eyeservice" essentially means "superficial" (*Colossians-Philemon*,
227). Not doing their work in a superficial way means that the Christian slaves in Colossae are to give their work their very best. Expecting slaves to do their work would not
have been anything revolutionary. But, slaves trying their hardest *voluntarily*, like they
were completing their tasks for God, was unheard of.

ecclesia, not as members of a household. This integrating power is something entirely new in ancient social history: masters and slaves have the same Lord and judge (Col 3:25b).[35]

Paul is addressing every person, regardless of gender, age, or status, as a responsible individual. They will be treated as responsible individuals by the Lord, and so Paul is expecting them to act like it now.

Also, as in the sections on husbands/wives and parents/children, there is a verse on how the masters are to behave. The command to masters, however, was very different from current thought. As with the sections on husbands and fathers, the privileges of the authoritative party are being reduced, and their responsibilities are being increased. Specifically, masters are to treat their slaves τὸ δίκαιον καὶ τὴν ἰσότητα (justly and fairly), because they also have a Master in heaven.

The word that jumps out is ἰσότητα (equally/fairly). The range of meaning for ἰσότης (equally/fairly) is pretty narrow. According to Bauer et al., it can mean one of two things: 1) the "state of matters being held in proper balance, *equality*" or 2) the "state of being fair, *fairness*."[36] Standhartinger says, "Embedded in the translation of the term 'fairly' is the notion of equality, ἰσότης . . . [which] does not merely represent what is reasonable, but in fact means equality between groups of varying status in ancient society."

Suggesting that Paul was calling for equality, however, may be going a bit too far. Dunn suggests a more moderated view of ἰσότης (equally/fairly). "The idea of equality of treatment for slave and free *in law* was an impossible thought for the time. However tempting, then, that Paul and Timothy have called for an effective abandonment of the legal status of slavery, it is much more probable that ἰσότης has the second sense of 'equity, fairness.'"[37]

Given that Rome was not a democracy and there was no opportunity for someone like Paul to change the law or even suggest a modification, it seems unlikely to think that ἰσότης (equally/fairly) meant the breaking down of *legal* barriers between classes. To suggest that would be outright

---

35. Balch, "Household Codes," 33–34. Henderson says, "What stands out here is not the concern with the conduct of the subjugated group—non-Christian literature also deals with inferior household members—but rather the use of direct address . . . . By appealing in an unmediated manner to the lesser parties, the writer imputes to them a degree of autonomy . . . . In each case, then, the writer addresses wives, children, and slaves not as passive and silent members to be controlled by their superiors, but rather as those endowed with the capacity for choice, especially in regard to their interaction with the powerful figures in their lives" ("Taking Liberties," 424–25).

36. Bauer et al., ἰσότης, *Greek English Lexicon*, 481.

37. Dunn, *Epistles to the Colossians*, 260.

revolution and would not have been good for the fledgling religion.[38] At this point in history, Christianity "was beginning a long journey of tenuous survival."[39] It is far more likely that Paul was telling the masters to treat their slaves fairly—above what the law required, but not outside of it—because they are slaves, too. The masters have a Master in heaven, and they should remember this as they deal with their own slaves.[40] Paul is saying, "Whether later or sooner, be one slave or slave-owner, all believers will ultimately be accountable to an impartial Master."[41]

MacDonald says, "While it is not usually conceived as such, the rhetorical strategy adopted by the author of Colossians in relation to slavery does involve a fundamental bestowal of honor: both slaves and masters are reminded of the distinction between the earthly master (lord) and the master (Lord) in heaven. Slaves and masters ultimately serve the same Lord and may experience the reward of inheritance or the punishments of final judgment."[42] While this would not put slaves and masters on the same level in this world, it does so for the next world.

Eschatologically, slaves had been emancipated, and that knowledge should have been enough to start their believing masters down the right path. This should remind the reader of 3:1–4, in which Paul said that Christians are to live for the world above. If there is no difference between slave and master in the Lord's eyes, and the Colossians are to live for the world above, it is implicit that the system under which they are currently living (which includes slavery) will end, so they shouldn't get too attached to it.

Paul also sends a message to both the slaves and masters at Colossae literally by the way he sends his message. One of the carriers of this letter was Onesimus (4:9), a runaway slave. Apparently, one's legal status as a slave was irrelevant to one's ability to serve in the body of Christ. The fact that a runaway slave was being sent to instruct the Colossians on slavery would not have been lost on them.

38. Lincoln says, "In Graeco-Roman culture, wives, children and slaves were expected to accept the religion of the *paterfamilias*, the male head of the household, and so religious groups that attracted women and slaves were seen as particularly likely to be subversive of social stability" ("Household Code," 101). Rome would get nervous simply at the attraction of women and slaves to a religious group. To then say there is no difference between slave and free would be extremely alarming.

39. MacDonald, "Slavery, Sexuality," 105.

40. Paul is also (implicitly) reminding them of the Golden Rule: "Do unto others as you would have them do unto you." This is essentially the point that he made in 3:17, and as was said previously, the household code is a case study. It is an example of how to work out the ethics of ch. 3 in practice.

41. Still, "Eschatology in Colossians," 129.

42. MacDonald, "Slavery, Sexuality," 108.

If Onesimus was the companion and messenger of Paul, then what one has here is a slave[43] in a position of authority over the people of Colossae (including those who are slaveowners). Since the carrier of a letter would have to explain questions about the letter, that means Onesimus was no mere postman; he was functioning as a representative of Paul the apostle and as a teacher to the slaveowners at Colossae. The one whom Paul considers to be τῷ πιστῷ καὶ ἀγαπητῷ ἀδελφῷ (a faithful and beloved brother) would have been seen as an example of the freedom to be found in Christ and as a representative of the new way of life.

One final unique point about what Paul says on slavery is that the promise of inheritance is given to slaves (3:24). "In the realm of Roman and Hellenistic law, slaves were excluded from the right to inherit."[44] MacDonald explains:

> Given the legal standing of slaves described above, the promise in Col 3:24 that slaves will receive inheritance (κληρονομία; cf. 1:12) offers a sign of the reversal of cultural expectations and is at the heart of the ideological justification for welcoming all—even the slaves of non-believers—as God's chosen ones (cf. Col 3:11–12) .... However difficult it is to determine how it was being lived—and much about the interaction between slaves and free persons appears to have been conventional—something has changed for slaves in house church communities. Col 3:11 suggests that this change was experienced in baptism and reaffirmed in worship through mutual admonition and the giving of thanks to a new patron, God the Father (Col 3:15–17).[45]

As mentioned before, there is a tension created between 3:11 and 3:22–4:1. In the former, Paul says that there is neither slave nor free. However, in the latter, he tells slaves that they should obey their masters, and masters should treat their servants fairly. With the left hand, he dismisses slavery, while with the right, he affirms it. How can this tension be resolved?

Standhartinger makes two points about the letter as a whole that help address this tension. She says first:

> The letter conspicuously avoids using the Pauline term "co-worker" (συνέργος) although this term is familiar (cf. 4:11). Instead of being designated "co-workers," Epaphras and Tychicus

43. Depending on when the letter was written, he could still have been a slave, or (if freed) he would have been a former slave. See also the letter to Philemon.

44. Standhartinger, "Origin and Intention," 127, and O'Brien, *Colossians-Philemon*, 229.

45. MacDonald, "Slavery, Sexuality," 108.

are referred to as "fellowservants" (σύνδουλος 1:7; 4:7; cf. 4:12). "Lord" (κύριος) in the Colossian epistle refers to Christ alone (1:3; 2:6; 3:12, 24). It is the responsibility of the "fellow servants" Epaphras and Tychicus to imitate Paul in word and deed, just as the whole congregation in turn imitates the Pauline party through 'teaching and admonition' (3:16; cf. 1:28).[46]

Later, she says the following:

> If the household code is read in the context of the letter as a whole, one discovers something surprising. Only one social group is mentioned both in the household code and in the letter, viz. that of masters and slaves. Christ is master alone. Apart from the household code there is no mention of masters again, only 'fellow servants' (1:17; 4:7, 12). In the congregation, which according to the letter is made up of spiritually renewed people (3:1–17), any differentiations between Jews and Gentiles, foreigners and indigenous, slaves and free persons are abolished. Thus it is likely that when the authors speak of 'fellow servants' they envisage not merely slaves but all members of the congregation. Their work for Christ (3:22–24) is to be rewarded with an inheritance; theirs is the promise of a fair judgment.[47]

The tension between the equality of 3:11 and the slavery of 3:22–4:1 can therefore be resolved by accepting three propositions.

1. *All Christians are slaves to their heavenly master, Christ.*

   The two quotes above from Standhartinger point towards this conclusion:[48] everyone is described as a slave.[49] Even Paul, who describes his afflictions, toil, and struggle (1:24–2:5), as well as his chains (4:18), is described as a slave.[50] The fact that one who is an apostle (1:1) and is sent by the Lord is not described as a master but rather as one who is subject to the will of the one he serves should make it clear to

---

46. Standhartinger, "Origin and Intention," 125.

47. Standhartinger, "Origin and Intention," 129.

48. Also, Lincoln, "Household Code," 105.

49. Standhartinger translates σύνδουλος as "fellow servant" ("Origin and Intention," 125). This is common, and one often sees this in modern translations. However, the root of the word is still δούλος, which means slave. The only change is that there is a σύν (with) added to the beginning, which makes the word σύνδουλος mean "slave with" or "fellow slave." The common translation "fellow servant" is probably meant to soften the language, but really, it means "fellow slave."

50. Paul implies this when he refers to people like Tychicus as fellow slaves (4:7).

the Colossians that they are not any better.[51] They are slaves, too. All Christians serve the Lord.

2. *The Colossians still lived in a society where the slave/master distinction held.*

In ancient society, slavery was assumed to be part of a functioning society. Slavery was simply a given, and there was no legal opportunity to change it. Paul and the Colossians did not live in the modern Western world where democracy exists and there is opportunity to push for one's views peacefully. Slavery was a reality that could not be changed without overthrowing the Roman empire (which was not a very practical idea).

3. *The commands in the Christian living section are about how to live for the world above while still acknowledging the realities of existing in this world.*

If there is truly no difference between slave and free for those in Christ (3:11), then the issue is how to live that out in a world in which slavery still exists. Because of practical constraints (such as fear of retaliation from Rome), it would not have been practical (or wise) for Paul to advocate freeing all slaves. A much better position for Paul to advocate was for Christians to demonstrate what they believed toward outsiders (4:2–6) while still obeying the law of the land. The way to do this had two parts: first, live within the earthly constraints that society placed on people (slavery); second, show others what the heavenly way looks like by acting better than was either required or normal. When slaves did their best work for their masters (not eyeservice, i.e., superficial obedience), even though they didn't have to, and masters treated their slaves fairly, even though they didn't have to, the Colossians would send a strong message to onlookers that they were different. The natural question that would have been asked by those who saw their actions was "Why?"

> To argue for the abolition of slavery within the Roman Empire would have been heard as a call for slaves to revolt. The slave revolts began in Italy immediately after the end of the Hannibalic War (201 B.C.) and occurred intermittently until 70 B.C.[52] However, while the slave rebellions might have ended in 70 B.C., the use of slaves for political purposes continued. Westermann says, "From 60 to 50 B.C. in Rome itself the use of slaves and freedmen to exert political pressure grew to scandalous

51. Lyall, "Roman Law," 76.
52. Westermann, *Slave Systems*, 63.

proportions."[53] Joshel says about the time after the revolts, "Although there were no more large-scale slave rebellions, the Romans constantly feared slave revolts. The truism of Roman slave-holders was *tot servi, quot hostes*—you have as many enemies as you have slaves."[54]

Because the issue of slavery remained explosive even during the time when there were no rebellions, Paul probably did not want Rome to view the fledgling Christian religion as attempting to use the power of slaves to rise up. It would not have been difficult for Rome to view Christianity that way if Paul were preaching emancipation, especially when one considers that the founder of the religion was crucified as the "King of the Jews." Parsons says, "It may be that the apostles realized the danger of advocating abolition in a civilization in which slavery was part of the framework of its social structure. The demand for freedom had been heard before. Three wars had been fought and lost over the issue, and the lot of the remaining slaves merely worsened. The difficulty in protesting was the fact that slaves had no peaceful, constitutional way of agitating for their liberty."[55]

Additionally, it is worth noting that even if the early Christians had the desire to start another slave rebellion (which is doubtful), they simply didn't have the manpower. Christianity in the mid-first century was quite small. For example, Fellows says, "The proportion of the Corinthian population that become Christians before the writing of 1 Corinthians was very small (probably between .06% and .25%)."[56] Even in one of the churches that was to gain so much attention from Paul, the population of Christians remained too small to achieve any change by force. There would have been little chance to change culture through numbers.

However, in discussing the letter to the Ephesians, Fowl gives a dissenting opinion to the view that Paul was concerned about stirring up too much trouble. He says, "Ephesians displays none of the apologetic concerns that comprise the scholarly consensus regarding the household codes. Indeed, Paul's willing acceptance of and frequent reference to his imprisonment for Christ's sake shows that he has little interest in masking the potentially disruptive costs and results of Christianity.

53. Westermann, *Slave Systems*, 66.

54. Joshel, *Slavery*, 64.

55. Michael Parsons, "Slavery," 90.

56. Fellows, "Renaming in Paul's Churches," 116.

Furthermore, in the light of 5:3–20, it is clear that Paul does not want the Ephesians to live according to the moral conventions of the world around them. Thus there is no reason to assume that when Paul addresses the ordering of Christian households in Ephesus, he has any interest in showing that Christians are not a threat to the order of the city."[57]

Given Paul's account of his suffering in Col 1, Fowl's point about Paul's lack of concern about stirring up trouble seems to apply to Colossians as well. Probably the best answer to this objection is that Paul was not *as* concerned with the structures of society as he was with how Christians lived within those structures. Christians were not to be concerned so much with their situation but with how to live as Christians within that situation. They were to make a difference by example. That means that they had to live in a society that they had no ability to change, but they were to do it in a way that made people sit up and take notice. It is this situation which Colossians addresses. As Parsons says, "The apostles, generally, are not making social comment on prevailing custom, they are asking the question, . . . 'What is the relationship between Christian freedom and social slavery?'"[58]

What Paul is doing with the household code is creating an alternate reality. The normal social reality is the one in which a person was a man, woman, child, slave, or master. However, in the text, Paul describes something different. He describes everyone as equal in Christ and says that all are responsible to the same master.[59] Paul presents the Colossians with an alternate reality that is very different than the one in which they live, and the norms of the heaven-focused reality do not look like the norms of their earth-focused reality.

It does not appear that Paul was suggesting that his new reality should replace the old one, as much as it looks like he intended it to be a correction

---

57. Fowl, *Ephesians*, 180.

58. Michael Parsons, "Slavery," 90.

59. Dale Martin says, "Surprising as it may seem to modern readers, Paul's slavery to Christ [as described in other letters] did not connote humility but rather established his authority as Christ's agent and spokesperson" (*Slavery as Salvation*, 147). The slaves in Colossae might be thinking of the upwardly mobile slaves that existed in the ancient world when Paul said that they had a master in heaven. Therefore, it might not simply have been an attempt at equality when Paul connected all the Colossians with a master in heaven; it might also have been an elevation in status for all parties. Even if one were a freeborn owner of slaves, becoming a slave would have been quite a a step up if, as a slave, you were a spokesperson for the creator God. For more information, see the rest of Martin's discussion that surrounds this quote on how Paul's slavery to Christ would have been heard by Greco-Roman city-dwellers.

(or at least a partial one). Normally, slaves are treated badly, but if one applies the heaven-focused reality, the situation is (somewhat) corrected. The application, though, does not mean that the first reality is done away with. Paul is not arguing for a slave rebellion and the overthrowing of the current world order. Rather, what he is offering is more like an update to a piece of software that is meant to fix the bugs in the current code rather than replace the code entirely.

The difference these changes make to the Colossians' lives can be found in restored relationships and functional fairness. Generating true fairness would mean changing Roman law, abolishing slavery, ending sexual and racial discrimination, etc. This was out of reach for an itinerant preacher of a fledgling religion.[60] However, while he could not change the system and reach true fairness, he could encourage people to be fair to one another, even though they didn't have to be. So, while he could not abolish slavery, if he could get Christians to view each other as brothers and sisters in Christ on a practical, day-to-day level, regardless of whether one was slave or free, people could transcend the normal boundaries and treat each other as equals. "And whatever you do, in word or deed, do everything in the name of the Lord Jesus, giving thanks to God the Father through him" (3:17).

Even though the Christian population was very small compared to the Roman empire as a whole (or even compared to the cities in which Christians lived), people who lived differently than those around them would have been noticed. Paul was planting a seed that had the potential to grow into something much larger. If the Christian community could live differently than those around them (according to heaven-focused norms), not only would the community itself be different, but those around them might catch the bug as well.

Before moving on, it is worth noting that there might have been an additional reason for the elongated section on slaves and masters. It is possible that the slavery section of the code was also being used to address the alternative philosophy by flattening the hierarchy. "Those who disqualify" (2:18) would logically be putting themselves in the role of judges and therefore *above* everyone else. In contrast, Paul puts himself *with* everyone else as a fellow servant (along with Epaphras and Tychicus—people, like Paul, who could have claimed status in the Christian community).

---

60. Of course, one could also ask, "Is God more interested in changing one's situation in life or changing who one is as a person?" From what Paul has said in this letter, it seems very likely that he would say God is more interested in renewing humans into his image than he is in making their lives easier.

IN THE LORD

There is a strong emphasis on Christ as *Lord* in the household code. "Whereas the term 'Christ' appears some twenty-five times in the letter, 'Lord' occurs only sixteen times, nine of which are found in the passage under consideration [3:18–4:1]. Particularly in matters that deal with social relationships, the writer asserts that all 'subjugation' occurs within the framework of Christ's lordship."[61] Because of their heavenly focus and their ongoing renewal by Christ, the "Lord" references were not "formal, meaningless platitudes, but evidence that Paul meant the influence of the risen Christ and the example of Jesus to guide the ethos of the Colossians."[62] Paul leaves many of the surface level things the same, making the household code look like other, contemporary codes. But, he changes what is underneath. This influence, this living for the heavenly, Christlike way, rather than the earthly way, is what is behind the phrase "in the Lord."

However, some commentators, like Osiek and Balch, say that, in Paul's version of the household code, not much has changed from other contemporary options. While they note the differences between the two, such as the active roles for subordinate members,[63] they say things like, "In great contrast to the leadership of women and their active participation in the worship of early Pauline assemblies, this pseudonymous letter assimilates Pauline household values to Aristotelian politics."[64]

What is funny about this is that this is exactly the sort of reaction that Paul hoped to cause among anyone who might casually read his letter or hear teaching based on this letter. Paul was trying to make real change happen while at the same time not look like he was a revolutionary—which would upset Rome. At a surface level, the code was meant to look like conventional wisdom on household management. The real changes are deeper. Commentators who think that Paul wasn't making any real changes are merely reading the code at a surface level and not appreciating either the differences between Paul and Aristotle nor the reason some of the code conformed to prevailing norms. They are reading the code the way Paul wanted *outsiders* to read it.

---

61. Henderson, "Taking Liberties," 424. It should be noted that only seven of the nine uses of κύριος (lord) in the code actually refer to Christ. The other two instances refer to earthly masters.

62. Witherington and Wessels, "Do Everything," 331.

63. Osiek and Balch, *Families*, 199.

64. Osiek and Balch, *Families*, 118.

Standhartinger says, "Most of the exhortations in Col 3:18–4:1 represent conventional formulations,"[65] but that is not necessarily a bad thing. While much of what one reads in ancient household codes is objectionable to modern ears, it would not have been to ancient ears. "Believers were being urged *not* to be different at this point, but to live fully in accord with high social ideals, widely esteemed by other ethicists of the time. The perspective and enabling might be different, but the goals were shared."[66]

The fact is, though, that while many of the ideals in the code were in line with high social ideas in the ancient world, there were quite a few differences between the two. Witherington and Wessels say the following:

> When one compares this material to either the ancient discussion of the household management in Aristotle and other such sources, or the Stoic or Greco-Roman codes, one is profoundly struck by not just the Christian elements but also the social engineering that is being undertaken here to limit the abuse of power by the head of the household, using Christian rationales to equalize and personalize, as well as Christianize, the relationship between the head and the rest of the family. The fact is that we do not find the exhortation to the head of the household to love their wives, or not break the spirit of their children, or treat their slaves with some equity and justice, in most of the parallel literature.[67]

Obviously, the code in Colossians conforms to the general pattern of household management that was considered to be ideal among his non-Christian contemporaries. However, "Paul has thoroughly Christianized the code, not just by adding 'in the Lord' at certain points, but by balancing carefully the duties and responsibilities of the various family members so that the stronger parties have duties as well as rights, and those who are in a position of submission are treated as responsible human beings with rights as well as duties."[68]

What Paul was doing in the code by relating everything one did to the Lord was placing a heavy emphasis on the person of Christ and making clear that everything one does should be done for him—especially the things one does not want to do. This points to a different motivation for one's actions than would have been found in contemporary codes. Aristotle

---

65. Standhartinger, "Origin and Intention," 122.

66. Dunn, *Epistles to the Colossians*, 245.

67. Witherington and Wessels, "Do Everything," 317.

68. N.T. Wright, *Colossians and Philemon*, 147.

appealed to "the cosmic scheme as the basis for household hierarchies."[69] He said that this is the way the world is, so it makes the best sense to order your house that way. Paul points to the person of Christ and says that in Christ, this (the order he lays out in the code) is the way to do things.

However, there is more to ordering one's house "according to the way of Christ" than it would appear at first glance. The commands in the household code are not commands for all time; they are tied to the situation of the Colossians. The Colossians have one foot in the world above and one foot in this world, and so telling them how to live is not a straightforward task. For which environment should they pattern their actions? If they patterned their lives according to the heavenly environment, there would be no slavery at all. If they patterned their lives according to the earthly environment, they might have a code that didn't look too different from Aristotle's. What are they to do?

The way Paul has explained the rationale for the Christian life from the beginning of ch. 3 up to this point has prepared the reader to be able to understand his answer. He began by explaining that Christians' focus should be on heavenly things, because that is where they are headed—to a world that is different from this one (3:1–4). They should, therefore, live for the world above, and, in fact, they are being prepared for that world now. They are being renewed in the image of their creator, Christ (3:9–10). This means that they should reflect Christ in this world and to this world.

Ultimately, then, the Christian's goal is to reflect and represent Christ in a world that does not know him. This is the idea behind Paul's version of the code. Paul wants Christians to live in the world's systems but to live better than those systems require. Who, for example, would expect slaves to really try their best at the tasks that their earthly masters give them? The very first question anyone would ask if they saw that would be "Why would they do that?" That is precisely the question that Paul wants people around Christians to be asking, because the answer is one that accomplishes the goal of Christians: reflecting Christ.

Given all this, it makes perfect sense why Paul would tell the Colossians to live in a manner that *somewhat* conforms with the pattern of this world. It is because by living in the world's systems but keeping one's focus on the world above and living better than those systems require that a Christian can reveal Christ to others. Ideally, this positive example that Christians are portraying will lead to those around them following Christ and becoming renewed themselves. These two things, revelation and renewal, constitute the whole responsibility of the Christian. What Paul has done is to show

69. Henderson, "Taking Liberties," 424.

the Colossians how to do their job in a situation that is not ideal. They accomplish it by doing everything ἐν κυρίῳ (in the Lord).

SIGNIFICANCE

The household code represents a delicate balance between opposing forces. Hull explains the situation:

> Any Christian group lives in a certain tension with its culture, at the same time reflecting the social norms and bringing the gospel to bear in such a way as to ultimately transform that society to be in line with the 'new creation in Christ.' Thus the household code in the New Testament mirrors a society in which patriarchal rule and the rights of masters over slaves are not only customary but also sanctioned by Roman law. For a powerless, minority religion to challenge this system head-on would be to condemn Christianity to an early death.[70]

On the one hand, it would be impossible for Paul to talk of being renewed in the image of Christ if there were not changes to be made at both an individual and communal level. On the other hand, as Hull and others have said, Rome would not have permitted this fledgling group to oppose them directly and make an attempt at empire-wide social change. The key word in the quote above is "transform." Christianity was seeking to *transform* society, not *replace* it or *live outside* of it. In other words, it was not attempting to be the new people of God by either overthrowing Rome (a common desire among many Jews at the time) or by separating from society (like the Essenes). They were trying to be in and among society while living differently from those who were a part of it.[71]

The end result of this is that, in order to transform the society in existence,[72] Christianity would have to adopt society's social structures. To completely reject them would be to live separately and have little to no impact on society. With the need to impact society as a constraint, it is not surprising at all that the code looks similar to contemporary thought on

---

70. Hull, "Family of Flesh," 26–27.

71. This sounds reminiscent of Jesus telling the people to be salt, which has to actually be in the food to change its taste.

72. As seen previously, the commands in 3:1–4:6 are not simply about individual morality. There is a strong interpersonal component to both the positive and negative commands. Furthermore, 4:2–6 emphasizes the need to walk in wisdom toward outsiders. The Christian life, as it is explained to the Colossians, is not simply about a personal morality. It is about living a renewed life both personally and communally.

household management. With the renewal that comes in Christ, it is also not surprising that one finds the code significantly modified from its ancient parallels (reciprocal duties, motivation/focus change, etc.). The path forward, it appears, was for the Colossians to live in society with its existing structures but to be different and focus on the things above.[73] Separation from society and complete replacement of its structures were not options.

The chief virtue described in the ethical section was ἀγάπη (love/ acting selflessly), and in the code, one finds a practical application of this virtue to daily life. Paul works through the standard structure whereby the more powerful party is in control, but he works against the selfishness that dominated that system. Husbands/fathers/masters no longer have unlimited rights. They must love those they lead and treat others as they would want to be treated—knowing that they, too, have a Master in heaven. "In each case, the Code subverts authoritarian power by setting ethical standards of love, compassion, and humility for those in the dominant social position."[74]

The code, therefore, is not merely a list of rules for how families should behave. The household code represents the application of the norms of a heaven-focused life to the prevailing customs of the family. In other words, by being part of the body of Christ, one should live differently as a wife/husband, child/parent, or slave/master. One's relationship with Christ should dominate all aspects of one's life and change every part with which it comes in contact. The commands in the ethical section were primarily relational commands; love, compassion, humility, patience, etc., are all relational. The impact of Christ, therefore, can be seen in how the Colossians live their daily lives in relation to one another.

It is also worth noting that in the code, there are no attempts to directly change the structures of the world.[75] Christians were not to focus on trying to change their situations; rather, Christians were to be extraordinary people in the world in which they were placed.[76] The ethical section and the household code were trying to help the Colossians towards right behavior, which meant doing everything *in the Lord*. Right behavior means

---

73. Henderson says, "The Colossians Code applies the logic of Christ's lordship to the writer's own cultural milieu, actively engaging the prevailing worldview in light of the cross. In these words, we find neither wholesale endorsement of secular Hellenistic values nor a prophetic indictment of stratified social structure. Instead, the writer refracts prevailing assumptions regarding household conduct through the lens of the Christian faith" ("Taking Liberties," 420–21).

74. Henderson, "Taking Liberties," 425.

75. There was little opportunity for this in the ancient world anyway. The structures in existence were, for the most part, fixed.

76. Michael Parsons, "Slavery," 90.

looking like Christ and being a good symbol/image/representation of him. When outsiders look at one of the Colossian Christians individually, they should be able to see Christ (3.9–10). When outsiders look at the Colossian church and the relationships between the members, they should be able to see Christ (4:5–6). In order for the Colossians to reach non-Christians, they had to live *in* society rather than be separate from it. Even if that meant that their social situation might have been less than ideal, reaching outsiders required one to live among them but be different.

It was said previously that revelation and renewal are the goals of Christians. These should be both received by Christians (believers should learn more about God and grow closer in their walk with Him) and shared by Christians (believers should share what they know about God with outsiders and hopefully lead them to a renewed life).[77] The household code demonstrates one of the main ways the Colossians were able to make sharing revelation and renewal happen. Living under the same system as their neighbors but transcending that system and living better than they had to showed what it means to be renewed by Christ. The Colossians would send a strong message if their relationships (especially hostile ones like those between slave and master) were characterized by love and peace. As images/symbols of Christ, they would be walking examples of Christ himself.

77. Very probably, renewal also includes one's duty to renew everything that is wrong with creation, but the focus in Colossians is on other humans.

13

The Essence of the Christian Worldview

PAUL'S MESSAGE TO THE Colossians has been investigated in detail, and it is now time to try to determine what he thought the essence of the Christian worldview is. There are at least two good ways to try to sort out what Paul thought was important from what he thought was unimportant.[1]

The first method is to look at the way he argued throughout the letter. Paul was trying to explain to the Colossians that Christianity was superior to the alternative philosophy. On what basis did he make those claims? How did he argue in favor of Christianity and against the philosophy?

The second method is to consider how essential each part of his worldview is using standard theological categories. In this method, each element (God, Christ, the church, etc.) will be isolated from the others, and then the questions will be asked, "What would happen if this element were removed? Would the Christian worldview (as seen in Colossians) collapse?" Those elements that would cause the Christian worldview to collapse if removed will be considered more important than those which would not cause the Christian worldview to collapse if removed.

Both of these methods will be employed and then compared in order to make final conclusions.

---

1. There could be more than these, but these are the ones that present themselves to the author.

PAUL'S ARGUMENT

The Truth of Christianity

Paul does not actually take any time in the letter to show why he thinks Christianity is true. This part of his argument is assumed. However, the picture he paints of the world begins with Christ *actually* being who Paul says he is and *actually* doing the things that Paul says he did.

If the things that Paul claims about Christ were not actually true, then the letter to the Colossians would not make any sense. Paul says that Christianity is better than the philosophy because its claims are better and because those claims are based in reality: they are true. One can see this in how Paul argues. Paul spends the entire letter trying to convince the Colossians that they should not accept the alternative philosophy, because Christianity is better. He does this on the basis that Christ actually is who Paul says he is and that Christ has actually done what Paul says he has done.

None of the things Paul tells the Colossians to do would make sense if Christianity were not actually true. Why would the Colossians live for another world, if that world were not real? Why would they conform their lives to the example of Christ, if Christ were not who Paul said he was? Why would they live in a manner that could potentially alienate them from their neighbors if they didn't have to?

In ch. 3 of the letter, Paul argued that because the Colossians have died and risen with Christ, they are headed to a heavenly world, and therefore their earthly lives should reflect those facts. Paul bases his argument on a real and different future as a result of what Christ has done. Of course, if Christianity is not true, then his argument makes absolutely no sense. If there is no heavenly world, then there is nothing to look forward to (at least as Christianity describes it). And, there is certainly no reason to follow Christ, if he is not who Paul claims he is and has not done what Paul claims he has done.

So, while Paul does not actually take space in the letter to argue for the truth of Christianity, this is, nevertheless, an essential point of his argumentation. If Christianity is not true, then nothing else Paul says makes any difference.

The Person and Work of Christ

All the central points about the person and work of Christ are found in the hymn. The rest of the letter shows how these points apply to the situation at Colossae.[2] In the hymn,[3] Christ is described as:

1. *The Image of the Invisible God*—Christ reveals God. He is the full and complete representation of God, and he is the way humanity "sees" God. Image of the invisible God also shows that Christ is related to God, but distinct from the invisible God.

2. *The Uncreated Creator*—Christ is responsible for all creation, yet he himself is uncreated. He stands on the creator side of the creator/ creation divide and is placed in a position that is usually reserved for God. When this is combined with Point 1, the result is early binitarian/trinitarian thought. Or more specifically, it is binitarian/trinitarian thought in pictorial language instead of propositional language. Christ is distinct from God, yet he is the uncreated creator.[4]

   The fact that Christ created the world means that the world will look different than it would if someone else (or no one else) had created it. Who created the cosmos matters and will have an impact on how people live. Also, given that Christ created all other beings, then his supremacy is for all times and places. Christianity therefore is not merely relevant to a single group; it is for all people, at all times, and in all places.

3. *The Temple of God*—In the Old Testament, God was described as present in all of creation, yet he was described as present in the temple in a special way. Christ is described in the same way as the temple, when the hymn says that God's fullness dwells in him (1:19). Like the Old Testament temple, then, Christ is the place man goes to "meet" God.

---

2. Basically, Paul lays out his theology in ch. 1, shows how that theology applies to the Colossians and why it's better than the alternative philosophy in ch. 2, and then explains how the Colossians should live as a result of Christian theology in ch. 3 and the beginning of ch. 4.

3. These statements are either directly taken from the hymn, or they are the essence of what the hymn says but explained in a way that is more understandable to a modern audience. Additionally, the order here is different from the order in the hymn. The order in the hymn occurred within a structure that itself carried meaning. When these statements are removed from that structure, they lose some of that meaning. Consequently, it makes better sense to present them in a different order, so as to keep them in logical order.

4. As discussed earlier, this is not an example of gnostic thought.

Furthermore, because the one in whom God's fullness dwells is also the one who died on the cross (1:20), the hymn is expressing genuine incarnational thought. It is simply expressing that thought in pictorial rather than propositional language. Christ is the place where God and man come together in a single person. He is the place where God and man meet.

4. *The Firstborn from the Dead*—Alhough it is not discussed in the hymn, there is an implied "fall" of creation. Everything was created good,[5] but it needs reconciliation. Christ's death and resurrection is what dealt with that problem. His death and resurrection lead to the future reconciliation of all things (Point 7), but immediately, they allowed for what was wrong with humanity (brokenness and separation from God) to be fixed. This leads to the next point.

5. *The Beginner of a New Humanity*—Those who follow Christ die and rise with him. By doing this, they receive forgiveness for their sins, freedom from the powers who stand against them, and entrance into the new people of God, the church. Beyond all this, those who follow Christ are also renewed into the image of their creator, Christ. It is not just that they are forgiven for their sins and then left to stay as they are; rather, Christ actually fixes what is wrong with them.

Through a process that begins in this life and is completed in the next, Christ renews those who follow him into being truly human. However, this renewal into the image of one's creator carries with it a responsibility. Just as Christ is the image of the invisible God and reflects and represents God, so Christians who are being renewed in the image of their creator are to reflect and represent Christ.

6. *The Head of the Body, the Church*—Renewal into the image of Christ is a vocation. To be the image of Christ is to reflect and represent Christ. Because Christ is not done with the world, those who are living as his images have work to do. Christ did not simply die, rise, and then leave the world. He is active in the world today, and he is working in the world through the church. Those who are a part of the church have received revelation and are being renewed. Then, after they have

---

5. This seems to follow from the fact that Christ is the image of the invisible God and that Christ is the uncreated creator. Assuming that God is good (which appears to be the assumption in the letter) and that Christ is a complete and faultless reflection of him, it is only logical to conclude that he made creation good rather than corrupted. That is why most commentators think that corruption entered into creation at a later point that is usually referred to today as the fall. For a more in-depth look at the fall, see the excursus in the discussion of 1:20.

received revelation and renewal, they are to share them with the rest of the world.

7. *The Reconciler of All Creation*—With the fall, everything in creation split into two kingdoms: the domain of darkness and the kingdom of Christ. The original creational order became broken, and humanity became hostile to God. Furthermore, those humans who are in the domain of darkness have their priorities out of order. Instead of placing God first and themselves second, they place themselves first and God second. As the reconciler of all creation, Christ will return all things to their original creational order. There will no longer be a domain of darkness, and humanity's hostility toward God will end.

However, there is a time element to reconciliation for individuals. Those who are reconciled in this life will also be renewed. Those who are reconciled after this life will not be renewed. Regardless of what happens with any particular individual, however, all creation will be reconciled.

If one thinks back over the letter to the Colossians, it should not be hard to see how these seven points represent the basis for Paul's argumentation in the rest of the letter. Essentially, the way the letter progresses is: 1) Christ is and has done all the things described above; 2) therefore, the Christian way is superior to the alternative philosophy (as well as every other worldview);[6] and 3) therefore, you Colossians should live in a manner that reflects and represents Christ.

Paul's own worldview (as discovered in Colossians) begins with the truth of Christianity and the facts about the person and work of Christ. He starts with true beliefs about the world. At this point, most people would expect he would move into actions, i.e., how to live a Christian life. But, there is an important step that comes before the Christian life that makes up a large part of Paul's worldview. The next major element in Paul's worldview is the connection of beliefs and actions.

---

6. Again, the fact that Paul's argument applies to all humanity and not just the Colossians or the alternative philosophy is based on the points in this section on the person and work of Christ. No one else is the image of the invisible God and the uncreated creator. There is no other place where God and man meet. No one else can take away people's sins or renew people in the image of their creator. Paul does not make an argument that Christianity applies to all people at all times in all places. He does not need to. The very facts about who Christ is and what he has done do that all by themselves.

Beliefs and Actions

On the one hand, connecting beliefs and actions (or theology and practice) was not unique to Christianity. It was common practice among moral teachers to say that one's actions should follow from one's beliefs. This fact, however, does not diminish the importance of this connection. The connection of beliefs and actions is critical for Paul's argument, because the actions he expects Christians to perform flow directly from Christian theology.

However, the connection between beliefs and actions does not just mean that one's actions and beliefs should line up. This connection also explains how daily actions lead to renewal, and it explains what Christians can expect from this life. It answers a lot of questions that don't have easy answers, like "Why does God care what humans do?" "Why does God command the actions he does?" "Why would a person want to follow God's commands in the first place?" This is a rarely discussed but very important part of the Christian worldview.

Unfortunately, there is no one place in the letter to find all the main points of connection between beliefs and actions like there was with the person and work of Christ in the hymn. However, the following points will explain the main ideas.

1. *The Beginning: God's Commands Are Based on Who He Is*—As the image of the invisible God, Christ reflects and represents God. Christ acts on God's behalf, and Christ's actions tell others who God is. Christians are being renewed in the image of their creator, Christ. They are to reflect and represent Christ in the same way that Christ reflects and represents God. Christians reflect Christ directly, and they reflect God indirectly (through Christ).

   God wants humans to represent him well. Therefore, the reason God commands the things he does is so humanity will reflect and represent him accurately. God bases his commands on his own nature so that when people look at Christians and (hopefully) see God, they will get the right idea.

2. *The Direction: Following God's Commands Helps People Know God Himself*—If God's commands are based on who he is, then by following those commands, a person experiences the character of God firsthand. When Christians love others, they experience firsthand the love God has for others. When Christians forgive others who have wronged them, they experience firsthand God's forgiveness for humans. By following God's commands, Christians get to know God himself better. Additionally, by following his commands, they will become more like

him (albeit in a limited way). How this actually happens is explained by the next point.

3. *The Spiral: Combining Beliefs and Actions Changes People*—Paul's imagery for renewal in the life of a Christian is an upward spiral. The knowledge of God's will enables the believer to know how to live a life that is pleasing to God. Practicing walking in a way that pleases God helps one to know God's will better. This brings one back to the starting point, only now the believer is in a better (higher) place than before. The result is an upward spiral in which the believer continually knows God more and walks with him more perfectly.

Although Paul does not talk about it, there is almost certainly a corresponding downward spiral that results when a person ignores or rejects knowledge of God and refuses to practice it. What the spiral imagery means, though, is that a person's life is not a static existence but a dynamic "walk" in which one either continually grows in one's knowledge of God and lives in a manner which reflects him more and more accurately, or one continually deteriorates in one's knowledge of God and reflects him less and less accurately.

4. *The Goal: Humans Are Being Renewed into the Image of Their Creator*— The upward spiral is headed to knowledge of God himself. After all, God's commands are based on who he is. However, because human actions are involved, this is no mere theoretical knowledge. Humans actually start to act like God. Of course, since humans were meant to reflect God, that means they actually become better humans. The end of the upward spiral is both knowledge of God himself *and* renewal into true humanity.

Unfortunately, Paul does not talk about the downward spiral. However, if it is the opposite of the upward spiral, then it leads to the loss of the knowledge of God and loss of one's humanity. The upward spiral leads to renewal into the image of one's creator, and the downward spiral leads to the loss of that image.

5. *The Focus: People Should Prepare for Life with God*—Whatever path a person begins in this life will be completed in the next life. Whether a person is spiraling up or down, moving toward God or moving away from God, one's path will be taken to its conclusion. The next life is focused on, shaped by, and centered around one's relationship with God—whether good or bad.

Because of that, it only makes sense to prepare for what is coming. That does not mean this world doesn't matter; it absolutely does.

It only means that humans are moving in a direction (up or down). Because of that, they should pay attention to where they're headed and prepare for life with God.

6. *The Fallout: The Christian Path Has Consequences*—Beliefs have consequences, whether those consequences are intended or not. Beliefs will make a person inflexible on certain points—even or especially if they are based on the truth. Some people will not like that. However, because Christian actions follow from Christian beliefs, many actions will be inflexible for the Christian as well. Some people will really not like that.[7] The Christian path is not an easy one. After all, it cost Christ his own life, and Jesus told people in the gospels, "Follow me." Representing Christ will have consequences in this world.

7. *The Reason: Thankfulness Is Why One Would Want to Follow the Christian Path*—Because God is God, it simply makes sense to do what he commands people to do. However, thankfulness explains why a person would *want* to follow God. Recognizing what God has done for believers through Christ is what causes thankfulness. Thankfulness is what keeps the spiral continually moving upward for the Christian.

The Christian Life

Paul's Christian worldview is based on what he considers to be true statements about the world. The section on theology gave and explained the most important of these statements. The section on beliefs and actions showed how theology and practice are connected. This section explains what Paul expected followers of Christ to actually do as a result of their beliefs.

1. *Receive Revelation and Renewal*—The process of renewal begins by knowing something about God. This occurs via revelation, because humans cannot reach up to God. God must reveal himself to humans if he is to be known. The path to renewal begins by receiving the revelation that God gives of himself through Christ. Following that, a person must follow the path towards renewal that God puts in front of him or her. This was described in the previous section through the upward spiral. To some degree, this will vary from person to person

---

7. This is why it is so important that Christianity is based on truth and why Christians need to be intentional about finding that truth. A closed-minded person who is certain that he or she is right can cause a lot of damage. On the other hand, a person who actively seeks the truth and then stands up for it (while remaining humble) can do a lot of good.

based on an individual's particular needs. However, many things will be the same for everyone, because all humans have some of the same problems (next point).

2. *Stop Acting Selfishly*—At its essence, selfishness is putting oneself in first place. The problem is that because Christ is the uncreated creator and God,[8] putting oneself in a position over him is idolatry. This is *the* problem that all humans have—idolatry/selfishness. In Paul's view, all other immoral actions (greed, sexual sins, anger, etc.) are specific instances of this one central sin. Therefore, the first thing that Christians should focus on in their renewal process is to stop acting selfishly.

3. *Start Acting Selflessly*—Acting selflessly is not the same thing as *not* acting selfishly. Merely avoiding selfish actions will lead to a person removing bad things from their life and not acting badly towards others. This is good, but it does not go far enough. Christians are to actively do good to others, rather than just avoid doing bad.

   In order to be able to represent Christ accurately, Christians need to actually act like Christ. Christ actively put others before himself when he died for those who were hostile to God in the doing of evil deeds (1:21). Likewise, Christians need to actively put others before themselves and do unto others as they would have others to do unto them. This means they need to start acting selflessly.

4. *Live for Where They're Headed*—Paul tells the Colossians that they need to focus on the things above, i.e., they need to live for where they're headed. It is easy to get distracted by the things of this world. But, if the goal is to know God himself and to become renewed in the image of one's creator, that is going to require a different orientation. A person can really aim at only one target at a time. It is not possible to aim at both success in this life and success in the next life. They are different targets. Paul tells the Colossians to aim for success in the next life and live for where they're headed.

5. *Live in the World, but Live Differently*—This new heavenly way of life that is characterized by acting selflessly is going to stand out from everyone else. However, Christians are not supposed to live separately from everyone else. Rather, Paul tells them to live among everyone else and live under the world's systems. They are to live in the same world as everyone else, but they are to live better than they have to. Others will

---

8. Think back to the discussion in 1:15–16 about how "the image of the invisible God" and "the firstborn over all creation" work together to explain how Christ is part of what would later be called the Trinity.

notice the difference and ask the question "Why?"[9] The answer itself is implied in the longer form of the question: "There is no earthly reason why someone would act that way. So, why would they?" Paul would say, "You are correct. There is no earthly reason a person would live that way. But, there is a heavenly reason."

6. *Focus on a Heavenly Measure of Success*—If the Christian is going to live in a different manner than those around him or her, there will be a disconnect (if not friction) between the two. The Christian life is not something that encourages earthly success, because it is about heavenly success. Furthermore, because the Christian is supposed to focus on heavenly things, earthly success should not be something that is even considered. Heavenly success is what matters.

As a result of this new focus, Christians will need to have a new measure of success—a heavenly measure of success. Everything they do should be done for the Lord. That means that the question "Am I following Christ?" is more important to the Christian than the question "Am I successful (according to the normal, earthly view of success)?" The Christian life results in a reordering of priorities, and that requires a new measure of success.

7. *Share Revelation and Renewal*—The primary goal for Christians is to become renewed in the image of their creator, which means that they are to represent Christ. Part of the Christian life is spent receiving revelation and renewal in order to actually be more like Christ. The other part of the Christian life is spent trying to share revelation and renewal. The more a Christian becomes like Christ, the more people look at him or her and see Christ. Christians actually become sources of revelation to the rest of the world. And because Christians are not mere reflections of Christ but his representatives as well, they are to share renewal with others and make the world around them a better, more heavenly place.

In the end, Paul's argument in the letter can be boiled down to four key parts: the truth of Christianity, the person and work of Christ, beliefs and actions, and the Christian life. These are like four links in a chain. All four links are necessary, and if even one of them breaks, his Christian worldview falls apart. However, this is only one method of determining what Paul thought was essential to the Christian worldview. There is another.

---

9. At least to themselves, if not directly to the Christian.

THE ESSENTIAL ELEMENTS OF PAUL'S WORLDVIEW

Now that the way that Paul argued in Colossians has been investigated, it is time to look at the second method to determine what he thought was essential to the Christian worldview. So, which elements did Paul think are essential? On what pillars does Christianity stand, and which ones will cause it to fall if removed?

God

The place to start is with God—not only because there can be no theology without a θεός (theos, God), but because everything else in Colossians relates back to God. Paul makes some statement about God at least every few verses throughout the letter, and sometimes he makes multiple statements in a single verse. Believers are to know his will (1:8) and increase in the knowledge of God (1:10). It is God who qualifies people (1:12) and delivers them from the domain of darkness and transfers them to the kingdom of his beloved Son (1:13). It is God who is responsible for rooting, establishing, and building the believer (2:7), and he is responsible for the circumcision, baptism, making alive, etc., those who are in Christ (2:11–15). God is the one who judges (3:5), and he is the one who should receive thanks (3:16). God is the one who opens a door for the word (4:3), and he is the ruler of the kingdom (4:11). In Paul's view, actions originate in and are directed to God. God is the beginning and end of all things.

If one attempted to take this God out of the picture and have Christianity without him, it would not work. Christianity would fall apart. Christ would not be anyone's visible image, and there would be no one for him to represent. There would be no one to qualify man or transfer him to a new kingdom. There would be no hostility between the Colossians and God (since there would be no God), and therefore no need for redemption. And, there would be no final judgment, since there would be no one to do the judging. Without God, the Christian worldview would fall apart.

If one were to substitute a different god or gods, perhaps some of these things would stay the same, but it would depend on which god(s). However, even a small change in which god(s) one is talking about makes a huge difference, because so much of what Paul talks about in the letter is related to the nature of the Jewish God and his continued interaction with humanity through his people, Israel. Deliverance of the Hebrew slaves from Egypt forms the background for the deliverance of humanity in 1:13. The resurrection that is described in the hymn and that features so prominently in the letter is the Jewish form of resurrection rather than the Greek version. Jewish wisdom theology forms the background for much of the theology of Christ in the letter. And, many of the concepts for how humans relate to God (walking with God, circumcision, sin, bearing fruit and increasing, etc.) have a Jewish background to them. If one were to change the god in question, none of this would make sense, and the theology would look radically different. For the Christian worldview to remain intact, there must be a god, and it must be the Jewish God.

Christ

The next place to look is Christ. Because he is the primary actor in Colossians and obviously not removable from Christianity, one needs to ask a more specific question: "What about the person and/or the work of Christ is essential to the Christian worldview?"

It might be best to start by asking whether Christ's representation of God is essential to the Christian worldview. There are two statements that directly speak to this: "He is the image of the invisible God" (1:15a) and "In him God's fullness was pleased to dwell" (1:19). Additionally, there is the background imagery about Wisdom.[10] The point is that Christ is the "place" where one finds full revelation of God and where one meets God. This thought is emphasized numerous times and undergirds the section on Christian living. If one could find full revelation of God somewhere other than "in Christ," much of the theology of Colossians and all of Paul's arguments against the alternative philosophy would no longer make sense. If there were another way to know/meet God than through Christ, then more than one road would lead to God, and Paul would be endorsing some form of pluralism. Even from a cursory reading of the letter, it is clear that that is not what Paul is advocating.

Continuing this thought, one must next look at exclusivism and particularism. Is Christ the only place where one can know God or the only place where one can know God fully? This was discussed in a few places, especially in ch. 2. In 2:16–17, Paul describes food, drink, festivals, new moons, and Sabbaths as "shadows" of things to come. But, he says, the substance belongs to Christ. In his view, things like these[11] point toward God, but they do not do it in the perfect, complete, or full manner that Christ does. Christ is not the only place where one can find revelation of God, but

---

10. The background imagery of the temple is part of God's fullness dwelling in Christ.

11. This is not the full extent of things that point toward God. Very probably, Paul thought that other things, such as the moral law, also pointed toward God.

he is the only place where one can find *full* revelation of God, because he is the only place where the fullness of deity dwells bodily (2:9). As such, one must say that Paul rejects exclusivism and holds to particularism. Furthermore, given the centrality of Christ's revelation of God to Paul's theology as well as his rejection of any other way as being sufficient, one must also say that particularism is an essential element to Paul's Christian worldview. Exclusivism would be a possible option, but it is not the position he takes. What is essential is that no less than particularism is part of his Christian worldview.

Christ is also described as the one in, through, and for whom all things were created—while he himself is uncreated. Christ is the agent of God and the one through whom he acts in the world. As far as original creation, though, one must ask whether it is central to Paul's Christian worldview that Christ was the one in whom all things were created. Paul makes it clear that Christ is the agent of God in the world. But, could creation have been made another way? What if God had made original creation without Christ, and then Christ stepped in later to reconcile and renew fallen creation? Would Christianity lose one of its central pillars?

Certainly, there is a sense of appropriateness and completion with Christ as responsible for both original creation and renewed creation that would be lost. But, this appropriateness all by itself is not a central pillar of the Christian worldview. On the other hand, one could look to the diminishing of Christ's representation of God if God created directly. If God worked in the world apart from Christ, then Christ might not reveal him fully. There would be works of God in the world that did not happen through Christ, and so man could learn something additional about God apart from Christ.

However, since Paul's Christianity rests on particularism rather than exclusivism, this is not actually a problem either. Paul's claim is not that the works of Christ are the only things that point to God in this world but that Christ is the only *full* representation of God. If God were responsible for creation and Christ were simply responsible for its reconciliation and renewal, Christ's representation of God *might* be diminished, but that would not necessarily be the case.

The question of whether or not it is essential that Christ was responsible for original creation rests (at least partly) on the importance of his supremacy. Both in the hymn that Paul quotes as well as throughout the entire letter, Paul heavily emphasizes the supremacy of Christ. Thinking through the argument of the hymn, if Christ were not the creator of all things, then he would not be the firstborn over all creation, since 1:16 gives the reason *why* he is the firstborn. The two firstborn statements provide a summary of all things in which Christ is first so that in 1:18, the hymn's author can make the statement (immediately following the second use of firstborn) that in all things Christ is first. If one were to take away half of that formula, Christ would be first in the reconciliation and renewal of the world, but he would not be first in all things. To remove this would be to remove a large part of the foundation of Paul's argument, and therefore a large part of the foundation of the Christian worldview. If Christ were not responsible for original creation, he would not be first in all things.

Beyond this, though, one might also ask whether reconciliation and renewal could be possible if Christ were not the creator. If Christ were not the creator, then it is difficult to understand how he could bridge the gap between God and man and fix what was wrong with creation. The ending of the hostility between God and man involves a being who can stand on both sides and bring the two parties together. If Christ were not creator as well as redeemer, it seems hard to understand how the gap between creator and creation could be bridged. Given the importance of Christ's supremacy in the letter as well as the need for someone to be able to end the hostilities between creator and creation, it seems essential that Christ be the uncreated creator.

The parallel to Christ's original creation is his work to reconcile and renew creation through the cross and his subsequent resurrection. There should not be much debate about whether or not the resurrection is central to the Christian worldview, though. Christ's reconciliation of all things and his renewal of humanity is based on the resurrection (1:18b-20), and if Christ did not rise from the dead, then neither of them would happen. If Christ did not rise from the dead, then there would be no peace between God and man (1:20), and disharmony would still exist in the cosmos. And, if Christ did not die and rise, then it would be impossible for believers to die and rise with him. In Paul's Christian worldview, the resurrection of Christ must have actually happened, because if it did not, many of the major elements of theology could not stand.[12]

Holy Spirit

At this point, it would be nice to address Paul's view on the Holy Spirit and investigate how it fits into his theology. However, that is a little hard to do when there is only one reference to "spirit" in Colossians (1:8); while it probably (though not definitely) refers to the Holy Spirit, Paul never brings it up

---

12. It does not take much space to say that the resurrection is central to Christianity. That does not mean, however, that one has investigated all the implications of the resurrection.

again.[13] In other letters, Paul attributes many roles and much importance to the Holy Spirit, but here, the Christian worldview is explained without almost any mention of the Holy Spirit.

It should be remembered that Paul is not giving a comprehensive picture of Christianity; rather, he is describing Christianity in response to a specific situation. More specifically, Paul is describing the Christian worldview *in comparison with* an alternative. The focus is therefore more external than internal. That means that some things that Paul would consider to be very important to theology or to the lives of believers may not be a part of his explanation here, because they are not the most helpful for comparison with another worldview.

An example of something that has more internal than external significance is the Lord's Supper. In 1 Cor 11, Paul places a high level of importance on it, but there is no mention of it in Colossians. A possible reason for that can be found in the passage itself. In 1 Cor 11, Paul says that it is for believers. In other words, it is something primarily of interest to Christians. The facts about the death and resurrection of Christ, on the other hand, have more relevance to outsiders than a practice meant for Christians that is based on those facts.[14] In a similar way to the Lord's Supper, theology concerning the Holy Spirit may, in Paul's view, have more application to the lives of believers than it does to non-believers. That would not mean that the Holy Spirit was not important to them. It would only mean that theology about the Holy Spirit is not the most useful for comparing the Christian worldview to the alternative worldview and discussing the merits of each view.

Unfortunately, without almost any data to go on, any attempt to explain why Paul left the Holy Spirit out of his description of the Christian worldview is only speculation. However, a plausible reason for this is that the theology of the Holy Spirit, like that of the Lord's Supper, is of more use to Christians than non-Christians. And, in Colossians, because Paul is comparing the Christian worldview with an alternative rather than simply explaining Christianity to Christians, it could be that the Holy Spirit was not the most helpful topic to bring up. Therefore, based on the argument that Paul uses in Colossians, while theology about the Holy Spirit may very well be essential to Christianity, it does not appear to be essential to the Christian worldview.

13. Bruce says, though, that it is possible that there are other indirect references (*Epistles to the Colossians*, 44–46).

14. That is not to say that the facts about the death and resurrection of Christ have no relevance for Christians.

Creation

In what he says about creation, Paul describes (or implies) three important phases in its existence. First, there is original creation, the point at which the cosmos came into existence. Second, there is the fall, in which humanity[15] ceased to exist in the harmony with God in which it was originally created. Third, there is the reconciliation of creation to its proper order. Unlike the first two phases, which happened in the past, the third one has past, present, and future elements. Paul thought the process of reconciliation began in the past, was ongoing at the time of his writing, and would be completed at some point in the future.

All three phases of creation are central to Christianity, because they are basic acts in the story of God and man.[16] In the beginning, Christ created everything perfect and in harmony, and if there were no creation, there would be nothing to discuss. The fall,[17] while only implied in the letter and not explicitly discussed, sets up the problem that is to be solved by Christ. Given that Christ created everything perfectly and in harmony, something had to happen for creation to need reconciliation. If the fall did not happen, there would be no need for reconciliation, which means there would be no need for Christ's death and resurrection. There would be no hostility between humanity and God, there would be no domain of darkness, and there would be no need for humans to be renewed in the image of their creator (because they would never have lost the image). Most of what Paul talks about when he describes Christianity is a repairing of the damage done at the fall. If the fall never happened, the Christianity he describes would not exist. Like original creation, the fall is a central pillar of the Christian worldview.

Similarly, the reconciliation of creation must also be a central pillar of the Christian worldview, because it is the restoring of creation to its proper order. If there were an original creation and then a fall into disharmony, but there were no reconciliation, one would find a very different theology. There would be no need to follow Christ, because he would have nothing to offer humanity. There may or may not be an afterlife, but even if there were,

---

15. What effects creation suffered as a result of the fall are not discussed in Colossians. There is reference to spiritual beings being reconciled, which implies that they fell as well, but the focus is almost exclusively on humans and their relationship with God.

16. For discussion on story, narrative, and worldview, see the excursus in ch. 2.

17. As mentioned earlier, the concept of a fall is certainly implied in the text, but no further information is given on the nature of this fall. The term "fall" continues to be used; however, one cannot know how much the term itself reflects later theological thought. See the excursus on the fall in the discussion of 1:20 for a fuller explanation.

humans would still exist in hostility towards God, and so there would be no hope of anything positive. Without reconciliation, Paul's theology and the moral life he lays out would look very different. For Christianity to have any meaning for humanity, there must be reconciliation of creation to creator.

Humanity

Paul says that those who follow Christ are being renewed in his image (3:9–10). This is an important statement, but it is not a simple one. In order for renewal to happen, several things have to be in place. First, there has to be an original (good) creation. Second, there has to be a fall from the original, harmonious state to one of estrangement and/or hostility between humanity and God. Third, this fall implies a negative anthropology in which humanity is inherently sinful (or at least partially so) rather than inherently good. Finally, Christ has to have risen from the dead to make a renewed humanity possible.

The first two of these points have already been discussed. This brings the discussion to Paul's belief in a negative anthropology. This means that after the fall, people are born at least somewhat flawed by default rather than perfect by default. The fact that Paul had a negative anthropology is not terribly debatable for two reasons. First, it is a direct consequence of the fall, which has already been demonstrated to be critical to Paul's Christian worldview. If man is born inherently perfect, then disharmony is not really present in creation—at least not in man.

Second, for man to be renewed, he must have to be renewed from some unrenewed state. This must imply something less than perfection, because otherwise Paul would not be talking about renewal but something else. All the language in the letter (especially things like Paul's desire to present the Colossians as holy, blameless, and above reproach) points towards them existing in an imperfect state. To what extent humans are sinful/fallen is a separate issue.[18] What is critical, though, is that humanity is imperfect and needs renewal. A negative anthropology is essential to Paul's Christian worldview.[19]

18. The question would be, "Are they completely sinful, evil, or broken, or are they only partially so?"

19. Though this technically is part of the fall, which was discussed earlier, this should be considered as a unique point. Partly, this is because the fall is something that affects all creation, and the nature of man is something fairly specific; but, also, it is worth pointing out for clarity's sake. It may not be obvious to all readers that the fall would necessarily result in a negative anthropology. Yet, Paul's argument views a negative anthropology as essential to the Christian worldview, so it should be made its own

To the final point, Christ must have risen from the dead in order to make renewal possible.[20] The hymn showed that Christ's resurrection not only makes him the firstborn from the dead but the beginner of a new humanity. A person becoming renewed in the image of his creator is the same thing as that person becoming a (re)new(ed) human.[21] If Christ had not risen from the dead, then he could not become the beginner of a new humanity; and if he had not become the beginner of a new humanity, then no humans could become renewed.

Related to this, it is important to understand that at least some humans must be renewed; otherwise, Christ's resurrection loses its main purpose. If there are not some people who are the "second-born" from the dead, then Christ is not the beginner of a new humanity, and his resurrection is of no consequence. Therefore, the renewal of at least some part of mankind is critical to Christianity, because without it, Christ's work produces nothing.

Also, the renewal of a person happens when he or she is "in Christ." As stated previously, this is a reference to which team or side a person is on, and the point that is consistently made throughout the letter is that renewal is only to be had by being in Christ. However, this is not actually a new point. This is only one of the implications of the resurrection. If Christ is actually the firstborn from the dead and the beginner of a new humanity, then it is only "in him" that one can expect to be renewed. Therefore, a central pillar of the Christian worldview is that renewal is found in Christ alone. To take this away would be to say that one can be renewed without the work of Christ, which goes against the entire argument of the letter.[22]

The other side of the coin to the believer in Christ is Christ in the believer. This refers to the work that Christ does in the world through those who are in him. This points back to the image language. Christ is the image of the invisible God, which means that Christ represents God to the world. Christians are being renewed in the image of their creator, which means that they represent Christ to the world (even if they don't do it perfectly, because they are not fully renewed).

---

point (for clarity, if for no other reason).

20. Previously, Christ's resurrection was described as essential. However, this particular application of his resurrection (renewal) has not been investigated. Only reconciliation has been considered.

21. See discussion on 3:9–10.

22. Beyond this, it would actually make any arguing pointless. What would be the point of Paul telling the Colossians not to follow the alternate philosophy if it could produce the same result as following Christ? There must be a difference (at least in Paul's mind) if he is going to bother making an argument.

Humans who are being renewed in the image of their creator are to become living and active representations of Christ. Just as Christ represents God, so humans are to represent Christ. Therefore, humanity's renewal does not mean that people go off somewhere to be holy all by themselves (either with or without other believers). The renewal of humanity means that humans are to function as they were meant to: living as Christ's representatives in the world, just as Christ is God's representative. Christ in the believer is essential to humans becoming the complete images of their creator, because it is into the representatives of Christ that they are being renewed.

It is worth pointing out that even though the believer in Christ and Christ in the believer are both essential, these really are not new points. Both of these flow directly from renewal and describe what it entails. The connection of the believer with Christ is essential to Christianity, but it is not a unique and/or separate point from renewal. Therefore, it might be more accurate to say that renewal of humanity in the image of Christ is essential to Christianity, and the various facets of humanity's connection with Christ (in Christ and Christ in you) explain what that renewal means.

Similar to this, one might also ask whether humanity's freedom from the powers that stand against them is an essential element of Christianity. Like the connection with Christ, it is and it isn't. It is essential to the Christian worldview that Christ is supreme; so humanity cannot be subject to any other powers,[23] or Christ would not be supreme. However, the freedom from the powers and authorities that Paul talks about is a consequence of Christ's supremacy and logically flows from it. In this determination of which elements of the Christian worldview are essential to Paul, the only ones that will be considered are the unique elements and not points that flow from them. In other words, this is a search for the necessary elements of the Christian worldview and not those elements which are contingent upon the necessary ones.

In the above case, that means that the supremacy of Christ is essential, but the freedom from the powers and authorities is not. The believer's freedom is an implication of the supremacy of Christ and is not a unique element on its own; it is the result of Christ's supremacy. Similarly, the believer being in Christ and Christ being in the believer are not essential elements. They certainly are unique features of the Christian worldview, but these are merely descriptions of what renewal into the image of Christ is. They are not separate points on their own. However, were they separate points and not

---

23. This would not be true if that authority were recognized by Christ as a legitimate sub-ruler under Christ. However, the question that is being asked is if there are any powers or authorities outside of Christ's sphere that the believer need worry about. If Christ is supreme, then the answer is no.

explanations of what renewal into the image of Christ means, then they also would be considered essential elements.

Moving on to another point, what about the moral lives of individuals? They are obviously an important part of Paul's worldview. Essentially, Paul says that Christ is to be at the center of one's life and that one's actions are to represent Christ. To act other than in a way that represents Christ and his character accurately is to be guilty of idolatry by putting oneself at the center of one's own universe, because that is where Christ belongs. But, must Christians *follow* this moral life for the Christian worldview not to fall apart?

Nowhere in the letter does Paul even give a hint that anything depends on the actions of humans. Rather, everything depends on Christ, and people are presented with two alternative paths, one according to Christ and the other not according to Christ. Which path they choose will impact their own future, but nowhere is there any indication that their choice will impact God's actions in the world through Christ. The renewal of humanity is part of Christ's renewal of creation, and if Christ is unable to accomplish renewal, then the Christian worldview falls apart. However, the renewal of those who are in Christ will be completed at the end of their life, whether they follow any particular moral command or not. Because of that, it seems that the answer to the question "Must Christians live the Christian life for the Christian worldview not to fall apart?" is "No." As stated previously, some humans must be renewed, but the actions they take after they are in Christ do not affect the success of Christ's work.

Here, the question must be asked, "Does Christ have to renew all humanity, and if so, then why is there still talk of another kingdom (the domain of darkness)?" It was seen previously that Christ's work on creation after the fall has two parts: reconciliation and renewal. Reconciliation is the returning of all things into the proper creational order (with Christ at the top), with or without the participants being reconciled willingly. Renewal, on the other hand, includes reconciliation but is above it, as the participants are remade into the image of their creator (and do so willingly). The reconciliation of creation is critical to Christianity, because without it, there still exists a domain of darkness that defies the order of original creation. Renewal, however, is a little more complicated.

There must be renewal of at least some part of humanity, because if everything were returned to its proper creational order but all of Christ's human creatures were still in rebellion at the point of final reconciliation, it would not be possible to say that he actually fixed any of them. However, nowhere does Paul indicate that all of humanity needs to be renewed for Christ's work to be accomplished. In many places, he makes it clear that there will be some portion of mankind which is not part of Christ's renewal. Unfortunately, *why* this is the case is not a topic of discussion in Colossians. It is merely presented as the way things are.

Some might suggest that it was God's plan to renew only part of humanity and that he has his own reasons for doing so. Others might suggest that there is an element of human choice involved and that some choose to follow Christ and some do not, resulting in only some portion of humanity experiencing renewal. Given that there is a strong polemical element in which Paul argues that the Christian way is superior to other ways, as well as a strong exhortation for Christians to follow the commands of Christ, it would seem that human choice is a factor (thus pointing to the latter option). However, it would take more information to decide between these two options (which may not be mutually exclusive anyway). It is simply not possible to tell from this letter alone.

For now, then, all that can be said is that the decision of individual humans on whether to follow Christ or not has no effect on the Christian worldview. While it is extremely important for humans to follow Christ for their own sake, if any particular one chooses not to follow Christ, the Christian worldview will not fall apart. All that must happen for the Christian worldview to remain intact is for at least some humans to experience renewal (though Paul gives no indication as to what that percentage that may be, or if a concept like percentage even applies). The Christian living section of the letter, then, is extremely important for individuals and their lives, and it gives one a picture both of what the earthly part of the renewal process looks like and insight into the nature of Christ. But, what individuals do or do not do in their lives is not critical to the Christian worldview, because an individual's actions cannot make the Christian worldview stand or fall. Paul's commands to Christians on how to live explain to them what renewal looks like in their individual and communal lives and how they are to participate in it, but that is all they do. If a person chooses to live an unrenewed life, the Christian worldview does not fall apart.

Church

The Church is something that has a great deal of importance, but it refers to a group of people that have already been discussed, those who have died and been raised with Christ. They are the body of Christ and the way he works in the world. This is of inestimable value to those who are a part of the church, just as the moral commands for Christ's people are of inestimable importance for how they live their lives. Again, though, just because something is important does not mean that it is critical to the Christian worldview. It is critical that humans are renewed only through relationship to Christ, and Paul says that those who undergo that renewal are part of the church. But, there is another attribute of the church that need to be discussed.

Paul says that the way that Christ works in the world is through the church. Is it an essential element of the Christian worldview that this is so? The answer to this is probably no, but only because it is a derivative concept.[24] If one assumes the Genesis accounts of creation (since it appears that Paul does), then humans were always meant to work in the world on behalf of God, because they were created in the image of God. For humans to be working in the world on their creator's behalf is simply to return to the original order of creation.[25] The return to the original order of creation through reconciliation and humans' renewal into the image of their creator are both foundational to Christianity. The church as a body of people who function as agents of their creator flows from these two concepts. The church is, therefore, a derivative concept.

Other important aspects of the church are similar to this, such as the descriptions of the church as the new people of God and the place where forgiveness happens. These are all explanations of what it looks like for man to be renewed. In the end, though, the church is the group of people who are in Christ and who participate in the renewal of humanity. Much of what is said about the church describes what renewal in Christ looks like, so while the return to the creational order (through Christ) of a part of humanity is central to Christianity, those descriptions are not. Again, this is not because they are not important but because they are derivative of renewal and describe what renewal entails. "The church" is a convenient way of describing what has already been discussed. It does not add any new content.

Eschatology

There is one final concept to cover before pulling everything together and making a summary. It is necessary to look at eschatology and the

---

24. As stated previously, only the foundational concepts will be considered in the search for the essential elements of the Christian worldview. Since derivative concepts flow from the foundational concepts, they should be considered as consequences of the foundational concepts rather than as foundational concepts themselves.

25. The renewal of those in Christ, however, may not be an *exact* return to the way creation originally was. Now that humans have gone through the fall and separation from God, what they return to will not be quite the same. While it may still be the image of their creator, no doubt, some things will be different than they were pre-fall.

future-oriented nature of Paul's theology, since so much of what he says about the present is based on what will happen in the future.

The focus, here, needs to be on the actual future nature of the events that have happened. Humanity's mere expectation of future transformation, renewal, etc., is not essential to the Christian worldview any more than whether or not a person lives the moral life. It might be helpful to an individual's walk or faith experience, but if a person is uninformed about what the future holds, that does not imply that the future will not happen. It might make one's life more difficult,[26] but the Christian worldview would not fall apart if people didn't know what was going to happen. One must, therefore, look at the actual facts of eschatology rather than a person's experience of those facts.

Much of what has been discussed up to this point has been about the reordering of the cosmos by Christ through his death and resurrection. The announcement of the way things will be has been made, but is there some reason that one sees a partially realized eschatology? Is it critical that the end of all things is not fully realized yet? Could humans be perfected now, or must they wait until the next life? Must they pass through death?

If there is some important reason for the delay in the final realization of the path those in Christ are on, then one might find that reason in what humans do during the intervening time, i.e., their earthly life. In other words, if it is important that humans are not immediately renewed and translated into their final state upon accepting Christ, then the task set before them in this life is the place to look for what is important enough to delay that final state. So, what is it that those who are in Christ are to do in this world?

Previously, it was said that the upward or downward spiral that humans begin during this life will be completed with the next. It seems like there needs to be time for individuals to choose which path to take (as well as possibly to what extent they will pursue that path). But, is there any reason to think that those who have already chosen Christ's path could not simply be renewed immediately? They are not renewed immediately, but this is given as a fact rather than explained as a necessary piece of the puzzle.[27]

The first question to ask is "What about people who die shortly after conversion and have no time to spiral up?" Paul seems to indicate that Christ will complete the renewal of anyone who has begun the upward spiraling

---

26. Of course, it is also very possible that *not* knowing the future would actually make a person's life easier.

27. It is possible that non-believers watching the process of believers being renewed and spiraling up would be more useful to Christ for reaching them than instant renewal would be, but that is just speculation.

process, since the end is presented as certain (as long as they continue in the faith, 1:21–23). That means that Christ will complete the process of a believer's renewal[28] regardless of how much time that person spends on earth or how far up the spiral he or she makes it.[29]

So, once the renewal process has begun, it will be finished. But, does that have to happen on earth? Could those who begin the renewal process be taken directly out of the world after they convert (and thereby become renewed immediately, though not in this world)? It seems possible; however, one should remember that those who are in Christ act as Christ's representatives on earth. If people were simply taken out of the world as soon as they converted, this could not happen. It seems therefore like there is a practical reason to keep those who are being renewed in the world through their natural lives.

However, it could be that there is actually a theological reason that they are kept in the world through the rest of their natural lives. It might be that in order for Christ's work to actually fix the problems brought on by the fall, at least some part of humanity must function as the image (Christ's representatives) on earth and not merely be whisked away to another world (though this is speculation). Unfortunately, there is not enough information in the text to answer this question, so it must remain unanswered.

There is still a final question, though: "Could man be perfected immediately and not have to wait for the next life?" The answer to this question seems like it is based on another question, "Must man pass through death?" Other places in the New Testament speak of the need for all humans to die, but it is just not discussed in Colossians. It is possible that one can find an answer in the Jewish form of resurrection that is assumed in the letter. In that view, sin and death are connected, and death is unnatural, because it is a curse. If all of those ideas are behind Paul's thought, then it is possible that the only way for a human to become free from the curse would be to pass through death and out the other side (since death would be required). However, because none of those topics is discussed in the letter, it might be too much to make that conclusion on the basis of the background material alone.

Again, because Paul was responding to a specific situation and not giving a full theology, some questions will go unanswered, because he did not

---

28. Or the opposite process of the complete loss of the image for those who are spiraling down.

29. This, however, is not something that is explicitly stated or discussed in great detail. It would be wise, therefore, to avoid being too dogmatic about this point. Furthermore, it is not discussed whether everyone's end result is the same or not. All who are headed up the spiral will be fully renewed, but will all renewed persons be exactly the same? This is not answered or even addressed.

need to cover them. A partially realized eschatology is clearly seen in Colossians, but this is presented as a fact. The audience is not given the reasons why this is the case or told if it is necessary.

RESULTS

Two methods for discovering what Paul thought was essential to the Christian worldview have now been applied. Here are the results from the first method, Paul's argument:

1. *The Truth of Christianity*—In Paul's view, the Christian life is based on its connection with theology, theology centers around the person and work of Christ, and the person and work of Christ is important because Christ actually is and has done what this letter claims. The starting point for Christianity is the truth of its theological claims. If these claims are not true, then Christianity is not worth following. However, if Christianity's claims are true, then they describe the way the world actually is, and people should follow it.

2. *The Person and Work of Christ*—In this letter, Christ is described as: 1) the image of the invisible God; 2) the uncreated creator; 3) the temple of God; 4) the firstborn from the dead; 5) the beginner of a new humanity; 6) the head of the body, the church; and 7) the reconciler of all creation. These points explain the essence of who Christ is and what he has done.

3. *Beliefs and Actions*—There are seven points that explain how the theology of the letter is connected to the practice of Christians. They are: 1) the Beginning—God's commands are based on who he is; 2) the Direction—following God's commands helps people know God himself; 3) the Spiral—combining beliefs and actions changes people; 4) the Goal—humans are being renewed into the image of their creator; 5) the Focus—people should prepare for life with God; 6) the Fallout—the Christian path has consequences; and 7) the Reason—thankfulness is why one would want to follow the Christian path.

4. *The Christian Life*—To live the Christian life, Christians need to: 1) receive revelation and renewal; 2) stop acting selfishly; 3) start acting selflessly; 4) live for where they're headed; 5) live in the world, but live differently; 6) focus on a heavenly measure of success; and 7) share revelation and renewal.

At their most basic level, these four points and their sub-points explain what makes the Christian worldview unique. However, these four points do something else, too. They point to a bigger picture. If Christ has made a difference in the world, there must have been something for him to make a difference in or on, and there was probably a reason to make that difference in the first place. This leads to the results from the second method for determining what Paul thought was essential to the Christian worldview—the search for what he considered to be the essential elements. They are as follows:

1. *God*—There actually is a God, and there is one God—the Jewish God. God is ultimately responsible for everything.

2. *Christ*—Christ is the representative and agent of God. He is the place where one finds full revelation of God and where one meets God. He is supreme and first in all things, both in original and reconciled creation. His resurrection from the dead forms the basis for reconciled creation as well as for the renewal of those who are reconciled during this life. Reconciliation happens because of Christ, and renewal is found only in Christ.

3. *Creation*—Creation has three phases which are distinguished by their relationship to the creator. In original creation, everything was created good and existed in harmony with its creator. At the fall, humans became hostile towards their creator, and disharmony entered creation. With the reconciliation of creation, all things will be returned to their original creational order, and the hostility will cease. However, not all creatures will return willingly, and not all creatures will be renewed.

4. *Humanity*—As a result of the fall, humanity is inherently broken and sinful (to some degree) rather than inherently perfect and good. Some portion of humanity is being renewed, and this group is called the church. Renewal is the remaking of a person into the image of God, which means that the believer is on the team of Christ and becomes Christ's representative.

In these points, one finds the basic elements in the Christian story of God and man.[30] This is especially obvious when one looks at the three phases of creation. The other elements help to explain certain parts in detail, but the main story is explained by original creation, the fall, and the reconciliation of creation. It is a story that effectively begins with the creation of

---

30. For an explanation of worldview, narrative, story, and the relationship between them, see the excursus in ch. 2.

the world, and while the end has been written by the actions of Christ and is being proclaimed and implemented by his Church, the story is still being played out by the individual actors.

Humans were created in the image of God but have since fallen from that image and are no longer acting as God's representatives. Through Christ, they can be renewed into the image of their creator (into true humans) and become the representatives of Christ. Alternatively, they can continue in their fallen state and lose what humanity they have left. This is the fork in the road at which all people find themselves. The final destination of each road has already been determined, and the story of God and humanity has already been written. Yet, individuals have two roads before them. The only question that remains is "Which one will they take?"

If the essence of the Christian worldview had to be summed up in a single phrase, it would be revelation and renewal. As the phrase itself implies, there is a bigger story—a bigger picture. There cannot be revelation if there is not someone to give it and someone to receive it, and there cannot be renewal if there are not already one or more things in existence that need to be renewed, as well as something into which they can be renewed. Christianity is not the whole of the story of God and man, but it is the turning point. It is the point at which God acted through Christ to fix what was wrong with creation and bring the whole story to a different conclusion.

Bibliography

Abbott, Thomas K. *A Critical and Exegetical Commentary on the Epistles to the Ephesians and to the Colossians.* New York: Charles Scribner's Sons, 1902.

Achtemeier, Paul J., ed. *Harper's Bible Dictionary.* San Francisco: HarperCollins, 1985.

Adeney, Walter F. "The Relation of New Testament Theology to Jewish Alexandrian Thought." *Biblical World* 26, no. 1 (1905) 41–54.

Aland, B. et al., eds. *The Greek New Testament.* 4th ed. Peabody, MA: Hendrickson, 2011.

Aletti, Jean-Noël. *Saint Paul Épître aux Colossiens.* Études Bibliques 20. Paris: J. Gabalda et Cie, 1993.

Alkier, Stefan. *Die Realität der Auferweckung in, nach und mit den Schriften des Neuen Testaments.* Tübingen, Germ.: Narr Francke Attempto, 2009.

Allison, Dale C. *Jesus of Nazareth: Millenarian Prophet.* Minneapolis: Fortress, 1998.

Altman, Rick. *A Theory of Narrative.* New York: Columbia University Press, 2008.

Altmann, Alexander. "'Homo Imago Dei' in Jewish and Christian Theology." *Journal of Religion* 48, no. 3 (1968) 235–259.

Armstrong, A.H. *An Introduction to Ancient Philosophy.* Totowa, New Jersey: Littlefield, Adams and Co., 1989.

Arzt, Peter. "The 'Epistolary Introductory Thanksgiving' in the Papyri and in Paul." *Novum Testamentum* 36, fasc. 1 (1994) 29–46.

Asad, Talal. "Anthropological Conceptions of Religion: Reflections on Geertz." in *Man,* n.s., 18, no. 2 (1983) 237–259.

Aune, David E. *The New Testament in Its Literary Environment.* Philadelphia: Westminster, 1987.

Bailey, James L. and Vander Broek, Lyle D. *Literary Forms in the New Testament: A Handbook.* Louisville: Westminster John Knox, 1992.

Balch, David L. "Household Codes." In *Greco-Roman Literature and the New Testament: Selected Forms and Genres,* edited by David E. Aune, 25–50. Atlanta: Scholars, 1988.

Balchin, John F. "Colossians 1:15–20: An Early Christian Hymn? The Arguments from Style." *Vox Evangelica* 15 (1985) 65–94.

Barcley, William B. *Christ in You: A Study in Paul's Theology and Ethics.* Lanham, MD: University Press of America, 1999.

Barram, Michael. "Colossians 3:1–17." *Interpretation* 59, no. 2 (2005) 188–190.

Bauckham, Richard. "Pseudo-Apostolic Letters." *Journal of Biblical Literature* 107, no. 3 (1988) 469–494.

Bauer, Walter, et al. *A Greek English Lexicon of the New Testament and Other Early Christian Literature*. 2nd ed. Chicago: University of Chicago Press, 2000.

Beale, Gregory K. *The Temple and the Church's Mission: A Biblical Theology of the Dwelling Place of God*. Downers Grove, IL: IVP Academic, 2004.

Beasley-Murray, G.R. *Baptism in the New Testament*. New York: Macmillan and Co., 1962.

———. "The Second Chapter of Colossians." *Review and Expositor* 70, no. 4 (1973) 469–479.

Becker, Jürgen, and Luz, Ulrich. *Die Briefe an die Galater, Epheser und Kolosser*. Göttingen, Germ.: Vandenhoeck & Ruprecht, 1998.

Bedard, Stephen J. "Hellenistic Influence on the Idea of Resurrection in Jewish Apocalyptic Literature." *Journal of Greco-Roman Christianity and Judaism* 5 (2008) 174–189.

Bevere, Allan R. *Sharing in the Inheritance: Identity and the Moral Life in Colossians*. London: Sheffield Academic, 2003.

Bing, Charles C. "The Warning in Colossians 1:21–23." *Bibliotheca Sacra* 164 (Jan.–Mar. 2007) 74–88.

Blomberg, Craig L. *From Pentecost to Patmos: An Introduction to Acts through Revelation*. Nashville: B&H, 2006.

Botha, J. "A Stylistic Analysis of the Christ Hymn: Colossians 1:15–20." In *A South African Perspective on the New Testament*, edited by Jacobus H. Petzer and Patrick J. Hartin, 238–251. Leiden, Neth.: Brill, 1986.

Brändl, Martin. *Der Agon bei Paulus: Herkunft und Profil paulinischer Agonmetaphorik*. Wissenschaftliche Untersuchungen zum Neuen Testament, 2nd ser., 222. Tübingen, Germ.: Mohr Siebeck, 2006.

Breytenbach, Cilliers. "Salvation of the Reconciled (with a Note on the Background of Paul's Metaphor of Reconciliation)." In *Salvation in the New Testament: Perspectives on Soteriology*, edited by Jan G. van der Watt, 171–186. Atlanta: Society of Biblical Literature, 2005.

———. "Versöhnung: Eine Studie zur paulinischen Soteriologie." *Wissenschaftliche Monographien zum Alten und Neuen Testament* 60 (1989) 225–239.

Briggs, Richard, S. *Words in Action: Speech Act Theory and Biblical Interpretation*. New York: T&T Clark, 2001.

Brown, Raymond E. *An Introduction to the New Testament*. New Haven, CT: Yale University Press, 1997.

Bruce, Frederick F. "Colossian Problems: Part 1: Jews and Christians in the Lycus Valley." *Bibliotheca Sacra* 141 (Jan.–Mar. 1984) 3–15.

———. "Colossian Problems: Part 2: The 'Christ Hymn' of Colossians 1:15–20" *Bibliotheca Sacra* 141 (Apr.–June 1984) 99–111.

———. "Colossian Problems: Part 3: The Colossian Heresy." *Bibliotheca Sacra* 141 (July–Sept. 1984) 195–208.

———. "Colossian Problems: Part 4: Christ as Conqueror and Reconciler." *Bibliotheca Sacra* 141 (Oct.–Dec. 1984) 291–302.

———. *The Epistles to the Colossians, to Philemon, and to the Ephesians*. New International Commentary on the New Testament. Grand Rapids: Eerdmans, 1984.

Bujard, Walter. *Stilanalytische Untersuchunger zum Kolosserbrief als Beitrag zur Methodik von Sprachvergleichen.* Göttingen, Germ.: Vandenhoeck & Ruprecht, 1973.

Burkert, Walter. *Ancient Mystery Cults.* Cambridge, MA: Harvard University Press, 1987.

Buttrick, George A. *The Interpreter's Dictionary of the Bible.* Nashville: Abingdon, 1962.

Caird, George B. *New Testament Theology.* Oxford, UK: Oxford University Press, 1995.

Campbell, Douglas A. "Unravelling Colossians 3:11b." *New Testament Studies* 42, no. 1 (Jan. 1996) 120–132.

Carr, Wesley. *Angels and Principalities: The Background, Meaning and Development of the Pauline Phrase* hai archai kai hai exousiai. Cambridge, UK: Cambridge University Press, 1981.

Carson, Donald A., and Douglas J. Moo. *An Introduction to the New Testament.* Grand Rapids: Zondervan, 1992.

Cavin, Robert L. *New Existence and Righteous Living: Colossians and 1 Peter in Conversation with 4QInstruction and the Hodayot.* Berlin: Walter de Gruyter, 2013.

Cerutti, Steven M. *Cicero's Accretive Style: Rhetorical Strategies in Judicial Speeches.* New York: University Press of America, 1996.

Charlesworth, James H. *The Historical Jesus.* Nashville: Abingdon Press, 2008.

Chester, Andrew. "The Relevance of Jewish Inscriptions for New Testament Ethics." In *Early Christian Ethics in Interaction with Jewish and Greco-Roman Contexts,* edited by Jan Willem van Henten and Joseph Verheyden, 107–146. Studies in Theology and Religion 17. Leiden, Neth.: Brill, 2012.

Clarke, Martin L. *Rhetoric at Rome: A Historical Survey.* London: Routledge, 1996.

Cohen, Abner. *Two-Dimensional Man: An Essay on the Anthropology of Power and Symbolism in Complex Society.* Los Angeles: University of California Press, 1976.

Collins, Raymond F. *The Letters That Paul Did Not Write: The Epistle to the Hebrews and the Pauline Pseudepigrapha.* Eugene, OR: Wipf & Stock, 1988.

Coloe, Mary L. *God Dwells with Us: Temple Symbolism in the Fourth Gospel.* Collegeville, MN: Liturgical, 2001.

Cullmann, Oscar. *Immortality of the Soul or Resurrection of the Dead: The Witness of the New Testament.* Eugene, OR: Wipf & Stock, 1964.

Daiute, Colette, and Lightfoot, Cynthia G., eds. *Narrative Analysis: Studying the Development of Individuals in Society.* Thousand Oaks, CA: Sage Publications, 2004.

De Jong, Irene J.F., René Nünlist, and Angus M. Bowie, eds. *Narrators, Narratees, and Narratives in Ancient Greek Literature: Studies in Ancient Greek Narrative.* Studies in Ancient Greek Narrative 1. Mnemoysne Supplements 257. Leiden, Neth.: Brill, 2004.

DeMaris, Richard E. *The Colossian Controversy: Wisdom in Dispute at Colossae.* Library of New Testament Studies. Sheffield, UK: Sheffield Academic, 1994.

DeSilva, David A. *An Introduction to the New Testament: Contexts, Methods, and Ministry Formation.* Downers Grove, IL: IVP Academic, 2004.

Dettwiler, Andréas. "L'Épître aux Colossiens: Un Exemple de Réception de la Théologie Paulinienne." *Foi et Vie* 94, no. 4 (1995) 26–40.

———. "La Lettre aux Colossiens: Une Théologie de la Mémoire." *New Testament Studies* 59, 1 (2013) 109–128.

———. "Das Verständnis des Kreuzes Jesu im Kolosserbrief." In *Kreuzestheologie im Neuen Testament,* edited by Andréas Dettwiler and Jean Zumstein, 81–105. Wissenschaftliche Untersuchungen zum Neuen Testament, 1st ser., 151. Tübingen, Germ.: Mohr Siebeck, 2002.

Dibelius, Martin. *Paulus*. Berlin: Walter de Gruyter, 1951.

Donelson, Lewis R. *Colossians, Ephesians, 1 and 2 Timothy, and Titus*. Louisville: Westminster John Knox, 1996.

Dübbers, Michael. *Christologie und Existenz im Kolosserbrief: Exegetische und semantische Untersuchungen zur Intention des Kolosserbriefes*. Wissenschaftliche Untersuchungen zum Neuen Testament, 2nd ser., 191. Tübingen, Germ.: Mohr Siebeck, 2005.

Duff, Tim. *Plutarch's Lives: Exploring Virtue and Vice*. Oxford: Oxford University Press, 1999.

Dunn, James D.G. "The 'Body' in Colossians." In *To Tell the Mystery: Essays on New Testament Eschatology in Honor of Robert H. Gundry*, edited by Thomas E. Schmidt and Moises Silva, 163–181. Sheffield, UK: Bloomsbury, 1994.

———. *Christology in the Making: A New Testament Inquiry into the Origins of the Doctrine of the Incarnation*. 2nd ed. Grand Rapids: Eerdmans, 1996.

———. *The Epistles to the Colossians and to Philemon*. New International Greek Testament Commentary. Grand Rapids: Eerdmans, 1996.

———. *The Theology of Paul the Apostle*. Grand Rapids: Eerdmans, 1998.

Du Toit, Andrie B. "Shaping a Christian Lifestyle in the Roman Capital." In *Identity, Ethics, and Ethos in the New Testament*, edited by Jan van der Watt, 167–198. Berlin: Walter de Gruyter, 2006.

Du Toit, Andrie B., ed. *Focusing on the Message: New Testament Hermeneutics, Exegesis, and Methods*. Pretoria, SA: Protea, 2009.

Eco, Umberto. *Semiotics and the Philosophy of Language*. Bloomington, IN: Indiana University Press, 1984.

Edsall, Benjamin, and Jennifer R. Strawbridge. "The Songs We Used to Sing? Hymn 'Traditions' and Reception in Pauline Letters." *Journal for the Study of the New Testament* 37, no. 3 (2015) 290–311.

Egger, Wilhelm. *How to Read the New Testament: An Introduction to Linguistic and Historical-Critical Methodology*. Peabody, MA: Hendrickson, 1996.

Eliade, Mircea. *The Quest: History and Meaning in Religion*. Chicago: University of Chicago Press, 1969.

Elwell, Walter A., and Philip W. Comfort, eds. *Tyndale Bible Dictionary*. Wheaton, IL: Tyndale House, 2001.

Erickson, Millard. *Christian Theology*. 2nd ed. Grand Rapids: Baker Books, 1998.

Evans, Craig A. *Jesus*. Grand Rapids: Baker Book House, 1992.

Faw, Chalmer E. "Death and Resurrection in Paul's Letters." *Journal of Bible and Religion* 27, no. 4 (1959) 291–298.

Fee, Gordon D. *New Testament Exegesis*. Louisville: Westminster John Knox, 2002.

Fellows, Richard G. "Renaming in Paul's Churches: The Case of Crispus-Sosthenes Revisited." *Tyndale Bulletin* 56, no. 1 (2005) 111–130.

Ferguson, Everett. *The Early Church at Work and Worship*. Vol. 1 of *Ministry, Ordination, Covenant, and Canon*. Eugene, OR: Cascade, 2013.

———. "Spiritual Circumcision in Early Christianity." *Scottish Journal of Theology* 41, no. 4 (Nov. 1988) 485–497.

Firth, Raymond. *Symbols: Public and Private*. New York: Routledge, 1973.

Fossum, Jarl. "Jewish-Christian Christology and Jewish Mysticism." *Vigiliae Christianae* 37, no. 3 (1983) 260–287.

Foulkes, Francis. *The Letter of Paul to the Ephesians: An Introduction and Commentary.* 2nd ed. Grand Rapids: Eerdmans, 1989.

Fowl, Stephen E. *Ephesians: A Commentary.* Louisville: Westminster John Knox, 2012.

———. *The Story of Christ in the Ethics of Paul: An Analysis of the Function of the Hymnic Material in the Pauline Corpus.* Sheffield, UK: Sheffield Academic, 1990

Frank, Nicole. *Der Kolosserbrief im Kontext des paulinischen Erbes: Eine intertextuelle Studie zur Auslegung und Fortschreibung der Paulustradition.* Wissenschaftliche Untersuchungen zum Neuen Testament, 2nd ser., 271. Tübingen, Germ.: Mohr Siebeck, 2009.

Freedman, David N., ed. *The Anchor Bible Dictionary.* New York: Doubleday, 1992.

———. *Eerdmans Dictionary of the Bible.* Grand Rapids: Eerdmans, 2000.

Gabathuler, Hans J. *Jesus Christus: Haupt der Kirche, Haupt der Welt.* Zürich: Zwingli, 1965.

Gamble, Harry. "The Redaction of the Pauline Letters and the Formation of the Pauline Corpus." *Journal of Biblical Literature* 94, no. 3 (1975) 403–418.

Geertz, Clifford. *The Interpretation of Cultures: Selected Essays.* New York: Basic Books, 1973.

———. "Religion as a Cultural System." In *Anthropological Approaches to the Study of Religion,* edited by Michael Banton, 1–44. London: Routledge, 1966.

Gill, Mary L., and Pierre Pellegrin, eds. *A Companion to Ancient Philosophy.* Malden, MA: Blackwell, 2006.

Gilmour, S. MacLean. "Church Consciousness in the Letters of Paul." *Journal of Religion* 18, no. 3 (1938) 289–302.

Gladd, Benjamin L. *Revealing the Mysterion: The Use of "Mystery" in Daniel and Second Temple Judaism with Its Bearing on First Corinthians.* Berlin: Walter de Gruyter, 2008.

Gnilka, Joachim. *Herders theologischer Kommentar zum Neuen Testament: Der Kolosserbrief.* Freiburg, Germ.: Herder, 1980.

Gordley, Matthew E. *The Colossian Hymn in Context: An Exegesis in Light of Jewish and Greco-Roman Hymnic and Epistolary Conventions.* Nehren, Germ.: Laupp & Göbel, 2007.

Gräbe, Petrus J. "Salvation in Colossians and Ephesians." In *Salvation in the New Testament: Perspectives on Soteriology,* edited by Jan G. van der Watt, 287–304. Supplements to Novum Testamentum. Atlanta: Society of Biblical Literature, 2005.

Gundry, Robert H. *Soma in Biblical Theology: With Emphasis on Pauline Anthropology.* Cambridge, UK: Cambridge University Press, 1976.

Gurtner, Daniel M. "Colossians." In *The Bible Knowledge Background Commentary: Acts-Philemon,* edited by Craig Evans, 587–608. Colorado Springs: Victor, 2004.

Habermas, Gary R. *The Historical Jesus: Ancient Evidence for the Life of Christ.* Joplin, MO: Thomas Nelson, 1996.

Hackenberg, Wolfgang. "Zukunft: Notizen zur Eschatologie im Kolosserbrief." In *Fragmentarisches Wörterbuch: Beiträge zur biblischen Exegese und christlichen Theologie,* edited by Kerstin Schriffner, Klaus Wengst, and Wener Zager, 442–456. Stuttgart, Germ.: Kolhammer, 2007.

Hadot, Pierre. *What Is Ancient Philosophy?* Translated by Michael Chase. 1995. Reprint. Cambridge, MA: Belknap, 2002.

Hahn, Scott, ed. *Catholic Bible Dictionary.* New York: Random House, 2009.

Hanegraaff, Woulter J. "Defining Religion in Spite of History." In *The Pragmatics of Defining Religion: Contexts, Concepts and Contests*, edited by Jan G. Platvoet and Arie Molendijk, 337–378. Numen Book 84. Leiden, Neth.: Brill, 1999.

Harris, Murray, J. *Colossians and Philemon. Exegetical Guide to the Greek New Testament.* Grand Rapids: Eerdmans, 1991.

Harrison, Everett F. *Introduction to the New Testament.* Grand Rapids: Eerdmans, 1971.

Hartman, Louis F. *Encyclopedic Dictionary of the Bible.* New York: McGraw-Hill, 1963.

Harvey, John D. "The 'With Christ' Motif in Paul's Thought." *Journal of the Evangelical Theological Society* 35, no. 3 (Sept. 1992) 329–340.

Hastings, James, ed. *A Dictionary of the Bible: Dealing with Its Language, Literature, and Contents, Including the Biblical Theology.* 5 vols. New York: Charles Scribner's Sons, 1903.

Hawthorne, Gerald F. *Paul's Letter to the Colossians.* Grand Rapids: Zondervan, 2010.

Hay, David M. *Colossians.* Nashville: Abingdon, 2000.

Heil, John P. *Colossians: Encouragement to Walk in All Wisdom as Holy Ones in Christ.* Atlanta: Society of Biblical Literature, 2010.

Helyer, Larry R. "Arius Revisited: The Firstborn over All Creation (Col 1:15)." *Journal of the Evangelical Theological Society* 31, no. 1 (Mar. 1988) 59–67.

———. "Colossians 1:15–20: Pre-Pauline or Pauline." *Journal of the Evangelical Theological Society* 26, no. 2 (June 1983) 167–179.

Henderson, Suzanne W. "God's Fullness in Bodily Form: Christ and Church in Colossians." *Expository Times* 118, no. 4 (2007) 169–173.

———. "Taking Liberties with the Text: The Colossians Household Code as Hermeneutical Paradigm." *Interpretation* 60, no. 4 (2006) 420–432.

Hoehner, Harold W. *Ephesians: An Exegetical Commentary.* Grand Rapids: Baker Academic, 2002.

Holladay, Carl R. "New Testament Christology: Some Considerations of Method." *Novum Testamentum* 25, no. 3 (1983) 257–278.

Hollenbach, Bruce. "Col. II. 23: Which Things Lead to the Fulfillment of the Flesh." *New Testament Studies* 25, no. 2 (1979) 254–261.

Horrell, David G. "From ἀδελφοί to οἶκος θεοῦ: Social Transformation in Pauline Christianity." *Journal of Biblical Literature* 120, no. 2 (2001) 293–311.

House, H. Wayne. "The Doctrine of Salvation in Colossians." *Bibliotheca Sacra* 151 (1994) 325–38.

Hughes, Frank W. *Early Christian Rhetoric and 2 Thessalonians.* Sheffield, UK: Sheffield Academic, 1989.

———. "The Rhetoric of Letters." In *The Thessalonians Debate: Methodological Discord or Methodological Synthesis?*, edited by Karl P. Donfried and Johannes Beutler, 194–240. Grand Rapids: Eerdmans, 2000.

Hull, Robert F., Jr. "The Family of Flesh and the Family of Faith: Reflections on the New Testament Household Codes." *Leaven* 9, no. 1 (2001) 23–28.

Jacobs, Andrew S. *Christ Circumcised: A Study in Early Christian History and Difference.* Philadelphia: University of Pennsylvania Press, 2012.

Josephus. *The New Complete Works of Josephus.* Translated by William Whiston. Grand Rapids: Kregel Academic & Professional, 1999.

Joshel, Sandra R. *Slavery in the Roman World.* Cambridge, UK: Cambridge University Press, 2010.

Jungbauer, Harry. *Ehre Vater und Mutter: Der Weg des Elterngebots in der biblischen Tradition.* Wissenschaftliche Untersuchungen zum Neuen Testament, 2nd ser., 146. Tübingen, Germ.: Mohr Siebeck, 2002.

Kalbhenn, Julia. "Realitätsverändernde Wirkung des Evangeliums?: Zur Normativität biblischer Überlieferung am Beispiel der Sklavenparänese des Kolosserbriefes." In *Diakonische Aussichten: Festschrift für Heinz Schmidt,* edited by Hermann Volker, 12–35. Heidelberg, Germ.: Diakoniewissenschaftliches Institut, 2003.

Käsemann, Ernst. "Unity and Diversity in New Testament Ecclesiology." *Novum Testamentum* 6, no. 4 (1963) 290–297.

Keck, Leander E. *Paul and His Letters.* Minneapolis: Fortress, 1988.

Keener, Craig. *The IVP Bible Background Commentary: New Testament.* 2nd ed. Downers Grove, IL: InterVarsity, 2014.

Keesmaat, Sylvia C. "Colossians." In *Theological Interpretation of the New Testament,* edited by Kevin J. Vanhoozer, 140–147. Grand Rapids: Baker Academic, 2008.

Kerr, Alan R. *The Temple of Jesus' Body: The Temple Theme in the Gospel of John.* Library of New Testament Studies. London: Sheffield Academic Press, 2002.

Kim, Jung H. *The Significance of Clothing Imagery in the Pauline Corpus.* New York: T&T Clark International, 2004.

Kittel, Gerhard, and Gerhard Friedrich, eds. *Theological Dictionary of the New Testament.* Translated by Geoffrey W. Bromiley. Grand Rapids: Eerdmans, 1964–1976.

Klauck, Hans-Josef. *Ancient Letters and the New Testament: A Guide to Content and Exegesis.* Translated by Daniel P. Bailey. Waco, TX: Baylor University Press, 2006.

Klawans, Jonathan. *Purity, Sacrifice, and the Temple: Symbolism and Supersessionism in the Study of Ancient Judaism.* Oxford: Oxford University Press, 2006.

Koch, Klaus. *Das Buch der Bücher: Die Entstehungsgeschichte der Bibel.* Berlin: Springer, 1970.

Koester, Helmut. *Introduction to the New Testament.* Vol. 2 of *History and Literature of Early Christianity.* 2nd ed. Berlin: Walter de Gruyter, 2000.

Kruger, Michael, J. *Canon Revisited: Establishing the Origins and Authority of the New Testament Books.* Wheaton, IL: Crossway, 2012.

Küchler, Max. "Aus seiner Fülle haben wir alle empfangen: Joh 1,16a als literarisches Pendant zum antiken Bildmotiv des überfließenden Füllhorns." In *Studien zu Matthäus und Johannes/Études sur Matthieu et Jean,* edited by Andreas Dettwiler and Uta Poplutz, 135–155. Zürich: Theologischer, 2009.

Kugel, James L., and Greer, Rowan A. *Early Biblical Interpretation.* Philadelphia: Westminster Press, 1986.

Kümmel, Werner G. *Einleitung in das Neue Testament.* Wiebelsheim, Germ.: Quelle & Meyer, 1983.

Lackhoff, George, and Mark Johnson. "The Metaphorical Structure of the Human Conceptual System." *Cognitive Science* 4 (Apr. 1980) 195–208.

Lamp, Jeffrey S. "Wisdom in Col 1:15–20: Contribution and Significance." *Journal of the Evangelical Theological Society* 41, no. 1 (Mar. 1998) 45–53.

Lampe, G. W. H. "The New Testament Doctrine of *Ktisis.*" *Scottish Journal of Theology* 17, no. 4 (Dec. 1964) 449–462.

Lane, William L. "Creed and Theology: Reflections on Colossians." *Journal of the Evangelical Theological Society* 21, no. 3 (Sept. 1978) 213–220.

Lapide, Pinchas. *The Resurrection of Jesus: A Jewish Perspective.* Translated by Wilhelm C. Linss. Eugene, OR: Wipf & Stock, 1982.

Lausberg, Heinrich. *Handbook of Literary Rhetoric: A Foundation for Literary Study.* Edited by David Orton and Dean Anderson. Leiden, Neth.: Brill, 1998.

Lenski, R. C. H. *The Interpretation of St. Paul's Epistles to the Colossians and Thessalonians.* Minneapolis: Augsburg Fortress, 2008.

Leppä, Outi. *The Making of Colossians: A Study on the Formation and Purpose of a Deutero-Pauline Letter.* Göttingen, Germ.: Vandenhoeck & Ruprecht, 2003.

Levinson, John R. "2 Apoc. Bar. 48:42–52:7 and the Apocalyptic Dimension of Colossians 3:1–6." *Journal of Biblical Literature* 108, no. 1 (Spring 1989) 93–108.

Lewis, C.S. *God in the Dock: Essays on Theology and Ethics.* Grand Rapids: Eerdmans, 2014.

Licona, Michael R. *The Resurrection of Jesus: A New Historiographical Approach.* Downers Grove, IL: IVP Academic, 2010.

Lightfoot, J.B. *St. Paul's Epistles to the Colossians and to Philemon: A Revised Text with Introductions, Notes, and Dissertations.* Cambridge, UK: Cambridge University Press, 1875.

Lincoln, Andrew T. "The Household Code and Wisdom Mode of Colossians." *Journal for the Study of the New Testament* 21, no. 74 (Oct. 1999) 93–112.

———. "The Spiritual Wisdom of Colossians in the Context of Graeco-Roman Spiritualities." In *The Bible and Spirituality: Exploratory Essays in Reading Scripture Spiritually,* edited by Andrew T. Lincoln and Gordon McConville, 212–232. Eugene, OR: Cascade, 2013.

Lincoln, Andrew T. and A.J.M. Wedderburn. *New Testament Theology: The Theology of the Later Pauline Letters.* Cambridge, UK: Cambridge University Press, 1993.

Lindemann, Andreas. *Der Kolosserbrief.* Zürcher Bibelkommentare. Zürich: Theologischer, 1983.

Loader, William R.G. "The Apocalyptic Model of Sonship: Its Origin and Development in New Testament Tradition." *Journal of Biblical Literature* 97, no. 4 (Dec. 1978) 525–554.

———. "The Significance of 2:15–17 for Understanding the Ethics of 1 John." In *Communities in Dispute: Current Scholarship on the Johannine Epistles,* edited by Alan R. Culpepper and Paul N. Anderson, 223–236. Atlanta: SBL Press, 2014.

Lohse, Eduard. *Die Briefe an die Kolosser und an Philemon.* Göttingen, Germ.: Vandenhoek & Ruprecht, 1971.

———. "Christusherrschaft und Kirche im Kolosserbrief." *New Testament Studies* 11, no. 3 (1965) 203–216.

———. *Die Einheit des Neuen Testaments: Exegetische Studien zur Theologie des Neuen Testaments.* 2nd ed. Göttingen, Germ.: Vandenhoeck & Ruprecht, 1973.

———. "Pauline Theology in the Letter to the Colossians." *New Testament Studies* 15, no. 2 (1969) 211–220.

Longfellow, Brenda. *Roman Imperialism and Civic Patronage: Form, Meaning, and Ideology in Monumental Fountain Complexes.* Cambridge, UK: Cambridge University Press, 2011.

Lyall, F. "Roman Law in the Writings of Paul: The Slave and the Freedman." *New Testament Studies* 17, no. 1 (1970) 73–79.

Macdonald, Janet M. *The Uses of Symbolism in Greek Art.* Chicago: University of Chicago Press, 1922

MacDonald, Margaret Y. *Colossians and Ephesians.* Sacra Pagina. Collegeville, MN: Liturgical, 2008.

————. "Slavery, Sexuality and House Churches: A Reassessment of Colossians 3:18–4:1 in Light of New Research on the Roman Family" *New Testament Studies* 53, no. 1 (Jan. 2007) 94–113.

Mach, Zdzislaw. *Symbols, Conflict, and Identity: Essays in Political Anthropology.* Albany: SUNY Press, 1993.

MaGee, Gregory S. *Portrait of an Apostle: A Case for Paul's Authorship of Colossians and Ephesians.* Eugene, OR: Pickwick, 2013

Maier, Harry O. "Roman Imperial Iconography, Moral Transformation, and the Construction of Christian Identity in the Lycus Valley." In *Colossae in Space and Time: Linking to an Ancient City,* edited by Alan H. Cadwallader and Michael Trainer, 212–231. Novum Testamentum et Orbis Antiquus/Studien zur Umwelt des Neuen Testaments 94. Göttingen, Germ.: Vandenhoeck & Ruprecht, 2011.

————. *Picturing Paul in Empire: Imperial Image, Text and Persuasion in Colossians, Ephesians, and the Pastoral Epistles.* New York: Bloomsbury T&T Clark, 2013.

Malan, F.S. "Church Singing According to the Pauline Epistles." *Neotestamentica* 32, no. 2 (1998) 509–524.

Malherbe, Abraham J. *Moral Exhortation: A Greco-Roman Sourcebook.* Philadelphia: Westminster, 1986.

Malina, Bruce J. *The New Testament World: Insights from Cultural Anthropology.* 3rd ed. Louisville: Westminster John Knox, 2001.

Malina, Bruce J., and Jerome H. Neyrey. *Portraits of Paul: An Archaeology of Ancient Personality.* Louisville: Westminster John Knox, 1996.

Martin, Dale. *Slavery as Salvation: The Metaphor of Slavery in Pauline Christianity.* New Haven, CT: Yale University Press, 1990.

Martin, Ralph P. *Colossians and Philemon.* New Century Bible. London: Oliphants, 1974.

————. *Colossians: The Church's Lord and the Christian's Liberty.* Grand Rapids: Zondervan, 1972.

————. "Reconciliation and Forgiveness in the Letter to the Colossians." In *Reconciliation and Hope: New Testament Essays on Atonement and Eschatology,* edited by Robert Banks, 104–124. Carlisle, UK: Paternoster, 1974.

Martin, Troy. "But Let Everyone Discern the Body of Christ." *Journal of Biblical Literature* 114, no. 2 (Summer 1995) 249–255.

————. *By Philosophy and Empty Deceit: Colossians as Response to a Cynic Critique.* Sheffield: Sheffield Academic, 1996.

Matera, Frank J. *New Testament Ethics: The Legacies of Jesus and Paul.* Louisville: Westminster John Knox, 1996.

McDonald, H. Dermot. *Commentary on Colossians and Philemon.* Waco, TX: Word Inc., 1980.

McKeon, Richard, ed. *The Basic Works of Aristotle.* New York: Random House, 2001.

Meeks, Wayne A. *The First Urban Christians: The Social World of the Apostle Paul.* 2nd ed. New Haven, CT: Yale University Press, 2003.

————. *The Origins of Christian Morality: the First Two Centuries.* New Haven, CT: Yale University Press, 1993.

Melick, Richard, R. *Philippians, Colossians, Philemon.* The New American Commentary. Nashville: B&H Publishing, 1991.

Metzger, Bruce M. *A Textual Commentary on the Greek New Testament.* Stuttgart, Germ.: Biblia-Druck, 1975.

Moo, Douglas J. *The Letters to the Colossians and to Philemon*. Pillar New Testament Commentary. Grand Rapids: Eerdmans, 2008.

Moreland, James P., and William Lane Craig. *Philosophical Foundations for a Christian Worldview*. Downers Grove, IL: InterVarsity, 2003.

Motyer, Stephen. "The Relationship between Paul's Gospel of 'All One in Christ Jesus' (Galatians 3:28) and the 'Household Codes.'" *Vox Evangelica* 19 (1989) 33–48.

Moule, C.F.D. *The Epistles to the Colossians and to Philemon*. The Cambridge Greek Testament Commentary. Cambridge, UK: Cambridge University Press, 1957.

———. "'Fulness' and 'Fill' in the New Testament." *Scottish Journal of Theology* 4, no. 1 (Mar. 1951) 79–86.

———. "The New Life in Colossians 3:1–17." *Review and Expositor* 70, no. 4 (Dec. 1973) 481–493.

Moule, H.C.G. *Colossian Studies: Lessons in Faith and Holiness from St. Paul's Epistles to the Colossians and Philemon*. New York: A.C. Armstrong and Son, 1898.

Mueller, Ekkehardt. "The Firstborn in Colossians 1:15." In *Biblical and Theological Studies on the Trinity*, edited by Paul Peterson and Rob McIver, 65–87. Adelaide, Aus.: Avondale Academic, 2014.

Murphy, James J., Richard A. Katula, and Michael Hoppmann. *A Synoptic History of Classical Rhetoric*. 4th ed. New York: Routledge, 2014.

Murphy-O'Connor, Jerome. *Paul the Letter-Writer: His World, His Options, His Skills*. Good New Studies. Collegeville, MN: Liturgical, 1995.

Neufeld, Vernon H. *The Earliest Christian Confessions*. New Testament Tools, Studies and Documents 5. Leiden, Neth.: Brill, 1963.

Norden, Eduard. *Agnostos Theos: Untersuchungen zur Formengeschichte religiöser Rede*. Darmstadt, Germ.: Wissenschaftliche, 1923.

O'Boyle, Aidan. *Towards a Contemporary Wisdom Christology: Some Catholic Christologies in German, English and French 1965–1995*. Tesi Gregoriana: Teologia. Rome: Gregorian University Press, 2001.

O'Brien, Peter T. *Introductory Thanksgivings in the Letters of Paul*. Eugene, OR: Wipf & Stock, 1977.

———. *The Letter to the Ephesians*. Pillar New Testament Commentary. Grand Rapids: Eerdmans, 1999.

———. *Colossians-Philemon*. Word Biblical Commentary. Nashville: Thomas Nelson, 1982.

O'Collins, Gerald. *Christology: A Biblical, Historical, and Systematic Study of Jesus*. Oxford: Oxford University Press, 2009.

Olbricht, Thomas H. "The Stoicheia and the Rhetoric of Colossians: Then and Now." In *Rhetoric, Scripture, and Theology: Essays from the 1994 Pretoria Conference*, edited by Stanley E. Porter and Thomas H. Olbricht, 308–328. Library of New Testament Studies. Sheffield, UK: Sheffield Academic, 1996.

Osiek, Carolyn. "What We Do and Don't Know about Early Christian Families." In *A Companion to Families in the Greek and Roman World*, edited by Beryl Rawson, 198–213 Chichester, UK: Blackwell, 2011.

Osiek, Carolyn A., and David L. Balch. *Families in the New Testament World: Households and House Churches*. Family, Religion, and Culture. Louisville: Westminster John Knox, 1997

Overfield, P.D. "Pleroma: A Study in Content and Context." *New Testament Studies* 25, no. 3 (Apr. 1979) 384–396.

Pao, David W. "Gospel within the Constraints of an Epistolary Form: Pauline Introductory Thanksgivings and Paul's Theology of Thanksgiving." In *Paul and the Ancient Letter Form*, edited by Stanley E. Porter and Sean A. Adams, 101–128. Pauline Studies 6. Leiden, Neth.: Brill, 2010.

Parsons, Michael. "Slavery and the New Testament: Equality and Submissiveness." *Vox Evangelica* 18 (1988) 90–96.

Parsons, Mikeal C. *Body and Character in Luke and Acts: The Subversion of Physiognomy in Early Christianity.* Grand Rapids: Baker Academic, 2006.

Perelman, Chaïm, and Olbrechts-Tyteca Lucie. *The New Rhetoric: A Treatise on Argumentation.* Translated by John Wilkinson and Purcell Weaver. Notre Dame, IN: University of Notre Dame Press, 1969.

Pernot, Laurent. "The Rhetoric of Religion." *Journal of the History of Rhetoric* 24, no. 3 (Summer 2006) 235–254.

Perkins, Pheme. *Ephesians.* Abingdon New Testament Commentaries. Nashville: Abingdon, 1997.

Perrin, Nicholas. "Sacraments and Sacramentality in the New Testament." In *The Oxford Handbook of Sacramental Theology*, edited by Hans Boersma and Matthew Levering, 52–67. Oxford: Oxford University Press, 2015.

Petersen, Norman R. "Pauline Baptism and 'Secondary Burial.'" *Harvard Theological Review* 79, no. 1 (Jan. 1986) 217–226.

Pfammatter, Josef. *Die Kirche als Bau: Eine exegetisch-theologische Studie zur Ekklesiologie der Paulusbriefe.* Analecta Gregoriana. Rome: Gregoriana, 1960.

Pollard, T.E. "Colossians 1:12–20: A Reconsideration." *New Testament Studies* 27, no. 4 (July 1981) 572–575.

Powell, Mark A. *What Is Narrative Criticism?* Minneapolis: Ausburg Fortress, 1990.

Quispel, Gilles. "Marcion and the Text of the New Testament." *Vigiae Christianae* 52, no. 4 (1998) 349–360.

Raphael, Simcha Paull. *Jewish Views of the Afterlife.* 2nd ed. New York: Rowman & Littlefield, 2009.

Rese, Martin. "Church and Israel in the Deuteropauline Letters." *Scottish Journal of Theology* 43, no. 1 (Feb. 1990) 19–32.

Resseguie, James L. *Narrative Criticism of the New Testament: An Introduction.* Grand Rapids: Baker Academic, 2005.

Ridderbos, Herman. *Paul: An Outline of His Theology.* Translated by John Richard de Witt. Grand Rapids: Eerdmans, 1997.

Roberts, J.H. "Jewish Mystical Experience in the Early Christian Era as Background to Understanding Colossians." *Neotestamentica* 32, no. 1 (1998) 161–189.

Robinson, James M. "A Formal Analysis of Colossians 1:15–20." *Journal of Biblical Literature* 76, no. 4 (Dec. 1957) 270–287.

Rodrigues, Hillary, and John S. Harding. *Introduction to the Study of Religion.* London: Routledge, 2009.

Rogers, Guy MacLean. *The Mysteries of Artemis of Ephesos: Cult, Polis, and Change in the Graeco-Roman World.* New Haven, CT: Yale University Press, 2012.

Roloff, Jürgen. *Die Kirche im Neuen Testament.* Grundrisse zum Neuen Testament 10. Göttingen, Germ.: Vandenhoeck & Ruprecht, 1993.

Roose, Hanna. "Die Hierarchisierung der Leib-Metapher im Kolosser und Epheserbrief als 'Paulinisierung': Ein Beitrag zur Rezeption Paulinischer Tradition in Pseudo-Paulinischen Briefen." *Novum Testamentum* 47, no. 2 (Jan. 2005) 117–141.

Rowland, Christopher. "Apocalyptic Visions and the Exaltation of Christ in the Letter to the Colossians." *Journal for the Study of the New Testament* 6, no. 19 (Sept. 1983) 73–83.

Rüpke, Jörg, ed. *Blackwell Companion to the Ancient World: A Companion to Roman Religion*. Malden, MA: Blackwell, 2007.

Ryan, Marie-Laure. "Toward a Definition of Narrative." In *The Cambridge Companion to Narrative*, edited by David Herman, 39–51. Cambridge, UK: Cambridge University Press, 2007

Sanders, E.P. *Jesus and Judaism*. Philadelphia: Fortress Press, 1985.

―――. "Literary Dependence in Colossians." *Journal of Biblical Literature* 85, no. 1 (Mar. 1966) 28–45.

Sanders, Jack T. *The New Testament Christological Hymns: Their Historical Religious Backgrounds*. Cambridge, UK: Cambridge University Press, 1971.

Sappington, Thomas J. *Revelation and Redemption at Colossae*. Sheffield, UK: Sheffield Academic, 1991.

Schnelle, Udo. *Theology of the New Testament*. Translated by M. Eugene Boring. Grand Rapids: Baker Academic, 2009.

Schrage, Wolfgang. "Zur Ethik Der neutestamentlichen Haustafeln." *New Testament Studies* 21, no. 1 (Oct. 1974) 1–22.

Schreiner, Thomas R. *Paul, Apostle of God's Glory in Christ: A Pauline Theology*. Downer's Grove, IL: IVP Academic, 2006.

Schweizer, Eduard. "Christus und Geist im Kolosserbrief." In *Christ and Spirit in the New Testament: Studies in Honour of Charles Francis Digby Moule*, edited by Barnabas Lindars and Stephen S. Smalley, 297–314. Cambridge, UK: Cambridge University Press, 1973.

―――. *The Letter to the Colossians: A Commentary*. Minneapolis: Ausburg, 1982.

―――. "Slaves of the Elements and Worshipers of Angels: Gal 4:3, 9 and Col 2:8, 18, 20." *Journal of Biblical Literature* 107, no. 3 (Sept. 1988) 455–468.

―――. "The Son of Man." *Journal of Biblical Literature* 79, no. 2 (June 1960) 119–129.

Sire, James W. *Naming the Elephant: Worldview as a Concept*. 2nd ed. Downers Grove, IL: InterVarsity, 2015.

―――. *The Universe Next Door*. 5th ed. Downers Grove, IL: IVP Academic, 2009.

Stambaugh, John E., and David L. Balch. *The New Testament in Its Social Environment*. Philadelphia: Westminster, 1986.

Standhartinger, Angela. "Colossians and the Pauline School." *New Testament Studies* 50, no. 4 (Oct. 2004) 572–593.

―――. "The Origin and Intention of the Household Code in the Letter to the Colossians." *Journal for the Study of the New Testament* 23, no. 79 (January 2001) 117–130.

Steiner, Deborah Tarn. *Images in Mind: Statues in Archaic and Classical Greek Literature and Thought*. Princeton, NJ: Princeton University Press, 2001.

Stettler, Christian. *Der Kolosserhymnus: Untersuchungen zu Form, traditionsgeschichtlichem Hintergrund und Aussage von Kol 1,15–20*. Wissenschaftliche Untersuchungen zum Neuen Testament, 2nd ser., 131. Tübingen, Germ.: Mohr Siebeck, 2000.

Stettler, Hanna. *Heiligung bei Paulus: Ein Beitrag aus biblisch-theologischer Sicht*. Wissenschaftliche Untersuchungen zum Neuen Testament, 2nd ser., 368. Tübingen, Germ.: Mohr Siebeck, 2014.

Still, Todd D. "Eschatology in Colossians: How Realized Is It?" *New Testament Studies* 50, no. 1 (Jan. 2004) 125–138.

Stowers, Stanley K. *Letter Writing in Greco-Roman Antiquity.* Edited by Wayne A. Meeks. Library of Early Christianity. Louisville: Westminster John Knox, 1986.

Strecker, Georg. *Theology of the New Testament.* Translated by Eugene M. Boring. Berlin: Walter de Gruyter, 2000.

Stuhlmacher, Peter. *Grundlegung: Von Jesus zu Paulus.* Vol. 1 of *Biblische Theologie des Neuen Testaments.* Göttingen: Vandenhoeck & Ruprecht, 2005.

Sumney, Jerry L. *Colossians: A Commentary.* New Testament Library Louisville: Westminster John Knox, 2008.

Tacitus. *Agricola.* Perseus under PhiloLogic, University of Chicago, 2018 edition. http://artflsrv02.uchicago.edu/cgi-bin/perseus/citequery3.pl?dbname=LatinSept18&query=Tac.%20Ag.%2030&getid=1.

Thackeray, Henry St. John, trans. *Josephus: Jewish Antiquites, Books 1–3.* Loeb Classical Library 242. Cambridge, MA: Harvard University Press, 1965.

Theobald, Michael. "Der Kolosserbrief." In *Einleitung in das Neue Testament*, edited by Martin Ebner and Stefan Schreiber, 425–439. Kohlhammer Studienbucher Theologie. Stuttgart, Germ.: Kohlhammer, 2008.

Thompson, Marianne M. *Colossians and Philemon.* Grand Rapids: Eerdmans, 2005.

Toolan, Michael. *Narrative: A Critical Linguistic Introduction.* 2nd ed. New York: Routledge, 2001.

Van Kooten, George H. *Cosmic Christology in Paul and the Pauline School.* Wissenschaftlich Untersuchungen zum Neuen Testament, 2nd ser., 171. Tübingen, Germ.: Mohr Siebeck, 2003.

Vermes, Geza. *The Resurrection: History and Myth.* New York: Doubleday, 2008.

Vielhauer, Philipp. *Geschichte der urchristlichen Literatur: Einleitung in das Neue Testament, die Apokryphen und die Apostolischen Väter.* De Gruyter Lehrbuch. Berlin: Walter de Gruyter, 1978.

Vorgrimler, Herbert. *Neues Theologisches Wörterbuch.* Freiburg, Germ.: Herder, 2008.

Wall, Robert W. *Colossians and Philemon.* The IVP New Testament Commentary Series. Downers Grove, IL: InterVarsity Press, 1993.

Wallace, Daniel B. *Greek Grammar Beyond the Basics: An Exegetical Syntax of the New Testament.* Grand Rapids: Zondervan, 1996.

Walsh, Brian J., and J. Richard Middleton. *The Transforming Vision: Shaping a Christian World View.* Downers Grove, IL: InterVarsity, 1984.

Walton, John H. *Ancient Near Eastern Thought and the Old Testament: Introducing the Conceptual World of the Hebrew Bible.* Grand Rapids: Baker Academic, 2006.

———. *The Lost World of Genesis One: Ancient Cosmology and the Origins Debate.* Downers Grove, IL: IVP Academic, 2009.

Wenham, Gordon J. *Genesis 1–15.* Word Biblical Commentary. Nashville: Thomas Nelson, 1987.

Wessels, G.F. "The Eschatology of Colossians and Ephesians." *Neotestamentica* 21, no. 2 (1987) 183–202.

Westermann, William L. *The Slave Systems of Greek and Roman Antiquity.* Philadelphia: American Philosophical Society, 1955.

Wiley, Galen W. "A Study of 'Mystery' in the New Testament." *Grace Theological Journal* 6 No. 2 (1985) 349–360.

Williams, A. Lukyn. *The Epistles of Paul the Apostle to the Colossians and to Philemon.* Cambridge Greek Testament for Schools and Colleges. London: Cambridge University Press, 1907.

Williams, Craig A. *Roman Homosexuality*. 2nd. ed. Oxford: Oxford University Press, 2010.

Wilson, Robert McLachlan. *Colossians and Philemon*. The International Critical Commentary. New York: T&T Clark International, 2005.

Wilson, Walter T. *The Hope of Glory: Education and Exhortation in the Epistle to the Colossians*. Novum Testamentum Supplements 88. New York: Brill, 1997.

Witherington, Ben, III. *Jesus the Sage: The Pilgrimage of Wisdom*. Minneapolis: Augsburg Fortress, 1994.

———. *The Letters to Philemon, the Colossians, and the Ephesians: A Socio-Rhetorical Commentary on the Captivity Epistles*. Grand Rapids: Eerdmans, 2007.

———. *New Testament Rhetoric: An Introductory Guide to the Art of Persuasion in and of the New Testament*. Eugene, OR: Cascade, 2009.

———. *Women and the Genesis of Christianity*. Cambridge, UK: Cambridge University Press, 1990.

Witherington, Ben, III, and G. Francois Wessels. "Do Everything in the Name of the Lord: Ethics and Ethos in Colossians." In *Identity, Ethics, and Ethos in the New Testament*, edited by Jan van der Watt, 303–334. Beihefte zur Zeitschrift für die neutestamentliche Wissenschaft, 141. Berlin: Walter de Gruyter, 2006.

Wolter, Michael. *Der Brief an die Kolosser/Der Brief an Philemon*. Gütersloh, Germ.: Gütersloher, 1993.

———. *Paul: An Outline of His Theology*. Translated by Robert L. Brawley. Waco, TX: Baylor University Press, 2015.

Wright, Christopher J.H. *The Mission of God*. Downers Grove, IL: InterVarsity Press, 2006.

Wright, N.T. *Colossians and Philemon*. Tyndale New Testament Commentaries. Grand Rapids: Eerdmans, 1986.

———. *The New Testament and the People of God*. Christian Origins and the Question of God 1. Minneapolis: Fortress, 1992.

———. "Poetry and Theology in Colossians 1:15–20." *New Testament Studies* 36, no. 3 (July 1990) 444–468.

———. *The Resurrection of the Son of God*. Christian Origins and the Question of God 3. Minneapolis: Fortress, 2003.

———. *Surprised by Scripture: Engaging Contemporary Issues*. New York: HarperOne, 2014.

Yamauchi, Edwin. "The Scythians: Who Were They? And Why Did Paul Include Them in Colossians 3:11?" *Priscilla Papers* 21, no. 4 (Autumn 2007) 13–18.

———. "Sectarian Parallels: Qumran and Colossae." *Bibliotheca Sacra* 121 (Apr.–June 1964) 141–152.

Yates, Roy. "Colossians 2:15: Christ Triumphant." *New Testament Studies* 37, no. 4 (Oct. 1991) 573–591.

———. "Colossians and Gnosis." *Journal for the Study of the New Testament* 8, no. 27 (Apr. 1986) 49–68.

———. "A Note on Colossians 1:24." *Evangelical Quarterly* 42, no. 2 (Apr.–June 1970) 88–92.

Made in the USA
Columbia, SC
02 June 2021